Circulation, Interlibrary Loan, Patron Use, and Collection Maintenance

HANDBOOKS FOR LIBRARY MANAGEMENT

Administration, Personnel, Buildings and Equipment
Acquisitions, Collection Development, and Collection Use
Reference Services and Library Instruction
Cataloging and Catalogs
Circulation, Interlibrary Loan, Patron Use, and Collection Maintenance
Library Education and Professional Issues

Circulation, Interlibrary Loan, Patron Use, and Collection Maintenance
A Handbook for Library Management

David F. Kohl

Foreword by Tom Alford

ABC·CLIO

Santa Barbara, California
Oxford, England

*This book is Smyth sewn and printed on acid-free paper to
meet library standards.*

Library of Congress Cataloging in Publication Data

Kohl, David F., 1942–
  Circulation, interlibrary loan, patron use, and
collection maintenance.

  (Handbooks for library management)
  Bibliography: p.
  Includes index.
  1. Libraries–Circulation, loans–Handbooks, manuals,
etc. 2. Library administration–Handbooks, manuals,
etc. 3. Inter-library loans–Handbooks, manuals, etc.
4. Libraries and readers–Handbooks, manuals, etc.
5. Library materials–Handbooks, manuals, etc.
I. Title. II. Series: Kohl, David F., 1942–
Handbooks for library management.
Z712.K59 1985   025.5'   85-15798
ISBN 0-87436-435-3 (v.5)
ISBN 0-87436-399-3 (set)

10   9   8   7   6   5   4   3   2

ABC-Clio, Inc.
2040 Alameda Padre Serra, Box 4397
Santa Barbara, California 93103

Clio Press Ltd.
55 St. Thomas Street
Oxford OX1 1JG, England

Manufactured in the United States of America

CONTENTS

1.

Circulation

2.

Interlibrary Loan

3.

Patron Use

4.

Collection Maintenance

FOREWORD

At certain times within an organization, opportunities arise to rearrange formulas and assumptions—not necessarily to get rid of the old, but more to profit from adding something new. Now is the time for library managers to look both forward and backward—back to the accomplishments of the last two decades and forward to the unmet challenge of the 1990s and the new century beyond. It is an opportune time to analyze current and future library needs and to adopt new ways and learn new things—to synthesize the familiar with the unfamiliar.

This book brings together knowledgeable and important data from both the public and private sectors to address the critical issues surrounding collection development and patron use. The professionals who have examined specific aspects of this topic are to be commended, since their efforts contribute much to this body of knowledge and its importance.

These examinations provide us with the framework with which to analyze past and current library trends. Also, they are the beginnings that will allow for more research on these and other related issues. More research promises to be professionally rewarding, for it comes at a time when far-reaching developments in the computer world will help meet the new challenges of our information-rich society.

Library managers are already responsible for allocating expensive resources—collections, equipment, personnel, space, etc. More and more, they will use computerized information to initiate, develop, and analyze many familiar and unfamiliar components of useful management information data collected from information environments, including functional and technical areas, and ranging from options to necessities and luxuries. Some of the important topics to be included in the process are planning, evaluation and selection, human behavior and training. Likewise, the future success of libraries may depend upon giving equal attention to some unfamiliar but special library management information. A topic deserving a prominent role is the development and maintenance of library collections and their utilization by patrons near and/or far away.

New learnings and perceptions come from many surprising sources. Our challenge is to break out of our limitations—self-imposed or otherwise—and accept the fact of a need for more information on how library collections are maintained and developed and how they are used by patrons.

Now is the time for the profession not to impose controls, but to set parameters defining the conditions under which librarianship may develop more competitive strategies. Likewise, an intelligent partnership of the familiar and unfamiliar by library managers can aid in further transforming libraries and information systems into more efficient, useful, and cost-effective organizations.

Our attitudes and philosophies fan out in an unlimited number of directions and so affect many thousands of libraries during our lifetimes. We truly have an obligation to make libraries the best humanly possible. Any new insight that will aid us to attain this goal is a benefit to all who use libraries. It may be our only hope for successfully addressing many of the critical issues that are affecting and will continue to affect libraries.

—Thomas E. Alford
Los Angeles Public Library

INTRODUCTION

The *Handbooks for Library Management* have been designed for library managers and decision makers who regularly need information, but who are chronically too short of time to do involved and time-consuming literature searches each time specific, quantitative information is desired. This unusual tool, rather than abstracting complete studies or providing only citations to research, instead presents summaries of individual research findings, grouped by subject. By looking under the appropriate subject heading in the *Handbook*, librarians can find summaries detailing the research findings on that topic. For example, what percentage of reference questions are answered correctly, and does it make a difference whether professional or nonprofessional staff are doing the answering? As a result, helpful information can be found in minutes and without an extensive literature review. Furthermore, if a more complete look at the study is desired, the user is referred to the bibliographic citation number so that the full study can be consulted.

Arrangement

The series consists of six volumes, with each volume covering two or more of the sixteen basic subject areas that divide the volumes into parts. While most of these basic subject divisions reflect such traditional administrative division of library work as administration, circulation, and reference, at least two subject areas go somewhat further. "Library Education" may be of interest, not just to library school administrators, but to faculty and students as well, and "Professional Issues" should be of interest to all career-oriented library professionals. Each basic subject division is further divided by specific subject headings, which are further subdivided by type of library: General (more than one library type), Academic, Public, School, and Special. For example, readers seeking information on book loss rates in academic libraries would consult the basic subject division "Collection Maintenance" and look under the specific subject heading "Loss Rates (Books)," in the "Academic" libraries subdivision. There they would find the summarized results of studies on book loss rates in academic libraries followed by the number referring to the full citation in the Bibliography of Articles.

Each volume in the series follows the same basic pattern: The introduction; a list of the journals surveyed; a detailed table of contents listing all subject headings used in that volume; the research findings arranged by subject; the complete bibliography of articles surveyed for the series with page numbers indicating locations of corresponding research summaries in the text; and an alphabetically arranged author index to the Bibliography of Articles.

The summaries of the research findings also tend to follow a standard format. First the study is briefly described by giving location, date, and, when appropriate, population or survey size and response rate. This information is provided to help users determine the nature, scope, and relevance of the study to their needs. The actual findings, signaled by an italicized *"showed that,"* follow and include, when appropriate, such supporting data as significance level and confidence interval. Information in brackets represents editorial comment, for example "[significance level not given]" or "[remaining cases not accounted for]," while information in parentheses merely represents additional data taken from the article.

The Sample Entries on page xxvii identify the elements and illustrate the interrelationships between the subject organization of the volume, research summaries of the text, corresponding article citations in the bibliography, and the author index entries.

Scope

In order to keep the *Handbook* series manageable, a number of scope limitations were necessary. The time period, 1960 through 1983, was selected since it covers the time when quantitative research began to come of age in library research. Only journal literature has been surveyed, because the bulk of quantitative library research is reported in that medium, and because the bulk of editorial and refereeing process required by most journals helps ensure the quality of the research reported. This limitation does ignore a number of important studies reported in monographic form, however, and we hope to cover this area at a later date. Further, only North American journals and research were reviewed since they constitute the main body of quantitative library research reported. Again, this ignores several journals reporting significant library research, particularly journals from Great Britain. We plan to expand our focus and include these in later editions or updates of the *Handbook* series.

Although we generally followed the principle that research good enough to publish was research worth including in the *Handbook* series, several caveats must be stated. First, no research findings with statistical significance exceeding .05 were reported. This follows general Social Science practice and, in recent years, almost universal library research practice. Second, occasional findings, and sometimes whole studies, were not reported in the *Handbook* series when there were serious problems with internal consistency and/or ambiguous and confusing text. At issue here is not the occasional typographical error or arithmetical miscalculation, but those situations where charts and text purportedly presenting the same information differed in substantial and unaccountable ways. Fortunately, such problems were not excessive. And third, as a general rule, only original and supported findings were used in the *Handbook* series. Findings that were reported second-hand, or where the study documentation was reported elsewhere (often the case with doctoral research), were generally not used in the series. Only in those instances when the second-hand data were used to show a pattern or otherwise resulted in new data by their juxtaposition, were such findings reported.

Finally, under the category of unsought limitations, we, like many library users, were not always able to find all the journal articles we needed in the time available to us. However, the excellent holdings and services of the University of Illinois Library Science Library provided us with access to almost all of the journal issues actually published and received by March 1984—a fact that should probably be listed as a record rather than as a limitation.

Acknowledgements

As might be expected, a project of this size required assistance from many quarters. Both the University of Illinois Library Research and Publication Committee and the University of Illinois Research Board provided invaluable assistance in the form of financial support for graduate assistants. The assistants themselves, Becky Rutter, Nicki Varyu, and Bruce Olsen, constituted a dedicated, bright, and hardworking team. The Undergraduate Library staff deserve special thanks for their support and cooperation, as do the Library Science Library staff, who were unfailingly courteous and helpful in making their truly outstanding collection available. The staff at ABC-Clio, particularly Gail Schlachter and Barbara Pope, provided much needed encouragement and good advice, even in the face of several delays and at least one nasty shock. And last, but by no means least, I would like to acknowledge the patience and support of my wife, Marilyn, and my son, Nathaniel, who have given up much in the way of a husband and father so that this *Handbook* series could be completed on schedule.

—*David F. Kohl*
Urbana, Illinois

SAMPLE ENTRIES

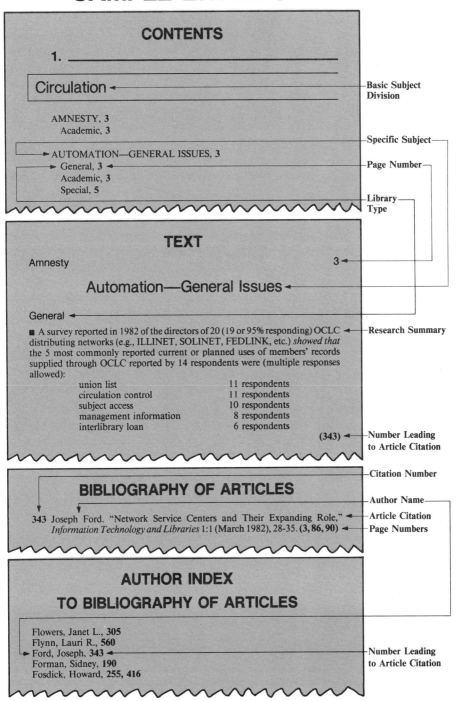

CONTENTS

1. _____

Circulation ◄——————————————————— Basic Subject Division

AMNESTY, **3**
Academic, **3**

Specific Subject

►AUTOMATION—GENERAL ISSUES, **3**
► General, **3** ◄ Page Number
Academic, **3**
Special, **5**

Library Type

TEXT

Amnesty   **3** ◄

Automation—General Issues ◄

General ◄

■ A survey reported in 1982 of the directors of 20 (19 or 95% responding) OCLC ◄—— Research Summary
distributing networks (e.g., ILLINET, SOLINET, FEDLINK, etc.) *showed that*
the 5 most commonly reported current or planned uses of members' records
supplied through OCLC reported by 14 respondents were (multiple responses
allowed):

union list	11 respondents
circulation control	11 respondents
subject access	10 respondents
management information	8 respondents
interlibrary loan	6 respondents

(343) ◄—— Number Leading to Article Citation

Citation Number

BIBLIOGRAPHY OF ARTICLES

Author Name

343 Joseph Ford. "Network Service Centers and Their Expanding Role," ◄—— Article Citation
Information Technology and Libraries 1:1 (March 1982), 28-35. **(3, 86, 90)** ◄—— Page Numbers

AUTHOR INDEX

TO BIBLIOGRAPHY OF ARTICLES

Flowers, Janet L., **305**
Flynn, Lauri R., **560**
► Ford, Joseph, **343** ◄
Forman, Sidney, **190**
Fosdick, Howard, **255**, **416**

Number Leading to Article Citation

xxvii

LIST OF JOURNALS SURVEYED

American Libraries. Chicago: American Library Association, 1970–. Monthly. LC 70-21767. ISSN 0002-9769. (Formerly *ALA Bulletin*, 1907-1969.)

American Society for Information Science. Journal. (JASIS) New York: John Wiley & Sons, 1970–. Bimonthly. LC 75-640174. ISSN 0002-8231. (Formerly *American Documentation*, 1950-1969.)

Canadian Library Journal. Ottawa: Canadian Library Association, 1969–. Bimonthly. LC 77-309891. ISSN 0008-4352. (Formerly *Bulletin*, 1944– March 1960; *Canadian Library*, 1960-1968.)

Catholic Library World. Haverford, PA: Catholic Library Association, 1929–. Monthly. LC 39-41. ISSN 0008-820X.

Collection Building. New York: Schuman, 1978–. Quarterly. LC 78-645190. ISSN 0160-4953.

Collection Management. New York: Haworth Press, 1975–. Quarterly. LC 78-640677. ISSN 0146-2679.

College and Research Libraries. Chicago: American Library Association, 1939–. Bimonthly. LC 42-16492. ISSN 0010-0870.

Drexel Library Quarterly. Philadelphia: Centrum Philadelphia, 1965–. Quarterly. LC 65-9911. ISSN 0012-6160.

Harvard Library Bulletin. Cambridge: Harvard University Library, 1947–. Quarterly. LC 49-1965//R802. ISSN 0017-8136.

International Journal of Legal Information. Camden, NJ: International Association of Law Libraries, 1982–. 6/yr. LC 82-643460. ISSN 0731-1265. (Formerly *Bulletin. International Association of Law Libraries*, 1960-1972; *International Journal of Law Libraries*, 1973-1979.)

International Library Review. London: Academic Press, 1969–. Quarterly. LC 76-10110. ISSN 0020-7837.

Journal of Academic Librarianship. Ann Arbor, MI: Mountainside Publishing, 1975–. Bimonthly. LC 75-647252. ISSN 0099-1333.

Journal of Education for Librarianship. State College, PA: Association of American Library Schools, 1960–. 5/yr. LC 63-24347. ISSN 0022-0604.

Journal of Library Administration. New York: Haworth Press, 1980–. Monthly. LC 80-644826. ISSN 0193-0826.

Journal of Library Automation. Chicago: American Library Association, 1968–. Quarterly. LC 68-6437//R82. ISSN 0022-2240.

Journal of Library History, Philosophy and Comparative Librarianship. Austin, TX: 1966–. Quarterly. LC 65-9989. ISSN 0275-3650. (Formerly *Journal of Library History,* 1966–1975.)

Law Library Journal. Chicago: American Association of Law Libraries, 1908–. Quarterly. LC 41-21688//R6. ISSN 0023-9283.

Library Acquisitions: Practice and Theory. Elmsford, NY: Pergamon Press, 1977–. Quarterly. LC 77-647728. ISSN 0364-6408.

Library Journal. New York: R.R. Bowker, 1876–. Semimonthly, except July–August. LC 76-645271. ISSN 0363-0277.

Library Quarterly. Chicago: University of Chicago, 1931–. Quarterly. LC 32-12448. ISSN 0024-2519.

Library Research. Norwood, NJ: Ablex Publishing, 1979–. Quarterly. LC 79-643718. ISSN 0164-0763.

Library Resources and Technical Services. Chicago: American Library Association, 1957–. Quarterly. LC 59-3198. ISSN 0024-2527. (Formed by the merger of *Serial Slants* and *Journal of Cataloging and Classification.*)

Library Trends. Champaign: University of Illinois at Urbana-Champaign, 1952–. Quarterly. LC 54-62638. ISSN 0024-2594.

Medical Library Association. Bulletin. Chicago: Medical Library Association, 1911–. Quarterly. LC 16-76616. ISSN 0025-7338.

Microform Review. Westport, CT: Meckler Publishing, 1972–. Quarterly. LC 72-620299. ISSN 0002-6530.

Notes. Philadelphia: Music Library Association, 1942–. Quarterly. LC 43-45299//R542. ISSN 0027-4380.

Online. Weston, CT: Online, 1977–. Quarterly. LC 78-640551. ISSN 0416-5422.

Public Libraries. Chicago: American Library Association, 1978–. 4/yr. ISSN 0163-5506. (Formerly *Just Between Ourselves,* 1962–1969; *PLA Newsletter,* 1962–1977.)

RQ. Chicago: American Library Association, 1960–. Quarterly. LC 77-23834. ISSN 0033-7072.

RSR Reference Services Review. Ann Arbor, MI: Perian Press, 1972–. LC 73-642283//R74. ISSN 0090-7324.

School Library Journal. New York: R.R. Bowker, 1954–. Monthly except June and July. LC 77-646483. ISSN 0362-8930.

School Library Media Quarterly. Chicago: American Library Association, 1981–. 4/yr. LC 82-640987. ISSN 0278-4823. (Formerly *School Libraries,* 1951–1972; *School Media Quarterly,* 1972–1980.)

Special Libraries. New York: Special Libraries Association, 1910– . 4/yr. LC 11-25280rev2*. ISSN 0038-6723.

Wilson Library Bulletin. Bronx, NY: H.W. Wilson, 1914– . Monthly except July and August. LC 80-9008(rev.42). ISSN 0043-5651.

1.

Circulation

Amnesty

Academic

■ A report published in 1977 of the experience of the University of Rhode Island that declared February 1976 as a 1-time amnesty *showed that* the library was able to clear 219 bills for overdue materials that year in February as compared to clearing 52 bills during February 1974 and 77 bills in February 1975 when no amnesty was in effect. **(003)**

Automation—General Issues

General

■ A survey reported in 1982 of the directors of 20 (19 or 95% responding) OCLC distributing networks (e.g., ILLINET, SOLINET, FEDLINK, etc.) *showed that* the 5 most commonly reported current or planned uses of members' records supplied through OCLC reported by 14 respondents were (multiple responses allowed):

union list	11 respondents
circulation control	11 respondents
subject access	10 respondents
management information	8 respondents
interlibrary loan	6 respondents **(343)**

Academic

■ A 1967 survey by the Institute of Higher Education at Teachers College, Columbia University, of innovative programs in libraries in academic institutions with liberal arts programs (sample size: 1,193; responding: 781 or 65%) *showed that* 100 (13%) of responding libraries reported having automated circulation systems, of which 11% had been installed since 1961. An additional 134 (16%) planned to install such systems at the time of the study. **(190)**

■ A 1979 survey of library automation in post-secondary educational institutions in Canada (survey size: 423 libraries; responding: 283 or 67%) *showed that*, of an average of 256 respondents for each of the following items, the distribution of automated activities was as follows (multiple responses allowed):

cataloging	47.2% respondents
online bibliographic searching	34.2% respondents

continued

COM catalog	24.2% respondents	
circulation	19.8% respondents	
ordering	16.5% respondents	
photo-sense ID	7.7% respondents	
online catalog	3.2% respondents	**(556)**

■ A 1980 survey of all Association of Research Libraries circulation managers (population: 98; 76 or 78% responding) *showed that* 30 or 39% of the circulation systems were manual (19% of the total respondents used McBee systems), 26 or 34% were batch, and 20 or 26% were online (15% of the total respondents used LIBS100 online systems). Manual systems were reported in use an average of 26 years, batch systems were reported in use an average of 8 years, and online systems were reported in use an average of 3 years.   **(338)**

Ibid. . . . *showed that* 74% of batch system respondents reported satisfaction with both their hardware and software, compared to 60% of the online system managers reporting satisfaction with hardware and 65% reporting satisfaction with software. Furthermore, 63% of the batch system managers reported downtime was no problem, compared to 75% of the online managers so reporting.   **(338)**

■ A 1980 survey of North American medical school libraries concerning automation of internal library operations (population: 139; responding: 93 or 69%) *showed that* 8 (8.6%) respondents reported online catalogs, 15 (16.1%) reported either batch or online automated circulation systems, and 20 (21.5%) reported using machine records to produce book or computer output microform (COM) catalogs. Further, 9 (9.7%) respondents reported plans to have online catalogs within a year or 2 of the survey, while 11 (11.8%) reported plans for automated circulation within a year or 2 of the survey.   **(741)**

■ A 1981 survey of faculty, students, staff, and community users of the University of Cincinnati Libraries (sample size: 4,074; responding: 912 or 22.4%, including 436 or 39% faculty response and 218 or 11% student response) *showed that*, when asked which should be automated first of 3 possibilities, faculty, university administrators, and community users picked the public card catalog as first priority with circulation second and periodicals third, while students and library staff picked circulation as first priority with the public card catalog second and periodicals third.   **(522)**

Special

■ A 1980 survey of North American medical school libraries concerning automation of internal library operations (population: 139; responding: 93 or 69%) *showed that* 8 (8.6%) respondents reported online catalogs, 15 (16.1%) reported either batch or online automated circulation systems, and 20 (21.5%) reported using machine records to produce book or computer output microform (COM) catalogs. Further, 9 (9.7%) respondents reported plans to have online catalogs within a year or 2 of the survey, while 11 (11.8%) reported plans for automated circulation within a year or 2 of the survey. **(741)**

Automation—Turnkey

Academic

■ A 1974 comparison of a semiautomated (Mohawk punched card system) vs. manual circulation system at Colorado State University *showed that* the unit costs of the manual system were $0.365 [per circulation transaction] vs. $0.474 [per circulation transaction] for the automated system, an increase of 29.9%. **(331)**

■ A study reported in 1980 comparing the costs of a manual and an automated circulation system (CLSI LIBS100) at the University of California, Davis, *showed that* direct labor costs were reduced by the computer equipment and maintenance costs more than offset this saving. However, since overall automated circulation costs were projected to increase more slowly than overall manual circulation costs, an increase in circulation activity of 20% would equal out the cost differences in the 2 systems. **(035)**

■ A 1980 survey of all Association of Research Libraries circulation managers (population: 98; 76 or 78% responding) *showed that* 30 or 39% of the circulation systems were manual (19% of the total respondents used McBee systems), 26 or 34% were batch, and 20 or 26% were online (15% of the total respondents used LIBS100 online systems). Manual systems were reported in use an average of 26 years, batch systems were reported in use an average of 8 years, and online systems were reported in use an average of 3 years. **(338)**

Automation-Manual Comparison

Academic

■ A 1974 comparison of a semiautomated (Mohawk punched card system) vs. manual circulation system at Colorado State University *showed that* the unit costs of the manual system were $0.365 [per circulation transaction] vs. $0.474 [per circulation transaction] for the automated system, an increase of 29.9%. **(331)**

■ A study reported in 1980 comparing the costs of a manual and an automated circulation system (CLSI LIBS100) at the University of California, Davis, *showed that* direct labor costs were reduced by the computer equipment and maintenance costs more than offset this saving. However, since overall automated circulation costs were projected to increase more slowly than overall manual circulation costs, an increase in circulation activity of 20% would equal out the cost differences in the 2 systems. **(035)**

■ A 1980 survey of all Association of Research Libraries circulation managers (population: 98; 76 or 78% responding) *showed that* 30 (39%) of the circulation systems were manual (19% of the total respondents used McBee systems), 26 (34%) were batch, and 20 (26%) were online (15% of the total respondents used LIBS100 online systems). Manual systems were reported in use an average of 26 years, batch systems were reported in use an average of 8 years, and online systems were reported in use an average of 3 years. **(338)**

Ibid. . . . *showed that* circulation managers of manual systems were 43% male vs. 57% female, that managers of batch systems were 54% male vs. 46% female, and that managers of online systems were 55% male vs. 45% female. **(338)**

Ibid. . . . *showed that* 3% of the manual system managers reported their system was "close to ideal," compared to 12% of batch system managers so reporting and 45% of online managers so reporting. **(338)**

Ibid. . . . *showed that* 16 (53%) of the manual system managers, 12 (47%) of the batch system managers, and 16 (80%) of the online system managers "agreed" or "strongly agreed" that their circulation systems were reliable. **(338)**

Ibid. . . . *showed that* that 9 (30%) of the manual system managers, 15 (54%) of the batch system managers, and 14 (70%) of the online system managers "agreed" or "strongly agreed" that their circulation system's records were "very accurate." **(338)**

Ibid. . . . *showed that* 56% of the manual system managers, 46% of the batch system managers, and 40% of the online system managers agreed with the statement "users tend to expect more service than the department can give." **(338)**

Ibid. . . . *showed that* 65% of the online managers, 48% of the batch managers, and 50% of the manual managers felt that patron complaints were "most often substantive," while 90% of online managers, 84% of batch managers, and 79% of manual managers rejected the statement that patrons "complain far too much." **(338)**

Ibid. . . . *showed that* 93% of the manual managers, 85% of the batch managers, and 70% of the online managers agreed with the statement "the circulation department should be oriented towards users' expectations." **(338)**

Books—General Issues

Academic

■ A 1-year study during 1964-65 at the Yale Medical Library concerning book and journal circulation (34,825 circulations) *showed that* journals accounted for 59.1% of the circulations while books accounted for 40.9% of the circulations. **(674)**

■ A study reported in 1977 at the University of Pittsburgh, based on the complete circulation history during the period October 1968-June 1976, *showed that* circulation was a good indicator of total book/monograph use. For example, based on 30-day samples of in-house use taken over a period of 2 academic terms and involving 29,098 items, 75% of the items used in-house had also circulated externally by the end of the sample period, with an additional 4% of the in-house items circulating the following year. Further, of 4,250 books/monographs loaned on interlibrary loan during the period January 1969-December 1975, 3,246 (76.4%) had external circulations, with the remaining 1,004 items accounting for only .34% of the total circulation during the period of the study. Finally, of 33,277 books/ monographs selected for reserve during the period January 1969-December 1975, 27,854 (83.7%) had external circulations, with the remaining 5,423 items accounting for only 1.84% of the total circulation during the period of this study. **(666)**

■ A study reported in 1979 at the Polk Library of the University of Wisconsin, Oshkosh, of books circulated to faculty and students during 6 sample days (1,371 titles circulated) *showed that* 157 (11%) books circulated every 30 days or more frequently, that 392 (29%) books circulated every 90 days or more frequently, that 879 (64%) books circulated once a year or more frequently, and that 1,360 (99.1%) circulated at least once every 8 years or more frequently. **(473)**

■ A study reported in 1980 at Emporia State University (Kansas) involving book and periodical use data for 1 year *showed that* the ratio between periodical and book use for the major subject areas was as follows: social/behavorial sciences, 9.1 to 1; life sciences, 3.4 to 1; pure/applied sciences, 3.1 to 1; and fine arts/humanities, 1.1 to 1. **(311)**

Ibid. . . . *showed that* the ratio between periodical and book use for the major user groups was as follows: undergraduate students, 2.1 to 1; graduate students, 1.6 to 1; and faculty, 7.4 to 1. **(311)**

■ A study reported in 1981 at DePauw University of circulation patterns over a 5-year period (1973-77) for a group of newly acquired monographs (sample size: 1,904 books) *showed that* in 5 years the following circulation pattern obtained:

no circulation	702 (36.9%)	books
1-5 circulations	951 (49.9%)	books
6-10 circulations	166 (8.7%)	books
11+ circulations	85 (4.5%)	books **(573)**

Ibid. . . . *showed that* there was a statistically significant difference in the circulation rates of gift books and those books purchased on the recommendation of classroom instructors or librarians, with the gift books circulating less than the purchased books (significant at the .01 level). For example, of 189 gift books, 121 (64.0%) did not circulate at all [during the 5-year period], while of 1,715 purchased books 581 (33.8%) did not circulate at all [during the 5-year period]. **(573)**

Ibid. . . . *showed that* there was a statistically significant difference in the circulation rates of books selected by the classroom instructors (1,542 books) and those books selected by librarians (173 books), with the books selected by the librarians circulating more (significant at the .01 level). For example, 74% of the librarian-selected books were either lightly circulated or not circulated at all compared to 87.3% of the books selected by classroom instructors, while 26% of the librarian-selected books were either moderately or heavily circulated compared to 12.7% of the books selected by classroom instructors.   **(573)**

Special

■ A 1-year study during 1964-65 at the Yale Medical Library concerning book and journal circulation (34,825 circulations) *showed that* journals accounted for 59.1% of the circulations while books accounted for 40.9% of the circulations.   **(674)**

Books—Age

Academic

■ A 1-year study during 1964-65 at the Yale Medical Library concerning book and journal circulation (34,825 circulations) *showed that* the importance of book currency varied considerably by subject area. For example, in the areas of biochemistry, neurology, and neoplasms, 90% of the circulations were accounted for by imprints going back 12 years, 17 years, and 17 years, respectively, while in the areas of surgery, biology, and infectious diseases, 90% of the circulations were accounted for by imprints going back 42 years, 39 years, and 37 years, respectively.   **(674)**

Ibid. . . . *showed that* currency was more important for journals than books. For example, 71% of the journals circulated had been published within the last 9 years, while only 66% of the books that circulated had been published within 9 years. Further, 90% of the journal circulations involved materials no more than 22 years old, while 90% of the book circulations required materials up to 28 years old.   **(674)**

■ A study reported in 1977 at the University of Pittsburgh, based on the complete circulation history during the period October 1968-June 1976, *showed that* approximately 40% of the new acquisitions did not circulate. Specifically, of 36,892 books/monographs acquired in 1969, 14,697 (39.8%) of the acquired materials had never circulated in a 7-year period. Further, of the 22,172 items that did circulate 1 or more times during the first 7 years, 72.76% were circulated 1 or more times during their first or second year in the library. "The six-year circulation history of all books and monographs acquired in the calendar year 1970 exhibited a strikingly similar pattern." **(666)**

Ibid. . . . *showed that*, if a book did not circulate within the first 2 years of ownership, "the chances of its ever being borrowed were reduced to less than 1 in 5." Further, if the book did not circulate within the first 6 years of ownership, its chances of "ever being borrowed were reduced to less than 1 chance in 50." **(666)**

■ A 1977 study of book circulation in Columbia-Greene Community College (sample size: 1,317 items or 6% of holdings) *showed that* as a group older materials tended to circulate less than newer materials. During a 15-month period 29% of a sample of 107 items purchased in 1969 circulated compared to 55% circulation in a sample of 162 items purchased in 1977, with a definite overall movement in the intervening years toward higher circulation rates for newer materials. **(229)**

■ A study reported in 1978 at the University of Pittsburgh of 98%+ of its circulation records for the book/monograph collection during the period October 1968-December 1975 (1,500,000 total circulations) *showed that* 16% of newly acquired items were used in the first year, 24% were used in the second year, and 8% in the third year. **(667)**

■ A study reported in 1979 at the Polk Library of the University of Wisconsin, Oshkosh, of a random sample of 1,098 books in the collection *showed that* 129 (11.8%) had been in the collection for at least 7.5 years and had not circulated, compared to 351 (32%) that had circulated and 618 (56.3%) that had not been in the collection that long. **(473)**

Ibid. . . . *showed that*, of the 129 books that had been in the collection for at least 7.5 years and not circulated, the reasons for their nonuse appeared to be:

specialized (historical sources, technical/scholarly, foreign language)	64 (49.6%) books
obsolete (superceded, outdated controversy)	35 (27.1%) books
out-of-fashion literature and art	23 (17.8%) books
irrelevant/no obvious reason	7 (5.4%) books **(473)**

■ A study reported in 1981 at DePauw University of circulation patterns over a 5-year period (1973-77) for a group of newly acquired monographs (sample size: 1,904 books) *showed that* generally circulation decreased with the books' length of time in the library. Comparing the circulation rate of the 1,904 books during the first 3 years with their circulation rate during the fourth and fifth years revealed that, while 356 (18.6%) increased their circulation rate, 719 (37.7%) had no change in circulation rate and 829 (43.5%) had a decrease in circulation rate. Further, 83.3% of the books uncirculated in years 1-3 remained uncirculated in years 4-5. **(573)**

Public

■ A study reported in 1979 at the Washington State Library based on 5 days' circulation information (1,878 items) and a shelflist sample of 159 titles, *showed that*:

90% of the user needs for monographs could be satisfied with monographs that had circulated within the past 35 months (these constituted 50% of the collection);

95% of the user needs for monographs could be satisfied with monographs that had circulated within the past 58 months (these constituted 60% of the collection);

and 99% of the user needs for monographs could be satisfied with monographs that had circulated within the past 131 months (these constituted 85% of the collection).

Data accurate to ±1.55 months at the .99 confidence level. **(527)**

Special

■ A 1-year study during 1964-65 at the Yale Medical Library concerning book and journal circulation (34,825 circulations) *showed that* the importance of book currency varied considerably by subject area. For example, in the areas of biochemistry, neurology, and neoplasms, 90% of the circulations were accounted for by imprints going back 12 years, 17 years, and 17 years, respectively, while in the areas of surgery, biology, and infectious diseases, 90% of the circulations were accounted for by imprints going back 42 years, 39 years, and 37 years, respectively. **(674)**

Ibid. . . . *showed that* currency was more important for journals than books. For example, 71% of the journals circulated had been published within the last 9 years, while only 66% of the books that circulated had been published within 9 years. Further, 90% of the journal circulations involved materials no more than 22 years old, while 90% of the book circulations required materials up to 28 years old. **(674)**

Books—Availability

Academic

■ A study reported in 1977 at Case Western Reserve concerning the impact of shortening the loan period at the Sears Library, containing 200,000 volumes in science, technology, and management, from a semester loan (in 1972) to a 4-week loan (in 1974) *showed that* 203 of 423 book requests (48%) were immediately satisfied under the semester loan system, while 245 of 437 book requests (56%) were immediately satisfied under the 4-week loan system. **(447)**

Ibid. . . . *showed that*, of the 423 requests studied during the semester loan system, 70 (16.5%) were unavailable because circulating, while of 437 requests studied during the 4-week loan system, 43 (9.8%) were unavailable because circulating. **(447)**

Ibid. . . . *showed that*, of the 220 book requests not immediately satisfied under the semester loan system and the 192 book requests not immediately satisfied under the 4-week loan system, reasons for failure were as follows:

	SEMESTER LOAN	4-WEEK LOAN
not owned by library	52 (23.6%)	38 (19.8%)
on loan or in-house use	81 (36.8%)	48 (25.0%)
library malfunctions	29 (13.2%)	45 (23.4%)
user errors	49 (22.3%)	50 (26.0%)
other	9 (4.1%)	11 (5.7%) **(447)**

■ A study reported in 1978 at the undergraduate library of the University of Tennessee, Knoxville, of patron success rate in finding books over a 5-week period (sample size: 1,010 patrons; responding: 503 or 49.5%, involving 2,375 titles) *showed that* the 828 titles not available involved 1,025 volumes. The 2 main reasons for unavailability were: volumes checked out (729 or 71.1%) and volumes unaccounted for (208 or 20.3%). Binding accounted for 22 (2.1%) volumes, while interlibrary loan accounted for 2 (0.2%) volumes. **(466)**

■ A study reported in 1983 at a medium-sized academic library, involving 504 volumes chosen at random from the card catalog, *showed that* 437 (86.7%) were available on the shelf, 25 (5.0%) were in circulation, and 42 (8.3%) were not available for other reasons. **(521)**

Books—Hardbound versus Paperback

Public

■ A study reported in 1979 at the Oklahoma City/County Metropolitan Library System *showed that* during FY 1978-79, for an uncataloged paperback collection of 76,862 items, each item circulated an average of 4.75 times during the year. This compared to an average circulation of 2.31 times per item during the same period for a collection of 465,326 cataloged hardback books. **(231)**

Ibid. . . . *showed that* during the month of July 1979 the average number of circulations per volume for 15,784 cataloged adult hardback volumes purchased in FY 1976-77 was .25, for 18,163 volumes purchased in FY 1977-78 was .33, and for 18,569 volumes purchased in FY 1978-79 was .64. This compared to the average number of circulations per volume for adult uncataloged paperbacks of .32 for a group of 6,743 volumes purchased in FY 1976-77, .54 for a group of 11,760 volumes purchased in FY 1977-78, and .87 for 19,138 volumes purchased in FY 1978-79. **(231)**

Ibid. . . . *showed that* during the month of July 1979 the average number of circulations per volume for 4,723 juvenile cataloged hardback volumes purchased in FY 1976-77 was 1.20, for 4,777 volumes purchased in FY 1977-78 was 1.18, and for 4,771 volumes purchased in 1978-79 was 1.28. This compares to the average number of circulations per volume for juvenile uncataloged paperbacks of .79 for 2,973 volumes purchased in FY 1976-77, 1.06 for 3,349 volumes purchased in 1977-78, and 1.09 for 3,037 volumes purchased in FY 1978-79. **(231)**

Ibid. . . . . *showed that* for 18,996 adult hardback books and 19,126 adult paperback books purchased in FY 1976-77 the cost ratio based on purchase price alone of hardback to paperback was 4.1 to 1 while the cost per circulation (again based on purchase price only) of hardback to paperback was 4.2 to 1. For slightly more materials in FY 1977-78 the cost ratio of hardbound to paperback was 3.7 to 1 and the cost per circulation was 3.89 to 1. **(231)**

Ibid. . . . *showed that* for 5,624 juvenile hardback books and 6,031 paperback books purchased in FY 1976-77 the cost ratio based on purchase price alone of hardback to paperback was 5.9 to 1 while the cost per circulation (again based on purchase price only) of hardback to paperback was 2.7 to 1. For approximately the same number of materials purchased in FY

1977-78 the cost ratio of hardbound to paperback was 4.8 to 1, and the cost per circulation was 2.6 to 1.   **(231)**

■ A 1982 survey of American and Canadian public libraries (sample size: 279; response rate: 68 or 24%) *showed that* approximately 27.4% (±5.9%, representing a 95% confidence interval for the population at large) of the books purchased by responding libraries were mass market paperbacks while approximately 11% (±6.3% representing a 95% confidence interval for the population at large) of the circulating collections were mass market paperbacks. These percentages of books purchased were statistically independent of the institutional characteristics (e.g., size of population served) of the libraries.   **(273)**

Ibid. . . . *showed that*, while approximately 11% of the circulating collections consisted of mass market paperbacks, these books accounted for approximately 18.2% of the book circulation, with hardcover books accounting for the rest.   **(273)**

Ibid. . . . *showed that* the circulation ratio of hardcover books to paperback books for matched titles in a given year was overall 1 to 1.3 while the overall ratio of cost of hardcover books to paperback books (purchase price only) was 1 to .26. The only large aberration in the overall circulation ratio when subcategories were considered was the subcategory "movie and tv tie-ins," which had a circulation ratio of hardback to paperback of 1 to 3.4.   **(273)**

Books—Subject

Academic

■ A 1-year study during 1964-65 at the Yale Medical Library concerning book and journal circulation (34,825 circulations) *showed that* the importance of book currency varied considerably by subject area. For example, in the areas of biochemistry, neurology, and neoplasms, 90% of the circulations were accounted for by imprints going back 12 years, 17 years, and 17 years, respectively, while in the areas of surgery, biology, and infectious diseases, 90% of the circulations were accounted for by imprints going back 42 years, 39 years, and 37 years, respectively.   **(674)**

Ibid. . . . *showed that* not all subject areas covered in the library are equally used. Specifically, of 67 subject fields covered in the library, "over half" of the book and journal circulations fell into 7 subject fields, while 82% of the circulations fell into 21 of the subject fields. **(674)**

Ibid. . . . *showed that* the ratio of book to journal circulations varied considerably by subject. For example, of 1,171 circulations in the area of experimental medicine, journals accounted for 98.8% of the circulations, while in the area of zoology, journals accounted for 14.3% of the circulations. **(674)**

■ 2 studies reported in 1971 and undertaken at the University of Southwestern Louisiana, comparing circulation by subject area with in-house use by subject area, *showed that* there was a strong positive correlation. In the first study 8,954 circulated books were compared with 4,532 books used in-house using finely delineated LC and Dewey class spans relating to academic departments. The overall Pearson correlation was r = .86 with a significance level no greater than .05. In the second study, 2,386 circulated books were compared to 1,102 books used in-house using broader subject areas based on LC first and second letters and Dewey tens. The overall Pearson correlation was r = .84 with a significance level no greater than .01. **(207)**

■ A 1977 study at the Music Library of the University of California, Berkeley, to investigate weeding criteria (based on a sample of 116 circulated volumes and a sample of 515 volumes from the shelf) *showed that* weeding on the basis of circulation activity in distinct subject areas was the most feasible idea. For example, the number of books that had never been charged out ranged from 5.6% of the books in "performance practice" to 35.0% of the books in "history." **(756)**

■ A study reported in 1980 at Emporia State University (Kansas) involving book and periodical use data for 1 year *showed that* the ratio between periodical and book use for the major subject areas was as follows: social/behavorial sciences, 9.1 to 1; life sciences, 3.4 to 1; pure/applied sciences, 3.1 to 1; and fine arts/humanities, 1.1 to 1. **(311)**

Special

■ A 1-year study during 1964-65 at the Yale Medical Library concerning book and journal circulation (34,825 circulations) *showed that* the importance of book currency varied considerably by subject area. For example, in the areas of biochemistry, neurology, and neoplasms, 90% of the circulations were accounted for by imprints going back 12 years, 17 years, and 17 years, respectively, while in the areas of surgery, biology, and infectious diseases, 90% of the circulations were accounted for by imprints going back 42 years, 39 years, and 37 years, respectively.   **(674)**

Ibid. . . . *showed that* not all subject areas covered in the library are equally used. Specifically, of 67 subject fields covered in the library, "over half" of the book and journal circulations fell into 7 subject fields, while 82% of the circulations fell into 21 of the subject fields.   **(674)**

Ibid. . . . *showed that* the ratio of book to journal circulations varied considerably by subject. For example, of 1,171 circulations in the area of experimental medicine, journals accounted for 98.8% of the circulations, while in the area of zoology, journals accounted for 14.3% of the circulations.   **(674)**

Circulation Rate

Academic

■ A 1970 study at Sir George Williams University (Canada) of mono-graphic circulation in the social sciences and humanities (sample size: 444 volumes) *showed that* 60% of the collection had circulated once in the last 3 years, that 25% had circulated more than 3 times in the last 3 years, and 10% had circulated more than 8 times in the last 3 years.   **(538)**

Ibid. . . . *showed that* 53% of the collection had circulated within the last 2 years, that 43% had circulated within the last year, and 15% had circulated within the last 3 months.   **(538)**

■ A sample of faculty patrons before (1971) and after (1972) the installation of departmental microfiche catalogs of the collection and an accompanying twice-daily book delivery system at Georgia Tech *showed that* the new system changed the way faculty retrieved books from the library. Phone requests increased from 0 to 21.6% of total checkouts, books obtained by going to the library decreased from 88% to 71.6% of total checkouts, and books obtained by sending someone else to the library decreased from 10.5% to 2.7%.   **(106)**

■ A study in 1974 of the relationship between book loan periods and use in the Physics Library at Ohio State University *showed that* reduction of the loan period of high-use items to 1 week increased circulation (and presumably the number of patrons having access to high-use items) over a year's time by 20.9%. Circulation in the previous 2 years had declined by 6 and 7%, respectively. **(128)**

■ A comparison reported in 1975 of circulation statistics at the Georgia Tech library for Spring quarter 1971 and Spring quarter 1972, before and after they had installed microfiche catalogs for the collection in 35 academic and research departments and an accompanying twice-daily book delivery service, *showed that* faculty book circulation as a percentage of total book circulation increased from 13% to 16%, a statistically significant difference. **(106)**

■ A 1977 study of book circulation in Columbia-Greene Community College (sample size: 1,317 items or 6% of holdings) *showed that* 35% of the titles circulated during a 15-month period. **(229)**

■ A study of 1977 survey information gathered by the National Center for Educational Statistics (U.S. Office of Education) concerning the degree to which 1,146 college and university libraries (Liberal Arts Colleges I and II; Comprehensive Universitites and Colleges I and II) met the 1975 Standards for College Libraries (ACRL) *showed that* the average number of loans per FTE student per year was 24 with a median of 19 loans, while the average number of directional and reference questions asked per FTE student per week was .33 with a median of .17 questions. **(486)**

■ A survey reported in 1978 of randomly selected 4-year college and university libraries in the U.S. (sample size: 1,001; responding: from 97 to 325 or 5.4% to 18%, depending on the amount of information supplied) *showed that* out of 292 libraries responding the annual circulation rate per FTE student was 25.4 books. **(487)**

■ A study reported in 1980 over a 6-year period (1973-78) at West Virginia University main library, concerning the effect of switching from closed to open stacks in 1976 with a collection of just under 1 million volumes of primarily humanities and social science materials, *showed that* annual nonreserve circulation decreased from 194,899 in 1973 to 146,949 in 1978. During this period a substantial growth in enrollment took place. **(484)**

■ A study reported in 1980 at the Health Sciences Library of the University of California, San Francisco, over a 21-week period in 1979 to determine the effects of limiting journal circulation *showed that*, when a 5-year backfile of all first-copy journals was made noncirculating, the average weekly circulation dropped 40.8% (from 2,971 items per week to 1,759 items per week) while the average in-house copying increased 135.7% (from 1,938 article equivalents, i.e., total copying divided by 8.5, to 4,567 article equivalents). **(731)**

■ A study reported in 1981 of data on 1,146 2-year colleges as reported in the 1977 Higher Education General Information Surveys and compared to the 1979 Association of College and Research Libraries standards *showed that* libraries in private schools averaged about 4 times as many loans per student per year as libraries in public schools. Specifically, overall the number of loans per FTE student per year averaged 14 with a median of 7, including privately supported schools (224 reporting), which averaged 36 with a median of 10, and publicly supported schools (906 reporting), which averaged 9 with a median of 7. **(500)**

■ A study reported in 1983 concerning costs among academic libraries based on data gathered by the National Center for Education Statistics for the year 1977 and various sources of institutional data (involving 3,057 institutions, including 2-year public, 2-year private, 4-year public, and 4-year private schools) *showed that* the strongest and most consistent correlation for all 4 types of libraries was between number of volumes held and number of items circulated. Specifically, the correlation coefficient by type of library was:

2-year public college libraries   r = .67
2-year private college libraries   r = .68
4-year public college and
    university libraries   r = .88
4-year private college and
    university libraries   r = .84

[No significance level reported.] **(797)**

■ A study reported in 1983 of 3 surveys made by the American Medical Association's Division of Library and Archival Services in 1969, 1973, and 1979 concerning the status of health sciences libraries in the U.S. (survey size for each survey ran between 12,000-14,000 health-related organizations with a response rate for each survey around 95%) *showed that* the average number of items circulated in 1979 in hospital health science libraries was 3,196 items per year, with circulation ranging from an average of 641 items per year for the libraries in the smallest hospitals to 8,007 items per year for the libraries in the largest hospitals. **(747)**

Public

■ A study in 1968 *showed that*, when overdue fines were eliminated in Virgo County Libraries (Terre Haute, Indiana) (overdue notices and replacement charges continued), borrowing increased by a monthly average of 19% while the number of individuals whose borrowing privileges were suspended for nonreturn of materials decreased by a monthly average of 38.8%. **(077)**

■ An attempt reported in 1982 to establish 4 input measures and 4 output measures for public libraries, based on published statistical reports for 301 New Jersey public libraries over a 6-year period (1974-79) and survey data for 96 public libraries in New Jersey, *showed that* (per capita based on number of residents in the library's service area):

INPUT MEASURES

The proportion of budget spent on materials averaged 19.9% with a standard deviation of .081 (based on 301 libraries).

The new volumes per capita averaged .181 with a standard deviation of .097 (based on 301 libraries).

The periodical titles per capita averaged .0094 with a standard deviation of .0054 (based on 301 libraries).

The circulation per volume averaged 1.79 with a standard deviation of .77 (based on 301 libraries).

OUTPUT MEASURES

The circulation per capita averaged 5.04 with a standard deviation of 3.07 (based on 301 libraries).

The patron visits per capita averaged 2.82 with a standard deviation of 1.82 (based on 96 libraries).

The reference questions per capita averaged 1.12 with a standard deviation of .79 (based on 96 libraries).

The in-library uses of materials per capita averaged 2.29 with a standard deviation of 2.02 (based on 96 libraries). **(576)**

■ A survey of 53 U.S. public libraries (all responding) reported in 1983 concerning circulation and expenditures *showed that*, using 1980 as a base year (index value = 100), circulation had increased in 1981 by 4% (index value = 104) and in 1982 by a further 3% (index value = 107). Further, between 1980 and 1982 the circulation ratio between adult and juvenile materials had remained unchanged, i.e., adult materials accounted for

69% of the circulation, and juvenile materials accounted for 31% of the circulation.   (791)

Special

■ A study reported in 1980 at the Health Sciences Library of the University of California, San Francisco, over a 21-week period in 1979 to determine the effects of limiting journal circulation *showed that* when a 5-year backfile of all first-copy journals was made noncirculating, the average weekly circulation dropped 40.8% (from 2,971 items per week to 1,759 items per week) while the average in-house copying increased 135.7% (from 1,938 article equivalents, i.e., total copying divided by 8.5, to 4,567 article equivalents).   (731)

■ A study reported in 1983 of 3 surveys made by the American Medical Association's Division of Library and Archival Services in 1969, 1973, and 1979 concerning the status of health sciences libraries in the U.S. (survey size for each survey ran between 12,000-14,000 health-related organizations with a response rate for each survey around 95%) *showed that* the average number of items circulated in 1979 in hospital health science libraries was 3,196 items per year, with circulation ranging from an average of 641 items per year for the libraries in the smallest hospitals to 8,007 items per year for the libraries in the largest hospitals.   (747)

Document Delivery

Academic

■ A survey in 1970 of the users of a library book delivery system for the campus of the University of Colorado (survey population: 377; responding: 208 or 55% [of whom 89% were resident teaching faculty]) *showed that* 33% of the faculty had used it during the first 18 months of its operation, with 68% of the respondents rating the service as excellent and 23% rating the service as good.   (123)

Ibid. . . . *showed that* of those responding 46% were in the humanities and social sciences; 36% were in the pure and applied sciences; 13% were in interdisciplinary institutes; and 4% were administrators or no answer.
                                                                            (123)

Ibid. . . . *showed that* 54% of the respondents reported that the campus book delivery system had changed their pattern of library use. The main reasons given were saved time, library easier to use, and library more convenient to use. **(123)**

Ibid. . . . *showed that* after 18 months of the campus book delivery operation 43% of the respondents assessed the service as either important or essential to their work. **(123)**

■ A sample of faculty patrons before (1971) and after (1972) the installation of departmental microfiche catalogs of the collection and an accompanying twice-daily book delivery system at Georgia Tech *showed that* the new system changed the way faculty retrieved books from the library. Phone requests increased from 0 to 21.6% of total checkouts, books obtained by going to the library decreased from 88% to 71.6% of total checkouts, and books obtained by sending someone else to the library decreased from 10.5% to 2.7%. **(106)**

■ A comparison reported in 1975 of circulation statistics at the Georgia Tech library for Spring quarter 1971 and Spring quarter 1972, before and after they had installed microfiche catalogs for the collection in 35 academic and research departments and an accompanying twice-daily book delivery service, *showed that* faculty book circulation as a percentage of total book circulation increased from 13% to 16%, a statistically significant difference. **(106)**

■ A study reported in 1977 at the University of Minnesota Twin Cities campus concerning attitudes held by heads of academic units toward departmental libraries independent of the university library system (sample size: 167; responding: 108 or 64.7%, including 67 respondents with independent departmental libraries and 41 respondents without such libraries) *showed that*, of the respondents with independent departmental libraries, a document delivery system was considered "helpful" by 79% [no raw number given] and "essential" by 15% [no raw number given], while of those respondents without an independent departmental library, a document delivery system was considered "helpful" by 66% [no raw number given] and "essential" by 17% [no raw number given]. **(451)**

■ A study reported in 1978 at Indiana University, Bloomington, of materials requested through a delivery service to faculty in the political science and economics departments during a 32-month period (October 1972-June 1975), involving 39 political scientists and 14 economists (40-50% of the faculty in the departments) and 5,478 articles from 620 different journals and newspapers, *showed that* availability of the materials requested on the delivery service, based on 2,544 requests and a library policy that did not allow periodicals to circulate outside of the library, was as follows:

90% of the material was immediately available;

98% of the material was ultimately available from the library's holdings;

and an additional 1% was available through interlibrary loan. **(421)**

Ibid. . . . *showed that* when the delivery service supplied copies of contents pages, 30.3% of all requests for material were the result of this current awareness service, which was used by 40 (64%) of the faculty.
(421)

Ibid. . . . *showed that* the chief reason for a journal being unavailable was reshelving, which accounted for 56% of the unavailable journals. **(421)**

Ibid. . . . *showed that* 9 titles accounted for 20.2% of the requests, while 43 titles accounted for 50.3% of the requests. **(421)**

Ibid. . . . *showed that* articles published after 1950 (the study concluded June 1975) accounted for 97.6% of the requests. **(421)**

Ibid. . . . *showed that* for economists 5 journal titles accounted for 25.5% of all requests, while 25 journal titles accounted for 60.1% of all requests. For political scientists 11 journal titles accounted for 25.9% of all requests, while 56 titles accounted for 60.1% of the requests. **(421)**

Fines and Penalties

Academic

■ A 1955 survey of university librarians in the U.S. and Canada (directed primarily though not exclusively to state-supported institutions) requesting information on faculty loan policies and practices (sample size: 120; responding: 84 or 70%) *showed that* 2 libraries reported that faculty were liable for fines while 81 reported they were not; 31 libraries reported that faculty were liable for lost book processing fees while 43 reported they were not; and 64 reported that faculty were liable for lost book replacement costs while 17 reported they were not. **(178)**

■ A survey reported in 1963 of faculty loan policies in the 62 ARL libraries and 62 libraries in small/medium undergraduate institutions (53 and 55 responding, respectively) *showed that* of responding libraries 52 ARL libraries and 55 college libraries reported that faculty members are not subject to an overdue fine. **(167)**

■ A study reported in 1974 of 4,361 book returns at Purdue University General Library under 3 different fine/reminder systems *showed that* there were statistically significant differences at the .001 level (ANOVA) in the return of books. The group that received both an overdue notice and a threat of encumbrance as well as the group that received only an overdue notice had a statistically significantly higher return rate than the group that received neither. No statistically significant difference was found between the group which received both an overdue notice and threat of encumbrance and the group which received only the overdue notice. **(098)**

■ A survey in 1976 conducted at Indiana University Library of 2,000 recalled books from the main (not undergraduate) collection *showed that* the average time it took to return recalled materials was 5.91 days for undergrads, 5.86 days for graduates, and 17.07 days for faculty. The large difference between faculty and student response was due to the excessively slow return rate of a small minority (46 individuals, 6%) of the faculty who took longer than 22 days to return recalled material. This was dramatically reduced in 1978 with the institution of recall fines for faculty. **(019)**

Public

■ A study in 1968 *showed that*, when overdue fines were eliminated in Virgo County Libraries (Terre Haute, Indiana) (overdue notices and replacement charges continued), 3,237 first overdue notices (3%) were sent out on circulation of 254,044 items in the first 7 months. The first notice was effective in 61% of the cases, with 1,247 (39%) requiring a second and final notice. The final notice was effective in 79% of the cases, leaving only 262 individuals who had their borrowing privileges suspended. **(077)**

Ibid. . . . *showed that* borrowing increased by a monthly average of 19% while the number of individuals whose borrowing privileges were suspended for nonreturn of materials decreased by a monthly average of 38.8%. **(077)**

Ibid. . . . *showed that*, in an informal survey of 315 patrons during the first month, the following was the response to the new policy:

strongly agree	156	(49.5%)
mildly agree	54	(17.1%)
no opinion	7	(2.2%)
mildly disapprove	44	(14.0%)
strongly disapprove	54	(17.1%)

(077)

■ A 1981 study of public libraries in North Carolina (58 or 74.3% responding) concerning the problem of overdue material *showed that* there was no statistically significant relationship between whether a library charged fines or not and its overdue rates. Specifically, of 47 libraries that charged fines, 16.52% of their material was not returned by date due; .74% of the material was not returned at the end of 1980-81 (based on 38 libraries charging fines); .65% of the material circulated in 1979-80 was not returned by the end of 1979-80 (based on 27 libraries charging fines); and .55% of the material circulated in 1978-79 was not returned by the end of 1978-79 (based on 21 libraries charging fines). This compared to 3 libraries who did not charge fines who reported that 26.81% of their material was not returned by the due date, that .7% of 1980-81's circulations were not returned at the end of 1980-81, that .44% of 1979-80's circulations were not returned by the end of 1979-80, and .55% of 1978-79's circulations were not returned by the end of 1978-79. **(274)**

Ibid. . . . *showed that* there was no statistically significant relationship between return of overdue materials and telephoning patrons with overdue materials, between overdue rates for libraries that renewed materials and libraries that did not, between the number of notices a library sends out and the overdue rate, only limited and ambiguous evidence of any difference in overdue rates between libraries who take patrons to court and those who do not, and no consistent evidence of a relationship between a library's loan period and its overdue rate. **(274)**

Ibid. . . . *showed that* there was no statistically significant relationship between whether a library restricted borrowing privileges of patrons with overdues or not and overdue rates (significant at the .05 level). Specifically, of 43 libraries with restriction policies, 17.52% of their material was not returned by date due while .74% of material circulated in 1980-81 was not returned by year's end (based on 36 responding libraries), .65% of material circulated in 1979-80 was not returned by year's end (based on 28 responding libraries), and .55% of the material circulated in 1978-79 was not returned by year's end (based on 23 responding libraries). This compared to 14.82% of the material not returned by due date in 7 nonrestricting libraries, .7% of material circulated in 1980-81 that was not returned by year's end (based on 5 nonrestricting libraries), 27% of material circulated in 1979-80 that was not returned by year's end (based on 2 nonrestricting libraries), and .57% of material circulated in 1978-79 that was not returned by year's end. **(274)**

General Issues

Academic

■ Studies at the University of Southwestern Louisiana and the South Dakota School of Mines and Technology on circulation data gathered during academic 1969-70 and 1967-68, respectively, *showed that* books whose class numbers matched profiles of class numbers associated with courses taught were more likely to circulate than books whose class numbers did not match the profiles. The Louisiana study was based on 56,828 items circulated vs. 115,201 items not circulated and was statistically significant at the .005 level. The South Dakota study was based on 7,696 items circulated vs. 40,433 items not circulated and was statistically significant at the .005 level. **(211)**

■ A 1972 study at a midwestern university comparing the titles that faculty checked out with the titles on the monthly list of new acquisitions sent to those faculty (only those faculty who had elected to receive acquisitions lists were involved) *showed that* within 30 days 7 titles out of 232 were charged out from 1 monthly list and 15 titles out of 280 were charged out from a second monthly list. **(130)**

■ A study at the University of Southeastern Louisiana reported in 1972 of 8,953 circulated books, 4,507 books left on tables, and 158,569 books left on the shelves *showed that* books whose class numbers matched profiles of class numbers associated with courses taught were more likely to be charged out after being taken from the shelves than left on the tables. (The study was statistically significant at the .005 level.) **(211)**

■ A study reported in 1974 comparing the effectiveness of collection development of librarians, teaching faculty, and approval plans in 5 academic libraries (3 college, 2 university) by comparing books bought by each of these groups with the books' subsequent circulation records

(7,213 books studied in total) *showed that* the circulation rates of the materials selected by each of the 3 groups was different to a statistically significant degree, with materials selected by librarians circulating most, materials selected by teaching faculty circulating next most often, and approval plan materials circulating the least. [Significance level not given.] **(628)**

■ A 1977 study at the Music Library of the University of California, Berkeley, to investigate weeding criteria (based on a sample of 116 circulated volumes and a sample of 515 volumes from the shelf) *showed that* weeding on the basis of circulation activity in distinct subject areas was the most feasible idea. For example, the number of books that had never been charged out ranged from 5.6% of the books in "performance practice" to 35.0% of the books in "history." **(756)**

■ A study reported in 1977 at the University of Pittsburgh, based on the complete circulation history during the period October 1968-June 1976, *showed that* over a 1-year period the circulation pattern showed a "log normal distribution." Further, during a 1-year period the number of items that circulated 2 times was roughly half the number of items that circulated once, the number of items that circulated 3 times was roughly half the number of items that circulated twice, and so on. For example, for 1974:

circulating 1 time	63,526 items
circulating 2 times	25,653 items
circulating 3 times	11,855 items
circulating 4 times	6,055 items
circulating 5 times	3,264 items **(666)**

■ A study at Washington State University reported in 1982 of a relatively homogeneous book collection (a recent social science collection of 100,000 volumes) *showed that* combining patron reports of missing items in a collection subject area with the circulation rate of that subject area produces a combined predictor of the actual number of missing items in that area that is a more powerful predictor than either of the 2 factors singly with an $r2 = .4892$. **(062)**

Ibid. . . . *showed that* circulation rate of a collection subject area was the second strongest predictor of the actual number of missing items in that area with an $r2 = .3187$. **(062)**

Ibid. . . . *showed that* patron reports of missing items in a collection subject area were the strongest single predictor of the actual number of missing items in that area with an r2 = .4049. **(062)**

Public

■ A questionnaire survey of 3,500 public library cardholders in 5 medium-sized Pennsylvania cities in conjunction with interviews of a randomly selected sample of householders in 1 city by the Institute of Public Administration (at Pennsylvania State University) under contract to the Pennsylvania State Library in 1965 *showed that* the major service provided by the library was book borrowing (60% of respondents), while reference/information was the next most important use made of the library (26% of respondents). **(084)**

■ A 1979 telephone survey of 1,046 New Orleans residents over the age of 12 *showed that* 37.6% report having visited the public library in the past 12 months. Of these, 28.2% visited the Central Library, and 71.8% visited the branches. The 1978 circulation figures indicated that the Central Library accounted for 28% of the overall circulation and the branches for 72% of the overall circulation. **(166)**

■ A study reported in 1980 of monthly library circulation data for the 12-year period 1965-76 for the Dallas public library system (main library and 14 branches), comparing circulation before and after the institution of the Nonresident Fee Card Program, *showed that* analysis by a series of statistical tests indicated strong evidence for statistically significant circulation declines in 3 libraries, moderate evidence for statistically significant declines in 2 libraries, weak evidence for declines in 4 libraries, and no evidence of statistically significant declines in 6 libraries. (Significance at the .05 level for all tests.) **(266)**

■ An attempt reported in 1982 to establish 4 input measures and 4 output measures for public libraries, based on published statistical reports for 301 New Jersey public libraries over a 6-year period (1974-79) and survey data for 96 public libraries in New Jersey, *showed that* (per capita based on number of residents in the library's service area):

INPUT MEASURES

The proportion of budget spent on materials averaged 19.9% with a standard deviation of .081 (based on 301 libraries).

The new volumes per capita averaged .181 with a standard deviation of .097 (based on 301 libraries).

The periodical titles per capita averaged .0094 with a standard deviation of .0054 (based on 301 libraries).

The circulation per volume averaged 1.79 with a standard deviation of .77 (based on 301 libraries).

OUTPUT MEASURES

The circulation per capita averaged 5.04 with a standard deviation of 3.07 (based on 301 libraries).

The patron visits per capita averaged 2.82 with a standard deviation of 1.82 (based on 96 libraries).

The reference questions per capita averaged 1.12 with a standard deviation of .79 (based on 96 libraries).

The in-library uses of materials per capita averaged 2.29 with a standard deviation of 2.02 (based on 96 libraries).   **(576)**

■ A survey of 53 U.S. public libraries (all responding) reported in 1983 concerning circulation and expenditures *showed that*, using 1980 as a base year (index value = 100), circulation had increased in 1981 by 4% (index value = 104) and in 1982 by a further 3% (index value = 107). Further, between 1980 and 1982 the circulation ratio between adult and juvenile materials had remained unchanged, i.e., adult materials accounted for 69% of the circulation, and juvenile materials accounted for 31% of the circulation.   **(791)**

Special

■ A study reported in 1968 of 6 months' library monographic circulation at the Air Force Cambridge research library (Massachusetts), involving 835 individuals who checked out at least 1 book out of 1,000 potential patrons and a total of 8,966 items checked out, *showed that* 12.5% of the 835 users accounted for 50% of the circulations while 50% of the 835 accounted for 90% of the circulations.   **(191)**

Gifts

Academic

■ A 1982 study at the University of Wisconsin, Milwaukee concerning the use of gift books in 2 separate parts of the collection, both the PS 3537-PS 3545 section (American literature, 1,039 nongift books and 104 gift books) and the QC 6-QC 75 section (physics, 1,023 nongifts and 16 gift books), *showed that* the average use of gift books was considerably lower than the use of nongift books. Specifically, nongift books in the PS section averaged 5.30 uses since added to the collection, while gift books averaged 1.23 uses; nongift books in the QC section averaged 5.31 uses since added to the collection, while gift books averaged 2.25 uses. **(807)**

Ibid. . . . *showed that* a higher percentage of gift books than nongift books did not circulate at all and that of the books that circulated at least once gift books circulated much less on the average than nongift books. Specifically, in the PS section 343 (33.0%) of the nongift books did not circulate compared to 59 (56.7%) of the gift books, while in the QC section 272 (26.6%) of the nongift books did not circulate compared to 6 (60.0%) of the gift books. Further, of the books that did circulate, the average number of uses for PS nongifts was 7.92 since added to the collection compared to 2.84 uses for gifts, while the average number of uses for QC nongifts was 7.23 since added to the collection compared to 3.60 uses for gifts. **(807)**

Ibid. . . . *showed that* the use of gift books followed a Bradford-like distribution. For example, in the PS section, the 14 (13.5%) most frequently used books accounted for 80 (62.5%) of the uses. **(807)**

Journals—General Issues

Academic

■ A 1-year study during 1964-65 at the Yale Medical Library concerning book and journal circulation (34,825 circulations) *showed that* journals accounted for 59.1% of the circulations while books accounted for 40.9% of the circulations. **(674)**

■ A 1971 study of journal availability at the Woodward Biomedical Library (University of British Columbia, Canada) during a 12-day period *showed that* the number of items not available due just to circulation was relatively small. Of 281 items not found (excluding items not held by UBC), 64 (22.8%) were circulating. These 64 items accounted for 4.7% of total circulation and 1.5% of total recorded journal use (including room use) during this period. **(692)**

■ A 1972-73 study of periodical usage in the Education-Psychology Library at Ohio State University *showed that*, based on 57,332 periodical circulation transactions generated over an almost complete academic year, 100 titles (out of 804) provided 72.4% of the materials circulated and 150 titles provided 83.8% of the materials circulated. Further, 23.9% of the

804 titles were not used at all, and 48% were used no more than 5 times. **(455)**

Ibid. . . . *showed that*, of the 360 periodical titles that circulated 11 or more times, 337 (93.6%) were indexed by at least 1 of the following services: *Readers' Guide, Education Index, Current Index to Journals in Education* and *Psychological Abstracts*. Further, all of the 50 most used titles were indexed in 1 of the 4 services mentioned, while only 34 (17.7%) of the 192 journals that did not circulate at all were indexed in 1 of the 4 services. **(455)**

■ A study reported in 1980 at Emporia State University (Kansas), involving book and periodical use data for 1 year, *showed that* the ratio between periodical and book use for the major subject areas was as follows: social/behavorial sciences, 9.1 to 1; life sciences, 3.4 to 1; pure/applied sciences, 3.1 to 1; and fine arts/humanities, 1.1 to 1. **(311)**

Ibid. . . . *showed that* the ratio between periodical and book use for the major user groups was as follows: undergraduate students, 2.1 to 1; graduate students, 1.6 to 1; and faculty, 7.4 to 1. **(311)**

■ A 1980 survey of 110 academic libraries (83 or 75.5% responding) of all types and sizes concerning their provision of a collection or services for the recreational reading interests of the campus community *showed that* 64.2% of the average recreational reading services collection (rrs) was fiction (79% of those with rrs responding), that 32.4% of the average rrs collection consisted of paperbacks (99% responding), that 42 (82.4%) of the respondents with rrs collections reported crafts and hobbies books in the collection, that the average size of the rrs collection was 1,636 titles with a median size of 700 titles, and that 18 (35.3%) libraries reported periodicals as part of their rrs collection (averaging 47 titles). 39% of these 18 libraries circulated their rrs periodicals. **(315)**

Special

■ A 1-year study during 1964-65 at the Yale Medical Library concerning book and journal circulation (34,825 circulations) *showed that* journals accounted for 59.1% of the circulations while books accounted for 40.9% of the circulations. **(674)**

■ A 1971 study of journal availability at the Woodward Biomedical Library (University of British Columbia, Canada) during a 12-day period *showed that* the number of items not available due just to circulation was relatively small. Of 281 items not found (excluding items not held by UBC), 64 (22.8%) were circulating. These 64 items accounted for 4.7% of total circulation and 1.5% of total recorded journal use (including room use) during this period.   **(692)**

Journals—Age

Academic

■ A 1-year study during 1964-65 at the Yale Medical Library concerning book and journal circulation (34,825 circulations) *showed that* the importance of journal currency varied considerably by subject area. For example, in the areas of nursing, science, and the cardiovascular system, 90% of the circulations were accounted for by 12 years, 13 years, and 15 years of backfiles of journal materials, respectively, while in the areas of anatomy, pathology, and psychology, 90% of the circulations required 30 years of backfiles of journal materials each.   **(674)**

Ibid. . . . *showed that* currency was more important for journals than books. For example, 71% of the journals circulated had been published within the last 9 years, while only 66% of the books that circulated had been published within 9 years. Further, 90% of the journal circulations involved materials no more than 22 years old, while 90% of the book circulations required materials up to 28 years old.   **(674)**

■ A 1972-73 study of periodical usage in the Education-Psychology Library at Ohio State University *showed that*, based on 7,623 periodical circulation transactions generated in just over a month, 5 years of holdings provided 75.6% of the materials circulated and 8 years of holdings provided 90.6% of the materials circulated.   **(455)**

■ A 1974 study at the Woodward Biomedical Library, University of British Columbia (Canada), involving circulation of individual issues of 106 journal titles out of both a 20-year and 5-year backfile (761 issues and 471 issues, respectively), *showed that* based on a single inventory only 3% of the issues in the 20-year backfile and 5% of the issues in the 5-year backfile were not available because they were circulating.   **(711)**

■ A study reported in 1978 at Indiana University, Bloomington, of materials requested through a delivery service to faculty in the political

science and economics departments during a 32-month period (October 1972-June 1975), involving 39 political scientists and 14 economists (40-50% of the faculty in the departments) and 5,478 articles from 620 different journals and newspapers, *showed that* articles published after 1950 (the study concluded June 1975) accounted for 97.6% of the requests.
(421)

Special

■ A 1-year study during 1964-65 at the Yale Medical Library concerning book and journal circulation (34,825 circulations) *showed that* the importance of journal currency varied considerably by subject area. For example, in the areas of nursing, science, and the cardiovascular system, 90% of the circulations were accounted for by 12 years, 13 years, and 15 years of backfiles of journal materials, respectively, while in the areas of anatomy, pathology, and psychology, 90% of the circulations required 30 years of backfiles of journal materials each.
(674)

Ibid. . . . *showed that* currency was more important for journals than books. For example, 71% of the journals circulated had been published within the last 9 years, while only 66% of the books that circulated had been published within 9 years. Further, 90% of the journal circulations involved materials no more than 22 years old, while 90% of the book circulations required materials up to 28 years old.
(674)

■ A 1974 study at the Woodward Biomedical Library, University of British Columbia (Canada), involving circulation of individual issues of 106 journal titles out of both a 20-year and 5-year backfile (761 issues and 471 issues, respectively), *showed that* based on a single inventory only 3% of the issues in the 20-year backfile and 5% of the issues in the 5-year backfile were not available because they were circulating.
(711)

Journals—Availability

Academic

■ A 1971 study of journal availability at the Woodward Biomedical Library (University of British Columbia, Canada) during a 12-day period *showed that* the number of items not available due just to circulation was relatively small. Of 281 items not found (excluding items not held by UBC), 64 (22.8%) were circulating. These 64 items accounted for 4.7% of total circulation and 1.5% of total recorded journal use (including room use) during this period.
(692)

Ibid. . . . *showed that*, out of 4,326 journal items, 370 (8.6%) were not found immediately. The reasons for unavailability were as follows:

title not held or issue not received	100 (27%) items	
in use or awaiting reshelving	98 (26%) items	
being bound	66 (18%) items	
user errors	41 (11%) items	
administrative reasons (on "hold" shelf, misshelved, etc.)	40 (11%) items	
unspecified reasons	25 (7%) items	**(692)**

■ A 1974 study at the Woodward Biomedical Library, University of British Columbia (Canada), involving circulation of individual issues of 106 journal titles out of both a 20-year and 5-year backfile (761 issues and 471 issues, respectively), *showed that* based on a single inventory only 3% of the issues in the 20-year backfile and 5% of the issues in the 5-year backfile were not available because they were circulating.   **(711)**

■ A study reported in 1978 at Indiana University, Bloomington, of materials requested through a delivery service to faculty in the political science and economics departments during a 32-month period (October 1972-June 1975), involving 39 political scientists and 14 economists (40-50% of the faculty in the departments) and 5,478 articles from 620 different journals and newspapers, *showed that* availability of the materials requested on the delivery service, based on 2,544 requests and a library policy that did not allow periodicals to circulate outside of the library, was as follows:

90% of the material was immediately available;

98% of the material was ultimately available from the library's holdings;

and an additional 1% was available through interlibrary loan. **(421)**

Ibid. . . . *showed that* the chief reason for a journal being unavailable was reshelving, which accounted for 56% of the unavailable journals. **(421)**

■ A study reported in 1983 at a medium-sized academic library, involving 504 volumes chosen at random from the card catalog, *showed that* 437 (86.7%) were available on the shelf, 25 (5.0%) were in circulation, and 42 (8.3%) were not available for other reasons. **(521)**

Special

■ A 1971 study of journal availability at the Woodward Biomedical Library (University of British Columbia, Canada) during a 12-day period *showed that* the number of items not available due just to circulation was relatively small. Of 281 items not found (excluding items not held by UBC), 64 (22.8%) were circulating. These 64 items accounted for 4.7% of total circulation and 1.5% of total recorded journal use (including room use) during this period. **(692)**

Ibid. . . . *showed that*, out of 4,326 journal items, 370 (8.6%) were not found immediately. The reasons for unavailability were as follows:

title not held or issue not received	100 (27%) items	
in use or awaiting reshelving	98 (26%) items	
being bound	66 (18%) items	
user errors	41 (11%) items	
administrative reasons (on "hold" shelf, misshelved, etc.)	40 (11%) items	
unspecified reasons	25 (7%) items	**(692)**

■ A 1974 study at the Woodward Biomedical Library, University of British Columbia (Canada), involving circulation of individual issues of 106 journal titles out of both a 20-year and 5-year backfile (761 issues and 471 issues, respectively), *showed that* based on a single inventory only 3% of the issues in the 20-year backfile and 5% of the issues in the 5-year backfile were not available because they were circulating. **(711)**

Journals—Subject

Academic

■ A 1-year study during 1964-65 at the Yale Medical Library concerning book and journal circulation (34,825 circulations) *showed that* the importance of journal currency varied considerably by subject area. For example, in the areas of nursing, science, and the cardiovascular system, 90% of the circulations were accounted for by 12 years, 13 years, and 15 years of backfiles of journal materials, respectively, while in the areas of anatomy, pathology, and psychology, 90% of the circulations required 30 years of backfiles of journal materials each.   **(674)**

Ibid. . . . *showed that* not all subject areas covered in the library are equally used. Specifically, of 67 subject fields covered in the library, "over half" of the book and journal circulations fell into 7 subject fields, while 82% of the circulations fell into 21 of the subject fields.   **(674)**

Ibid. . . . *showed that* the ratio of book to journal circulations varied considerably by subject. For example, of 1,171 circulations in the area of experimental medicine, journals accounted for 98.8% of the circulations, while in the area of zoology, journals accounted for 14.3% of the circulations.   **(674)**

■ A 1977 study at the Music Library of the University of California, Berkeley, to investigate weeding criteria (based on a sample of 116 circulated volumes and a sample of 515 volumes from the shelf) *showed that* weeding on the basis of circulation activity in distinct subject areas was the most feasible idea. For example, the number of books that had never been charged out ranged from 5.6% of the books in "performance practice" to 35.0% of the books in "history."   **(756)**

■ A study reported in 1978 at Indiana University, Bloomington, of materials requested through a delivery service to faculty in the political science and economics departments during a 32-month period (October 1972-June 1975), involving 39 political scientists and 14 economists (40-50% of the faculty in the departments) and 5,478 articles from 620 different journals and newspapers, *showed that* for economists 5 journal titles accounted for 25.5% of all requests, while 25 journal titles accounted for 60.1% of all requests. For political scientists 11 journal titles accounted for 25.9% of all requests, while 56 titles accounted for 60.1% of the requests.   **(421)**

■ A study reported in 1980 at Emporia State University (Kansas) involving book and periodical use data for 1 year *showed that* the ratio between periodical and book use for the major subject areas was as follows: social/behavorial sciences, 9.1 to 1; life sciences, 3.4 to 1; pure/applied sciences, 3.1 to 1; and fine arts/humanities, 1.1 to 1. **(311)**

Special

■ A 1-year study during 1964-65 at the Yale Medical Library concerning book and journal circulation (34,825 circulations) *showed that* the importance of journal currency varied considerably by subject area. For example, in the areas of nursing, science, and the cardiovascular system, 90% of the circulations were accounted for by 12 years, 13 years, and 15 years of backfiles of journal materials, respectively, while in the areas of anatomy, pathology, and psychology, 90% of the circulations required 30 years of backfiles of journal materials each.   **(674)**

Ibid. . . . *showed that* not all subject areas covered in the library are equally used. Specifically, of 67 subject fields covered in the library, "over half" of the book and journal circulations fell into 7 subject fields, while 82% of the circulations fell into 21 of the subject fields.   **(674)**

Ibid. . . . *showed that* the ratio of book to journal circulations varied considerably by subject. For example, of 1,171 circulations in the area of experimental medicine, journals accounted for 98.8% of the circulations, while in the area of zoology, journals accounted for 14.3% of the circulations.   **(674)**

Library Budget Issues

Academic

■ A study reported in 1977 at the Purdue University Libraries and Audio-Visual Center to determine and allocate library and audiovisual costs to teaching departments and user groups *showed that*, based upon library use as determined by circulation of materials, library and AV center costs would be allocated as follows:

undergraduates	43.9% of the costs
graduate students	36.7% of the costs
faculty	9.5% of the costs
other (includes staff)	9.9% of the costs **(459)**

Public

■ A study reported in 1977 of 32 county libraries in Florida that related 4 variables (level of education in county, potential users, per capita operating cost, and per capita library collection) *showed that* allocating library budgets on the basis of circulation was likely to favor communities with higher levels of education and strong collections since both level of education and per capita collection were highly correlated with per capita circulation. Specifically, while the 4 variables taken together accounted for "about 74%" of the variance in per capita library circulation, the 2 most important variables were "level of education" (beta weight = .60) and "per capita library collection" (beta weight = .44). The regression coefficients of both of these variables were reported as statistically significant although no significance level was reported. **(617)**

Loan Periods

Academic

■ A 1955 survey of university librarians in the U.S. and Canada (directed primarily though not exclusively to state-supported institutions) requesting information on faculty loan policies and practices (sample size: 120; responding: 84 or 70%) *showed that* 3 libraries reported no limit on length of faculty loans, 1 reported faculty loan period of 3 years, 45 reported an annual audit, 13 reported semester/quarter/term loans, and the rest reported miscellaneous periods under 1 year. **(178)**

■ A survey reported in 1963 of faculty loan policies in the 62 ARL libraries and 62 libraries in small/medium undergraduate institutions (53 and 55 responding, respectively) *showed that* 27 of the ARL respondents and 26 of the college respondents reported faculty loan periods of indefinite length, 10 ARL and 17 college reported faculty loan periods of an academic year, and 15 ARL and 10 college reported faculty loan periods of a semester/quarter. **(167)**

■ A study in 1974 of the relationship between book loan periods and use in the Physics Library at Ohio State University *showed that* reduction of the loan period of high-use items to 1 week increased circulation (and presumably the number of patrons having access to high-use items) over a year's time by 20.9%. Circulation in the previous 2 years had declined by 6 and 7%, respectively. **(128)**

■ A study reported in 1977 at Case Western Reserve concerning the impact of shortening the loan period at the Sears Library, containing 200,000 volumes in science, technology, and management, from a semester loan (in 1972) to a 4-week loan (in 1974) *showed that* 203 of 423 book requests (48%) were immediately satisfied under the semester loan system while 245 of 437 book requests (56%) were immediately satisfied under the 4-week loan system. **(447)**

Ibid. . . . *showed that*, of the 423 requests studied during the semester loan system, 70 (16.5%) were unavailable because circulating, while of 437 requests studied during the 4-week loan system, 43 (9.8%) were unavailable because circulating. **(447)**

Ibid. . . . *showed that*, of the 220 book requests not immediately satisfied under the semester loan system and the 192 book requsts not immediately satisfied under the 4-week loan system, reasons for failure were as follows:

	SEMESTER LOAN	4-WEEK LOAN
not owned by library	52 (23.6%)	38 (19.8%)
on loan or in-house use	81 (36.8%)	48 (25.0%)
library malfunctions	29 (13.2%)	45 (23.4%)
user errors	49 (22.3%)	50 (26.0%)
other	9 (4.1%)	11 (5.7%) **(447)**

■ A study reported in 1980 at the Health Sciences Library of the University of California, San Francisco, over a 21-week period in 1979 to determine the effects of limiting journal circulation *showed that* when a 5-year backfile of all first-copy journals was made noncirculating the average weekly circulation dropped 40.8% (from 2,971 items per week to 1,759 items per week) while the average in-house copying increased 135.7% (from 1,938 article equivalents, i.e., total copying divided by 8.5, to 4,567 article equivalents). **(731)**

Public

■ A 1981 study of public libraries in North Carolina (58 or 74.3% responding) concerning the problem of overdue material *showed that* there was no statistically significant relationship between return of overdue materials and telephoning patrons with overdue materials, between overdue rates for libraries that renewed materials and libraries that did not, between the number of notices a library sends out and the overdue rate, only limited and ambiguous evidence of any difference in overdue rates between libraries who take patrons to court and those who do not, and no consistent evidence of a relationship between a library's loan period and its overdue rate. **(274)**

Special

■ A study reported in 1980 at the Health Sciences Library of the University of California, San Francisco, over a 21-week period in 1979 to determine the effects of limiting journal circulation *showed that* when a 5-year backfile of all first-copy journals was made noncirculating the average weekly circulation dropped 40.8% (from 2,971 items per week to 1,759 items per week) while the average in-house copying increased 135.7% (from 1,938 article equivalents, i.e., total copying divided by 8.5, to 4,567 article equivalents). **(731)**

Maps

Academic

■ A 1972 study of Map Room use at Southern Illinois University during Summer and Fall quarters, involving the circulation of 2,721 maps and aerial photos to 223 borrowers, *showed that* the stated purpose of 60% of the loans was research. **(403)**

Ibid. . . . *showed that* borrowers were: undergraduates (44%), graduate students (32%), and faculty (19%). However, graduate students accounted for 72% of the loans, undergraduates for 16%, and faculty for 10%. **(403)**

Ibid. . . . *showed that* borrowers were "widely scattered in approximately 40 departments." The largest number of borrowers came from the Forestry Department and involved 23 individuals or 10% of the borrowing population. **(403)**

Ibid. . . . *showed that,* in terms of broad areas, 58 (26%) borrowers came from the social sciences, 52 (23%) from the sciences, 37 (17%) from the applied sciences, 24 (11%) from education, and 22 (10%) from humanities. **(403)**

■ A 1972-75 study at Southern Illinois University, Carbondale, of map and aerial photograph circulation from the Map Room *showed that* for all 3 years (1972-73, 1973-74, and 1974-75) undergraduate circulation consistently increased with academic status. Freshmen borrowed less than sophomores, sophomores less than juniors, and juniors less than seniors. **(420)**

Ibid. . . . *showed that* the main general trend over the 3-year period was a decrease in social science use (from 26% of the borrowers and 22% of the borrowing in 1972-73 to 16% of the borrowers and 8% of the borrowing in 1974-75) and an increase in science use (from 22% of the borrowers and 39% of the borrowing in 1972-73 to 25% of the borrowers and 46% of the borrowing in 1974-75). **(420)**

Ibid. . . . *showed that* for 2,699 loans in 1972-73 the purpose of borrowing the material was as follows:

class use	741 (27%)	items
research	544 (20%)	items
recreation	512 (19%)	items
travel	460 (17%)	items
theses and dissertations	271 (10%)	items
other	170 (06%)	items **(420)**

Ibid. . . . *showed that* over the 3-year period the region covered by the maps and photos borrowed was: southern Illinois (37-53% of the borrowing), northern and central Illinois (3-5% of the borrowing), nearby states (10-20% of the borrowing), U.S. (24-31% of the borrowing), and other including space maps (6-13% of the borrowing). **(420)**

Ibid. . . . *showed that* over the 3-year period undergraduates made up 49-52% of the borrowers in any given year, graduate students made up of 25-28% of the borrowers, faculty made up 12-15% of the borrowers, and "other" made up 8-11% of the borrowers. **(420)**

Ibid. . . . *showed that* over the 3-year period undergraduates accounted for 34-38% of the borrowing in any given year, graduates accounted for 30-38% of the borrowing, faculty accounted for 14-22% of the borrowing, and "other" accounted for 8-14% of the borrowing. **(420)**

Ibid. . . . *showed that* over the 3-year period 5 departments accounted for 33-37% of the borrowers and 45-50% of the borrowing. These were: forestry, geology, geography, zoology, and botany. The other borrowers were scattered throughout 80 other departments. **(420)**

Ibid. . . . *showed that* each year the proportion of male to female borrowers was "about 80% male, 20% female, although university enrollment was 36-38% female during this period."   **(420)**

Overdues

Academic

■ A survey reported in 1963 of faculty loan policies in the 62 ARL libraries and 62 libraries in small/medium undergraduate institutions (53 and 55 responding, respectively) *showed that* of responding libraries 52 ARL libraries and 55 college libraries reported that faculty members are not subject to an overdue fine.   **(167)**

■ A study reported in 1974 of 4,361 book returns at Purdue University General Library under 3 different fine/reminder systems *showed that* there were statistically significant differences at the .001 level (ANOVA) in the return of books. The group that received both an overdue notice and a threat of encumbrance as well as the group that received only an overdue notice had a statistically significantly higher return rate than the group that received neither. No statistically significant difference was found between the group that received both an overdue notice and threat of encumbrance and the group that received only the overdue notice.   **(098)**

■ A survey in 1976 conducted at Indiana University Library of 2,000 recalled books from the main (not undergraduate) collection *showed that* the average time it took to return recalled materials was 5.91 days for undergrads, 5.86 days for graduates, and 17.07 days for faculty. The large difference between faculty and student response was due to the excessively slow return rate of a small minority (46 individuals, 6%) of the faculty who took longer than 22 days to return recalled material. This was dramatically reduced in 1978 with the institution of recall fines for faculty.   **(019)**

Public

■ A study in 1968 *showed that*, when overdue fines were eliminated in Virgo County Libraries (Terre Haute, Indiana) (overdue notices and replacement charges continued), 3,237 first overdue notices (3%) were sent out on circulation of 254,044 items in the first 7 months. The first notice was effective in 61% of the cases, with 1,247 (39%) requiring a second and final notice. The final notice was effective in 79% of the cases,

leaving only 262 individuals who had their borrowing privileges suspended.
(077)

Ibid. . . . *showed that* borrowing increased by a monthly average of 19%
while the number of individuals whose borrowing privileges were suspended for nonreturn of materials decreased by a monthly average of
38.8%.   (077)

Ibid. . . . *showed that*, in an informal survey of 315 patrons during the first
month, the following was the response to the new policy:

strongly agree	156 (49.5%)	
mildly agree	54 (17.1%)	
no opinion	7 (2.2%)	
mildly disapprove	44 (14.0%)	
strongly disapprove	54 (17.1%)	(077)

■ A 1981 study of public libraries in North Carolina (58 or 74.3%
responding) concerning the problem of overdue material *showed that* there
was no statistically significant relationship between whether a library
charged fines or not and its overdue rates. Specifically, of 47 libraries that
charged fines, 16.52% of their material was not returned by date due, .74%
of the material was not returned at the end of 1980-81 (based on 38
libraries charging fines), .65% of the material circulated in 1979-80 was not
returned by the end of 1979-80 (based on 27 libraries charging fines), and
.55% of the material circulated in 1978-79 was not returned by the end of
1978-79 (based on 21 libraries charging fines). This compares to 3 libraries
who did not charge fines who reported that 26.81% of their material was
not returned by the due date, that .7% of 1980-81's circulations were not
returned at the end of 1980-81, that .44% of 1979-80's circulations were not
returned by the end of 1979-80, and .55% of 1978-79's circulations were
not returned by the end of 1978-79.   (274)

Ibid. . . . *showed that* there was no statistically significant relationship
between whether a library restricted borrowing privileges of patrons with
overdues or not and overdue rates (significant at the .05 level). Specifically,
of 43 libraries with restriction policies, 17.52% of their material was not
returned by date due, while .74% of material circulated in 1980-81 was not
returned by year's end (based on 36 responding libraries), .65% of material
circulated in 1979-80 was not returned by year's end (based on 28
responding libraries), and .55% of the material circulated in 1978-79 was
not returned by year's end (based on 23 responding libraries). This
compared to 14.82% of the material not returned by due date in 7

nonrestricting libraries, .7% of material circulated in 1980-81 that was not returned by year's end (based on 5 nonrestricting libraries), 27% of material circulated in 1979-80 that was not returned by year's end (based on 2 nonrestricting libraries), and .57% of material circulated in 1978-79 that was not returned by year's end.   **(274)**

Ibid. . . . *showed that* there was no statistically significant relationship between return of overdue materials and telephoning patrons with overdue materials, between overdue rates for libraries that renewed materials and libraries that did not, between the number of notices a library sends out and the overdue rate, only limited and ambiguous evidence of any difference in overdue rates between libraries who take patrons to court and those who do not, and no consistent evidence of a relationship between a library's loan period and its overdue rate.   **(274)**

Ibid. . . . *showed that* there was a statistically significant relationship between population served and long-term overdue rate (significant at the .05 level). Specifically, long-term overdue rates (percentage of books circulated during the year but not returned by the end of the year for 1980-81, 1979-80, and 1978-79) for libraries serving populations over 100,000 were significantly greater than for libraries serving populations under 100,000. These rates were .62% (based on 27 libraries) vs. 1.28% (based on 6 libraries), .60% (based on 19 libraries) vs. 1.08% (based on 3 libraries) and .52% (based on 15 libraries) vs. 1.21% (based on 3 libraries), respectively. Although the difference between short-term overdue rate (percentage of books returned after due date) for the 2 kinds of libraries was not statistically significant, it was greater for those libraries serving populations over 100,000 (namely, 25.01% vs. 15.97%).   **(274)**

Ibid. . . . *showed that* libraries that sent the first overdue notice within 14 days of when the material was due had a statistically significant lower short-term overdue rate than libraries that did not (significant at the .05 level). Specifically, the short-term overdue rate for libraries sending the notice was 15.12% (based on 25 libraries), while the rate for the other libraries was 25.87% (based on 14 libraries). Findings for long-term overdue rates were mixed with only the differences for 1978-79 statistically significant (at the .05 level), although overdue rates for the other 2 years were lower for libraries sending such notices. The overdue rates themselves were (going from 1980-81 to 1978-79):

.61% (based on 19 libraries) vs. .94% (based on 14 libraries),

.50% (based on 14 libraries) vs. .97% (based on 8 libraries), and

.36% (based on 10 libraries) vs. .95% (based on 6 libraries).   **(274)**

Ibid. . . . *showed that* overall respondents reported that approximately 96% of the materials that were overdue as of the last due date would be returned within 1 year of that due date. **(274)**

Patron Restrictions

Academic

■ A 1968 survey of junior colleges by ACRL's Committee on Community Use of Academic Libraries (sample size: 689; responding: 308 or 45%) *showed that* 282 (91%) permit in-building use of library materials by persons other than students, faculty, staff, and their immediate family, 19 (6%) did not permit such use, and 7 (2%) did not answer. **(197)**

Ibid. . . . *showed that* 217 (70%) circulate library material to individuals not associated with the junior college while 88 (28%) did not. 3 institutions did not answer. However, when asked if borrowing privileges or in-building use privileges were extended to all members of the public, 60% replied yes, 38% replied no, and 2% did not answer. **(197)**

Ibid. . . . *showed that* 19 (6%) libraries required a fee or deposit in order to borrow materials, 80% required neither, and 39 (13%) indicated that the question did not apply. **(197)**

Patron Type—Faculty

Academic

■ A study of all library books (2,898) checked out by the faculty (441) of a midwestern university during Spring semester, 1962 *showed that* the checkout rate did not vary greatly from rank to rank, with full professors having the lowest checkout rate (5.6 books per individual) and associate professors having the highest checkout rate (7.9). The overall average number of books checked out per faculty member was 6.6. **(130)**

Ibid. . . . *showed that* the highest per capita faculty book checkout rates were in physics (21.7), library science (20.5), and English (17.0), whereas in the departments of sociology, anthropology, chemistry, library science, and philosophy every faculty member checked out at least 1 book during the semester. **(130)**

■ A 1-year study during 1964-65 at the Yale Medical School Library concerning patron use patterns of library materials (based on 34,825 book/journal circulations) *showed that* 20,563 journal circulations were distributed among members of the medical school as follows (accounting for 74.6% of the journal use):

full-time faculty	32.0% journal uses
students	27.2% journal uses
house officers	11.6% journal uses
part-time faculty	3.8% journal uses **(675)**

Ibid. . . . *showed that* 14,262 book circulations were distributed among members of the medical school as follows (accounting for 51.7% of the book use):

students	24.6% book uses
full-time faculty	17.6% book uses
house officers	6.5% book uses
part-time faculty	3.0% book uses **(675)**

Ibid. . . . *showed that* the per capita book and journal use (over 1 year's time) was as follows:

students	10.0 journals; 6.3 books
full-time faculty	11.9 journals; 4.6 books
house officers	7.9 journals; 3.1 books
part-time faculty	1.6 journals; 0.8 books **(675)**

■ A 1972 study of Map Room use at Southern Illinois University during Summer and Fall quarters, involving the circulation of 2,721 maps and aerial photos to 223 borrowers, *showed that* borrowers were: undergraduates (44%), graduate students (32%), and faculty (19%). However, graduate students accounted for 72% of the loans, undergraduates for 16%, and faculty for 10%. **(403)**

Ibid. . . . *showed that* borrowers (students and faculty) were "widely scattered in approximately 40 departments." The largest number of borrowers came from the Forestry Department and involved 23 individuals or 10% of the borrowing population.   **(403)**

Ibid. . . . *showed that,* in terms of broad areas, 58 (26%) borrowers (students and faculty) came from the social sciences, 52 (23%) from the sciences, 37 (17%) from the applied sciences, 24 (11%) from education, and 22 (10%) from humanities.   **(403)**

■ A 1972-75 study at Southern Illinois University, Carbondale, of map and aerial photograph circulation from the Map Room *showed that* over the 3-year period undergraduates made up 49-52% of the borrowers in any given year, graduate students made up of 25-28% of the borrowers, faculty made up 12-15% of the borrowers, and "other" made up 8-11% of the borrowers.   **(420)**

Ibid. . . . *showed that* over the 3-year period undergraduates accounted for 34-38% of the borrowing in any given year, graduates accounted for 30-38% of the borrowing, faculty accounted for 14-22% of the borrowing, and "other" accounted for 8-14% of the borrowing.   **(420)**

■ A study reported in 1978 at the University of Pittsburgh of 98%+ of its circulation records for the book/monograph collection during the period October 1968-December 1975 (1,500,000 total circulations) *showed that* book/monograph usage by academic status was as follows:

undergraduates	40% total usage
graduate students	33% total usage
faculty	4-5% total usage
all others	15% total usage **(667)**

■ A study reported in 1980 at Emporia State University (Kansas), involving book and periodical use data for 1 year, *showed that* the ratio between periodical and book use for the major user groups was as follows: undergraduate students, 2.1 to 1; graduate students, 1.6 to 1; and faculty, 7.4 to 1.   **(311)**

Special

■ A 1-year study during 1964-65 at the Yale Medical School Library concerning patron use patterns of library materials (base d on 34,825 book/journal circulations) *showed that* 20,563 journal circulations were distributed among members of the medical school as follows (accounting for 74.6% of the journal use):

full-time faculty	32.0% journal uses	
students	27.2% journal uses	
house officers	11.6% journal uses	
part-time faculty	3.8% journal uses	**(675)**

Ibid. . . . *showed that* 14,262 book circulations were distributed among members of the medical school as follows (accounting for 51.7% of the book use):

students	24.6% book uses	
full-time faculty	17.6% book uses	
house officers	6.5% book uses	
part-time faculty	3.0% book uses	**(675)**

Ibid. . . . *showed that* the per capita book and journal use (over 1 year's time) was as follows:

students	10.0 journals; 6.3 books	
full-time faculty	11.9 journals; 4.6 books	
house officers	7.9 journals; 3.1 books	
part-time faculty	1.6 journals; 0.8 books	**(675)**

Patron Type—Student

Academic

■ A 1962 study repeated the following year of all book charges in a 1-month period in the middle of the semester at Eastern Illinois University *showed that* a higher percentage of freshmen checked out books than upperclassmen, with 44% (451) of the freshmen checking books out during this 1-month period in 1962, 35% (238) of the sophomores, 36% (226) of the juniors, 35% (15) of the seniors, and 28% (42) of the graduate students. The per capita number of books checked out in each group was 1.8, 1.2, 1.6, 1.4, 1.7, respectively.   **(172)**

Ibid. . . . *showed that* during the month 63% (1,849) of the students borrowed no books from the library in 1962 and 62% (2,318) borrowed no books in 1963.   **(172)**

■ A study in academic 1963-64 at the Grand Canyon College (Phoenix, Arizona; 1963 enrollment: 479) of circulation records for 9 weeks *showed that* 468 students checked out a total of 3,181 books. Median per capita = 3 books; average per capita = 6.7 books. Half of the student borrowers—the most active half—accounted for 3,024 circulations (95.1% of the total). **(179)**

■ A study during winter quarter 1964 of the book circulation records of 50% of the 742 members of the 1963-64 entering freshman class at the California State Polytechnic College (Pomona) *showed that,* while only 63% of the freshman class returned the following Fall, of those students who had used the library 73.7% returned, compared to the 57% return rate for non-library users. **(183)**

■ A 1-year study during 1964-65 at the Yale Medical School Library concerning patron use patterns of library materials (based on 34,825 book/journal circulations) *showed that* 20,563 journal circulations were distributed among members of the medical school as follows (accounting for 74.6% of the journal use):

full-time faculty	32.0%	journal uses
students	27.2%	journal uses
house officers	11.6%	journal uses
part-time faculty	3.8%	journal uses	**(675)**

Ibid. . . . *showed that* 14,262 book circulations were distributed among members of the medical school as follows (accounting for 51.7% of the book use):

students	24.6%	book uses
full-time faculty	17.6%	book uses
house officers	6.5%	book uses
part-time faculty	3.0%	book uses	**(675)**

Ibid. . . . *showed that* the per capita book and journal use (over 1 year's time) was as follows:

students	10.0 journals; 6.3 books
full-time faculty	11.9 journals; 4.6 books
house officers	7.9 journals; 3.1 books
part-time faculty	1.6 journals; 0.8 books	**(675)**

■ A 1972 study of Map Room use at Southern Illinois University during Summer and Fall quarters, involving the circulation of 2,721 maps and aerial photos to 223 borrowers, *showed that* borrowers were: undergraduates (44%), graduate students (32%), and faculty (19%). However, graduate students accounted for 72% of the loans, undergraduates for 16%, and faculty for 10%. **(403)**

Ibid. . . . *showed that* borrowers (students and faculty) were "widely scattered in approximately 40 departments." The largest number of borrowers came from the Forestry Department and involved 23 individuals or 10% of the borrowing population. **(403)**

Ibid. . . . *showed that*, in terms of broad areas, 58 (26%) borrowers (students and faculty) came from the social sciences, 52 (23%) from the sciences, 37 (17%) from the applied sciences, 24 (11%) from education, and 22 (10%) from humanities. **(403)**

■ A 1972-75 study at Southern Illinois University, Carbondale, of map and aerial photograph circulation from the Map Room *showed that* for all 3 years (1972-73, 1973-74, and 1974-75) undergraduate circulation consistently increased with academic status. Freshmen borrowed less than sophomores, sophomores less than juniors, and juniors less than seniors. **(420)**

Ibid. . . . *showed that* over the 3-year period undergraduates made up 49-52% of the borrowers in any given year, graduate students made up of 25-28% of the borrowers, faculty made up 12-15% of the borrowers, and "other" made up 8-11% of the borrowers. **(420)**

Ibid. . . . *showed that* over the 3-year period undergraduates accounted for 34-38% of the borrowing in any given year, graduates accounted for 30-38% of the borrowing, faculty accounted for 14-22% of the borrowing, and "other" accounted for 8-14% of the borrowing. **(420)**

Ibid. . . . *showed that* each year the proportion of male to female borrowers was "about 80% male, 20% female, although university enrollment was 36-38% female during this period." **(420)**

■ A study of business students (undergraduates and graduates) at University of Delaware, University of Maryland, and Wright State University in 1975 *showed that* less than 50% of the students rated themselves frequent borrowers of library materials.   **(049)**

■ A study reported in 1978 at the University of Pittsburgh of 98% + of its circulation records for the book/monograph collection during the period October 1968-December 1975 (1,500,000 total circulations) *showed that* book/monograph usage by academic status was as follows:

undergraduates	40% total usage
graduate students	33% total usage
faculty	4-5% total usage
all others	15% total usage **(667)**

■ A study reported in 1980 at Emporia State University (Kansas), involving book and periodical use data for 1 year, *showed that* the ratio between periodical and book use for the major user groups was as follows: undergraduate students, 2.1 to 1; graduate students, 1.6 to 1; and faculty, 7.4 to 1.   **(311)**

Special

■ A 1-year study during 1964-65 at the Yale Medical School Library concerning patron use patterns of library materials (based on 34,825 book/journal circulations) *showed that* 20,563 journal circulations were distributed among members of the medical school as follows (accounting for 74.6% of the journal use):

full-time faculty	32.0% journal uses
students	27.2% journal uses
house officers	11.6% journal uses
part-time faculty	3.8% journal uses **(675)**

Ibid. . . . *showed that* 14,262 book circulations were distributed among members of the medical school as follows (accounting for 51.7% of the book use):

students	24.6% book uses
full-time faculty	17.6% book uses
house officers	6.5% book uses
part-time faculty	3.0% book uses **(675)**

Ibid. . . . *showed that* the per capita book and journal use (over 1 year's time) was as follows:

students	10.0 journals; 6.3 books
full-time faculty	11.9 journals; 4.6 books
house officers	7.9 journals; 3.1 books
part-time faculty	1.6 journals; 0.8 books **(675)**

Patron Type—Other

Academic

■ A 1-year study during 1964-65 at the Yale Medical School Library concerning patron use patterns of library materials (based on 34,825 book/journal circulations) *showed that* 20,563 journal circulations were distributed among members of the medical school as follows (accounting for 74.6% of the journal use):

full-time faculty	32.0% journal uses
students	27.2% journal uses
house officers	11.6% journal uses
part-time faculty	3.8% journal uses **(675)**

Ibid. . . . *showed that* 14,262 book circulations were distributed among members of the medical school as follows (accounting for 51.7% of the book use):

students	24.6% book uses
full-time faculty	17.6% book uses
house officers	6.5% book uses
part-time faculty	3.0% book uses **(675)**

Ibid. . . . *showed that* the per capita book and journal use (over 1 year's time) was as follows:

students	10.0 journals; 6.3 books
full-time faculty	11.9 journals; 4.6 books
house officers	7.9 journals; 3.1 books
part-time faculty	1.6 journals; 0.8 books **(675)**

■ A 1968 survey of junior colleges by ACRL's Committee on Community Use of Academic Libraries (sample size: 689; responding: 308 or 45%) *showed that*, on a typical day, 1/3 of the libraries responded that they estimated that they had either no outside users or not more than 1; another 1/3 estimated that 1-4 outsiders visited them on a typical day; 14%

estimated the number between 5 and 9; and 10% estimated that more than
10 outsiders a day visited the library.   **(197)**

■   A study reported in 1978 at the University of Pittsburgh of 98%+ of its
circulation records for the book/monograph collection during the period
October 1968-December 1975 (1,500,000 total circulations) *showed that*
book/monograph usage by academic status was as follows:

undergraduates	40% total usage
graduate students	33% total usage
faculty	4-5% total usage
all others	15% total usage	**(667)**

Special

■   A 1-year study during 1964-65 at the Yale Medical School Library
concerning patron use patterns of library materials (based on 34,825
book/journal circulations) *showed that* 20,563 journal circulations were
distributed among members of the medical school as follows (accounting
for 74.6% of the journal use):

full-time faculty	32.0% journal uses
students	27.2% journal uses
house officers	11.6% journal uses
part-time faculty	3.8% journal uses	**(675)**

Ibid. . . . *showed that* 14,262 book circulations were distributed among
members of the medical school as follows (accounting for 51.7% of the
book use):

students	24.6% book uses
full-time faculty	17.6% book uses
house officers	6.5% book uses
part-time faculty	3.0% book uses	**(675)**

Ibid. . . . *showed that* the per capita book and journal use (over 1 year's
time) was as follows:

students	10.0 journals; 6.3 books
full-time faculty	11.9 journals; 4.6 books
house officers	7.9 journals; 3.1 books
part-time faculty	1.6 journals; 0.8 books	**(675)**

Policy and Procedures

Academic

■ A 1955 survey of university librarians in the U.S. and Canada (directed primarily though not exclusively to state-supported institutions) requesting information on faculty loan policies and practices (sample size: 120; responding: 84 or 70%) *showed that* 32 (39%) libraries reported requiring the physical return of the book as part of the audit process. **(178)**

■ A survey reported in 1968 of 32 urban universities (32 responding; 24 usable responses) concerning faculty studies ("a small enclosed area of individual study; not an open study station") in the library *showed that* 66% of responding libraries do not use a separate circulation policy for faculty studies. **(180)**

■ A 1968 survey of junior colleges by ACRL's Committee on Community Use of Academic Libraries (sample size: 689; responding: 308 or 45%) *showed that* 282 (91%) permit in-building use of library materials by persons other than students, faculty, staff, and their immediate family, 19 (6%) did not permit such use, and 7 (2%) did not answer. **(197)**

Ibid. . . . *showed that* 217 (70%) circulate library material to individuals not associated with the junior college while 88 (28%) did not. 3 institutions did not answer. However, when asked if borrowing privileges or in-building use privileges were extended to all members of the public, 60% replied yes, 38% replied no, and 2% did not answer. **(197)**

Ibid. . . . *showed that* 19 (6%) libraries required a fee or deposit in order to borrow materials, 80% required neither, and 39 (13%) indicated that the question did not apply. **(197)**

■ A survey reported in 1977 of moderate sized (120,000-500,000 volumes) U.S. academic libraries listed in the 1972-73 *American Library Directory* (survey size: 200; responding: 147 or 74%) *showed that* 44% responding libraries circulated current issues of periodicals while 53% reported that they did not. Further, 53% of the libraries reported that they circulated bound volumes of periodicals, while 44% reported that they did not. **(454)**

■ A study reported in 1978 at Indiana University, Bloomington, of materials requested through a delivery service to faculty in the political science and economics departments during a 32-month period (October 1972-June 1975), involving 39 political scientists and 14 economists (40-50% of the faculty in the departments) and 5,478 articles from 620 different journals and newspapers, *showed that* availability of the materials requested on the delivery service, based on 2,544 requests and a library policy that did not allow periodicals to circulate outside of the library, was as follows:

90% of the material was immediately available;

98% of the material was ultimately available from the library's holdings;

and an additional 1% was available through interlibrary loan. **(421)**

■ A 1978 survey of academic law libraries concerning the issue of faculty libraries (a separate collection or library set aside for the use of the law faculty) (survey size: 169 libraries; responding: 115 or 68.0%) *showed that*, of the 70 respondents with faculty libraries, 41 (58.6%) allowed checkout privileges from the main collection to the faculty library. **(795)**

■ A 1980 survey of 110 academic libraries (83 or 75.5% responding) of all types and sizes concerning their provision of a collection or services for the recreational reading interests of the campus community *showed that* 64.2% of the average recreational reading services collection (rrs) was fiction (79% of those with rrs responding), that 32.4% of the average rrs collection consisted of paperbacks (99% responding), that 42 (82.4%) of the respondents with rrs collections reported crafts and hobbies books in the collection, that the average size of the rrs collection was 1,636 titles with a median size of 700 titles, and that 18 (35.3%) libraries reported periodicals as part of their rrs collection (averaging 47 titles). 39% of these 18 libraries circulated their rrs periodicals. **(315)**

■ A 1981 survey of academic libraries selected randomly from OCLC academic library participants concerning the issue of university collections, i.e., collections of publications by the university's own faculty and affiliates (sample size: 184; responding: 103 or 56%) *showed that* 61% of the respondents reported their university collections were housed in closed-access areas, with 79% reporting that the material was noncirculating. However, 86 (83%) did report purchasing duplicates of the university collection for circulation. **(647)**

Public

■ A survey reported in 1968 of Michigan public libraries (559 libraries or branches queried; 462 or 82% responding) receiving periodicals from the state *showed that* the smaller the library the more likely it is to circulate current issues of periodicals, with an overwhelming majority of libraries of all sizes circulating back issues.   **(133)**

■ A 1981 study of public libraries in North Carolina (58 or 74.3% responding) concerning the problem of overdue material *showed that* there was no statistically significant relationship between return of overdue materials and telephoning patrons with overdue materials, between overdue rates for libraries that renewed materials and libraries that did not, between the number of notices a library sends out and the overdue rate, only limited and ambiguous evidence of any difference in overdue rates between libraries who take patrons to court and those who do not, and no consistent evidence of a relationship between a library's loan period and its overdue rate.   **(274)**

Ibid. . . . *showed that* libraries that sent the first overdue notice within 14 days of when the material was due had a statistically significant lower short-term overdue rate than libraries that did not (significant at the .05 level). Specifically, the short-term overdue rate for libraries sending the notice was 15.12% (based on 25 libraries), while the rate for the other libraries was 25.87% (based on 14 libraries). Findings for long-term overdue rates were mixed, with only the differences for 1978-79 statistically significant (at the .05 level), although overdue rates for the other 2 years were lower for libraries sending such notices. The overdue rates themselves were (going from 1980-81 to 1978-79):

.61% (based on 19 libraries) vs. .94% (based on 14 libraries),

.50% (based on 14 libraries) vs. .97% (based on 8 libraries),

.36% (based on 10 libraries) vs. .95% (based on 6 libraries). **(274)**

Ibid. . . . *showed that* there was no statistically significant relationship between whether a library restricted borrowing privileges of patrons with overdues or not and overdue rates (significant at the .05 level). Specifically, of 43 libraries with restriction policies, 17.52% of their material was not returned by date due, while .74% of material circulated in 1980-81 was not returned by year's end (based on 36 responding libraries), .65 % of material circulated in 1979-80 was not returned by year's end (based on 28 responding libraries), and .55% of the material circulated in 1978-79 was not returned by year's end (based on 23 responding libraries). This compared to 14.82% of the material not returned by due date in 7 nonrestricting libraries, .7% of material circulated in 1980-81 that was not returned by year's end (based on 5 nonrestricting libraries), 27% of material circulated in 1979-80 that was not returned by year's end (based on 2 nonrestricting libraries) and .57% of material circulated in 1978-79 that was not returned by year's end. **(274)**

Special

■ A 1974 survey of a random sample of U.S. museum libraries (including history, art, and science museums) listed in the 1973 *Official Museum Directory* (population: 2,556; sample size: 856; responding: 374 or 43.7%) *showed that*, 46% reported open stacks, 49% reported closed stacks, and 5% reported open stacks with restrictions. Further, 76% of the libraries did not lend books. **(412)**

■ A 1978 survey of academic law libraries concerning the issue of faculty libraries (a separate collection or library set aside for the use of the law faculty) (survey size: 169 libraries; responding: 115 or 68.0%) *showed that*, of the 70 respondents with faculty libraries, 41 (58.6%) allowed checkout privileges from the main collection to the faculty library. **(795)**

Recalls

Academic

■ A semester-long study in 1974-75 in the Economics and Political Science Library of Indiana University *showed that* 51% of the books recalled by faculty members were checked out to other faculty members. **(012)**

■ A survey in 1976 conducted at Indiana University Library of 2,000 recalled books from the main (not undergraduate) collection *showed that* the average time it took to return recalled materials was 5.91 days for undergrads, 5.86 days for graduates, and 17.07 days for faculty. The large difference between faculty and student response was due to the excessively slow return rate of a small minority (46 individuals, 6%) of the faculty who took longer than 22 days to return recalled material. This was dramatically reduced in 1978 with the institution of recall fines for faculty.   **(019)**

Ibid. . . . *showed that* students returned recalled books faster than faculty. At the end of 7 days 69% of the recalled materials charged to students had been returned vs. 65% of the material charged to faculty; at the end of 14 days it was 93% return rate for students vs. 85% return rate for faculty.   **(019)**

Ibid. . . . *showed that* 67.3% of all recalled materials were returned within 7 days of the recall notice being sent and 89.5% of all recalled materials were returned within 14 days of the recall notice being sent.   **(019)**

Ibid. . . . *showed that*, while only 6% of the total user population was faculty and only 8% of all circulation charges were to faculty, 41% of all recalled materials were already charged to faculty.   **(019)**

Ibid. . . . *showed that* undergraduates recalled 17.4% of the books and had 16.3% of the books recalled from them, that graduates recalled 3.5 times more books than the faculty, whereas 41% of all recalled material were charged out to faculty.   **(019)**

Public

■ A 1966 survey of 21,385 adult (12 years old or older) public library users in the Baltimore-Washington metropolitan region of Maryland conducted during a 6-week period of patrons entering the library (79.1% of patrons approached filled out the survey instrument) *showed that*, of the unsatisfied respondents, 5,104 (66%) planned to continue their quest. Of these, 59.3% planned to go to another library, 19.9% put a reserve on the book, 7.7% made arrangements for the library to get the material from another library, and 13.1% planned to use other alternatives (e.g., buying the book or borrowing it from friends).   **(301)**

Relation to Catalog Use

Academic

■ A 1976-70 study in the Main Library at Yale University, involving 2,100 interviews at the card catalog during a 1-year period, *showed that* weekly charting of card catalog use and book circulation revealed by inspection that card catalog use and book borrowing always remained in the same proportion.   **(248)**

■ A 1979 study at Iowa State University concerning queuing at the public card catalog during a month and a half period, involving 2,327 sample counts of patrons at the catalog, *showed that* the correlation between card catalog use and exit counts, books circulated, and number of individuals checking out books, while statistically significant (significance level less than .001) in all 3 cases was so low as to be negligible. The highest R^2 (exit count with card catalog use), for example, was .075. With a 1-hour differential between card catalog use counts and number of books circulated, the correlation began to be substantial with an R^2 of 22%. [No significance level given.] **(497)**

Ibid. . . . *showed that*, when the Friday and Sunday counts (there were no Saturday counts) of card catalog patrons were ignored, there was no statistically significant difference among the daily means during Monday through Thursday. For example, the average number of arrivals at the card catalog during a 10-minute period during any of these 4 days ranged from 11.9 patrons (Wednesday) to 12.9 patrons (Monday). **(497)**

Ibid. . . . *showed that* there were statistically significant differences between patron counts at the card catalog by hour of the day, especially when Friday and Sunday (there were no Saturday counts) were excluded. Arrivals at the card catalog during 10-minute periods averaged 9.7 patrons at 10:00 a.m. and rose regularly until a high of 18.0 patrons was reached at 2:00 p.m. and then fell to 8.8 patrons at 4:00 p.m. [No significance level was given.] **(497)**

Relation to Grades

Academic

■ A 1962 study repeated the following year of all book charges in a 1-month period in the middle of the semester at Eastern Illinois University *showed that* inspection suggested a relationship between number of books checked out during this period and grade point average, with 62% (75) of A average students, 44% (399) of B average, 39% (529) of C average, 22% (16) of D average, and 14% (1) of F average students checking out at least 1 book. **(172)**

■ A study in academic 1963-64 at the Grand Canyon College (Phoenix, Arizona; 1963 enrollment: 479) of circulation records for 9 weeks, *showed that* checking books out of the library and GPA did not seem by inspection to be correlated. The average GPA of 150 students who had no recorded use of the library was 1.43, while the average GPA of the 150 students who checked the most books out of the library (7-55 volumes each) was 1.47. **(179)**

■ A study during Winter quarter 1964 of the book circulation records of 50% of the 742 members of the 1963-64 entering freshman class at the California State Polytechnic College (Pomona) *showed that* students who borrowed no books during the quarter earned an average GPA of 2.00 (on a 4.00 scale), while library users earned an average GPA of 2.22. This was a statistically significant difference. **(183)**

Ibid. . . . *showed that* library use and GPA were not equally correlated among majors. No statistically significant GPA accrued to engineering or science majors who used the library, while among arts majors the advantage was 2.37 GPA for library users compared to 2.10 for nonusers, and for agriculture majors the advantage was 2.13 GPA vs. 1.70 for nonusers. **(183)**

Ibid. . . . *showed that*, while only 63% of the freshman class returned the following Fall, of those students who had used the library 73.7% returned, compared to the 57% return rate for non-library users. **(183)**

Relation to Reference Use

Public

■ A study of the gross annual circulation statistics and gross annual reference statistics for the 30 large and medium-large public libraries for the years 1972-73-74, as reported in the *Bowker Annual* 1976, *showed that* there was a fairly strong positive correlation between the 2 figures, with a correlation coefficient of +.80 for 1972, +.75 for 1973, and +.76 for 1974. [No significance level reported.] **(156)**

Reserve Unit

Academic

■ An academic year 1968-69 study of central reserve use at the city campus of the University of Nebraska, Lincoln, *showed that*, of 3,586 titles placed on reserve Fall semester and 3,196 titles placed on reserve Spring semester, 42% of the Fall semester titles did not circulate and 36% of the

Spring semester titles did not circulate. On the other hand 18% of the Fall semester titles and 22% of the Spring semester titles circulated 9 times or more.   **(203)**

Ibid. . . . *showed that*, on the average for the 2 semesters, 33% of the titles coming from lists with 1 to 20 items did not circulate at all, while 42% of the titles from lists with 21 or more items did not circulate.   **(203)**

■   A study in 1972 of reserve reading assignments at the University of Alberta in Edmonton involving 8 classes, 4 where faculty presented students with 1 large list of readings and 4 where faculty presented students with shorter, multiple lists, throughout the semester, *showed that* the materials on the shorter lists were used more frequently (81% of materials on shorter, frequent lists was circulated a number of times equal to or greater than 66% of the class size, while 42% of the materials on the long lists circulated on equal percentages of the class size); a higher number of the items on the shorter, more frequent lists were used (92% of the items on the shorter, more frequent lists were used compared to 57% of the items on the long lists); and use of materials was more evenly spread throughout the semester than with the classes given 1 long list.   **(100)**

■   A study reported in 1977 at the University of Pittsburgh, based on the complete circulation history during the period October 1968-June 1976, *showed that* circulation was a good indicator of total book/monograph use. For example, based on 30-day samples of in-house use taken over a period of 2 academic terms and involving 29,098 items, 75% of the items used in-house had also circulated externally by the end of the sample period, with an additional 4% of the in-house items circulating the following year. Further, of 4,250 books/monographs loaned on interlibrary loan during the period January 1969-December 1975, 3,246 (76.4%) had external circulations, with the remaining 1,004 items accounting for only .34% of the external circulation during the period of the study. Finally, of 33,277 books/monographs selected for reserve during the period January 1969-December 1975, 27,854 (83.7%) had external circulations, with the remaining 5,423 items accounting for only 1.84% of the external circulation during the period of this study.   **(666)**

■   A study reported in 1978 at the undergraduate library of the University of Tennessee, Knoxville, of patron success rate in finding books over a 5-week period (sample size: 1,010 patrons; responding: 503 or 49.5%, involving 2,375 titles) *showed that*, of the 1,097 titles not immediately found, 117 (10.7%) titles were on reserve, 152 (13.9%) were actually on the shelf, and 828 (75.5%) were actually not available in the library. Of the

2,375 titles patrons searched for, 34.9% were actually not available in the library. **(466)**

Reshelving

Academic

■ A 1971 study of journal availability at the Woodward Biomedical Library (University of British Columbia, Canada) during a 12-day period *showed that*, out of 4,326 journal items, 370 (8.6%) were not found immediately. The reasons for unavailability were as follows:

title not held or issue not received	100 (27%) items
in use or awaiting reshelving	98 (26%) items
being bound	66 (18%) items
user errors	41 (11%) items
administrative reasons (on "hold" shelf, misshelved, etc.)	40 (11%) items
unspecified reasons	25 (7%) items **(692)**

■ A study reported in 1978 at Indiana University, Bloomington, of materials requested through a delivery service to faculty in the political science and economics departments during a 32-month period (October 1972-June 1975), involving 39 political scientists and 14 economists (40-50% of the faculty in the departments) and 5,478 articles from 620 different journals and newspapers, *showed that* the chief reason for a journal being unavailable was reshelving, which accounted for 56% of the unavailable journals. **(421)**

Special

■ A 1971 study of journal availability at the Woodward Biomedical Library (University of British Columbia, Canada) during a 12-day period *showed that*, out of 4,326 journal items, 370 (8.6%) were not found immediately. The reasons for unavailability were as follows:

title not held or issue not received	100 (27%) items
in use or awaiting reshelving	98 (26%) items

continued

being bound	66 (18%) items
user errors	41 (11%) items
administrative reasons (on "hold" shelf, misshelved, etc.)	40 (11%) items
unspecified reasons	25 (7%) items	**(692)**

Restricted Materials

Academic

■ A survey reported in 1977 of moderate-sized (120,000-500,000 volumes) U.S. academic libraries listed in the 1972-73 *American Library Directory* (survey size: 200; responding: 147 or 74%) *showed that* 44% responding libraries circulated current issues of periodicals, while 53% reported that they did not. Further, 53% of the libraries reported that they circulated bound volumes of periodicals, while 44% reported that they did not. **(454)**

■ A 1980 survey of 110 academic libraries (83 or 75.5% responding) of all types and sizes concerning their provision of a collection or services for the recreational reading interests of the campus community *showed that* 64.2% of the average recreational reading services collection (rrs) was fiction (79% of those with rrs responding), that 32.4% of the average rrs collection consisted of paperbacks (99% responding), that 42 (82.4%) of the respondents with rrs collections reported crafts and hobbies books in the collection, that the average size of the rrs collection was 1,636 titles with a median size of 700 titles, and that 18 (35.3%) libraries reported periodicals as part of their rrs collection (averaging 47 titles). 39% of these 18 libraries circulated their rrs periodicals. **(315)**

■ A study reported in 1980 at the Health Sciences Library of the University of California, San Francisco, over a 21-week period in 1979 to determine the effects of limiting journal circulation *showed that*, when a 5-year backfile of all first-copy journals was made noncirculating, the average weekly circulation dropped 40.8% (from 2,971 items per week to 1,759 items per week) while the average in-house copying increased 135.7% (from 1,938 article equivalents, i.e., total copying divided by 8.5, to 4,567 article equivalents). **(731)**

■ A 1981 survey of academic libraries selected randomly from OCLC academic library participants concerning the issue of university collections, i.e., collections of publications by the university's own faculty and affiliates (sample size: 184; responding: 103 or 56%) *showed that* 61% of the respondents reported their university collections were housed in closed-access areas, with 79% reporting that the material was noncirculating. However, 86 (83%) did report purchasing duplicates of the university collection for circulation.   **(647)**

Public

■ A survey reported in 1968 of Michigan public libraries (559 libraries or branches queried; 462 or 82% responding) receiving periodicals from the state *showed that* the smaller the library the more likely it is to circulate current issues of periodicals, with an overwhelming majority of libraries of all sizes circulating back issues.   **(133)**

Special

■ A 1974 survey of a random sample of U.S. museum libraries (including history, art, and science museums) listed in the 1973 *Official Museum Directory* (population: 2,556; sample size: 856; responding: 374 or 43.7%) *showed that* 46% reported open stacks, 49% reported closed stacks, and 5% reported open stacks with restrictions. Further, 76% of the libraries did not lend books.   **(412)**

■ A study reported in 1980 at the Health Sciences Library of the University of California, San Francisco, over a 21-week period in 1979 to determine the effects of limiting journal circulation *showed that*, when a 5-year backfile of all first copy journals was made noncirculating, the average weekly circulation dropped 40.8% (from 2,971 items per week to 1,759 items per week) while the average in-house copying increased 135.7% (from 1,938 article equivalents, i.e., total copying divided by 8.5, to 4,567 article equivalents).   **(731)**

Self-charging

Academic

■ A 1968-69 study at Loretto Heights College (a women's college with an enrollment of 900 located in Denver, Colorado), comparing a traditional charge-out system operated by staff with a patron self-charge system, *showed that* fewer students reported taking books out of the library without charging them and fewer books were taken out of the library without charging them out under the self-charge system of circulation.

During a comparable 1-month period 32.1% (1,183) of the books returned to the library had not been charged out under the self-serve system compared to 51.0% (2,324) under the traditional system. Further, 32.2% (176) of a sample of 546 students reported taking library materials out of the library without charging them under the self-serve system compared to 40.6% (103) of a sample of 254 students reporting similarly under the traditional system. Both changes in books returned and student reports of behavior are statistically significant according to Chi Square tests at the .001 significance level. **(206)**

Staff Attitudes

Academic

■ A 1980 survey of all Association of Research Libraries circulation managers (population: 98; 76 or 78% responding) *showed that* 3% of the manual system managers reported their system was "close to ideal," compared to 12% of batch system managers so reporting and 45% of online managers so reporting. **(338)**

Ibid. . . . *showed that* 16 (53%) of the manual system managers, 12 (47%) of the batch system managers, and 16 (80%) of the online system managers "agreed" or "strongly agreed" that their circulation systems were reliable. **(338)**

Ibid. . . . *showed that* that 9 (30%) of the manual system managers, 15 (54%) of the batch system managers, and 14 (70%) of the online systems managers "agreed" or "strongly agreed" that their circulation system's records were "very accurate." **(338)**

Ibid. . . . *showed that* 56% of the manual system managers, 46% of the batch system managers, and 40% of the online system managers agreed with the statement "users tend to expect more service than the department can give." **(338)**

Ibid. . . . *showed that* 65% of the online managers, 48% of the batch managers, and 50% of the manual managers felt that patron complaints were "most often substantive," while 90% of online managers, 84% of batch managers, and 79% of manual managers rejected the statement that patrons "complain far too much." **(338)**

Ibid. . . . *showed that* 93% of the manual managers, 85% of the batch managers, and 70% of the online managers agreed with the statement "the circulation department should be oriented towards users' expectations." **(338)**

■ A survey reported in 1983 of circulation professionals in public and academic libraries with more than 50,000 volumes concerning their interest in and use of management data (e.g., loss rates, effectiveness of fines) and the formal methods by which management data was generated (e.g., sampling, statistical tests) (survey size: 200 professionals; responding: 132 or 66%) *showed that* there was more interest in management data itself than in the methods by which it could be generated. Specifically, while 57 (43%) respondents felt "strongly" that use of management data was important for their particular responsibilities, only 41 (31%) felt "strongly" that techniques were likewise important. Further, while 60 (45%) respondents reported they would "definitely" make more use of management data if more were available, only 37 (28%) reported they would "definitely" make more use of techniques to generate management data if information on their use were more easily available. **(807)**

Ibid. . . . *showed that*, both in order to find management information and to acquaint themselves with the techniques for generating such information, respondents most frequently used and found most helpful the published literature. Specifically, the information sources used in the last year (prior to the survey) in descending order of importance were:

1. professional library literature
2. other literature
3. local and regional workshops
4. ALA conferences
5. formal academic classes
6. ALA preconference programs and workshops

The usefulness of each of these sources of information according to the personal experience of the respondents was (in descending order of importance):

1. professional library literature
2. local and regional workshops
3. other literature
4. formal academic classes
5. ALA conferences
6. ALA preconferences and workshops **(807)**

Ibid. . . . *showed that* circulation professionals supported the idea of national standards only in a general way. Specifically, when asked only about national standards, 45% of the respondents reported that they were "very important" or "important." However, when ranked in importance with 11 other specific items, national standards was ranked last in importance. **(807)**

Ibid. . . . *showed that* circulation professionals felt more strongly about the importance of management data and the methods for generating it than they perceived their institutions felt. Specifically, while 57 (43%) respondents felt "strongly" that the use of management data was important for their responsibilities and 41 (31%) felt "strongly" that formal methods for generating such data were important for their responsibilities, only 38 (29%) felt that their institution attached a "great deal" of importance to either the use of management data or to the methods for generating it. **(807)**

Ibid. . . . *showed that* the average monthly time spent by circulation professionals in increasing their awareness of management data or the techniques for generating such data was as follows (including both personal and professional time):

no hours per month	10 (7.6%) respondents	
1-5 hours per month	68 (51.5%) respondents	
6-10 hours per month	28 (21.2%) respondents	
11-30 hours per month	14 (10.6%) respondents	
no answer	12 (9.1%) respondents	**(807)**

Ibid. . . . *showed that* the greatest obstacles to greater use of management data or techniques for generating such data were as follows (in descending order of importance):

1. lack of time
2. lack of appropriate management data
3. lack of training in the formal techniques that could be used to generate management data
4. difficulty in locating appropriate data or sources of skills
5. lack of interest personally **(807)**

Ibid. . . . *showed that* the 5 most highly ranked areas (out of 12) in which more management data was needed were as follows (in descending order of importance):
1. relationship between collection use and collection development

2. collection loss
3. staff training

  4. impact of fines and penalties on book return
  5. automation costs vs. manual circulation costs   (807)

Public

■ A survey reported in 1983 of circulation professionals in public and academic libraries with more than 50,000 volumes concerning their interest in and use of management data (e.g., loss rates, effectiveness of fines) and the formal methods by which management data was generated (e.g., sampling, statistical tests) (survey size: 200 professionals; responding: 132 or 66%) *showed that* there was more interest in management data itself than in the methods by which it could be generated. Specifically, while 57 (43%) respondents felt "strongly" that use of management data was important for their particular responsibilities, only 41 (31%) felt "strongly" that techniques were likewise important. Further, while 60 (45%) respondents reported they would "definitely" make more use of management data if more were available, only 37 (28%) reported they would "definitely" make more use of techniques to generate management data if information on their use were more easily available.   (807)

Ibid. . . . *showed that*, both in order to find management information and to acquaint themselves with the techniques for generating such information, respondents most frequently used and found most helpful the published literature. Specifically, the information sources used in the last year (prior to the survey) in descending order of importance were:

  1. professional library literature
  2. other literature
  3. local and regional workshops
  4. ALA conferences
  5. formal academic classes
  6. ALA preconference programs and workshops

The usefulness of each of these sources of information according to the personal experience of the respondents was (in descending order of importance):

  1. professional library literature
  2. local and regional workshops
  3. other literature
  4. formal academic classes
  5. ALA conferences
  6. ALA preconferences and workshops   (807)

Ibid. . . . *showed that* circulation professionals supported the idea of national standards only in a general way. Specifically, when asked only about national standards, 45% of the respondents reported that they were "very important" or "important." However, when ranked in importance with 11 other specific items, national standards was ranked last in importance. **(807)**

Ibid. . . . *showed that* circulation professionals felt more strongly about the importance of management data and the methods for generating it than they perceived their institutions felt. Specifically, while 57 (43%) respondents felt "strongly" that the use of management data was important for their responsibilities and 41 (31%) felt "strongly" that formal methods for generating such data were important for their responsibilities, only 38 (29%) felt that their institution attached a "great deal" of importance to either the use of management data or to the methods for generating it. **(807)**

Ibid. . . . *showed that* the average monthly time spent by circulation professionals in increasing their awareness of management data or the techniques for generating such data was as follows (including both personal and professional time):

no hours per month	10 (7.6%) respondents
1-5 hours per month	68 (51.5%) respondents
6-10 hours per month	28 (21.2%) respondents
11-30 hours per month	14 (10.6%) respondents
no answer	12 (9.1%) respondents **(807)**

Ibid. . . . *showed that* the greatest obstacles to greater use of management data or techniques for generating such data were as follows (in descending order of importance):

1. lack of time
2. lack of appropriate management data
3. lack of training in the formal techniques that could be used to generate management data
4. difficulty in locating appropriate data or sources of skills
5. lack of interest personally **(807)**

Ibid. . . . *showed that* the 5 most highly ranked areas (out of 12) in which more management data was needed were as follows (in descending order of importance):

1. relationship between collection use and collection development
2. collection loss
3. staff training

4. impact of fines and penalties on book return
5. automation costs vs. manual circulation costs   (807)

Staffing

Academic

■ A study reported in 1976 of 4 academic libraries in the Southern California area *showed that* patrons almost always chose to approach a standing reference or circulation staff member rather than a seated one if both were exhibiting similar nonverbal behavior.   **(050)**

Ibid. . . . *showed that* reference personnel exhibited positive nonverbal behavior a higher percentage of the time than circulation desk personnel.
(050)

Ibid. . . . *showed that* patrons chose to approach a female rather than male staff member in reference or circulation if both were seated or standing or exhibiting similar nonverbal behavior.   **(050)**

■ A survey in 1978 of circulation staff (including supervisors, clerks, and students) activity at the University of Illinois, Urbana, based on 4,304 random checks of activity during 44 randomly selected days, *showed that* over half of the staff's time was spent on 4 activities: 15.4% on patron interaction; 14.8% on discharging; 11.8% on filing; and 9.4% on charging/renewing.   **(119)**

Ibid. . . . *showed that* the activity that accounted for the largest percentage of time for circulation student staff was absenteeism, which involved 26.4% of student staff time.   **(119)**

■ A 1980 survey of all Association or Research Libraries circulation managers (population: 98; 76 or 78% responding) *showed that* circulation managers had held their positions an average of 5 years, that 38 of the managers were women and 38 were men, and that 70% of the managers held an M.L.S.   **(338)**

Ibid. . . . *showed that* circulation managers of manual systems were 43% male vs. 57% male, that managers of batch systems were 54% male vs. 46% female, and that managers of online systems were 55% male vs. 45% female.   **(338)**

Ibid. . . . *showed that* 57% of responding circulation managers reported spending more than 25% of their time on noncirculation concerns, while 23% reported spending over 50% of their time on noncirculation matters.
(338)

Unit Costs

Academic

■ A 1974 comparison of an semiautomated (Mohawk punched card system) vs. manual circulation system at Colorado State University *showed that* the unit costs of the manual system were $0.365 [per circulation transaction] vs. $0.474 [per circulation transaction] for the automated system, an increase of 29.9%.   **(331)**

■ A comparison of periodical costs—1975 cost data including subscription costs (actual), ordering (estimated), receiving (estimated), processing (estimated), accounting and shelving costs (estimated), binding preparation and binding costs (estimated)—and use rates (based on use during the period 1972-75) in an academic library (unspecified) *showed that* for the 25 most requested journals out of 528 political science journals (use determined by an earlier study, 421) the cost for each use of the periodical ranged from $.17 to $4.98 with a median of $.53 per use.   **(307)**

Ibid. . . . *showed that* the cost per individual user (many users made multiple requests, see above) of the 25 most requested jourals out of 528 political science journals (use determined by an earlier study, 421) ranged from $.78 to $4.64 per user with a median of $2.27 per user.   **(307)**

Public

■ A study reported in 1979 at the Oklahoma City/County Metropolitan Library System *showed that* for 18,996 adult hardback books and 19,126 adult paperback books purchased in FY 1976-77 the cost ratio based on purchase price alone of hardback to paperback was 4.1 to 1, while the cost per circulation (again based on purchase price only) of hardback to paperback was 4.2 to 1. For slightly more materials in FY 1977-78 the cost ratio of hardbound to paperback was 3.7 to 1, and the cost per circulation was 3.89 to 1.   **(231)**

Ibid. . . . *showed that* for 5,624 juvenile hardback books and 6,031 paperback books purchased in FY 1976-77 the cost ratio based on purchase price alone of hardback to paperback was 5.9 to 1, while the cost per circulation (again based on purchase price only) of hardback to paperback was 2.7 to 1. For approximately the same number of materials purchased in FY 1977-78 the cost ratio of hardbound to paperback was 4.8 to 1, and the cost per circulation was 2.6 to 1. **(231)**

2.

Interlibrary Loan

Age of Material

General

■ A survey of the literature on interlibrary loan in 1972-73 for the Association of Research Libraries *showed that* there was general agreement in the literature that approximately 20% of the ILL items requested had been published within the last 3 years and just over half of the items requested had been published within the last 10 years.   **(096)**

■ A 1976 study of interlibrary loan requests sent to the Library of Congress during 1975 (sample size: 1,114 requests) *showed that* the publication date of requested material was as follows:

pre-1900	16.7% of total
1900-49	38.0% of total
1950-69	23.8% of total
1970-75	21.5% of total

Material that was no more than 3 years old accounted for 10% of the LC requests, compared to a range of 17-25% of the requests in other, non-LC interlibrary loan studies.   **(469)**

Academic

■ A study by the Joint Libraries Committee on Fair Use in Photocopying on single-copy photocopy requests (not necessarily ILL requests) in 10 libraries (3 governmental, 3 public, and 4 university) in 1959, with more detailed analysis of photocopy requests in NYPL, University of Chicago, and Princeton University, *showed that* in 3 major research libraries the following pattern of photocopy requests by age of material prevailed:

PUBLICATION DATE	NYPL	PRINCETON	CHICAGO	
20th century	91.0%	83.7%	95.1%	
within last 10 years	57.9%	47.4%	37.0%	
within last 1 year	13.3%	2.5%	6.0%	**(067)**

■ A study reported in 1975 of interlibrary loan requests submitted to the Information Dissemination Service (serving the information needs of health professionals in a surrounding 9-county area) located in the Health Sciences Library of the State University of New York, Buffalo, broken down into 2 samples (sample A: all requests during a 3-month period in 1972 from 4 major teaching hospitals, 1,802 interlibrary loan requests;

sample B: a 10% random sample of all requests from a broad group of health professionals over a 3-year period, 1970-73, 2,280 interlibrary loan requests), *showed that* requests for materials less than 5 years old were as follows: sample A (60.4% journal requests; 40.2% book requests), and sample B (70.6% journal requests; 53.6% book requests).   **(708)**

Special

■ A study reported in 1975 of interlibrary loan requests submitted to the Information Dissemination Service (serving the information needs of health professionals in a surrounding 9-county area) located in the Health Sciences Library of the State University of New York, Buffalo, broken down into 2 samples (sample A: all requests during a 3-month period in 1972 from 4 major teaching hospitals, 1,802 interlibrary loan requests; sample B: a 10% random sample of all requests from a broad group of health professionals over a 3-year period, 1970-73, 2,280 interlibrary loan requests), *showed that* requests for materials less than 5 years old were as follows: sample A (60.4% journal requests; 40.2% book requests), and sample B (70.6% journal requests; 53.6% book requests).
(708)

■ A 1975 study of interlibrary loan requests initiated by 21 hospitals in central and western Massachusetts for their patrons during 1975 (4,368 requests for copies of periodical articles from 1,071 different journals) *showed that* the age of requested items was as follows:

5 years old or less	2,729 (62.48%) items
10 years old or less	3,501 (80.15%) items
20 years old or less	4,086 (93.54%) items
30 years old or less	4,262 (97.57%) items

This compared to the number of requested items 5 years old or less in 4 other studies reported in the literature, which ranged from 50-65%, and the number of requested items that were 10 years old or less in 3 other studies reported in the literature, which ranged from 69-85%.   **(718)**

Availability

Special

■ A 1967 survey of the physician staff of 16 osteopathic hospitals in southeastern Michigan (813 physicians) *showed that* physician staff in only 3 hospitals had "dependable interlibrary loan service" that allowed access to the library resources of the community. This involved "a few more than 300" of the physicians or "less than 40%." **(683)**

Causes of Failure

General

■ A 1976 study of interlibrary loan requests sent to the Library of Congress during 1975 (sample size: 1,114 requests) *showed that* the fill rate for interlibrary loan requests was 54%. 3 main reasons caused failure to fill requests: material was noncirculating (35% of failures); material in internal or external use (32% of failures); and material not owned (24% of failures). **(469)**

Academic

■ A 1-year study (academic 1969-70) of 7,126 interlibrary loan transactions among RAILS members (11 state-assisted university libraries in Ohio) *showed that* 17.4% of the ILL requests were not filled. A detailed analysis of a 10% sample (N = 708) involving 125 unfilled requests indicated that the reasons for failure were: not owned (46.4%), item missing (21.6%), issue not received (19.2%), in use (8.8%), noncirculating (3.2%), and other (0.8%). The in-use figure suggests a relatively low rate of overlap between local and ILL use. **(204)**

Center for Research Libraries

Academic

■ A 1976-77 study of the requests sent by the library at the University of North Carolina, Chapel Hill, to the Center for Research Libraries *showed that*, of the 524 requests sent in a 14-month period, 371 (70.8%) were filled by CRL. Of the 524 requests 160 (31%) were sent on behalf of faculty, 275 (52%) were on behalf of graduate students, 75 (14%) were on behalf of library staff, and the remaining 14 (3%) were on behalf of other community members. **(302)**

Ibid. . . . *showed that* the Journals Access Service was the service most successfully used, with 58.5% of the materials received coming from this CRL service. Average receipt time for photocopied materials through this service was 10-13 days. **(302)**

Collection Efficiency

Special

■ A study reported in 1975 of interlibrary loan requests submitted to the Information Dissemination Service (serving the information needs of health professionals in a surrounding 9-county area) located in the Health Sciences Library of the State University of New York, Buffalo, broken down into 2 samples (sample A: all requests during a 3-month period in 1972 from 4 major teaching hospitals, 1,802 interlibrary loan requests; sample B: a 10% random sample of all requests from a broad group of health professionals over a 3-year period, 1970-73, 2,280 interlibrary loan requests), *showed that* for both samples 3% of the journal titles satisfied "approximately 20%" of the journal requests.   **(708)**

■ A 1975 study of interlibrary loan requests initiated by 21 hospitals in central and western Massachusetts for their patrons during 1975 (4,368 requests for copies of periodical articles from 1,071 different journals), *showed that*:

> 12 (1.12%) journal titles accounted for 439 (10.05%) requested articles;

> 47 (4.39%) journal titles accounted for 1,059 (24.24%) requested articles;

> 160 (14.94%) journal titles accounted for 2,227 (50.98%) requested articles;

> 1,071 (100%) journal titles accounted for 4,368 (100%) requested articles.   **(718)**

■ A 1977 study at the Treadwell Library of the Massachusetts General Hospital investigating all requests for journals (both circulation use and interlibrary loan requests) over a year's time (79,369 requests) *showed that* the 647 journal titles held in the library satisfied 75,039 (94.5%) of the requests, while interlibrary loan had to be used to satisfy the remaining 4,330 (5.5%) requests. To satisfy these interlibrary loan requests itself the library would have had to subscribe to an additional 1,352 journals. **(733)**

Collection Size

Academic

■ A 1-year study (academic 1969-70) of 7,126 interlibrary loan transactions among RAILS members (11 state-assisted university libraries in Ohio) *showed that* there was no statistically significant correlation between volume of ILL requests and size of collection. There was also no statistically significant correlation between ILL use and number of subscriptions or enrollment. **(204)**

■ A study reported in 1981 concerning the relationship between interlibrary loan activity and collection size in major academic libraries, based on 5 years of statistics (academic year 1973-74 through 1977-78) from 82 Association for Research Libraries members, *showed that* there was a statistically significant but not particularly strong correlation between collection size and ILL lending, with the larger libraries tending to lend more and the smaller libraries tending to lend less. The correlation ranged from r = .444 in academic 1973-74 to r = .605 in academic 1974-75. (Significant at the .05 level in all 5 cases.) **(575)**

Ibid. . . . *showed that* there was a statistically significant but only weak correlation between collection size and ILL borrowing, with the smaller libraries tending to borrow more and the larger libraries tending to borrow less. The correlation ranged from r = .291 in academic 1973-74 to r = .393 in academic 1977-78. (Significant at the .05 level in all 5 cases.) **(575)**

Copyright

Academic

■ A study by the Joint Libraries Committee on Fair Use in Photocopying on single-copy photocopy requests (not necessarily ILL requests) in 10 libraries (3 governmental, 3 public, and 4 university) in 1959, with more detailed analysis of photocopy requests in NYPL, University of Chicago, and Princeton University, *showed that* in meeting research demand participating libraries neither could nor did adjust their duplicating services to the complexities of copyright law and status. **(067)**

Ibid. . . . *showed that* photocopy demand was widely dispersed, with no correlation with copyright status or the advertising policies of publishers. **(067)**

Ibid. . . . *showed that* in 3 major research libraries the following pattern of photocopy requests by age of material prevailed:

PUBLICATION DATE	NYPL	PRINCETON	CHICAGO	
20th century	91.0%	83.7%	95.1%	
within last 10 years	57.9%	47.4%	37.0%	
within last 1 year	13.3%	2.5%	6.0%	**(067)**

Ibid. . . . *showed that* in 3 major research libraries the following pattern of requests by format of material prevailed:

TYPE OF MATERIAL	NYPL	PRINCETON	CHICAGO	
books	5.4%	25.8%	17.0%	
periodicals	92.1	49.8	71.9	
maps	0.2	5.1	–	
music text	0.05	–	–	
music notation	0.3	–	–	
manuscripts	0.3	14.2	–	
prints, pictures				
& illustrations	0.55	5.1	–	
theses	–	–	11.1	**(067)**

■ A 1-year study (academic year 1969-70) of the 7,126 interlibrary loan transactions among RAILS members (11 state-assisted university libraries in Ohio) *showed that* approximately 71.3% of the ILL requests were for photocopies (almost exclusively journal articles) and 28.7% were for monographs.   **(204)**

■ A study during fiscal year 1971-72 at California State University, Fullerton, involving interlibrary loan requests generated by CSUF patrons for 527 books and 697 periodicals not in the CSUF collection, *showed that* 73% of the journal titles were requested once, 14% of the titles twice, 6% of the titles 3 times, 3% of the titles 4 times, and 4% of the titles 5 or more times.   **(629)**

■ A review of ILL photocopy requests filled by other libraries for Millikan Library at the California Institute of Technology during the calendar year 1978 *showed that* 87.3% of the 865 requests required no more than 5 photocopies per title. (CONTU guidelines state that libraries should not request more than 5 photocopies per title per year for articles published within 5 years of the reprinting date.)   **(018)**

Public

■ A study by the Joint Libraries Committee on Fair Use in Photocopying on single-copy photocopy requests in 10 libraries (3 governmental, 3 public, and 4 university) in 1959, with more detailed analysis of photocopy requests (not necessarily ILL requests) in NYPL, University of Chicago, and Princeton University, *showed that* in meeting research demand participating libraries neither could nor did adjust their duplicating services to the complexities of copyright law and status.   **(067)**

Ibid. . . . *showed that* in 3 major research libraries the following pattern of photocopy requests by age of material prevailed:

PUBLICATION DATE	NYPL	PRINCETON	CHICAGO	
20th century	91.0%	83.7%	95.1%	
within last 10 years	57.9%	47.4%	37.0%	
within last 1 year	13.3%	2.5%	6.0%	**(067)**

Ibid. . . . *showed that* photocopy demand is widely dispersed, with no correlation with copyright status or the advertising policies of publishers. **(067)**

Ibid. . . . *showed that* in 3 major research libraries the following pattern of photocopy requests by format of material prevailed:

TYPE OF MATERIAL	NYPL	PRINCETON	CHICAGO	
books	5.4%	25.8%	17.0%	
periodicals	92.1	49.8	71.9	
maps	0.2	5.1	–	
music text	0.05	–	–	
music notation	0.3	–	–	
manuscripts	0.3	14.2	–	
prints, pictures & illustrations	0.55	5.1	–	
theses	–	–	11.1	**(667)**

Costs—Time and Money

General

■ A survey reported in 1982 of libraries participating in the Florida Library Information Network (FLIN) including academic, public, school, and special libraries (survey size: "approximately 530"; responding: 372 or 70%) *showed that* the average number of hours per week spent on interlibrary loan operation in individual libraries by type of institution was as follows:

college/university libraries	52.2 hours/week
public libraries	15.6 hours/week
state institutions	11.1 hours/week
government libraries	9.5 hours/week
corporation libraries	9.3 hours/week

community college/junior college libraries	5.6 hours/week	
military libraries	2.5 hours/week	
school libraries	1.3 hours/week	
other	12.7 hours/week	(513)

Academic

■   A study of ILL operations during the first 2 months of 1972 at Trent University Library in Peterborough, Ontario, *showed that* the average ILL request to borrow materials outside of Trent took 35.6 minutes (31.5 minutes nonprofessional time and 4.9 minutes of professional time), while ILL loans to other libraries of Trent material took 11.1 minutes of nonprofessional time. Total average time spent on all ILL transactions was 29.5 minutes each.   **(142)**

Ibid. . . . *showed that* the average ILL request to borrow materials outside of Trent took more staff time (professional and nonprofessional combined) for faculty requests (42.5 minutes each) than for undergraduate requests (29.4 minutes each).   **(142)**

■   A review of interlibrary loan costs at Carnegie-Mellon University *showed that* the average per unit transaction cost in 1976 was $4.15, with a borrowing per unit cost of $5.28 and a lending per unit cost of $3.02. **(032)**

Fill Rate

General

■   A study of ILL in New England of all types of libraries in 1976 (sample size: 191; usable responses: 113 or 58%), of requests generated in a month, *showed that* the overall fill rate for ILL requests was 93.6%, although this reflects only the final transactions and many items may have been referred several times.   **(122)**

■   A 1976 study of interlibrary loan requests sent to the Library of Congress during 1975 (sample size: 1,114 requests) *showed that* the fill rate for interlibrary loan requests was 54%. 3 main reasons caused failure to fill requests: material was noncirculating (35% of failures); material in internal or external use (32% of failures); and material not owned (24% of failures).   **(469)**

■ A study reported in 1980 of interlibrary borrowing of monographs among 7 libraries in west-central Illinois (West-Central Illinois Library Cooperative), involving 4,146 blind search requests for materials during a 1-year period in 1977-78, *showed that* the fill rate was 2,114 items or 51%.
(479)

Ibid. . . . *showed that* the fill rate for 426 items that could not be obtained through the Cooperative and were subsequently requested via the ALA form from a single location known to have the item was 284 items or 66.7% with an average delivery time of 15.9 days. This compares to use of the OCLC/ILL subsystem for 70 requests sent up to 5 known locations, which had a fill rate of 65 items (92.9%) with an average delivery time of 10.8 days.
(479)

Ibid. . . . *showed that* the fill rate for 68 requests using the OCLC/ILL subsystem but where the first 2 locations were blind requests to Cooperative members and the subsequent 3 locations were known to have the monograph was 59 (86.8%). 27 (39.7%) of the requests were filled by 1 of these first 2 blind locations, thus allowing faster delivery time [although no delivery times were given].
(479)

■ A 1980-81 study of interlibrary loan requests generated through the OCLC Library during a 7-month period, involving 254 serial requests and 255 monographic requests (total requests: 509), *showed that,* of the requests bibliographically verified in the OCLC Online Union Catalog, 96.3% of the serials and 88.5% of the monographs were filled.
(437)

Ibid. . . . *showed that* of those items found within 5 attempts the fill rate by position in the lender string was as follows:

1st library	64.4% serials;	49.3% monographs filled
2nd library	20.1% serials;	30.4% monographs filled
3rd library	9.9% serials;	11.1% monographs filled
4th library	4.3% serials;	6.4% monographs filled
5th library	1.3% serials;	2.8% monographs filled **(437)**

■ A survey reported in 1982 of libraries participating in the Florida Library Information Network (FLIN) including academic, public, school, and special libraries (survey size: "approximately 530"; responding: 372 or 70%) *showed that* the average fill rate for photocopied articles for the most recent reporting year was 86%, while the average fill rate for monographs for the most recent reporting year was 82%.
(513)

Academic

■ A 1969 study of 1,148 ILL transactions in the Maryland Interlibrary Loan Network gathered during a 1-week period in January *showed that* there was a system success rate of 677 items (59%). Of the 232 requests received by the first-level area library, 47.4% (110) were filled; of the 1,038 requests received by the second-level Pratt Library (a large number of requests were sent directly to Pratt in addition to the requests referred from the first-level libraries), 47.4% (492) were filled; and of the 149 requests received by the third-level University of Maryland Library, 50.3% (75) were filled.   **(205)**

■ A 1-year study (academic 1969-70) of 7,126 interlibrary loan transactions among RAILS members (11 state-assisted university libraries in Ohio) *showed that* 17.4% of the ILL requests were not filled. A detailed analysis of a 10% sample (N = 708) involving 125 unfilled requests indicated that the reasons for failure were: not owned (46.4%), item missing (21.6%), issue not received (19.2%), in use (8.8%), noncirculating (3.2%), and other (0.8%). The in-use figure suggests a relatively low rate of overlap between local and ILL use.   **(204)**

■ A study of ILL operations during the first 2 months of 1972 at Trent University Library in Peterborough, Ontario, *showed that*, of 625 requests for material off campus, 326 (52.1%) were requested by undergraduates and 299 (47.9%) were requested by faculty. Of these, 237 (72.7%) of the undergraduate requests were filled, while 285 (95.3%) of the faculty requests were filled.   **(142)**

■ A study reported in 1973 at the University of Calgary Library (Canada) comparing interlibrary loan requests sent to the National Lending Library for Science and Technology (England) and those sent to Canadian (and sometimes U.S.) libraries (sample size: 50 requests to each) *showed that* the National Lending Library filled 46 (92%) requests in an average time of 19.5 days, while the Canadian (and U.S.) libraries filled 47 (94%) requests in an average time of 14.4 days.   **(541)**

Ibid. . . . *showed that*, of a further 8 articles that were requested from the National Lending Library using a Xerox Telecopier (photocopy sent over the phone lines), the time required to fill the requests from the time the telex was sent until the photocopy was received ranged from a half hour to 3 days. All requests were filled. Further, transmission was at the rate of 6 minutes per page in order to get readable copies.   **(541)**

■ A study reported in 1975 of interlibrary loan requests submitted to the Information Dissemination Service (serving the information needs of health professionals in a surrounding 9-county area) located in the Health Sciences Library of the State University of New York, Buffalo, broken down into 2 samples (sample A: all requests during a 3-month period in 1972 from 4 major teaching hospitals, 1,802 interlibrary loan requests; sample B: a 10% random sample of all requests from a broad group of health professionals over a 3-year period, 1970-73, 2,280 interlibrary loan requests), *showed that* the fill rate (books and journals combined) for sample A was 89.5% and for sample B was 97.1%. Further, 89.2% of the requests in sample A and 68.3% of the requests for sample B were filled within 2 working days.   **(708)**

■ A review of interlibrary loan statistics over a 4-year period, 1975-78, at Carnegie Mellon University *showed that* the success rate in filling unverified ILL requests sent to Carnegie Mellon dropped from 72% in 1975 to 58% in 1978, while the success rate for filling ILL requests sent to Carnegie Mellon that had been verified by OCLC increased from 75% to 96%.   **(032)**

Ibid. . . . *showed that* the library was able to fill almost 62% of the interlibrary loan requests made to it.   **(032)**

■ A 1976-77 study of the requests sent by the library at the University of North Carolina, Chapel Hill, to the Center for Research Libraries *showed that*, of the 524 requests sent in a 14-month period, 371 (70.8%) were filled by CRL. Of the 524 requests 160 (31%) were sent on behalf of faculty, 275 (52%) were on behalf of graduate students, 75 (14%) were on behalf of library staff, and the remaining 14 (3%) were on behalf of other community members.   **(302)**

■ A study reported in 1982 at the Paul Klapper Library in Queens College, CUNY, comparing ILL requests for off-campus material requested during a 3-month period in Fall 1979 (200 requests) and a 3-month period during Spring 1981 (333 requests), *showed that* the success rate in 1979 and 1981, respectively, for TWX requests from other CUNY units was 100% (for 11 requests) and 94% (for 36 requests), for OCLC was 100% (for 79 requests) and 95% (for 130 requests), for the New York State ILL system was 86% (for 35 requests) and 84% (for 57 requests), and for the ALA procedure and form was 74% (for 75 requests) and 76% (for 110 requests).   **(346)**

Special

■ A study reported in 1975 of interlibrary loan requests submitted to the Information Dissemination Service (serving the information needs of health professionals in a surrounding 9-county area) located in the Health Sciences Library of the State University of New York, Buffalo, broken down into 2 samples (sample A: all requests during a 3-month period in 1972 from 4 major teaching hospitals, 1,802 interlibrary loan requests; sample B: a 10% random sample of all requests from a broad group of health professionals over a 3-year period, 1970-73, 2,280 interlibrary loan requests), *showed that* the fill rate (books and journals combined) for sample A was 89.5% and for sample B was 97.1%. Further, 89.2% of the requests in sample A and 68.3% of the requests for sample B were filled within 2 working days.   **(708)**

General Issues

General

■ A survey in 1974 of the 47 charter members of the OCLC network, including site visits and interviews (148) with all levels of library personnel in member libraries, *showed that*, of the charter members, 12 libraries reported no particular objectives for joining the OCLC network, 15 were principally interested in faster cataloging, 10 were principally interested in reducing cataloging costs, 7 in improved ILL, and 3 in miscellaneous objectives. The directors of 80% of the libraries reported their primary objectives had been met.   **(112)**

■ A survey reported in 1982 of the directors of 20 (19 or 95% responding) OCLC distributing networks (e.g., ILLINET, SOLINET, FEDLINK, etc.) *showed that* the 5 most commonly reported current or planned uses of members' records supplied through OCLC reported by 14 respondents were (multiple responses allowed): union list (11 respondents), circulation control (11 respondents), subject access (10 respondents), management information (8 respondents), and interlibrary loan (6 respondents). **(343)**

Academic

■ A survey reported in 1972 of 2,600 U.S. colleges and universities (usable responses: 1,516) *showed that* the 4 activities common to at least half of the academic library consortia were as follows: reciprocal borrowing privileges, 78% (97 consortia); expanded interlibrary loan service, 64% (80); union catalogs or lists, 62% (78); and photocopying services, 58% (72).   **(212)**

■ A 1979 study at the University of North Dakota of faculty willingness to cancel journal titles and rely on interlibrary loan (3,030 periodical titles considered; responses from 32 of 47 departments) *showed that* teaching faculty were willing to cancel not only periodicals they rated as marginally important but even substantial numbers of periodicals they rated as moderately important and a few they rated as essential. Specifically, of 1,721 periodical titles rated "essential," of 832 periodical titles rated "of moderate value," and of 418 periodical titles rated "of marginal value" by the faculty respondents, the average number of subscriptions that faculty would be willing to cancel in each group (weighted to reflect the different number of journals considered by each responding department) was 1.2% of the "essential" journal titles, 17.9% of the "of moderate value" journal titles, and 82.8% of the "of marginal value" titles. **(645)**

Special

■ A study reported in 1975 of interlibrary loan requests submitted to the Information Dissemination Service (serving the information needs of health professionals in a surrounding 9-county area) located in the Health Sciences Library of the State University of New York, Buffalo broken down into 2 samples (sample A: all requests during a 3-month period in 1972 from 4 major teaching hospitals, 1,802 interlibrary loan requests; sample B: a 10% random sample of all requests from a broad group of health professionals over a 3-year period, 1970-73, 2,280 interlibrary loan requests), *showed that* the main bibliographic sources of requests in sample B were INDEX MEDICUS (17.3% of the requests) and SUNY [online] searches (12.7% of the requests). The main patron sources of requests in sample B were physicians (67.5% of the requests) and nurses (8.2% of the requests). The 2 main channels used by patrons in sample B to submit requests were hospitals (77% of requests) and universities (13.3% of requests). **(708)**

Ibid. . . . *showed that* for both samples 3% of the journal titles satisfied "approximately 20%" of the journal requests. **(708)**

Language of Material

General

■ A survey of the literature on interlibrary loan in 1972-73 for the Association of Research Libraries *showed that* there was general agreement in the literature that most of the items requested on ILL were in

English, with the percentage of such items ranging from 67% to 99%.
                                                                    (096)

Special

■ A study reported in 1975 of interlibrary loan requests submitted to the Information Dissemination Service (serving the information needs of health professionals in a surrounding 9-county area) located in the Health Sciences Library of the State University of New York, Buffalo, broken down into 2 samples (sample A: all requests during a 3-month period in 1972 from 4 major teaching hospitals, 1,802 interlibrary loan requests; sample B: a 10% random sample of all requests from a broad group of health professionals over a 3-year period, 1970-73, 2,280 interlibrary loan requests), *showed that* English-language materials accounted for 1,535 (85.2%) requests in sample A and for 1,903 (83.5%) requests for sample B. The next most frequent language was German with 46 (2.6%) requests in sample A and 53 (2.3%) requests in sample B.   **(708)**

National Lending Library

Academic

■ A study reported in 1973 at the University of Calgary Library (Canada) comparing interlibrary loan requests sent to the National Lending Library for Science and Technology (England) and those sent to Canadian (and sometimes U.S.) libraries (sample size: 50 requests to each) *showed that* the National Lending Library filled 46 (92%) requests in an average time of 19.5 days, while the Canadian (and U.S.) libraries filled 47 (94%) requests in an average time of 14.4 days.   **(541)**

Ibid. . . . *showed that*, of a further 8 articles that were requested from the National Lending Library using a Xerox Telecopier (photocopy sent over the phone lines), the time required to fill the requests from the time the telex was sent until the photocopy was received ranged from a half hour to 3 days. All requests were filled. Further, transmission was at the rate of 6 minutes per page in order to get readable copies.   **(541)**

OCLC

General

■ A survey in 1974 of the 47 charter members of the OCLC network, including site visits and interviews (148) with all levels of library personnel in member libraries, *showed that*, of the charter members, 12 libraries reported no particular objectives for joining the OCLC network, 15 were principally interested in faster cataloging, 10 were principally interested in reducing cataloging costs, 7 in improved ILL, and 3 in miscellaneous objectives. The directors of 80% of the libraries reported their primary objectives had been met. **(112)**

Ibid. . . . *showed that* 95% of the charter members made at least some use of the OCLC data base for ILL work. 59% searched all Roman alphabet requests in the data base, while 41% used it on a more limited basis for ILL verification and location finding. **(112)**

Ibid. . . . *showed that* indications from limited data suggested that use of the OCLC data base for ILL verification was successful 75 to 80% of the time in medium- to small-sized libraries (libraries with budgets for printed materials under $500,000), while 1 large library (printed materials budget $500,000+) showed a verification success rate of 24% for pre-1950 imprints, 34% for 1950-67 imprints, and 60% for 1968 imprints. **(112)**

Ibid. . . . *showed that* 44% of the ILL librarians indicated that use of the OCLC data base resulted in noticeable, though slight, decreases in the processing and receipt time for monographs. **(112)**

■ A study of ILL in New England of all types of libraries in 1976 (sample size: 191; usable responses: 113 or 58%), of requests generated in a month, *showed that* on the average 28% of all ILL transactions were verified on the OCLC data base. **(122)**

■ A study reported in 1980 of interlibrary borrowing of monographs among 7 libraries in west-central Illinois (West-Central Illinois Library Cooperative), involving 4,146 blind search requests for materials during a 1-year period in 1977-78, *showed that* the fill rate for 426 items that could not be obtained through the Cooperative and were subsequently requested via the ALA form from a single location known to have the item was 284 items or 66.7% with an average delivery time of 15.9 days. This compares to use of the OCLC/ILL subsystem for 70 requests sent up to 5 known locations, which had a fill rate of 65 items (92.9%) with an average delivery time of 10.8 days. **(479)**

Ibid. . . . *showed that* the fill rate for 68 requests using the OCLC/ILL subsystem but where the first 2 locations were blind requests to Coopera-tive members and the subsequent 3 locations were known to have the monograph was 59 (86.8%). 27 (39.7%) of the requests were filled by 1 of these first 2 blind locations, thus allowing faster delivery time [although no delivery times were given]. **(479)**

■ A 1980-81 study of interlibrary loan requests generated through the OCLC Library during a 7-month period, involving 254 serial requests and 255 monographic requests (total requests: 509), *showed that*, of the requests bibliographically verified in the OCLC Online Union Catalog, 96.3% of the serials and 88.5% of the monographs were filled. **(437)**

Ibid. . . . *showed that* 242 (95.3%) of the serial requests and 243 (95.3%) of the monographic requests could be bibliographically verified in the OCLC Online Union Catalog, while of these items, 237 (97.9%) of the serials and 242 (99.6%) of the monographs could be verified as to holding institution in the OCLC Online Union Catalog. **(437)**

Ibid. . . . *showed that* of those items found within 5 attempts the fill rate by position in the lender string was as follows:

1st library	64.4% serials;	49.3% monographs filled
2nd library	20.1% serials;	30.4% monographs filled
3rd library	9.9% serials;	11.1% monographs filled
4th library	4.3% serials;	6.4% monographs filled
5th library	1.3% serials;	2.8% monographs filled **(437)**

Ibid. . . . *showed that* of those items found the time lag between the date of request and the date of receipt was 11.6 days. **(437)**

■ A survey reported in 1982 of the directors of 20 (19 or 95% responding) OCLC distributing networks (e.g., ILLINET, SOLINET, FEDLINK, etc.) *showed that* the 5 most commonly reported current or planned uses of members' records supplied through OCLC reported by 14 respondents were (multiple responses allowed): union list (11 respondents), circulation control (11 respondents), subject access (10 respondents), management information (8 respondents) and interlibrary loan (6 respondents). **(343)**

■ A survey reported in 1982 of 144 libraries contracting for OCLC services through the Bibliographic Center for Research (126 or 87.5% responding) *showed that*, when 2 or more copies of a work were acquired at

1 time, 44.4% of the respondents reported they would not indicate multiple-copy ownership in the OCLC record if all copies went into the same collection, while 30.2% reported they would not indicate multiple-copy ownership even if copies went into different collections.   **(342)**

Ibid. . . . *showed that*, when a subsequent copy of a title cataloged earlier on OCLC was purchased, 70.6% of the respondents reported they would not enter information on the subsequent copy into the OCLC record if the copy were going into the same collection as the earlier copy, while 30.2% reported they would not enter information on the subsequent copy even if it were going into a different collection from the earlier copy.   **(342)**

Ibid. . . . *showed that*, when the only copy of a work in the library was withdrawn, 70.6% of the respondents reported canceling the holdings recorded in the OCLC data base, while 19.8% reported they did not, 6.4% reported varying practices, and 3.2% did not reply to the question.
    (342)

Ibid. . . . *showed that*, when 1 of several copies of a work in the library that were previously cataloged on OCLC was withdrawn, 21.4% of the respondents reported that the OCLC holdings were updated, while 65.9% of the respondents reported that the holdings were not, 4.8% reported that their practice varied, and 7.9% did not answer.   **(342)**

Academic

■ A review of interlibrary loan statistics over a 4-year period, 1975-78, at Carnegie Mellon University *showed that* the success rate in filling unverified ILL requests sent to Carnegie Mellon dropped from 72% in 1975 to 58% in 1978, while the success rate for filling ILL requests sent to Carnegie Mellon that had been verified by OCLC increased from 75% to 96%.
    (032)

■ A study reported in 1982 at the Paul Klapper Library in Queens College, CUNY, comparing ILL requests for off-campus material requested during a 3-month period in Fall 1979 (200 requests) and a 3-month period during Spring 1981 (333 requests), *showed that* the success rate in 1979 and 1981, respectively, for TWX requests from other CUNY units was 100% (for 11 requests) and 94% (for 36 requests), for OCLC was 100% (for 79 requests) and 95% (for 130 requests), for the New York State

ILL system was 86% (for 35 requests) and 84% (for 57 requests), and for the ALA procedure and form was 74% (for 75 requests) and 76% (for 110 requests).   (346)

Special

■ A 1977-78 study of acquisitions in 3 Canadian addictions libraries (Alberta Alcoholism and Drug Abuse Commission, British Columbia Alcohol and Drug Commission, Addiction Research Foundation of Ontario) over a 10-month period that were then searched in the OCLC data base (601 titles) *showed that* overall 422 (70.2%) were found in OCLC. Hit rates for the individual libraries were 67%, 68%, and 74%.   (643)

Ibid. . . . *showed that* 76% of the items were U.S. materials while 19.5% were Canadian titles. The hit rate in OCLC for U.S. materials only was 78.9%, while the hit rate in OCLC for Canadian materials only (117 items) was 40 or 34.2%.   (643)

Organization

Academic

■ A survey reported in 1965 of ILL staffing in college and university libraries (sample: 45; responding: 40, usable: 35) *showed that* ILL was part of reference in 17 libraries, part of circulation in 8, a separate unit in 3, and dispersed among divisions in 2, and in miscellaneous arrangements in a further 5.   (173)

Photocopies

Academic

■ A study by the Joint Libraries Committee on Fair Use in Photocopying on single-copy photocopy requests (not necessarily ILL requests) in 10 libraries (3 governmental, 3 public, and 4 university) in 1959, with more detailed analysis of photocopy requests in NYPL, University of Chicago, and Princeton University, *showed that* in meeting research demand participating libraries neither could nor did adjust their duplicating services to the complexities of copyright law and status.   (067)

Ibid. . . . *showed that* photocopy demand was widely dispersed with no correlation with copyright status or the advertising policies of publishers. **(067)**

Ibid. . . . *showed that* in 3 major research libraries the following pattern of photocopy requests by age of material prevailed:

PUBLICATION DATE	NYPL	PRINCETON	CHICAGO	
20th century	91.0%	83.7%	95.1%	
within last 10 years	57.9%	47.4%	37.0%	
within last 1 year	13.3%	2.5%	6.0%	**(067)**

Ibid. . . . *showed that* in 3 major research libraries the following pattern of requests by format of material prevailed:

TYPE OF MATERIAL	NYPL	PRINCETON	CHICAGO	
books	5.4%	25.8%	17.0%	
periodicals	92.1	49.8	71.9	
maps	0.2	5.1	–	
music text	0.05	–	–	
music notation	0.3	–	–	
manuscripts	0.3	14.2	–	
prints, pictures,				
& illustrations	0.55	5.1	–	
theses	–	–	11.1	**(067)**

■ A 1-year study (academic year 1969-70) of the 7,126 interlibrary loan transactions among RAILS members (11 state-assisted university libraries in Ohio) *showed that* approximately 71.3% of the ILL requests were for photocopies (almost exclusively journal articles) and 28.7% were for monographs. **(204)**

■ A review of ILL photocopy requests filled by other libraries for Millikan Library at the California Institute of Technology during the calendar year 1978 *showed that* 87.3% of the 865 requests required no more than 5 photocopies per title. (CONTU guidelines state that libraries should not request more than 5 photocopies per title per year for articles published within 5 years of the reprinting date.) **(018)**

Public

■ A study by the Joint Libraries Committee on Fair Use in Photocopying on single-copy photocopy requests in 10 libraries (3 governmental, 3 public, and 4 university) in 1959, with more detailed analysis of photocopy requests (not necessarily ILL requests) in NYPL, University of Chicago, and Princeton University, *showed that* in meeting research demand partici-pating libraries neither could nor did adjust their duplicating services to the complexities of copyright law and status.   **(067)**

Ibid. . . . *showed that* in 3 major research libraries the following pattern of photocopy requests by age of material prevailed:

PUBLICATION DATE	NYPL	PRINCETON	CHICAGO	
20th century	91.0%	83.7%	95.1%	
within last 10 years	57.9%	47.4%	37.0%	
within last 1 year	13.3%	2.5%	6.0%	**(067)**

Ibid. . . . *showed that* photocopy demand is widely dispersed with no correlation with copyright status or the advertising policies of publishers.
                                                                              (067)

Ibid. . . . *showed that* in 3 major research libraries the following pattern of photocopy requests by format of material prevailed:

TYPE OF MATERIAL	NYPL	PRINCETON	CHICAGO	
books	5.4%	25.8%	17.0%	
periodicals	92.1	49.8	71.9	
maps	0.2	5.1	–	
music text	0.05	–	–	
music notation	0.3	–	–	
manuscripts	0.3	14.2	–	
prints, pictures,				
& illustrations	0.55	5.1	–	
theses	–	–	11.1	**(667)**

Procedures

General

■ A survey in 1974 of the 47 charter members of the OCLC network, including site visits and interviews (148) with all levels of library personnel in member libraries, *showed that* 95% of the charter members made at least some use of the OCLC data base for ILL work. 59% searched all Roman alphabet requests in the data base, while 41% used it on a more limited basis for ILL verification and location finding. **(112)**

Ibid. . . . *showed that* indications from limited data suggested that use of the OCLC data base for ILL verification was successful 75 to 80% of the time in medium- to small-sized libraries (libraries with budgets for printed materials under $500,000), while 1 large library (printed materials budget $500,000+) showed a verification success rate of 24% for pre-1950 imprints, 34% for 1950-67 imprints, and 60% for 1968 imprints. **(112)**

Ibid. . . . *showed that* 44% of the ILL librarians indicated that use of the OCLC data base resulted in noticeable, though slight, decreases in the processing and receipt time for monographs. **(112)**

■ A study of ILL in New England of all types of libraries in 1976 (sample size: 191; usable responses: 113 or 58%), of requests generated in a month, *showed that* on the average 28% of all ILL transactions were verified on the OCLC data base. **(122)**

■ A survey reported in 1982 of 144 libraries contracting for OCLC services through the Bibliographic Center for Research (126 or 87.5% responding) *showed that* when 2 or more copies of a work were acquired at 1 time 44.4% of the respondents reported they would not indicate multiple-copy ownership in the OCLC record if all copies went into the same collection, while 30.2% reported they would not indicate multiple-copy ownership even if copies went into different collections. **(342)**

Ibid. . . . *showed that* when a subsequent copy of a title cataloged earlier on OCLC was purchased 70.6% of the respondents reported they would not enter information on the subsequent copy into the OCLC record if the copy were going into the same collection as the earlier copy, while 30.2% reported they would not enter information on the subsequent copy even if it were going into a different collection from the earlier copy.   **(342)**

Ibid. . . . *showed that* when the only copy of a work in the library was withdrawn 70.6% of the respondents reported canceling the holdings recorded in the OCLC data base, while 19.8% reported they did not, 6.4% reported varying practices, and 3.2% did not reply to the question.

(342)

Ibid. . . . *showed that*, when 1 of several copies of a work in the library that were previously cataloged on OCLC was withdrawn, 21.4% of the respondents reported that the OCLC holdings were updated, while 65.9% of the respondents reported that the holdings were not, 4.8% reported that their practice varied, and 7.9% did not answer.   **(342)**

■   A survey reported in 1982 of libraries participating in the Florida Library Information Network (FLIN) including academic, public, school and special libraries (survey size: "approximately 530"; responding: 372 or 70%) *showed that* the average number of hours per week spent on interlibrary loan operation in individual libraries by type of institution was as follows:

college/university libraries	52.2 hours/week
public libraries	15.6 hours/week
state institutions	11.1 hours/week
government libraries	9.5 hours/week
corporation libraries	9.3 hours/week
community college/junior college libraries	5.6 hours/week
military libraries	2.5 hours/week
school libraries	1.3 hours/week
other	12.7 hours/week **(513)**

Academic

■   A study of ILL operations during the first 2 months of 1972 at Trent University Library in Peterborough, Ontario, *showed that* the average ILL request to borrow materials outside of Trent took 35.6 minutes (31.5 minutes nonprofessional time and 4.9 minutes of professional time) while ILL loans to other libraries of Trent material took 11.1 minutes of nonprofessional time. Total average time spent on all ILL transactions was 29.5 minutes each.   **(142)**

Ibid. . . . *showed that* the average ILL request to borrow materials outside of Trent took more staff time (professional and nonprofessional combined) for faculty requests (42.5 minutes each) than for undergraduate requests (29.4 minutes each).   **(142)**

Quality of Tools

General

■   A 1980-81 study of interlibrary loan requests generated through the OCLC Library during a 7-month period and involving 254 serial requests and 255 monographic requests (total requests: 509) *showed that* 242 (95.3%) of the serial requests and 243 (95.3%) of the monographic requests could be bibliographically verified in the OCLC Online Union Catalog, while of these items, 237 (97.9%) of the serials and 242 (99.6%) of the monographs could be verified as to holding institution in the OCLC Online Union Catalog.   **(437)**

Special

■   A 1977-78 study of acquisitions in 3 Canadian addictions libraries (Alberta Alcoholism and Drug Abuse Commission, British Columbia Alcohol and Drug Commission, Addiction Research Foundation of Ontario) over a 10-month period that were then searched in the OCLC data base (601 titles) *showed that* overall 422 (70.2%) were found in OCLC. Hit rates for the individual libraries were 67%, 68%, and 74%.   **(643)**

Ibid. . . . *showed that* 76% of the items were U.S. materials while 19.5% were Canadian titles. The hit rate in OCLC for U.S. materials only was 78.9%, while the hit rate in OCLC for Canadian materials only (117 items) was 40 or 34.2%.   **(643)**

Relationship to Local Use

General

■   A 1976 study of interlibrary loan requests sent to the Library of Congress during 1975 (sample size: 1,114 requests) *showed that* the fill rate for interlibrary loan requests was 54%. 3 main reasons caused failure to fill requests: material was noncirculating (35% of failures); material in internal or external use (32% of failures); and material not owned (24% of failures).   **(469)**

Academic

■ A 1-year study (academic 1969-70) of 7,126 interlibrary loan transactions among RAILS members (11 state-assisted university libraries in Ohio) *showed that* 17.4% of the ILL requests were not filled. A detailed analysis of a 10% sample (N = 708) involving 125 unfilled requests indicated that the reasons for failure were: not owned (46.4%), item missing (21.6%), issue not received (19.2%), in use (8.8%), noncirculating (3.2%), and other (0.8%). The in-use figure suggests a relatively low rate of overlap between local and ILL use.   **(204)**

■ A study reported in 1977 at the University of Pittsburgh, based on the complete circulation history during the period October 1968-June 1976, *showed that* circulation was a good indicator of total book/monograph use. For example, based on 30-day samples of in-house use taken over a period of 2 academic terms and involving 29,098 items, 75% of the items used in-house had also circulated externally by the end of the sample period, with an additional 4% of the in-house items circulating the following year. Further, of 4,250 books/monographs loaned on interlibrary loan during the period January 1969-December 1975, 3,246 (76.4%) had external [local] circulations, with the remaining 1,004 items accounting for only .34% of the total circulation during the period of the study. Finally, of 33,277 books/monographs selected for reserve during the period January 1969-December 1975, 27,854 (83.7%) had external circulations, with the remaining 5,423 items accounting for only 1.84% of the total circulation during the period of this study.   **(666)**

■ A study reported in 1978 at the undergraduate library of the University of Tennessee, Knoxville, of patron success rate in finding books over a 5-week period (sample size: 1,010 patrons; responding: 503 or 49.5%, involving 2,375 titles) *showed that* the 828 titles not available involved 1,025 volumes. The 2 main reasons for unavailability were: volumes checked out (729 or 71.1%) and volumes unaccounted for (208 or 20.3%). Binding accounted for 22 (2.1%) volumes, while interlibrary loan accounted for 2 (0.2%) volumes.   **(466)**

Relationship to Online Searching

Academic

■ A 1974 study over a 4-month period (January-April) of free MED-LINE use at Oakland University (Rochester, Michigan), a university without a medical school, involving 21 faculty and students for a total of 36 searches, *showed that*, although 54% of the citations considered relevant by the user were not available in the university library, only 4.1% of the citations were requested through ILL. **(411)**

■ A survey reported in 1977 concerning online searching at the U.S. Army Construction Engineering Research Laboratory library (Champaign, Illinois), involving both users of the service (sample size: 27; responding: 26 or 96.3%) and nonusers of the service (sample size: 19; responding: 13 or 68.4%), *showed that*, of 25 user respondents, 11 (44%) reported ordering "many" of the documents for the citations from the online search through the library; 9 (36%) reported ordering "a few"; and 5 (20%) reported ordering "none." **(416)**

■ A 1978 survey of North American health sciences libraries that were users of the National Library of Medicine search services in November 1977 (survey size: 708 libraries; responding: 376; usable: 345 or 48.7%) *showed that*, of 337 respondents, 316 (93.8%) libraries "agreed" or "strongly agreed" that online searching had made it possible to serve more users, while of 330 respondents, 311 (94.2%) libraries "agreed" or "strongly agreed" that online searching had caused an increase in interlibrary loan borrowing. **(724)**

■ A study reported in 1978 of LEXIS subscribers in 4 different cities (Cleveland, Chicago, New York City, and Washington, D.C.) (sample size: 62; responding: 39; usable: 38 or 61.3%), involving 35 law firms, 2 law schools, and 1 government agency, *showed that* 6 (15.8%) respondents reported an increase in interlibrary loan borrowing since they began to use LEXIS, 1 (2.6%) reported that interlibrary loan borrowing decreased after they began to use LEXIS, 30 (79.0%) reported no change in interlibrary loan borrowing, and 1 did not reply to this question. **(359)**

Special

■ A 1974 study over a 4-month period (January-April) of free MED-LINE use at Oakland University (Rochester, Michigan), a university without a medical school, involving 21 faculty and students for a total of 36 searches, *showed that*, although 54% of the citations considered relevant by the user were not available in the university library, only 4.1% of the citations were requested through ILL.   **(411)**

■ A 1976-77 study at the Russell Research Center Library (USDA, Athens, Georgia) of the relationship between online literature searches and interlibrary loan activity *showed that* during the 18-month period in which retrospective online seaching was initiated (314 searches) interlibrary loan requests compared to the 6-month period just prior to the online searching (858 requests) increased 167.7% (2,297 requests) during the first 6 months, 85.5% (1,592 requests) during the second 6 months, and 120.0% (1,888 requests) during the last 6 months.   **(419)**

■ A survey reported in 1977 concerning online searching at the U.S. Army Construction Engineering Research Laboratory library (Champaign, Illinois), involving both users of the service (sample size: 27; responding: 26 or 96.3%) and nonusers of the service (sample size: 19; responding: 13 or 68.4%), *showed that*, of 25 user respondents, 11 (44%) reported ordering "many" of the documents for the citations from the online search through the library; 9 (36%) reported ordering "a few"; and 5 (20%) reported ordering "none."   **(416)**

■ A 1978 survey of North American health sciences libraries that were users of the National Library of Medicine search services in November 1977 (survey size: 708 libraries; responding: 376; usable: 345 or 48.7%) *showed that*, of 337 respondents, 316 (93.8%) libraries "agreed" or "strongly agreed" that online searching had made it possible to serve more users, while of 330 respondents, 311 (94.2%) libraries "agreed" or "strongly agreed" that online searching had caused an increase in interlibrary loan borrowing.   **(724)**

■ A study reported in 1978 of LEXIS subscribers in 4 different cities (Cleveland, Chicago, New York City, and Washington, D.C.) (sample size: 62; responding: 39; usable: 38 or 61.3%), involving 35 law firms, 2 law schools, and 1 government agency, *showed that* 6 (15.8%) respondents reported an increase in interlibrary loan borrowing since they began to use LEXIS, 1 (2.6%) reported that interlibrary loan borrowing decreased after they began to use LEXIS, 30 (79.0%) reported no change in interlibrary loan borrowing, and 1 did not reply to this question.   **(359)**

Remote Facilities

Academic

■ A 1976-77 study of the requests sent by the library at the University of North Carolina, Chapel Hill, to the Center for Research Libraries *showed that*, of the 524 requests sent in a 14-month period, 371 (70.8%) were filled by CRL. Of the 524 requests 160 (31%) were sent on behalf of faculty, 275 (52%) were on behalf of graduate students, 75 (14%) were on behalf of library staff, and the remaining 14 (3%) were on behalf of other community members.   **(302)**

Ibid. . . . *showed that* the Journals Access Service was the service most successfully used, with 58.5% of the materials received coming from this CRL service. Average receipt time for photocopied materials through this service was 10-13 days.   **(302)**

Speed

General

■ A survey in 1974 of the 47 charter members of the OCLC network, including site visits and interviews (148) with all levels of library personnel in member libraries, *showed that* 44% of the ILL librarians indicated that use of the OCLC data base resulted in noticeable, though slight, decreases in the processing and receipt time for monographs.   **(112)**

■ A study of ILL in New England of all types of libraries in 1976 (sample size: 191; usable responses: 113 or 58%), of requests generated in a month, *showed that* the average in-house turnaround time (from receipt of request to mailing item) was 2.5 days, with more than 85% of all requests answered within 3 days and 32% answered in less than a day.   **(122)**

■ A study reported in 1980 of interlibrary borrowing of monographs among 7 libraries in west-central Illinois (West-Central Illinois Library Cooperative) involving 4,146 blind search requests for materials during a 1-year period in 1977-78 *showed that* the fill rate for 426 items that could not be obtained through the Cooperative and were subsequently requested via the ALA form from a single location known to have the item was 284 items or 66.7% with an average delivery time of 15.9 days. This compared to use of the OCLC/ILL subsystem for 70 requests sent up to 5 known locations, which had a fill rate of 65 items (92.9%) with an average delivery time of 10.8 days.   **(479)**

■ A 1980-81 study of interlibrary loan requests generated through the OCLC Library during a 7-month period, involving 254 serial requests and 255 monographic requests (total requests: 509), *showed that* of those items found the time lag between the date of request and the date of receipt was 11.6 days.   **(437)**

Academic

■ A study reported in 1973 at the University of Calgary Library (Canada) comparing interlibrary loan requests sent to the National Lending Library for Science and Technology (England) and those sent to Canadian (and sometimes U.S.) libraries (sample size: 50 requests to each) *showed that* the National Lending Library filled 46 (92%) requests in an average time of 19.5 days, while the Canadian (and U.S.) libraries filled 47 (94%) requests in an average time of 14.4 days.   **(541)**

Ibid. . . . *showed that*, of a further 8 articles that were requested from the National Lending Library using a Xerox Telecopier (photocopy sent over the phone lines), the time required to fill the requests from the time the telex was sent until the photocopy was received ranged from a half hour to 3 days. All requests were filled. Further, transmission was at the rate of 6 minutes per page in order to get readable copies.   **(541)**

■ A 1976-77 study of the requests sent by the library at the University of North Carolina, Chapel Hill, to the Center for Research Libraries *showed that* the Journals Access Service was the service most successfully used, with 58.5% of the materials received coming from this CRL service. Average receipt time for photocopied materials through this service was 10-13 days.   **(302)**

■ A study reported in 1982 at the Paul Klapper Library in Queens College, CUNY, comparing ILL requests for off-campus material requested during a 3-month period in Fall 1979 (200 requests) and a 3-month period during Spring 1981 (333 requests), *showed that* the average number of calendar days between generating the ILL request and receipt of the item for 1979 and 1981, respectively, was 10.09 and 13.70 days using TWX service with other CUNY units, 17.01 and 16.33 days using OCLC, 19.50

and 19.60 days using the New York State ILL system, and 27.39 and 22.13 days using the ALA ILL procedure and form. **(346)**

Special

■ A study reported in 1975 of interlibrary loan requests submitted to the Information Dissemination Service (serving the information needs of health professionals in a surrounding 9-county area) located in the Health Sciences Library of the State University of New York, Buffalo, broken down into 2 samples (sample A: all requests during a 3-month period in 1972 from 4 major teaching hospitals, 1,802 interlibrary loan requests; sample B: a 10% random sample of all requests from a broad group of health professionals over a 3-year period, 1970-73, 2,280 interlibrary loan requests), *showed that* the fill rate (books and journals combined) for sample A was 89.5% and for sample B was 97.1%. Further, 89.2% of the requests in sample A and 68.3% of the requests for sample B were filled within 2 working days. **(708)**

Use Patterns—Format of Material

Academic

■ A study by the Joint Libraries Committee on Fair Use in Photocopying on single-copy photocopy requests (not necessarily ILL requests) in 10 libraries (3 governmental, 3 public, and 4 university) in 1959, with more detailed analysis of photocopy requests in NYPL, University of Chicago, and Princeton University, *showed that* in 3 major research libraries the following pattern of requests by format of material prevailed:

TYPE OF MATERIAL	NYPL	PRINCETON	CHICAGO
books	5.4%	25.8%	17.0%
periodicals	92.1	49.8	71.9
maps	0.2	5.1	–
music text	0.05	–	–
music notation	0.3	–	–
manuscripts	0.3	14.2	–
prints, pictures, & illustrations	0.55	5.1	–
theses	–	–	11.1

(067)

■ A study reported in 1962 at Southern Illinois University of 503 interlibrary loan requests made by SIU faculty and graduate students over a 3-year period (1958-60) *showed that* 344 (68%) were for serial articles,

105 (21%) were for theses and dissertations, and 54 (11%) were for books.
(397)

Ibid. . . . *showed that* faculty requested 64% of the 503 ILL requests including 87% of the books, 40% of the theses, and 67% of the serials.
(397)

Ibid. . . . *showed that*, of the 344 serial requests, 257 (74.7%) were for different serial titles. 203 (79%) titles were borrowed 1 time, 34 (13.2%) were borrowed 2 times, 11 (4.3%) were borrowed 3 times, 5 (1.9%) were borrowed 4 times, and 4 (1.6%) were borrowed 5 times or more.   **(397)**

■ A 1-year study (academic year 1969-70) of the 7,126 interlibrary loan transactions among RAILS members (11 state-assisted university libraries in Ohio) *showed that* approximately 71.3% of the ILL requests were for photocopies (almost exclusively journal articles) and 28.7% were for monographs.   **(204)**

■ A study during fiscal year 1971-72 at California State University, Fullerton, involving interlibrary loan requests generated by CSUF patrons for 527 books and 697 periodicals not in the CSUF collection, *showed that* the book requests were not equally distributed among the LC class numbers, suggesting specific weaknesses in the collection. (Difference between the expected and observed distribution of interlibrary loan requests among LC class numbers was statistically significant at the .02 level.)   **(629)**

Ibid. . . . *showed that* 73% of the journal titles were requested once, 14% of the titles twice, 6% of the titles 3 times, 3% of the titles 4 times, and 4% of the titles 5 or more times.   **(629)**

Public

■ A study by the Joint Libraries Committee on Fair Use in Photocopying on single-copy photocopy requests in 10 libraries (3 governmental, 3 public, and 4 university) in 1959, with more detailed analysis of photocopy requests (not necessarily ILL requests) in NYPL, University of Chicago, and Princeton University, *showed that* in 3 major research libraries the following pattern of photocopy requests by format of material prevailed:

TYPE OF MATERIAL	NYPL	PRINCETON	CHICAGO	
books	5.4%	25.8%	17.0%	
periodicals	92.1	49.8	71.9	
maps	0.2	5.1	–	
music text	0.05	–	–	
music notation	0.3	–	–	
manuscripts	0.3	14.2	–	
prints, pictures,				
& illustrations	0.55	5.1	–	
theses	–	–	11.1	**(667)**

Special

■ A study reported in 1975 of interlibrary loan requests submitted to the Information Dissemination Service (serving the information needs of health professionals in a surrounding 9-county area) located in the Health Sciences Library of the State University of New York, Buffalo, broken down into 2 samples (sample A: all requests during a 3-month period in 1972 from 4 major teaching hospitals, 1,802 interlibrary loan requests; sample B: a 10% random sample of all requests from a broad group of health professionals over a 3-year period, 1970-73, 2,280 interlibrary loan requests), *showed that* in sample A 1,623 (90.1%) requests were for journals with 179 (9.9%) requests for books, while in sample B 2,060 (90.4%) of the requests were for journals with 220 (9.6%) requests for books. **(708)**

Use Patterns—Institutions

General

■ A survey of the literature on interlibrary loan in 1972-73 for the Association of Research Libraries *showed that* there was considerable disagreement in the literature as to which kind of libraries originated most of the requests. Studies focused on academic libraries revealed that 60 to 75% of ILL requests originated from academic libraries, compared to 17 to 19% from special libraries and only 5 to 8% from public libraries. A major New York state study showed 74% of ILL loans originating from public libraries and only 24% of ILL from academic libraries, while studies involving other systems showed 59 to 63% of the requests originating from state and public libraries. **(096)**

■ A study of ILL in New England of all types of libraries in 1976 (sample size: 191; usable responses: 113 or 58%), of requests generated in a month, *showed that* 29% of all lending came from 5 very large libraries (collections over 1 million volumes) who themselves accounted for only 11% of the borrowing. **(122)**

Ibid. . . . *showed that* by inspection no clear pattern of net borrowing or lending was shown for the 85 libraries with collections under 300,000; (59%) were net borrowers and 35 (41%) were net lenders with no relationship to size. **(122)**

Ibid. . . . *showed that* public libraries transacted 80% of their ILL with other public libraries and academic libraries transacted 66% of their ILL with other academic libraries. Special and academic libraries borrowed at an almost even rate from each other. **(122)**

Ibid. . . . *showed that* 40% of the ILL requests recorded during the survey period were for materials published in the last 3 years. Only 10% of the requests were for items published more than 20 years ago. **(122)**

Ibid. . . . *showed that* 79% of all ILL transactions in New England took place within state boundaries. **(122)**

■ A 1976 study of interlibrary loan requests sent to the Library of Congress during 1975 (sample size: 1,114 requests) *showed that* requests by type of library were as follows:

academic/research libraries	63% of total	
foreign libraries	18% of total	
federal libraries	10% of total	
special libraries	5% of total	
public libraries	4% of total	
other governmental libraries	1% of total	**(469)**

Ibid. . . . *showed that* requests by type of material requested were as follows:

humanities	44% of total	
science	24% of total	
social Sciences	19% of total	
other	13% of total	**(469)**

Ibid. . . . *showed that* there was a statistically significant correlation between type of library and type of material requested (significant at the 0.0

[sic] level). Specifically, federal libraries requested fewer humanities materials than expected, while academic libraries requested more; federal and special libraries requested more science materials than expected, while academic libraries requested fewer. **(469)**

Ibid. . . . *showed that* the 4 most frequent languages of publication were: English (64% requests), Russian (8.4% requests), German (8.1% requests), and French (6.7% requests). **(469)**

■ A survey reported in 1982 of libraries participating in the Florida Library Information Network (FLIN) including academic, public, school, and special libraries (survey size: "approximately 530"; responding: 372 or 70%) *showed that* the 3 types of institutions that requested the most interlibrary loan items were: college/university libraries (44% of the total interlibrary loans), public libraries (26% of the total), and "other" libraries (16% of the total). Further, 100% of the college and university ILL requests were sent to other colleges and universities. **(513)**

Ibid. . . . *showed that* college/university libraries and public libraries accounted for most of the ILL volume. These 2 types of libraries together borrowed 66% of the total ILL items and lent 88% of the total items and in fact were the only net lenders of 9 types of libraries. Further, the ratio of borrowing to lending was 1 to 1.6 for academic libraries and 1 to 1.1 for public libraries. **(513)**

Academic

■ A study of ILL in New England of all types of libraries in 1976 (sample size: 191; usable responses: 113 or 58%), of requests generated in a month, *showed that* public libraries transacted 80% of their ILL with other public libraries and academic libraries transacted 66% of their ILL with other academic libraries. Special and academic libraries borrowed at an almost even rate from each other. **(122)**

Public

■ A study of ILL in New England of all types of libraries in 1976 (sample size: 191; usable responses: 113 or 58%), of requests generated in a month, *showed that* public libraries transacted 80% of their ILL with other public libraries and academic libraries transacted 66% of their ILL with other academic libraries. Special and academic libraries borrowed at an almost even rate from each other. **(122)**

Use Patterns—Patron Groups

Academic

■ A study during academic 1958-59 at the Columbia University Medical Library involving interlibrary loan requests originated at Columbia (712 requests, 248 patrons) *showed that* a small number of users accounted for a large share of the services. Specifically, 50% of the total requests came from 10% of the users; 34% of the requests came from 4% of the users; and 22% of the requests came from 2% of the users.   **(671)**

Ibid. . . . *showed that* the "repeat requester" was the major user of interlibrary loans. Specifically, 40% of the total requesters were repeat requesters, who accounted for 79% of all requests.   **(671)**

■ A study reported in 1962 at Southern Illinois University of 503 interlibrary loan requests made by SIU faculty and graduate students over a 3-year period (1958-60) *showed that* faculty requested 64% of the 503 ILL requests including 87% of the books, 40% of the theses, and 67% of the serials.   **(397)**

Ibid. . . . *showed that*, of the 344 serial requests, 257 (74.7%) were for different serial titles. 203 (79%) titles were borrowed 1 time, 34 (13.2%) were borrowed 2 times, 11 (4.3%) were borrowed 3 times, 5 (1.9%) were borrowed 4 times, and 4 (1.6%) were borrowed 5 times or more.   **(397)**

■ A 1971 survey of owners (primarily academics) of personal library collections (sample selected from authors of 300 single-author articles published during 1969-70 in one of 3 broad areas: humanities, social science, and science; 178 authors responding, of which 175 owned personal collections) *showed that* cited material received through interlibrary loan accounted for only 38 (0.7%) items.   **(258)**

■ A study of ILL operations during the first 2 months of 1972 at Trent University Library in Peterborough, Ontario, *showed that* of 625 requests for material off campus 326 (52.1%) were requested by undergraduates and 299 (47.9%) were requested by faculty. Of these, 237 (72.7%) of the undergraduate requests were filled, while 285 (95.3%) of the faculty requests were filled.   **(142)**

■ A 1974 study over a 4-month period (January-April) of free Medline use at Oakland University (Rochester, Michigan), a university without a medical school, involving 21 faculty and students for a total of 36 searches, *showed that* although 54% of the citations considered relevant by the user were not available in the university library, only 4.1% of the citations were requested through ILL. **(411)**

■ A 1976-77 study of the requests sent by the library at the University of North Carolina at Chapel Hill to the Center for Research Libraries, *showed that* of the 524 requests sent in a 14-month period, 371 (70.8%) were filled by CRL. Of the 524 requests 160 (31%) were sent on behalf of faculty, 275 (52%) were on behalf of graduate students, 75 (14%) were on behalf of library staff and the remaining 14 (3%) were on behalf of other community members. **(302)**

Public

■ A 1966 survey of 21,385 adult (12 years old or older) public library users in the Baltimore-Washington metropolitan region of Maryland conducted during a 6-week period of patrons entering the library (79.1% of patrons approached filled out the survey instrument) *showed that*, of the unsatisfied respondents, 5,104 (66%) planned to continue their quest. Of these, 59.3% planned to go to another library, 19.9% put a reserve on the book, 7.7% made arrangements for the library to get the material from another library, and 13.1% planned to use other alternatives (e.g., buying the book or borrowing it from friends). **(301)**

Special

■ A study during academic 1958-59 at the Columbia University Medical Library involving interlibrary loan requests originated at Columbia (712 requests, 248 patrons) *showed that* a small number of users accounted for a large share of the services. Specifically, 50% of the total requests came from 10% of the users; 34% of the requests came from 4% of the users; and 22% of the requests came from 2% of the users. **(671)**

Ibid. . . . *showed that* the "repeat requester" was the major user of interlibrary loans. Specifically, 40% of the total requesters were repeat requesters, who accounted for 79% of all requests. **(671)**

■ A 1974 study over a 4-month period (January-April) of free Medline use at Oakland University (Rochester, Michigan), a university without a medical school, involving 21 faculty and students for a total of 36 searches, *showed that* although 54% of the citations considered relevant by the user were not available in the university library, only 4.1% of the citations were requested through ILL.   **(411)**

■ A study reported in 1975 of interlibrary loan requests submitted to the Information Dissemination Service (serving the information needs of health professionals in a surrounding 9-county area) located in the Health Sciences Library of the State University of New York, Buffalo, broken down into 2 samples (sample A: all requests during a 3-month period in 1972 from 4 major teaching hospitals, 1,802 interlibrary loan requests; sample B: a 10% random sample of all requests from a broad group of health professionals over a 3-year period, 1970-73, 2,280 interlibrary loan requests), *showed that* the main bibliographic source of requests in sample B were INDEX MEDICUS (17.3% of the requests) and SUNY [online] searches (12.7% of the requests). The main patron sources of requests in sample B were physicians (67.5% of the requests) and nurses (8.2% of the requests). The 2 main channels used by patrons in sample B to submit requests were hospitals (77% of requests) and universities (13.3% of requests).   **(708)**

Volume

General

■ A survey of the literature on interlibrary loan in 1972-73 for the Association of Research Libraries *showed that* a conservative estimate for the total quantity of interlibrary loans would be around 6 to 7 million requests a year.   **(096)**

Academic

■ A study reported in 1983 of 3 surveys made by the American Medical Association's Division of Library and Archival Services in 1969, 1973, and 1979 concerning the status of health sciences libraries in the U.S.(survey size for each survey ran between 12,000-14,000 health-related organizations, with a response rate for each survey around 95%) *showed that* the number of items borrowed through interlibrary loan per year in 1979 averaged 569 items per hospital (an average of 6.6 items per year per hospital were loaned), with the libraries in the largest hospitals borrowing the most items. For example, while libraries in hospitals with 99 or fewer beds borrowed an average of 142 items per year per hospital, libraries in hospitals with 500 or more beds borrowed 1,364 items per year per hospital.   **(747)**

Special

■ A study reported in 1978 of LEXIS subscribers in 4 different cities (Cleveland, Chicago, New York City, and Washington, D.C.) (sample size: 62; responding: 39; usable: 38 or 61.3%), involving 35 law firms, 2 law schools, and 1 government agency, *showed that* 6 (15.8%) respondents reported an increase in interlibrary loan borrowing since they began to use LEXIS, 1 (2.6%) reported that interlibrary loan borrowing decreased after they began to use LEXIS, 30 (79.0%) reported no change in interlibrary loan borrowing, and 1 did not reply to this question.   **(359)**

■ A study reported in 1983 of 3 surveys made by the American Medical Association's Division of Library and Archival Services in 1969, 1973, and 1979 concerning the status of health sciences libraries in the U.S.(survey size for each survey ran between 12,000-14,000 health-related organizations, with a response rate for each survey around 95%) *showed that* the number of items borrowed through interlibrary loan per year in 1979 averaged 569 items per hospital (an average of 6.6 items per year per hospital were loaned), with the libraries in the largest hospitals borrowing the most items. For example, while libraries in hospitals with 99 or fewer beds borrowed an average of 142 items per year per hospital, libraries in hospitals with 500 or more beds borrowed 1,364 items per year per hospital.   **(747)**

3.

Patron Use

Adult Services—General Issues

Special

■ A survey reported in 1980 of the largest medical library in each state (sample size: 51; responding: 37) *showed that* 26 (91%) reported that they were open to the public, 8 (22%) reported they were partly open to the public, and 3 (8%) reported they were not open to the public.   **(236)**

Ibid. . . . *showed that*, in terms of providing medical information to nonmedical or nonallied health professionals, patients, or laymen, 7 (20%) reported a completely open policy, 24 (65%) reported they were open to the public with limited services, 1 (3%) reported open to some of the public, 1 (3%) reported open to the public through the public library, and 3 (8%) reported not being open to the public at all.   **(236)**

Ibid. . . . *showed that* 12 (32%) reported they would like to serve the public extensively, 7 (19%) reported they would perhaps like to serve the public extensively, and 10 (27%) reported they would not like to serve the public extensively.   **(236)**

Ibid. . . . *showed that* in order to provide priority service to the public, 20 (54%) libraries reported the need for additional personnel, 22 (59%) reported the need for additional materials such as patient education books, 7 (19%) reported the need for malpractice insurance, and 17 (46%) reported the need for additional building size, space, and facilities.   **(236)**

Ibid. . . . *showed that* 21 (57%) respondents referred questions from the public to public libraries, 8 (22%) referred questions to the local medical association, 10 (27%) referred questions to a physician, and 3 (8%) referred questions to other libraries.   **(236)**

Attitudes—Automation

Academic

■ A 1980 study at Washington University School of Medicine Library over a 13-week period to investigate the feasibility of substituting an online version of *Chemical Abstracts* for the print copy *showed that* such a substitution was not feasible. Specifically, 53 times during this period when patrons began to use the print copy of *Chemical Abstracts* and were offered a free online search instead, on 32 (60.4%) occasions patrons indicated that they did not want an online search. Further, of the 21 (39.6%) occasions when patrons did take the free online search, 13 (61.9%) of these times patrons reported that they still planned to use the printed copies later for looking up the abstracts (available only in the printed copies). **(737)**

Ibid. . . . *showed that* the 4 most frequent reasons given for refusing the online search (out of 8) were:

wanted to browse printed copy	12 occasions
manual search quicker (searching for a specific citation or compound)	8 occasions
previous online searches unsatisfactory	4 occasions
did not want to wait for an online search (a wait of up to 24 hours was required)	4 occasions **(737)**

■ A 1981 survey of faculty, students, staff, and community users of the University of Cincinnati Libraries (sample size: 4,074; responding: 912 or 22.4%, including 436 or 39% faculty response and 218 or 11% student response) *showed that*, when asked which should be automated first of 3 possibilities, faculty, university administrators, and community users picked the public card catalog as first priority with circulation second and periodicals third, while students and library staff picked circulation as first priority with the public card catalog second and periodicals third.   **(522)**

Attitudes—Catalogs on Microform

Academic

■ A 1979 study comparing lookup time of the same catalog (Anoka County, Minnesota, with a collection size of 110,000 titles with almost 500,000 entries) in fiche format (using a NMI-90 fiche reader) vs. microfilm format (ROM 3 mechanized reader) *showed that*, of 39 respondents in the patron group and 31 respondents in the library staff group, 10 (26%) of the patron group favored the fiche reader vs. 14 (45%) of the library staff group, 10 (26%) of the patron group had no preference vs. 1 (3%) of the library staff group and 19 (49%) of the patron group favored the ROM vs. 16 (52%) of the library staff group.   **(267)**

Attitudes—Catalogs Online

Academic

■ A 1982 online survey of MELVYL patrons from all 9 UC campuses conducted over a 2-month period for each 25th user of the system (1,259 questionnaires collected; 72.2 questionnaires complete and usable) *showed that*, in relation to what they were looking for during the search in which they were queried, 32.7% of the respondents judged MELVYL "very satisfactory," 33.5% judged it "somewhat satisfactory," 14.9% judged it "somewhat unsatisfactory," and 18.9% judged it "very unsatisfactory."

(349)

Ibid. . . . *showed that* 70.8% of the respondents reported that their general attitude toward the computer catalog was "very favorable," 22.1% reported their attitude as "somewhat favorable," 3.2% reported "somewhat unfavorable," and 3.9% reported "very unfavorable."   **(349)**

Ibid. . . . *showed that* 68.3% of the respondents reported that the computer catalog was better than other library (i.e., card) catalogs, 17.3% reported that it was equal to other library catalogs, and 14.4% reported that it was worse than other library catalogs.   **(349)**

Public

■ A 1980 survey of card catalog and information desk patrons in the Pikes Peak Library District Library over a 2-week period (sample size: 97; responding: 91) *showed that* 85.4% reported a preference for online catalog searching over the traditional manual approach to the card catalog. The main reason given for preferring the online catalog was its ease of use and the speed with which searches could be conducted.   **(345)**

Attitudes—Censorship

General

■ A reanalysis of a 1970 survey of 2,486 American adults undertaken by the Commission on Obscenity and Pornography, based on dividing the sample into those favoring library censorship, i.e., librarians keeping sexually explicit materials off the shelves (1,877 respondents) and those opposing such censorship (473 respondents) (data were missing on the remaining 136 individuals), *showed that* there was a statistically significant difference between the 2 groups in the following areas, with people who opposed censorship by librarians:

expressing more liberal sexual attitudes and claiming more exposure to erotica in the 2 years preceding the survey;

reporting an average educational attainment of "some college" (12.8 years) as opposed to 11.3 years of education;

reporting an average age of 38.5 versus an average age of 45.4 years;

scoring higher on reported consumption of mass media (books, magazines, and movies) and on the willingness to take citizen's actions on important social or political problems;

reporting church attendance an average of 1.8 times a month versus 3.1 times a month.

(All differences significant at the .001 significance level.)   **(781)**

Ibid. . . . *showed that* older age groups were more likely to favor sexual censorship by librarians (women: gamma $-.32$; men: gamma $-.44$), while increasing levels of education (women: gamma .37; men: gamma .48), increasing levels of mass media consumption, i.e., books, magazines, and movies (women: gamma .24; men: gamma .40), and increasing levels of recent exposure to erotica (women: gamma .38; men: gamma .40) were associated with a tendency to oppose sexual censorship by librarians. (All findings significant at the .001 level.)   **(781)**

Ibid. . . . *showed that* there was no statistically significant relationship between either of the 2 groups (for or against library censorship) and sexual activity or degree of satisfaction with one's sex life. "Opposition to [or advocacy of] censorship is apparently not explained by people's sex lives."   **(781)**

Attitudes—Circulation

Academic

■ A 1980 survey of all Association of Research Libraries circulation managers (population: 98; 76 or 78% responding) *showed that* 56% of the manual system managers, 46% of the batch system managers, and 40% of the online system managers agreed with the statement "users tend to expect more service than the department can give."   **(338)**

Ibid. . . . *showed that* 65% of the online managers, 48% of the batch managers, and 50% of the manual managers felt that patron complaints were "most often substantive," while 90% of online managers, 84% of batch managers, and 79% of manual managers rejected the statement that patrons "complain far too much." **(338)**

Attitudes—Classification Systems

Special

■ A study reported in 1974 of U.S. libraries that had switched to the National Library of Medicine classification system between 1959 and 1973 (survey size: 25 libraries; responding: 25 or 100%) *showed that* the effects of switching to NLM classification were minimal. For example, of 23 libraries, 8 (34.8%) libraries reported patrons had expressed a preference for the NLM classification system, none had expressed a preference for the previous system, and 15 (65.2%) libraries reported patrons had not expressed a preference. **(701)**

Attitudes—Clinical Medical Librarianship

Academic

■ A survey reported in 1978 at the Yale-New Haven Hospital of clinicians concerning their attitudes toward the clinical medical librarian program (4 reference librarians assigned to the departments of pediatrics, psychiatry, internal medicine, and surgery) (survey size: 98 hosptial clinicians; responding: 73 or 74%) *showed that* the program was primarily viewed as education-oriented rather than as supporting patient care. **(723)**

Ibid. . . . *showed that* respondents reported that the "information provided was exceptionally relevant" (overall average of 3.45 on a scale of 1-4) and that the literature searches were highly accurate (overall average of 3.48 on a scale of 1-4). **(723)**

Ibid. . . . *showed that* the degree to which respondents reported that the clinical medical librarian had been integrated into their unit was as follows:

not at all	0 (00%)	respondents
slightly	7 (10%)	respondents

continued

mostly   36 (49%) respondents
fully   30 (41%) respondents   **(723)**

Ibid. . . . *showed that* the methods by which 73 respondents wished to
contact the clinical medical librarian were as follows:

in person at conferences
  in the hospital   38 (52%) respondents
in person in the library   10 (14%) respondents
by phone   22 (30%) respondents
through a 3rd person   0 (0%) respondents
other (no preference)   3 (4%) respondents   **(723)**

Special

■ A survey reported in 1978 at the Yale-New Haven Hospital of
clinicians concerning their attitudes toward the clinical medical librarian
program (4 reference librarians assigned to the departments of pediatrics,
psychiatry, internal medicine, and surgery) (survey size: 98 hosptial
clinicians; responding: 73 or 74%) *showed that* the program was primarily
viewed as education-oriented rather than as supporting patient care.
(723)

Ibid. . . . *showed that* respondents reported that the "information provided was exceptionally relevant" (overall average of 3.45 on a scale of 1-4)
and that the literature searches were highly accurate (overall average of
3.48 on a scale of 1-4).   **(723)**

Ibid. . . . *showed that* the degree to which respondents reported that the
clinical medical librarian had been integrated into their unit was as follows:

not at all   0 (00%) respondents
slightly   7 (10%) respondents
mostly   36 (49%) respondents
fully   30 (41%) respondents   **(723)**

Ibid. . . . *showed that* the methods by which 73 respondents wished to
contact the clinical medical librarian were as follows:

in person at conferences
  in the hospital   38 (52%) respondents
in person in the library   10 (14%) respondents

continued

by phone   22 (30%) respondents
through a 3rd person   0 (0%) respondents
other (no preference)   3 (4%) respondents   **(723)**

Attitudes—Collection Location

Academic

■ A survey during the 1974-75 academic year at the Queen's University in Kingston (Canada) and Trent University in Peterborough (Canada) of part-time students (survey size: 1,143 students at Trent and 1,408 students at Queen's; responding: 286 or 25.1% students at Trent and 480 or 34.1% students at Queen's) *showed that* the 3 locations most frequently chosen by students as their first choice for location of the library collection (or a suitable academic collection) was as follows:

41.7% of the Queen's students and 41.6% of the Trent students selected the university;

24.0% of the Queen's students and 21.3% of the Trent students selected the place of instruction (often not the university);

14.8% of the Queen's students and 21.0% of the Trent students selected the local public library.   **(545)**

Attitudes—Continuing Education

Public

■ A 1974-75 study of the independent learning program (a program jointly sponsored by public libraries and the College Entrance Examination Board and designed to provide information service to adults interested in gaining college credit by examination) provided by the Atlanta Public Library and involving 132 learners *showed that* 43% of the learners were between the ages of 26-35 while 71% of the learners were between the ages 18-35.   **(147)**

Ibid. . . . *showed that* 47% of the learning projects were in the humanities-related areas while 32% were in the science/technology area.   **(147)**

Ibid. . . . *showed that* 63% of the learners reported their goals to be personal development, 28% had job-related goals, and 9% were interested in academic credit.   **(147)**

Ibid. . . . *showed that* the length of the learning projects ranged from 1 to 239 days with an average length of 12.2 days.   **(147)**

Special

■ A 1970 survey of practicing physicians in 2 urban (Bridgeport, Connecticut) hospitals and 3 rural (northwest rural area) hospitals (population: 510; responding: 299 or 58%) *showed that* by self-report urban physicans devoted 39.7 hours per month and rural physicans 33.6 hours per month to educational activities.   **(402)**

Ibid. . . . *showed that* both urban and rural physicans reported that half of their educational activities consisted of reading. 74% of the reading time was spent on personal subscription journals and textbooks, 12-14% on unsolicited medical literature, and 12-14% on library materials.   **(402)**

Ibid. . . . *showed that*, when asked to rank preferred methods for continuing medical education, both urban and rural physicans ranked hospital-based programs first, medical-based programs second, and improvement of hospital library a distant third.   **(402)**

Attitudes—Departmental Libraries

Academic

■ A study reported in 1977 at the University of Minnesota Twin Cities campus concerning attitudes held by heads of academic units toward departmental libraries independent of the university library system (sample size: 167; responding: 108 or 64.7%, including 67 respondents with independent departmental libraries and 41 respondents without such libraries), *showed that* 67% [no raw number given] of the respondents with independent departmental libraries reported finding materials sought after in the official library more than 50% of the time, while 83% [no raw number given] of the respondents without independent departmental libraries reported finding desired materials more than 50% of the time.
(451)

Ibid. . . . *showed that* 34% [no raw number given] of the respondents with independent departmental libraries considered the offical library they used most frequently small and crowded, while only 27% [no raw number given] reported similar feelings about the official library they most frequently used. Further, 22 (33%) of the respondents with independent departmental libraries felt that the official library they most frequently used was "too far" from their office, while only 24% [no raw number given] of the respondents without independent departmental libraries felt similarly. Both groups rated the official library collection "adequate," while more than 90% [no raw numbers given] rated the library staff courteous and helpful. **(451)**

Ibid. . . . *showed that*, of the respondents with independent departmental libraries, a document delivery system was considered "helpful" by 79% [no raw number given] and "essential" by 15% [no raw number given], while of those respondents without an independent departmental library a document delivery system was considered "helpful" by 66% [no raw number given] and "essential" by 17% [no raw number given]. **(451)**

Ibid. . . . *showed that*, while 88% [no raw number given] of both groups indicated that an online terminal for interface with the official library system would be "helpful" or "essential," 31% [no raw number given] of the respondents with independent department libraries and 20% [no raw numbers given] of the respondents without independent departmental libraries rated the terminals as "essential." **(451)**

Attitudes—Document Delivery

Academic

■ A survey in 1970 of the users of a library book delivery system for the campus of the University of Colorado (survey population: 377; responding: 208 or 55% [of whom 89% were resident teaching faculty]) *showed that* after 18 months of the campus book delivery operation 43% of the respondents assessed the service as either important or essential to their work. **(123)**

■ A study reported in 1977 at the University of Minnesota Twin Cities campus concerning attitudes held by heads of academic units toward departmental libraries independent of the university library system (sample size: 167; responding: 108 or 64.7%, including 67 respondents with independent departmental libraries and 41 respondents without such libraries) *showed that* of the respondents with independent departmental libraries a document delivery system was considered "helpful" by 79% [no raw number given] and "essential" by 15% [no raw number given], while of those respondents without an independent departmental library a document delivery system was considered "helpful" by 66% [no raw number given] and "essential" by 17% [no raw number given].   **(451)**

Public

■ A survey reported in 1977 based on a stratified random sample of 300 households (response rate: 251 or 83%) in the Piedmont area of North Carolina *showed that* 122 or 49% (67 or 55% of rural respondents; 21 or 36% of small town respondents; and 34 or 49% of urban respondents) of the full sample of respondents reported an interest in bookmobile service; 115 or 46% (53 or 43% of rural respondents; 20 or 34% of small town respondents; and 42 or 61% of urban respondents) of the full sample of respondents reported an interest in being able to order library materials over the phone and have them delivered; while 90 or 36% (45 or 37% of rural respondents; 14 or 24% of small town respondents; and 31 or 45% of urban respondents) of the full sample of respondents reported an interest in ordering library materials by mail.   **(225)**

Special

■ A 1979 study and survey of physicians in nonmetropolitan areas of the Pacific northwest who were offered an opportunity to receive, without charge, table of contents pages from 18 journals relating to cancer research as well as the option to request a photocopy of any article of interest identified through the service (1-day turnaround guaranteed) (study and survey size: 126 physicians, including 63 randomly selected physicians and 63 physicians identified as having a special interest in cancer research and patient care) *showed that*, of 56 physicians who had not responded to the original offer of the service but who did respond to a subsequent survey 6 months later, the reasons for not participating were as follows:

access to the journals elsewhere	38% physicians
did not receive the letter offering the service (conjecture: thrown out by staff before seen by physician)	38% physicians
too busy	16% physicians
seldom saw cancer patients	9% physicians **(735)**

Ibid. . . . *showed that*, of the 29 physicians who participated in the service but who did not request articles (96% did respond to a subsequent survey 6 months later), the following reasons were given for not requesting articles:

access to the journals elsewhere	11 (40%) physicians
saw no journals of interest	8 (30%) physicians

continued

too busy	6 (22%) physicians	
seldom saw cancer patients	2 (7%) physicians	**(735)**

Attitudes—Fines and Penalties

Public

■ In 1968 when overdue fines were eliminated in the Virgo County Libraries (Terre Haute, Indiana) (overdue notices and replacement charges continued), an informal survey of 315 patrons during the first month *showed that* patrons:

strongly agree	156 (49.5%)	
mildly agree	54 (17.1%)	
no opinion	7 (2.2%)	
mildly disapprove	44 (14.0%)	
strongly disapprove	54 (17.0%)	**(077)**

Attitudes—Foreign Languages

Academic

■ A survey reported in 1979 of a large plant pathology department at the University of Minnesota concerning language skills (sample size: 100; responding: 43 or 42%) *showed that* only 27% of the respondents reported reading or speaking proficiency in any 1 foreign language. 39.5% reported proficiency in German; 25.5% reported proficiency in French; 18.6% reported proficiency in Spanish; and 6.2% reported proficiency in Russian.

(426)

Ibid. . . . *showed that*, although *Translations Register Index* and *World Transindex* were readily available in the library, only 7% of the respondents were familiar with either index. **(426)**

■ A survey reported in 1981 of historians listed in the 1978 *Directory of American Scholars* concerning their use of and attitudes toward periodicals (survey size: 767 historians, although not all questionnaires could be delivered; responding: 360 or 46.9%, with respondents tending to be younger and with a higher scholarly productivity record than nonrespondents) *showed that* 58% of the respondents "do not attempt to keep up with research published in foreign languages." Further, when asked if they felt their research was restricted in any way because of a language problem, 334 respondents reported as follows:

no restriction	138 (41.3%)	respondents
slight restriction	136 (40.7%)	respondents
moderate restriction	42 (12.6%)	respondents
substantial restriction	18 (5.4%)	respondents

Finally, when encountering a reference in a foreign language they did not read, respondents reported the following responses:

try to get article translated	30.3%	respondents	
search for summary or abstract	21.7%	respondents	
try to get gist on own	34.7%	respondents	
ignore	13.3%	respondents	**(780)**

Attitudes—Government Documents

Academic

■ A 1982 survey of economics and political science faculty members in 9 colleges and universities serving as academic depository institutions in Massachusetts for the Government Printing Office (sample size: 216, including 105 economists and 111 political scientists; responding: 155 or 71.8%, including 86 economists and 69 political scientists) *showed that*, for the 125 respondents who used federal documents if the kinds of federal documents that faculty respondents used frequently were only available on microform, 41 (32.8%) reported they would adapt (albeit "grudgingly") to the format change, 40 (32%) reported they would no longer consult the documents but instead look for the information elsewhere or do without, and 18 (14.4%) reported they would use the documents less frequently.
(316)

Ibid. . . . *showed that*, when informed that microfiche was now the primary format for the distribution of federal govenment publications to depository libraries, 75 (60%) of the 125 faculty respondents who used federal documents felt that their information-gathering patterns would be affected, 45 (36%) thought that their information-gathering patterns would not be affected, and 5 (4%) could not speculate on the effect.   **(316)**

Ibid. . . . *showed that*, if a promising document were in microformat, 66 (52.8%) of the 125 respondents who reported using documents reported that they would look at the document to determine its value to them,

38.4% reported that they would not bother checking the library's micro-form copy and instead contact their congressional representative or the issuing agency (to get hard copy), 6 (4.8%) suggested they would not use the document at all, and 5 (4%) reported an interest in having their own personal copy of microtext.   **(316)**

Ibid. . . . *showed that* 87 (69.6%) of the 125 respondents who reported using federal government documents reported that they felt, even with the increased number of federal documents which the microform program made available, this use of microform format would decrease their use of documents, 14 (11.2%) thought that with more material available their use of documents might increase, 18 (14.4%) would not speculate on how their frequency of use of federal documents might change, and 6 (4.8%) thought their use of documents would not change.   **(316)**

Attitudes—Librarians

Academic

■ A 1972 survey of patrons selected at random over a 167-day period at Syracuse University's Carnegie Library (sample size: 160 patrons; 119 or 74.4% responding) *showed that* 49 (41%) had questions and of these 32 (65%) reported that they would not ask a librarian for help.   **(139)**

Ibid. . . . *showed that* the main reasons why responding patrons were reluctant to ask for assistance from librarians were dissatisfaction with past service from the librarian (10), the question was too simple for the librarian (7), or they did not want to bother the librarian (7).   **(139)**

■ A 1973 survey of physicists in 6 universities of the greater Boston area (Boston University, Brandeis, Brown, Harvard, MIT, and Northeastern) to determine how they meet their information needs (sample size: 339; responding: 179 or 52.8%) *showed that* 83.2% reported always or usually finding what they want when assisted by a librarian, compared to 76.6% who reported always or usually finding what they want without assistance from a librarian.   **(404)**

■ A 1975 study at the University of Nebraska, Omaha, concerning student perceptions of academic librarians and involving a stratified sample of full-time students (sample size: 700; responding: 362 or 51.7%), *showed that* 40.7% [no raw number given] of the students were unsure or did not think that academic reference librarians have subject specialities, although 41.4% [no raw number given] reported that librarians "frequently" or "always" have the same "mastery of research methodology in subject areas as instructors." **(449)**

Ibid. . . . *showed that* only 31.6% [no raw number given] felt that the verbal interchange between student and librarian was "frequently" or "always" a learning experience, 22.5% [no raw number given] of the students felt that librarians should not locate answers and materials for them (59.4% [no raw number given] answered "sometimes"), and 11.6% [no raw number given] "frequently" or "always" wished their questions answered briefly without additional information. **(449)**

Ibid. . . . *showed that* 61.6% [no raw number given] believed that librarians performed a teaching function while 38.4% [no raw number given] did not. No statistically significant differences were found in the response to this question by sex, age, subject area, or class level. **(449)**

■ A study reported in 1976 of 4 academic libraries in the southern California area *showed that* patrons chose to approach a female rather than a male staff member in reference or circulation if both were seated or standing and exhibiting similar nonverbal behavior. **(050)**

■ A survey reported in 1981 of historians listed in the 1978 *Directory of American Scholars* concerning their use of and attitudes toward periodicals (survey size: 767 historians, although not all questionnaires could be delivered; responding: 360 or 46.9%, with respondents tending to be younger and with a higher scholarly productivity record than nonrespondents) *showed that* historians tend not to use the invisible college for discovering relevant published information for research. Specifically, the 3 most highly rated methods (out of 10) of discovering relevant published information for research (based on a rating scale of 1 to 5, where 5 was most highly rated) were:

bibliographies or references in books or journals	4.36 rating
specialized bibliographies	4.01 rating
book review	3.85 rating

While "discussion or correspondence with acquaintances elsewhere" ranked sixth with a rating of 3.14, "consulting a known expert" ranked eighth (2.87 rating), and "discussion with colleague at own institution" ranked ninth (2.6 rating). "Consulting librarian" ranked tenth (2.16 rating). **(780)**

■ A study reported in 1981 at Southern Illinois University, Carbondale, investigating teaching faculty perception of librarians (survey size: 507; responding: 386; usable: 384 or 75.7%) *showed that* 24% of the teaching faculty reported that the librarian was "indispensable" to their teaching and research, 25% reported that the librarian was "very important," 29% reported that the librarian was "important," and 22% reported that the librarian was of "little" or "no importance" to their teaching and research.
(493)

Ibid. . . . *showed that* librarians appeared to be more appreciated by senior teaching faculty. Specifically, 34% of the [full] professors reported that librarians were indispensable to their teaching and research, while 21% of the associate professors and 22% of the assistant professors reported the same. Further, in terms of help received from librarians in the library itself, 19% of the [full] professors reported such help was indispensable, while 14% of the associate professors and 12% of the assistant professors so reported.
(493)

Ibid. . . . *showed that*, in terms of help received from librarians in the library itself, 13% of the teaching faculty reported that it was indispensable, 44% reported it was "very helpful," 33% reported it was "helpful," and 10% reported it was of "little" or "no help."
(493)

Ibid. . . . *showed that* 18% of the teaching faculty reported that the librarians contributed a "very substantial" amount to student instruction, 33% reported that librarians contributed a "substantial" amount, 31% reported librarians contributed "some," and 18% reported that librarians contributed "very little" or "none."
(493)

Ibid. . . . *showed that* 17% of the teaching faculty felt librarians should conduct research on practical topics related to improving service, 2% felt librarians should conduct research on scholarly library topics, 56% felt librarians should conduct research on both of the previously mentioned topics, 8% felt librarians should not conduct research, and 16% felt that librarians should decide whether they should conduct research on not.
(493)

Ibid. . . . *showed that* 13% of the teaching faculty felt librarians should be given no research time, 21% felt librarians should be given 4 hours of research time per week, 31% felt librarians should be given 8 hours of research time per week, 8% felt librarians should be given 12 hours of research time per week, while 27% felt the amount of research time to be given depended upon the needs of the research project.   **(493)**

Ibid. . . . *showed that* 28% of the teaching faculty saw librarians as equal to teaching faculty, 65% saw librarians as "professionals rather than faculty," and 7% saw librarians as "nonprofessional or equal to clerical or secretarial help."   **(493)**

Ibid. . . . *showed that* 201 (57%) of the teaching faculty felt that librarians should have faculty rank and status whereas 148 (43%) felt librarians should not. Of these 148 (multiple responses allowed), 58% gave as their reason for denying librarians faculty rank and status "insufficient teaching," 40% gave "insufficient research and publication," 13% gave "insufficient service," and 27% gave "insufficient education." 37% gave a variety of other reasons.   **(493)**

Special

■ A 1976 survey of physicians associated with hospitals in a 17-county region of upstate New York (Health Service Area V) based on a systematic sample of "approximately 40%" of the physicians in each county (survey size: 592 physicians; responding: 258 or 45.6%) *showed that*, of the 61% physicians who had asked a medical librarian for work-related information within the past year, 61.8% rated the information received as "adequate," 28.9% as "more than adequate," and 9.2% as "less than adequate." Further, 84.9% of the physicians had requested the information themselves, while 15.1% had used an intermediary (e.g., secretary).   **(720)**

Attitudes—Libraries

Academic

■ A study of library instruction involving "approximately 190" students in a general biology class at Earlham College, reported in 1971, *showed that* there was no statistically significant difference in students' ability to use the library or in their development of positive attitudes toward the library regardless of whether instruction was presented by a librarian in a 2-hour lecture/demonstration or via a guided self-paced exercise undertaken by individual students.   **(208)**

■ A 1977 survey of faculty at Clark University, the College of the Holy Cross, and the Worcester Polytechnic Institute (population: 474; sample size: 121; responding: 87 or 72%) concerning faculty perception of academic libraries *showed that* faculty length of time at an institution tended to be correlated with positive attitudes toward the library. Specifically:

43 (89.6%) of the faculty with 7 or more years of service at their institution felt their students' library needs were being satisfied, compared to 19 (55.9%) of the faculty with less than 7 years of service (a statistically significant difference at the .001 level);

37 (86.0%) of the faculty with 7 or more years of service at their institution ranked the helpfulness of the library staff high in terms of importance to their use of the library compared to 21 (63.6%) of the faculty with less service (a statistically significant difference at the .04 level);

of the faculty with 7 or more years of service at their institution, 38 (92.7%) gave high ratings to the adequacy of the speed of cataloging, while 40 (83.3%) gave high ratings to the adequacy of the quality of the collection in their field, compared to 18 (69.2%) and 13 (43.3%), respectively, of the faculty with less service (a statistically significant difference at the .04 and .03 levels, respectively). **(478)**

■ A survey reported in 1982 of educators teaching in accredited B.A. and higher-degree nursing programs in the southern U.S. (survey size: 1,715 faculty; responding: 790 or 46.1%) *showed that* 65.7% respondents rated adequate library facilities as "extremely important" while 33.3% rated them as "very important." **(742)**

Ibid. . . . *showed that* the distribution of faculty satisfaction ratings with their libraries was as follows:

very satisfied	15.1%	respondents
satisfied	42.0%	respondents
uncertain	8.8%	respondents
dissatisfied	25.1%	respondents
very dissatisfied	9.0%	respondents **(742)**

Ibid. . . . *showed that* faculty who perceived their schools and departments to have open organizational climates ("lively organization working toward goals through genuinely satisfying social interactions") were more satisfied with their libraries to a statistically significant degree than faculty who perceived their schools and departments to have other kinds of organizational structures (i.e., "paternal" or "familiar"—highly personal but undercontrolled). (Significant at the .05 level.)   (742)

Public

■ A questionnaire survey of 3,500 public library cardholders in 5 medium-sized Pennsylvania cities in conjunction with interviews of a randomly selected sample of householders in 1 city by the Institute of Public Administration (at Pennsylvania State University) under contract to the Pennsylvania State Library in 1965 *showed that* library users ranked the financial needs of the library and the public schools higher than all other local public services. In 3 cities the public schools were ranked highest, and in 2 cities the library was ranked highest.   (084)

Ibid. . . . *showed that* the most consistent criticism of the library was the absence of adequate patron parking space. Criticism of the building, the collection, and the reference materials all took second place to parking. The importance of parking was also shown in that improved parking accommodations were given more often as the most important change patrons recommended for improving library service in 4 out of 5 cities.   (084)

■ A 1979 telephone survey of 1,046 New Orleans residents over the age of 12 *showed that* reasons given by nonusers for not using the library were "no need" (71.9%), "too busy" (8.65%), and (7.5%) found books elsewhere.   (166)

■ A 1980 survey of 623 adult patrons using the Ramsey County (Minnesota) Public Library during a 5-day period in November *showed that* there was a moderately strong correlation between a user's evaluation of the library and satisfaction with the library (.71 correlation with .50 variance). This does not replicate the findings of an earlier study.   (270)

Ibid. . . . *showed that* 4 specific service factors were statistically important in accounting for how patrons evaluated the library. More specifically, the 4 factors accounted for 24% of the variance of the library grade scale in addition to the 23% already accounted for by demographic variables, and each of the 4 new factors had a continuing cumulative effect, as follows ($R2$ scores): satisfaction with the physical facilities index (37%), quality of collections index (42%), satisfaction with the staff index (46%), and convenience of the hours (47%). (Significant at the .001 level.)   (270)

Ibid. . . . *showed that* user evaluation of the availability of library materials was not statistically significantly related to user's overall evaluation of the library. **(270)**

Ibid. . . . *showed that* the user satisfaction scale appears to measure "a generalized, positive reaction to the library" and consequently "does not appear useful for diagnosing the performance of individual services within the library." More specifically, the range among the coefficients of the significance variables was so small that "the addition or deletion of a few subjects could easily have changed the magnitude of the coefficients just enough to alter dramatically the results of the regression analysis."
(270)

Ibid. . . . *showed that* there is no statistically significant relationship between measures of library use and either patrons' evaluation of the library (library grade scale) or patrons' satisfaction with the library (user satisfaction score). The measures of library use involved were: frequency of visits, number of services used during the visit, duration of visit, fiction circulation, nonfiction circulation, and combined circulation. This replicates earlier findings. **(270)**

Ibid. . . . *showed that* 4 demographic variables were statistically important factors in accounting for patron evaluation of the library. More specifically, the 4 factors account for 23% of the variance of the library grade scale scores, and each had a cumulative effect, as follows (R^2 scores): age (13%), educational level (inversely correlated, 17%), importance of visit (22%), and style of use—book borrowing in contrast to in-house use (23%). (Significant at the .001 level.) **(270)**

Ibid. . . . *showed that* 4 demographic variables were satistically important factors in accounting for patron satisfaction with the library. More specifically, the 4 factors account for 16% of the variance of the user satisfaction scale scores, and each had a cumulative effect, as follows (R^2 scores): importance of visit (7%), age (11%), educational level (inversely correlated, 15%), and purpose of visit—recreation in contrast to research (16%). (Significant at the .001 level.) **(270)**

Special

■ A survey reported in 1978 of private law firm libraries (sample size: 278; responding: 141 or 51%) concerning budgeting practices *showed that* 71% of the respondents reported that their firms regarded the library as a "justifiable expenditure" while 11% reported that the libraries were considered a "necessary evil." **(361)**

■ A survey reported in 1982 of educators teaching in accredited B.A. and higher-degree nursing programs in the southern U.S. (survey size: 1,715 faculty; responding: 790 or 46.1%) *showed that* 65.7% respondents rated adequate library facilities as "extremely important" while 33.3% rated them as "very important." **(742)**

Ibid. . . . *showed that* the distribution of faculty satisfaction ratings with their libraries was as follows:

very satisfied	15.1% respondents	
satisfied	42.0% respondents	
uncertain	8.8% respondents	
dissatisfied	25.1% respondents	
very dissatisfied	9.0% respondents	**(742)**

Ibid. . . . *showed that* faculty who perceived their schools and departments to have open organizational climates ("lively organization working toward goals through genuinely satisfying social interactions") were more satisfied with their libraries to a statistically significant degree than faculty who perceived their schools and departments to have other kinds of organizational structures (i.e., "paternal" or "familiar"—highly personal but undercontrolled). (Significant at the .05 level.) **(742)**

Attitudes—Microforms

Academic

■ A survey reported in 1976 of 120 randomly selected patrons of the Bobst Library Microform Center of New York University *showed that*, given the statement "when I find what I want it makes no difference whether it is in regular form or microform," 64 (53%) respondents reported "strongly agree" or "agree," 19 (16%) gave no opinion, and 37 (31%) reported "disagree" or strongly disagree." However, when given the statement "the advantages of microforms outweigh the disadvantages," 102 (85%) reported "strongly agree" or "agree," 12 (10%) gave no opinion, and 6 (5%) reported "disagree" or "strongly disagree." **(224)**

Ibid. . . . *showed that* given the statement "working with microforms usually bothers my eyes," 33 (28%) reported "strongly agree" or "agree," 10 (8%) gave no opinion, and 77 (64%) reported "disagree" or "strongly disagree." **(224)**

Ibid. . . . *showed that* 55 (46%) used the center either seldom or occasionally, while 65 (54% used it often (at least once a month) or frequently (at least once a week). 15 (13%) reported spending 30 minutes or less per session; 24 (20%) spent 30 minutes to 1 hour; 39 (33%) spent 1-2 hours; 28 (23%) spent 2-4 hours; and 14 (12%) spent more than 4 hours. **(224)**

■ A 1982 survey of economics and political science faculty members in 9 colleges and universities serving as academic depository institutions in Massachusetts for the Government Printing Office (sample size: 216, including 105 economists and 111 political scientists; responding: 155 or 71.8%, including 86 economists and 69 political scientists) *showed that* 125 (80.6%) had made some use of federal government documents during the past year while 53 (42.2%) reported citing a federal government publication in 1 or more of their scholarly writings in the past 3 years. **(316)**

Ibid. . . . *showed that*, for the 125 respondents who used federal documents if the kinds of federal documents that faculty respondents used frequently were only available on microform, 41 (32.8%) reported they would adapt (albeit "grudgingly") to the format change, 40 (32%) reported they would no longer consult the documents but instead look for the information elsewhere or do without, and 18 (14.4%) reported they would use the documents less frequently. **(316)**

Ibid. . . . *showed that*, when informed that microfiche was now the primary format for the distribution of federal govenment publications to depository libraries, 75 (60%) of the 125 faculty respondents who used federal documents felt that their information-gathering patterns would be affected, 45 (36%) thought that their information-gathering patterns would not be affected, and 5 (4%) could not speculate on the effect. **(316)**

Ibid. . . . *showed that*, if a promising document were in microformat, 66 (52.8%) of the 125 respondents who reported using documents reported that they would look at the document to determine its value to them, 38.4% reported that they would not bother checking the library's microform copy and instead contact their congressional representative or the issuing agency (to get hard copy), 6 (4.8%) suggested they would not use the document at all, and 5 (4%) reported an interest in having their own personal copy of microtext. **(316)**

Ibid. . . . *showed that* 87 (69.6%) of the 125 respondents who reported using federal government documents reported that they felt, even with the increased number of federal documents that the microform program made available, this use of microform format would decrease their use of documents, 14 (11.2%) thought that with more material available their use of documents might increase, 18 (14.4%) would not speculate on how their frequency of use of federal documents might change, and 6 (4.8%) thought their use of documents would not change.   **(316)**

Special

■ A study reported in 1978 in an industrial R & D laboratory evaluating the shift from use of a hard copy of *Chemical Abstracts* to use of a microfilm copy, involving 33 laboratory professionals who had used both formats, *showed that* the microfilm was considered to be less accessible than hard copy to a statistically significant degree. Specifically, on a scale of 1 to 10 where 1 was "very accessible" and 10 was "not very accessible," the average rating for the hard copy version was 2.55, while the average rating for the microfilm copy was 4.12. (This difference was statistically significant at the .001 level.)   **(524)**

Ibid. . . . *showed that* the microfilm was considered to be less easy to use than hard copy to a statistically significant degree. Specifically, on a scale of 1 to 10 where 1 was "very easy to use" and 10 was "not very easy to use," the average rating for the hard copy version was 3.36, while the average rating for the microfilm copy was 4.97 . (This difference was statistically significant at the .01 level.)   **(524)**

Attitudes—Mutilation

Academic

■ A study reported in 1969 of a staged book mutilation episode in 2 libraries at Miami University, involving 82 students either singly or in groups, *showed that* 9 (11%) of the student bystanders responded to stop or report the incident. 38 (46%) reported that they had noticed the mutilation but chose to do nothing about it, while 35 (43%) reported that they had not noticed the obvious, nearby student tearing pages out of a book.   **(194)**

Ibid. . . . *showed that* of those who admitted witnessing the book mutilation but who had chosen not to do anything about it the reasons given for inaction were primarily: desire for noninvolvement (30%), vacillation (27%), and irrelevant, i.e., "I thought he had permission," "I thought it wasn't a library book" (24%).   **(194)**

■ A survey in 1973 of 168 students in introductory psychology and social psychology at Kent State University *showed that* 36.6% of the nonmutilators who saw someone tearing an article out of a journal would ask them to stop or would report the action. **(099)**

Ibid. . . . *showed that* students' estimates of the percentage of students who tore or cut articles from journals was high. 92.9% of the mutilators and 78.5% of the nonmutilators judged that 21% or higher of the student body tore or cut articles from library journals. **(099)**

Ibid. . . . *showed that* mutilators and nonmutilators alike generally had positive attitudes toward the library. 100% of the mutilators and 92.9% of the nonmutilators reported positive or neutral feelings toward the library; 57.2% of mutilators and 64.7% of nonmutilators disagreed with the statement that the library was a cold and anonymous place; and 92.9% of the mutilators and 90.8% of the nonmutilators found the library staff to be "quite friendly and helpful." **(099)**

Ibid. . . . *showed that* mutilators seem to be aware of the inconvenience that their action causes others. Only 7.1% of the mutilators agreed that no harm was done by tearing or cutting articles from journals since no one else was likely to need that article, while 71.5% disagreed with the statement. However, the perception of inconvenience was statistically significantly higher among nonmutilators. **(099)**

Ibid. . . . *showed that* according to the students the greatest deterrent to having articles torn or cut from journals would be:

	MUTILATORS	NONMUTILATORS
free copying	85.7%	83.9%
2-week periodical checkout	71.4%	71.8%
warning sign ($500 fine or 30 days in jail)	64.3%	61.5% **(099)**

■ Interviews in 1973 with 3 students at Kent State University who admitted cutting or tearing articles from library journals *showed that* all 3 went to the library with no prior intention of mutilating journals, that 2 of the 3 cut or tore the articles because the library was closing (and journals could not be checked out), that all 3 used carrels for cutting or tearing the articles from the journals, that all 3 had been previously angered or upset to find articles gone from journals and that they would not cut or tear material from books because they were much more expensive. **(099)**

■ A 1978 survey of 201 undergraduate students in a large urban university concerning book theft and mutilation *showed that* 17 (8%) students reported "sneaking" books out of the library while 18 (9%) students reported mutilating books or periodicals. Only 2 students were in both groups.   **(499)**

Ibid. . . . *showed that* a statistically significantly greater number of students who reported doing well academically also reported stealing or mutilating library materials. 37 (22%) of the nonviolators reported doing "very well" academically, while 14 (42%) of the violators reported doing "very well" (significant at the .05 level).   **(499)**

Ibid. . . . *showed that* neither feeling poorly served by the library nor lack of access to a copy machine appeared to be related to the theft or mutilation of library materials. Specifically, 61 (37%) of the nonviolators and 11 (33%) of the violators felt "served well" by the library. Further, 111 (67%) of the nonviolators and 21 (70%) of the violators reported that the cost of the copy machine was "never too expensive," while 30 (21%) of the nonviolators and 6 (19%) of the violators reported that they were "never inconvenienced" by a broken copy machine.   **(499)**

Ibid. . . . *showed that* there was a statistically significant difference between violators and nonviolators in their perception of the ease of ripping out pages of library material. 103 (61%) of the nonviolators and 25 (76%) of the violators reported it was "very easy" to rip pages out of library material (significant at the .05 level).   **(499)**

Ibid. . . . *showed that* the reasons given for stealing or mutilating library materials were as follows (multiple responses allowed):

Do not consider the needs of others	45% violators
Need the photographs or charts in books and cannot photocopy them	36% violators
Do not think about the act but steal and mutilate casually and thoughtlessly	30% violators
Are not aware of the cost of theft and mutilation to the library	27% violators
Cannot afford the copy machine or price of a book but want to own a copy	24% violators

continued

Steal and mutilate books as an
expression of hostility toward
the library and the university   18% violators   **(499)**

Attitudes—Online Bibliographic Searching

Academic

■ A 1973 survey of patrons using MEDLINE at 7 information centers
(University of Illinois Medical Center, Chicago; Indiana University; University of Chicago; University of Illinois, Urbana; Cleveland Health
Sciences Library; Mayo Clinic; and Wayne State University) during
April-September 1973 (survey size: 1,017 patrons; responding: 904 or
88.9%) *showed that* of 895 respondents the helpfulness of the search was
judged as follows:

not helpful	9.7% respondents	
moderately helpful	29.4% respondents	
helpful	34.6% respondents	
very helpful	26.3% respondents	**(715)**

Ibid. . . . *showed that* of 706 respondents there was a statistically significant relationship between the number of useful references received and the
perception that the search was helpful (significant at the .001 level).
Specifically, 80% of the respondents who received a high number of useful
references (6 or more) judged the search helpful, compared to 40% of the
users so reporting who received a low number of references (less than 6).
(715)

Ibid. . . . *showed that* of 795 respondents there was a statistically significant relationship between patron perception that relevant references were
missed in a search and patron perception of the search as helpful
(significant at the .001 level). Specifically, 70% of the patrons who
perceived that no references had been missed in the search reported the
search helpful, compared to 49.0% patrons so reporting who perceived
that 1 or more references had been missed.   **(715)**

■ A survey reported in 1974 at the University of Virginia Medical Center
of MEDLINE users (primarily faculty, house staff, outside health professionals, and graduate students) during a 6-month period in 1972-73 (survey
size: 428 users; responding: 246 or 58%) *showed that* 188 (76%) respon-

dents reported they would continue to use MEDLINE even if charged for the service ($1.50 per simple search; $3.00 per more complex search), 5 (2%) reported they would not continue to use MEDLINE, and 53 (22%) were undecided. **(696)**

■ A 1974 study over a 4-month period (January-April) of free MED-LINE use at Oakland University (Rochester, Michigan), a university without a medical school, involving 21 faculty and students for a total of 36 searches, *showed that*, of 27 (75%) search evaluation forms returned, 25 indicated the search to be of "major" or "considerable" value to the user; 2 searches were reported to be of "minor" value to the user. **(411)**

■ An analysis reported in 1978 of records of online bibliographic data base searching at Florida State University Chemistry Department and Monsanto Textiles Company in Pensacola, Florida (353 searches conducted at FSU and 345 conducted at Monsanto) *showed that* there were no statistically significant differences of opinion on the currency of citations, with 44% of FSU researchers reporting "very satisfactory" compared to 35% of Monsanto researchers and 43% of FSU researchers reporting "satisfactory" compared to 49% of Monsanto researchers. **(155)**

Ibid. . . . *showed that* there were no statistically significant differences of opinion on the utility of the searches, with 54% of the FSU researchers reporting "very useful" compared to 50% of the Monsanto researchers and 24% of the FSU researchers reporting "of some use" compared to 25% of the Monsanto researchers. **(155)**

■ A 1980 study at Washington University School of Medicine Library over a 13-week period to investigate the feasibility of substituting an online version of *Chemical Abstracts* for the print copy *showed that* such a substitution was not feasible. Specifically, 53 times during this period when patrons began to use the print copy of *Chemical Abstracts* and were offered a free online search instead, on 32 (60.4%) occasions patrons indicated that they did not want an online search. Further, of the 21 (39.6%) occasions when patrons did take the free online search, 13 (61.9%) of these times patrons reported that they still planned to use the printed copies later for looking up the abstracts (available only in the printed copies). **(737)**

Ibid. . . . *showed that* the 4 most frequent reasons given for refusing the online search (out of 8) were:

wanted to browse printed copy   12 occasions
manual search quicker (searching for
  a specific citation or compound)   8 occasions
previous online searches
  unsatisfactory   4 occasions
did not want to wait for an online
  search (a wait of up to 24
  hours was required)   4 occasions   **(737)**

■ A study reported in 1982 at the University of Iowa Health Sciences Library concerning the effect of the patron's presence during MEDLINE searches, based on searches for 100 different patrons (each search was conducted twice by different staff members, once with and once without the patron) and subsequent survey (100% responding) of those patrons, *showed that* 80% of the patrons reported that the quality of the search where they were present was worth the extra time it cost them (17% reported it was not worth the extra time, and 3% gave no response). Further, 80% of the patrons reported they preferred to be present during their next search, while 12% reported they preferred to be absent, and 8% did not respond or did not care either way.   **(743)**

Special

■ A 1973 survey of patrons using MEDLINE at 7 information centers (University of Illinois Medical Center, Chicago; Indiana University; University of Chicago; University of Illinois, Urbana; Cleveland Health Sciences Library; Mayo Clinic; and Wayne State University) during April-September 1973 (survey size: 1,017 patrons; responding: 904 or 88.9%) *showed that* of 895 respondents the helpfulness of the search was judged as follows:

not helpful	9.7%	respondents
moderately helpful	29.4%	respondents
helpful	34.6%	respondents
very helpful	26.3%	respondents	**(715)**

Ibid. . . . *showed that* of 706 respondents there was a statistically significant relationship between the number of useful references received and the perception that the search was helpful (significant at the .001 level). Specifically, 80% of the respondents who received a high number of useful references (6 or more) judged the search helpful, compared to 40% of the users so reporting who received a low number of references (less than 6).

(715)

Ibid. . . . *showed that* of 795 respondents there was a statistically significant relationship between patron perception that relevant references were
missed in a search and patron perception of the search as helpful
(significant at the .001 level). Specifically, 70% of the patrons who
perceived that no references had been missed in the search reported the
search helpful, compared to 49.0% patrons so reporting who perceived
that 1 or more references had been missed.   **(715)**

■ A survey reported in 1974 at the University of Virginia Medical Center
of MEDLINE users (primarily faculty, house staff, outside health professionals, and graduate students) during a 6-month period in 1972-73 (survey
size: 428 users; responding: 246 or 58%) *showed that* 188 (76%) respondents reported they would continue to use MEDLINE even if charged for
the service ($1.50 per simple search; $3.00 per more complex search), 5
(2%) reported they would not continue to use MEDLINE, and 53 (22%)
were undecided.   **(696)**

■ An analysis reported in 1978 of records of online bibliographic data
base searching at Florida State University Chemistry Department and
Monsanto Textiles Company in Pensacola, Florida (353 searches conducted
at FSU and 345 conducted at Monsanto) *showed that* there were no
statistically significant differences of opinion on the currency of citations,
with 44% of FSU researchers reporting "very satisfactory" compared to
35% of Monsanto researchers and 43% of FSU researchers reporting
"satisfactory" compared to 49% of Monsanto researchers.   **(155)**

Ibid. . . . *showed that* there were no statistically significant differences of
opinion on the utility of the searches, with 54% of the FSU researchers
reporting "very useful" compared to 50% of the Monsanto researchers
and 24% of the FSU researchers reporting "of some use" compared to
25% of the Monsanto researchers.   **(155)**

■ A 1980 study at Washington University School of Medicine Library
over a 13-week period to investigate the feasibility of substituting an online
version of *Chemical Abstracts* for the print copy *showed that* such a
substitution was not feasible. Specifically, 53 times during this period
when patrons began to use the print copy of *Chemical Abstracts* and were
offered a free online search instead, on 32 (60.4%) occasions patrons
indicated that they did not want an online search. Further, of the 21
(39.6%) occasions when patrons did take the free online search, 13
(61.9%) of these times patrons reported that they still planned to use the
printed copies later for looking up the abstracts (available only in the
printed copies).   **(737)**

Ibid. . . . *showed that* the 4 most frequent reasons given for refusing the online search (out of 8) were:

wanted to browse printed copy	12 occasions
manual search quicker (searching for a specific citation or compound)	8 occasions
previous online searches unsatisfactory	4 occasions
did not want to wait for an online search (a wait of up to 24 hours was required)	4 occasions **(737)**

■ A study reported in 1982 at the University of Iowa Health Sciences Library concerning the effect of the patron's presence during MEDLINE searches, based on searches for 100 different patrons (each search was conducted twice by different staff members, once with and once without the patron) and subsequent survey (100% responding) of those patrons, *showed that* 80% of the patrons reported that the quality of the search where they were present was worth the extra time it cost them (17% reported it was not worth the extra time, and 3% gave no response). Further, 80% of the patrons reported they preferred to be present during their next search, while 12% reported they preferred to be absent, and 8% did not respond or did not care either way. **(743)**

Attitudes—Outreach

Public

■ A survey reported in 1977 based on a stratified random sample of 300 households (response rate: 251 or 83%) in the Piedmont area of North Carolina *showed that* 122 or 49% (67 or 55% of rural respondents; 21 or 36% of small town respondents; and 34 or 49% of urban respondents) of the full sample of respondents reported an interest in bookmobile service; 115 or 46% (53 or 43% of rural respondents; 20 or 34% of small town respondents; and 42 or 61% of urban respondents) of the full sample of respondents reported an interest in being able to order library materials over the phone and have them delivered; while 90 or 36% (45 or 37% of rural respondents; 14 or 24% of small town respondents; and 31 or 45% of urban respondents) of the full sample of respondents reported an interest in ordering library materials by mail. **(225)**

Special

■ A 1972 survey of physicians who referred patients to the Medical College of Virginia and received short lists of references from the Virginia Medical Information System relevant to the problems of the patients referred (as described in the physicians' letter of referral) (survey size: 123 physicians; responding: 61 or 49.6%) *showed that* while 6 (10%) physicians did not want to continue receiving the service, 55 (90%) reported that the service was "a good idea and wanted to continue receiving it." 75% of the 55 reported they would be willing to pay for the service in all or some instances. **(695)**

■ A survey reported in 1978 at the University of Texas Medical Branch (Galveston) of the popularity of various elements of an in-house library publication as rated by UTMB faculty members (survey size: 489 faculty; responding: 295 or 60%) *showed that* the popularity of elements was as follows (in descending order of popularity):

1. new acquisitions
2. faculty publications
3. historical article
4. news and notes
5. meet our staff

Further, of the 4 faculty ranks the the faculty rank most interested in the historical article was "full professors." **(721)**

■ A 1979 study and survey of physicians in nonmetropolitan areas of the Pacific northwest who were offered an opportunity to receive, without charge, table of contents pages from 18 journals relating to cancer research as well as the option to request a photocopy of any article of interest identified through the service (1-day turnaround guaranteed) (study and survey size: 126 physicians, including 63 randomly selected physicians and 63 physicians identified as having a special interest in cancer research and patient care) *showed that*, of 56 physicians who had not responded to the original offer of the service but who did respond to a subsequent survey 6 months later, the reasons for not participating were as follows:

access to the journals elsewhere	38% physicians
did not receive the letter offering the service (conjecture: thrown out by staff before seen by physician)	38% physicians
too busy	16% physicians
seldom saw cancer patients	9% physicians **(735)**

Ibid. . . . *showed that*, of the 29 physicians who participated in the service but who did not request articles (96% did respond to a subsequent survey 6 months later), the following reasons were given for not requesting articles:

access to the journals elsewhere	11 (40%) physicians	
saw no journals of interest	8 (30%) physicians	
too busy	6 (22%) physicians	
seldom saw cancer patients	2 (7%) physicians	**(735)**

Attitudes—Personal Collections of Journals

Academic

■ A 1978-79 study underwritten by the NSF Division of Information Science and Technology of academic and research journal subscription and cancellation for both individuals and libraries (individual questionnaires: 2,817; usable responses: 1,190; library questionnaires: 4,997; usable responses: 1,905) of journals at least 5 years old *showed that* the top 6 reasons individuals reported for cancelling journal subscriptions (multiple responses permitted: N = 705) were as follows: 200 individuals (41.2%) cancelled journal subscriptions because of changed focus of interest, 91 (18.8%) because it did not contain the kind of information expected, 81 (16.7%) substituted a more appropriate journal, 71 (14.6%) were no longer a member of the society through which they received the journal, 65 (13.4%) due to financial reasons, 53 (10.9%) library purchased a subscription they could use. **(264)**

Ibid. . . . *showed that* only 6% of the individual respondents reported that the availability of a library copy was the only reason they cancelled their personal subscription, while only 5.1% reported that they might resubscribe if they lost access to the library's copy. **(264)**

Special

■ A 1970 survey of practicing physicians in 2 urban (Bridgeport, Connecticut) hospitals and 3 rural (northwest rural area) hospitals (population: 510; responding: 299 or 58%) *showed that* both urban and rural physicans reported that half of their educational activities consisted of reading. 74% of the reading time was spent on personal subscription journals and textbooks, 12-14% on unsolicited medical literature, and 12-14% on library materials. **(402)**

Attitudes—Reading

School

■ A survey reported in 1964 of 239 12th-grade students from 4 upper socioeconomic level high schools and 4 lower socioeconomic high schools (10% sample from each school) *showed that* students in both groups preferred to use the public library rather than the school library but that students in the lower socioeconomic schools read less and borrowed fewer books than their counterparts in the higher socioeconomic category.

(072)

Ibid. . . . *showed that*, when asked to indicate books they might like to read, the lower socioeconomic students were more likely to choose that category of books on how to be a more popular or successful person than their higher socioeconomic counterparts.   **(072)**

■ A survey reported in 1977 of selected 7th-grade students (257 readers, i.e., read 2 books a week or more, and 230 nonreaders, i.e., read 2 books a year or less) in Regina (Canada) concerning the amount of voluntary reading undertaken by these 2 groups *showed that* speaking a second language seemed to have no effect on a student's reading. Specifically, of 254 readers and 230 nonreaders, 47 (18.5%) of the readers spoke a second language while 42 (18.26%) of the nonreaders spoke a second language.

(547)

Ibid. . . . *showed that*, in terms of reading preference, nonreaders were more likely to mention nonfiction than readers. Overall, 21% of the nonreaders chose nonfiction compared to 10% of the readers. Further, when first, second, and third choices were combined for nonreaders, 94 (40.9%) chose comics, 55 (23.9%) chose joke books, and 51 (22.2%) chose sports books. When first, second, and third choices were combined for readers, 113 (44.0%) chose mysteries, 73 (28.4%) chose love stories, and 62 (24.1%) chose science fiction.   **(547)**

Ibid. . . . *showed that* only 13% of both groups reported never reading comic books while 87% reported reading them sometimes. 111 (42%) of the readers and 117 (51.1%) of the nonreaders read comic books once a week or more.   **(547)**

Ibid. . . . *showed that* of 254 readers and 226 nonreaders, the format of book preferred by readers was as follows:

paperback 168 (66.14%) students
hardcover 74 (29.13%) students
comic 9 (3.54%) students
magazine 3 (1.18%) students

While the format of book preferred by nonreaders was as follows:

comic 91 (40.27%) students
paperback 77 (34.07%) students
magazine 40 (17.70%) students
hardcover 18 (7.96%) students **(547)**

Special

■ A 1970 survey of practicing physicians in 2 urban (Bridgeport, Connecticut) hospitals and 3 rural (northwest rural area) hospitals (population: 510; responding: 299 or 58%) *showed that* both urban and rural physicans reported that half of their educational activities consisted of reading. 74% of the reading time was spent on personal subscription journals and textbooks, 12-14% on unsolicited medical literature, and 12-14% on library materials. **(402)**

Attitudes—Reference Service

Academic

■ A 1972 survey of patrons selected at random over a 167-day period at Syracuse University's Carnegie Library (sample size: 160 patrons; 119 or 74.4% responding) *showed that* 49 (41%) had questions, and of these 32 (65%) reported that they would not ask a librarian for help. **(139)**

Ibid. . . . *showed that* the main reasons why responding patrons were reluctant to ask for assistance from librarians were dissatisfaction with past service from the librarian (10), the question was too simple for the librarian (7), or they did not want to bother the librarian (7). **(139)**

■ A 1973 survey of physicists in 6 universities of the greater Boston area (Boston University, Brandeis, Brown, Harvard, MIT, and Northeastern) to determine how they meet their information needs (sample size: 339; responding: 179 or 52.8%) *showed that* 83.2% reported always or usually finding what they want when assisted by a librarian, compared to 76.6% who reported always or usually finding what they want without assistance from a librarian. **(404)**

■ A 1975 study at the University of Nebraska, Omaha, concerning student perceptions of academic librarians, involving a stratified sample of full-time students (sample size: 700; responding: 362 or 51.7%), *showed that* 40.7% [no raw number given] of the students were unsure or did not think that academic reference librarians have subject specialities, although 41.4% [no raw number given] reported that librarians "frequently" or "always" have the same "mastery of research methodology in subject areas as instructors." **(449)**

Ibid. . . . *showed that* only 31.6% [no raw number given] felt that the verbal interchange between student and librarian was "frequently" or "always" a learning experience, 22.5% [no raw number given] of the students felt that librarians should not locate answers and materials for them (59.4% [no raw number given] answered "sometimes"), and 11.6% [no raw number given] "frequently" or "always" wished their questions answered briefly without additional information. **(449)**

Ibid. . . . *showed that* 70.1% [no raw number given] of the students did not perceive the reference desk as a major barrier while 20.1% [no raw number given] "sometimes" felt it was. Further, 34.4% [no raw number given] of the students stated that they were bothered about asking the same librarian for further information. **(449)**

Ibid. . . . *showed that* 61.6% [no raw number given] believed that librarians performed a teaching function while 38.4% [no raw number given] did not. No statistically significant differences were found in the response to this question by sex, age, subject area, or class level. **(449)**

■ A study reported in 1976 of 4 academic libraries in the southern California area, *showed that* patrons chose to approach a female rather than a male staff member in reference or circulation if both were seated or standing and exhibiting similar nonverbal behavior. **(050)**

■ A survey reported in 1980 of a representative sample of 100 Drexel University students using conjoint analysis to determine the relative importance of various elements of reference service to these students *showed that* they ranked reference service elements from most to least important: (1) completeness of answer, (2) data base service, (3) attitude of reference librarian, (4) hours of service, (5) interlibrary loans, (6) knowledge of reference librarian, (7) time needed to answer, (8) wait for service. **(263)**

Ibid. . . . *showed that* students' school level, subject discipline, sex, use of the library, and place of residence made no difference in which of the 3 elements of reference service they ranked most important or in the order in which they ranked them.

(263)

■ A survey reported in 1981 of historians listed in the 1978 *Directory of American Scholars* concerning their use of and attitudes toward periodicals (survey size: 767 historians, although not all questionnaires could be delivered; responding: 360 or 46.9%, with respondents tending to be younger and with a higher scholarly productivity record than nonrespondents) *showed that* historians tend not to use the invisible college for discovering relevant published information for research. Specifically, the 3 most highly rated methods (out of 10) of discovering relevant published information for research (based on a rating scale of 1 to 5, where 5 was most highly rated) were:

bibliographies or references
   in books or journals   4.36 rating
   specialized bibliographies   4.01 rating
   book review   3.85 rating

While "discussion or correspondence with acquaintances elsewhere" ranked sixth with a rating of 3.14, "consulting a known expert" ranked eighth (2.87 rating), and "discussion with colleague at own institution" ranked ninth (2.6 rating). "Consulting librarian" ranked tenth (2.16 rating).

(780)

■ A study reported in 1981 at Southern Illinois University, Carbondale, investigating teaching faculty perception of librarians (survey size: 507; responding: 386; usable: 384 or 75.7%) *showed that* 24% of the teaching faculty reported that the librarian was "indispensable" to their teaching and research, 25% reported that the librarian was "very important," 29% reported that the librarian was "important," and 22% reported that the librarian was of "little" or "no importance" to their teaching and research.

(493)

Ibid. . . . *showed that* librarians appeared to be more appreciated by senior teaching faculty. Specifically, 34% of the [full] professors reported that librarians were indispensable to their teaching and research, while 21% of the associate professors and 22% of the assistant professors reported the same. Further, in terms of help received from librarians in the library itself, 19% of the [full] professors reported such help was indispensable, while 14% of the associate professors and 12% of the assistant professors so reported.

(493)

Ibid. . . . *showed that*, in terms of help received from librarians in the library itself, 13% of the teaching faculty reported that it was indispensable, 44% reported it was "very helpful," 33% reported it was "helpful," and 10% reported it was of "little" or "no help." **(493)**

Ibid. . . . *showed that* 18% of the teaching faculty reported that the librarians contributed a "very substantial" amount to student instruction, 33% reported that librarians contributed a "substantial" amount, 31% reported librarians contributed "some," and 18% reported that librarians contributed "very little" or "none." **(493)**

Special

■ A 1976 survey of physicians associated with hospitals in a 17-county region of upstate New York (Health Service Area V) based on a systematic sample of "approximately 40%" of the physicians in each county (survey size: 592 physicians; responding: 258 or 45.6%) *showed that*, of the 61% physicians who had asked a medical librarian for work-related information within the past year, 61.8% rated the information received as "adequate," 28.9% as "more than adequate," and 9.2% as "less than adequate." Further, 84.9% of the physicians had requested the information themselves, while 15.1% had used an intermediary (e.g., secretary). **(720)**

■ A survey reported in 1978 at the Yale-New Haven Hospital of clinicians concerning their attitudes toward the clinical medical librarian program (4 reference librarians assigned to the departments of pediatrics, psychiatry, internal medicine, and surgery) (survey size: 98 hosptial clinicians; responding: 73 or 74%) *showed that* respondents reported that the "information provided was exceptionally relevant" (overall average of 3.45 on a scale of 1-4) and that the literature searches were highly accurate (overall average of 3.48 on a scale of 1-4). **(723)**

Attitudes—Reference Use of Media

Special

■ A 1975-77 study of the use of a drug information service (including closed-circuit TV capability for sending answers) originating from the Health Sciences Library at the University of Cincinnati to provide information about drugs, chemicals, and poisons to health professionals in 14 local hospitals (2,294 questions researched; TV used to help provide the answer in 460 instances) *showed that* 79% of the information providers rated the contribution of the television medium as "excellent" or "good" while 74%

of the information users rated the television medium as "essential" or "very useful." **(422)**

Ibid. . . . *showed that* information users rated the information received as "very helpful" in 75.9% of the cases, as "satisfactory" in 19.9% of the cases, and as "poor" in 4.2% of the cases. **(422)**

Attitudes—SDI

Academic

■ A survey reported in 1972 at the University of Saskatchewan of participants in the SELDOM service (a selective dissemination of information service for new English-language monographs based on MARC records) (sample size: 121; responding: 77; usable: 71 or 58.6%) *showed that* 25.8% of the respondents reported the SDI lists "very useful," 48.5% reported them "useful," while 8.5% reported them inconsequential for their purposes. **(322)**

Ibid. . . . *showed that* 23.6% of the respondents reported that in most cases items of interest on the SELDOM lists were previously unknown to them while 45.8% reported that items of interest from the list were frequently new to them. **(322)**

Ibid. . . . *showed that* 83.5% of the respondents indicated that the information provided (MARC data only) was sufficient to determine whether they were interested in the item or not. The 3 most important data elements in making such determinations were, in decending order of importance: title, author/editor, and subject headings. 55.8% of the respondents reported they needed no more than 10 minutes per week to scan the SDI printouts. **(322)**

Ibid. . . . *showed that* 88.6% of the respondents wished the SDI service to continue, with 11.3% of the respondents rating the service "very high," 33.8% rating it "high," 42.2% rating it "medium," and 12.7% rating it "low." **(322)**

■ A survey reported in 1974 at the Hershey Medical Center Library of Pennsylvania State University comparing medical faculty views of a manually generated selective dissemination of information service with SDILINE (Selective Dissemination of Information Online, from the

National Library of Medicine) *showed that* of 8 faculty who had used both systems 88.9% preferred SDILINE and reported that it covered their subject area best. **(705)**

■ A 1974 study of current awareness methods used by Canadian academic chemists in 34 institutions (survey size: 170; responding: 134 or 80%) *showed that* only 19% of the respondents subscribed to a selective dissemination of information service. Among the reasons given for not subscribing were: ignorance of the existence of such services (15% respondents), not needed because of the nature of their work (15%), cost (25%), and personal preference (45%). **(636)**

Ibid. . . . *showed that* there was a statistically significant relationship between perception of scatter of information (number of different sources that respondents felt it necessary to consult in order to stay up-to-date in a speciality) and time spent on current awareness, with time spent on current awareness higher in specialities where information was perceived as being more scattered (significant at beyond the .001 level). However, there was no statistically significant relationship between perception of scatter of information and subscribing to an SDI service. **(636)**

Ibid. . . . *showed that* there was no statistically significant relationship (inverse) between perceived scatter of information and success in keeping up-to-date. The reason for this was the increased time spent on current awareness by respondents in specialities with high information scatter. There was a statistically significant inverse relationship between scatter of information and efficiency (success divided by time spent) in keeping up-to-date (significant at the .01 level). **(636)**

Public

■ A 1973 study of an experimental SDI service in the Mideastern Michigan Library Cooperative (sample size: 96, responding: 42 or 44%) *showed that* 43% of the respondents indicated they found the service "very useful," while an additional 45% reported that they found the service "of some use." 52% indicated that they thought that at least half of the books suggested fit their interests. **(144)**

Special

■ A survey reported in 1974 at the Hershey Medical Center Library of Pennsylvania State University comparing medical faculty views of a manually generated selective dissemination of information service with SDILINE (Selective Dissemination of Information Online, from the

National Library of Medicine) *showed that* of 8 faculty who had used both systems 88.9% preferred SDILINE and reported that it covered their subject area best.   (705)

■ A 1974 user survey of the Bristol Laboratory library (Syracuse, New York) involving 32 individuals (14% sample size) from 21 departments, including 18 directors and 14 nondirectors, *showed that* 72% of the respondents rejected the need for a personalized selective dissemination of information service. The main reason given (38% respondents) was that interests were too broad and changing. 28% reported that their present method of keeping up with the literature was satisfactory, and 6% reported a need for personal contact with the literature.   (407)

■ A survey reported in 1977 concerning online searching at the U.S. Army Construction Engineering Research Laboratory library (Champaign, Illinois), involving both users of the service (sample size: 27; responding: 26 or 96.3%) and nonusers of the service (sample size: 19; responding: 13 or 68.4%), *showed that*, of 25 user respondents, 7 (28%) indicated an interest in periodic update searches on their research topic; 11 (44%) indicated they would not; and 7 (28%) indicated they were uncertain.   (416)

■ A survey reported in 1978 of the current awareness service provided at the General Electric Corporate Research and Development library (Schenectady, New York) involving the Chemical Abstracts CONDENSATES data base (sample size: 65; responding: 60.0% [no raw number given]) and the Engineering Index COMPENDEX data base (sample size: 68; responding: 38.2% [no raw number given]) *showed that* 84.6% of the CONDENSATES users and 88.5% of the COMPENDEX users reported that the service had a "major" or "moderate" value, while 87.2% of the CONDENSATES users and 84.6% of the COMPENDEX users reported that "many" or "most" of the references retrieved by their profiles were relevant.   (424)

Ibid. . . . *showed that* the 3 main professional benefits resulting from the current awareness service for CONDENSATES users were: made aware of others in the field (53.8% respondents), provided new research leads (43.6% respondents), and made more time available for research (25.6% respondents).   (424)

Ibid. . . . *showed that* the 3 main professional benefits resulting from the current awareness service for COMPENDEX users were: made aware of others in the field (50.0% respondents), provided new research leads

(30.7% respondents), and prevented duplication of research conducted elsewhere (19.2% respondents).   **(424)**

■ A 1979 study and survey of physicians in nonmetropolitan areas of the Pacific northwest who were offered an opportunity to receive, without charge, table of contents pages from 18 journals relating to cancer research as well as the option to request a photocopy of any article of interest identified through the service (1-day turnaround guaranteed) (study and survey size: 126 physicians, including 63 randomly selected physicians and 63 physicians identified as having a special interest in cancer research and patient care) *showed that,* of 56 physicians who had not responded to the original offer of the service but who did respond to a subsequent survey 6 months later, the reasons for not participating were as follows:

access to the journals elsewhere	38% physicians
did not receive the letter offering the service (conjecture: thrown out by staff before seen by physician)	38% physicians
too busy	16% physicians
seldom saw cancer patients	9% physicians **(735)**

Ibid. . . . *showed that,* of the 29 physicians who participated in the service but who did not request articles (96% did respond to a subsequent survey 6 months later), the following reasons were given for not requesting articles:

access to the journals elsewhere	11 (40%) physicians
saw no journals of interest	8 (30%) physicians
too busy	6 (22%) physicians
seldom saw cancer patients	2 (7%) physicians **(735)**

Attitudes—Sources of Information

General

■ A 1970 survey of psychiatrists randomly selected from the 1968 membership of the American Psychiatric Association (survey size: 394; responding: 290 or 74%) *showed that* the 4 most frequently reported prime information sources (out of 11) were:

journals	55% respondents
books and monographs	16% respondents
colleagues	9% respondents
no preference indicated	9% respondents **(690)**

Academic

■ A 1964 study at the Yale Medical Library involving patron use of books (survey size: 831 borrowers; responding: 430) during a 5-month period *showed that* respondents reported learning about library books from the following sources (multiple responses allowed):

library	117 (24.2%) respondents
chance	104 (21.5%) respondents
citations from another	
published source	97 (20.0%) respondents
previous use	72 (14.9%) respondents
personal recommendation	60 (12.4%) respondents
miscellaneous	34 (7.0%) respondents

Further, a breakdown of the library sources was as follows:

card catalog	77 (16.0%) respondents	
monthly accessions list	22 (4.6%) respondents	
new book shelf	15 (3.0%) respondents	
asked librarian for help	3 (0.6%) respondents	**(672)**

■ A 1969 study of physicians on the faculty of the School of Medicine, Case Western Reserve University, who were also members of the Cleveland Medical Library Association (survey size: 615 physicians; responding: 418 or 62%) concerning their pattern of searching for professional information *showed that* the ratio of informal information sources (colleagues, etc.) to formal information sources (INDEX MEDICUS, etc.) used varied in a statistically significant way among 6 medical school departments (medicine, pathology, pediatrics, psychiatry, biology, and surgery). The main difference came between surgery (high use of formal sources) and psychiatry (high use of informal sources). (Significant at the .01 level.)

(609)

Ibid. . . . *showed that* the ratio of informal information sources (colleagues, etc.) to formal information sources (INDEX MEDICUS, etc.) used varied in a statistically significant way among 5 specialities (internal medicine, surgery, pediatrics, pathology, and psychiatry). The main difference came between surgery (high use of formal sources) and psychiatry (high use of informal sources). (Significant at the .05 level.) **(609)**

■ A survey reported in 1969 of a representative sample of agricultural economists in universities and the USDA (sample size: 590; response rate:

379 or 64%) *showed that* the 3 top reported methods of communicating scientific information were: conversations at work (35.9% rated excellent), discussions at meetings (27.9% rated excellent), and periodical of AFEA (complete texts) (22.8% rated excellent). **(245)**

■ A 1973 survey of physicists in 6 universities of the greater Boston area (Boston University, Brandeis, Brown, Harvard, MIT, and Northeastern) to determine how they meet their information needs (sample size: 339; responding: 179 or 52.8%) *showed that* at all universities physicists rated formal publications (i.e., journals primarily) their most important source of information and reference materials their least important source of information with semiformal publications, meetings and conferences, and informal oral communication in between. **(404)**

Ibid. . . . *showed that* preferred study areas were (multiple responses allowed): library (114 or 63.7%), departmental reading room (99 or 55.3%), colleague's collection (26 or 14.5%), and other (11 or 6.1%). **(404)**

Ibid. . . . *showed that* the reasons given for not using the library by 173 respondents (Harvard chemistry respondents included) were: no need (77 or 44.5%), time (59 or 34.1%), physical location (18 or 10.4%), and other (19 or 11.0%). **(404)**

■ A survey during the 1974-75 academic year at the Queen's University in Kingston (Canada) and Trent University in Peterborough (Canada) of part-time students (survey size: 1,143 students at Trent and 1,408 students at Queen's; responding: 286 or 25.1% students at Trent and 480 or 34.1% students at Queen's) *showed that*, of the 480 respondents to the Queen's University survey, 282 (58.8%) of the students reported obtaining their course readings primarily through the purchase of books. In contrast, 15.8% of the students reported that the university library was the primary source of their readings, while 5.2% reported that the public library was the primary source of their readings. A list of 8 options was provided. **(545)**

■ A 1975 study at the University of Nebraska, Omaha, concerning student perceptions of academic librarians, involving a stratified sample of full-time students (sample size: 700; responding: 362 or 51.7%) *showed that* only 16.1% reported "frequently" or "always" seeking assistance immediately when searching for library materials or information. (449)

■ A 1975-77 study of the use of a drug information service (including closed-circuit TV capability for sending answers) originating from the Health Sciences Library at the University of Cincinnati to provide information about drugs, chemicals, and poisons to health professionals in 14 local hospitals (2,294 questions researched; TV used to help provide the answer in 460 instances) *showed that* 79% of the information providers rated the contribution of the television medium as "excellent" or "good" while 74% of the information users rated the television medium as "essential" or "very useful." (422)

Ibid. . . . *showed that* information users rated the information received as "very helpful" in 75.9% of the cases, as "satisfactory" in 19.9% of the cases, and as "poor" in 4.2% of the cases. (422)

■ A 1978-79 study underwritten by the NSF Division of Information Science and technology of academic and research journal subscription and cancellation for both individuals and libraries (individual questionnaires; 2,817; usable responses: 1,190; library questionnaires: 4,997; usable responses: 1,905) of journals at least 5 years old *showed that* only 8 respondents (1.1%) placed a subscription because the library had cancelled its subscription, and this reason in every case was combined with other reasons. (264)

Ibid. . . . *showed that* the top 5 means through which individuals reported learning about a journal (multiple responses permitted; N = 705) were as follows: 254 individuals (36%) became aware of the journal while in school, 241 (34.2%) through professional contacts, 225 (31.9%) through references in the literature, 116 (16.5%) through browsing in the library, and 24 (3.4%) through promotional activity by publisher. (264)

■ A survey reported in 1981 of historians listed in the 1978 *Directory of American Scholars* concerning their use of and attitudes toward periodicals (survey size: 767 historians, although not all questionnaires could be delivered; responding: 360 or 46.9%, with respondents tending to be younger and with a higher scholarly productivity record than nonrespondents) *showed that* historians tended not to use the invisible college for discovering relevant published information for research. Specifically, the 3 most highly rated methods (out of 10) of discovering relevant published information for research (based on a rating scale of 1 to 5, where 5 was most highly rated) were:

bibliographies or references
in books or journals   4.36 rating
specialized bibliographies   4.01 rating
book review   3.85 rating

While "discussion or correspondence with acquaintances elsewhere" ranked sixth with a rating of 3.14, "consulting a known expert" ranked eighth (2.87 rating), and "discussion with colleague at own institution" ranked ninth (2.6 rating). "Consulting librarian" ranked tenth (2.16 rating). **(780)**

Ibid. . . . *showed that* respondents clearly preferred bibliographic tools providing abstracts over those providing simple author and title entries. Specifically, when asked to compare the value of bibliographic tools providing abstracts in contrast to simple author and title entries, 23.7% reported the abstracts "about the same," 46.4% reported the abstracts "somewhat more satisfactory," and 29.9% reported the abstracts "much more satisfactory." **(780)**

Ibid. . . . *showed that* the invisible college was also not important in making accidental discoveries. For example, the 3 most frequently reported ways of making frequent accidental discoveries (out of 6) were:

scanning current periodicals   173 (48.1%) respondents
looking up a given reference
and spotting something else   151 (41.9%) respondents
wandering along library shelves   108 (30.0%) respondents

"In conversation with colleagues" ranked fourth with 78 (21.7%) respondents. **(780)**

Ibid. . . . *showed that* the degree of importance to their research of knowing as soon as possible after publication what had been published was as follows:

very important   40.7% respondents
moderately important   47.8% respondents
not very important   11.5% respondents   **(780)**

Ibid. . . . *showed that* 58% of the respondents "do not attempt to keep up with research published in foreign languages." Further, when asked if they felt their research was restricted in any way because of a language problem, 334 respondents reported as follows:

no restriction	138 (41.3%) respondents
slight restriction	136 (40.7%) respondents
moderate restriction	42 (12.6%) respondents
substantial restriction	18 (5.4%) respondents

Finally, when encountering a reference in a foreign language that they did not read, respondents reported the following responses:

try to get article translated	30.3% respondents
search for summary or abstract	21.7% respondents
try to get gist on own	34.7% respondents
ignore	13.3% respondents **(780)**

Public

■ Self-studies conducted in 1957 in 3 western Kansas counties by public libraries *showed that* respondents gave parallel answers to the question, Where do you and your family get the materials you read? The largest percentage reported getting their reading materials and books through subscription and book clubs; the second largest percentage reported getting their books by borrowing from or exchanging with friends; the third highest percentage was from libraries. **(064)**

■ A survey reported in 1977 based on a stratified random sample of 300 households (response rate: 251 or 83%) in the Piedmont area of North Carolina *showed that* 97 or 39% (10 or 30% of respondents who had never used a library) of the full sample of respondents reported they would turn to the library for the names, locations, and phone numbers for health services (e.g., hospitals, clinics, prenatal care) were such information available through the library. **(225)**

Ibid. . . . *showed that* 71 or 28% (8 or 24% of respondents who had never used a library) of the full sample of respondents reported they would turn to the library for the names, locations, and phone numbers of emergency services (e.g., fire and policy departments, civil defense, poisonings) were such information available through the library. **(225)**

Ibid. . . . *showed that* 60 or 24% (5 or 15% of respondents who had never used a library) of the full sample of respondents reported they would turn to the library for the names, locations, and phone numbers for social services (e.g., foster homes, food stamps, Medicare) were such information available through the library. **(225)**

School

■ A 1978 survey of a random sample of teachers, administrators, and support personnel representative of educators in the 12 regions of British Columbia (Canada) (survey size: 1,640; responding: 1,078 or 65.7% individuals) *showed that* the 3 most frequently reported sources of information (out of 13) in descending order of importance were:

1. conversations with colleagues
2. notes, files, books in my office
3. books or textbooks

"School or district libraries" was ranked fifth, while "public or university libraries" was ranked eleventh.   **(658)**

Special

■ A 1964 study at the Yale Medical Library involving patron use of books (survey size: 831 borrowers; responding: 430) during a 5-month period *showed that* respondents reported learning about library books from the following sources (multiple responses allowed):

library	117 (24.2%) respondents
chance	104 (21.5%) respondents
citations from another published source	97 (20.0%) respondents
previous use	72 (14.9%) respondents
personal recommendation	60 (12.4%) respondents
miscellaneous	34 (7.0%) respondents

Further, a breakdown of the library sources was as follows:

card catalog	77 (16.0%) respondents	
monthly accessions list	22 (4.6%) respondents	
new book shelf	15 (3.0%) respondents	
asked librarian for help	3 (0.6%) respondents	**(672)**

■ A 1969 study of physicians on the faculty of the School of Medicine, Case Western Reserve University, who were also members of the Cleveland Medical Library Association (survey size: 615 physicians; responding 418 or 62%) concerning their pattern of searching for professional information *showed that* the ratio of informal information sources (colleagues, etc.) to formal information sources (INDEX MEDICUS, etc.) used varied in a statistically significant way among 6 medical school departments (medicine, pathology, pediatrics, psychiatry, biology, and surgery). The main difference came between surgery (high use of formal sources) and

psychiatry (high use of informal sources). (Significant at the .01 level.)
(609)

Ibid. . . . *showed that* the ratio of informal information sources (colleagues, etc.) to formal information sources (INDEX MEDICUS, etc.) used varied in a statistically significant way among 5 specialities (internal medicine, surgery, pediatrics, pathology, and psychiatry). The main difference came between surgery (high use of formal sources) and psychiatry (high use of informal sources). (Significant at the .05 level.)   **(609)**

■ A 1970 survey of psychiatrists randomly selected from the 1968 membership of the American Psychiatric Association (survey size: 394; responding: 290 or 74%) *showed that* the 4 most frequently reported prime information sources (out of 11) were:

journals	55% respondents
books and monographs	16% respondents
colleagues	9% respondents
no preference indicated	9% respondents **(690)**

■ A 1975-77 study of the use of a drug information service (including closed-circuit TV capability for sending answers) originating from the Health Sciences Library at the University of Cincinnati to provide information about drugs, chemicals, and poisons to health professionals in 14 local hospitals (2,294 questions researched; TV used to help provide the answer in 460 instances) *showed that* 79% of the information providers rated the contribution of the television medium as "excellent" or "good" while 74% of the information users rated the television medium as "essential" or "very useful."
(422)

Ibid. . . . *showed that* information users rated the information received as "very helpful" in 75.9% of the cases, as "satisfactory" in 19.9% of the cases, and as "poor" in 4.2% of the cases.   **(422)**

■ A 1976 survey of physicians associated with hospitals in a 17-county region of upstate New York (Health Service Area V) based on a systematic sample of "approximately 40%" of the physicians in each county (survey size: 592 physicians; responding: 258 or 45.6%) *showed that* the 3 most frequently used sources of information as reported by the physicians were (in descending order of importance):

1. papers in journals
2. personal contact with colleagues
3. books

As an information source used by physicians "library reference services" ranked 7 out of a list of 19.   **(720)**

Attitudes—Theft

Academic

■ A 1978 survey of 201 undergraduate students in a large urban university concerning book theft and mutilation *showed that* 17 (8%) students reported "sneaking" books out of the library while 18 (9%) students reported mutilating books or periodicals. Only 2 students were in both groups.   **(499)**

Ibid. . . . *showed that* a statistically significantly greater number of students who reported doing well academically also reported stealing or mutilating library materials. 37 (22%) of the nonviolators reported doing "very well" academically while 14 (42%) of the violators reported doing "very well" (significant at the .05 level).   **(499)**

Ibid. . . . *showed that* neither feeling poorly served by the library nor lack of access to a copy machine appeared to be related to the theft or mutilation of library materials. Specifically, 61 (37%) of the nonviolators and 11 (33%) of the violators felt "served well" by the library. Further, 111 (67%) of the nonviolators and 21 (70%) of the violators reported that the cost of the copy machine was "never too expensive," while 30 (21%) of the nonviolators and 6 (19%) of the violators reported that they were "never inconvenienced" by a broken copy machine.
                                                                          (499)

Ibid. . . . *showed that* there was a statistically significant difference between violators and nonviolators in their perception of the odds of getting caught "sneaking" a book out of the library. 126 (71%) of the nonviolators and 7 (44%) of the violators (only those who reported "sneaking" books out of the library) reported the odds of getting caught as 1 in 10, while 52 (29%) of the nonviolators and 9 (56%) of the violators reported the odds of getting caught as 1 in 100 (significant at the .05 level).
                                                                          (499)

Ibid. . . . *showed that* there was a statistically significant difference between violators and nonviolators in their perception of whether their friends steal books. None of the nonviolators reported that their friends steal books, while 3 (9%) of the violators reported that their friends steal books (significant at the .05 level). **(499)**

Ibid. . . . *showed that* 82 (53%) of the nonviolators and 15 (52%) of the violators reported the perception that 10% or less of the student body stole books, while 72 (47%) of the nonviolators and 15 (48%) of the violators reported the perception that 25% or more of the student body stole books. **(499)**

Ibid. . . . *showed that* the reasons given for stealing or mutilating library materials were as follows (multiple responses allowed):

Do not consider the needs of others	45% violators
Need the photographs or charts in books and cannot photocopy them	36% violators
Do not think about the act but steal and mutilate casually and thoughtlessly	30% violators
Are not aware of the cost of theft and mutilation to the library	27% violators
Cannot afford the copy machine or price of a book but want to own a copy	24% violators
Steal and mutilate books as an expression of hostility toward the library and the university	18% violators **(499)**

Attitudes—Use of the Library

Academic

■ A 1964 study at the Yale Medical Library involving patron use of books (survey size: 831 borrowers; responding: 430) during a 5-month period *showed that* 11% of the books were reported used in lecture preparation, while 89% appeared to be "associated with research activites." Further, 28% of the books were reported used to "acquire general information to keep up with the field." **(672)**

■ A 1964-67 study of northern California university, 4-year college, and 2-year college libraries (including 1 Oregon library) *showed that* the top 6 reasons a sample of 1,563 students at 16 institutions gave for studying in the library were: quiet (51%), convenience or proximity (29%), materials (27%), atmosphere conducive to study (21%), few distractions, little movement (20%), and concentrate better (10%). **(244)**

Ibid. . . . *showed that* the main disadvantage to studying in the library given by "1 out of 8" of a sample of 1,563 students at 16 institutions was noise from other people. **(244)**

Ibid. . . . *showed that* the top 4 major distractions reported by 279 students at 7 institutions were (multiple responses allowed): people coming in and out (73%), other students talking (65%), thinking of other things (62%), and noises other than talking (41%). **(244)**

Ibid. . . . *showed that* the 3 aspects of the physical library environment that 1,112 students at 16 institutions most often rated as needing improvements were: snack facilities (53%), number of carrels (44%), and quietness (44%). **(244)**

■ A survey reported in 1970 of library patrons at Purdue University (6,568 sampled; 6,323 usable responses) and statistically analyzed by Chi Square tests *showed that* the 3 patron groupings (faculty, graduate, and undergraduate) gave statistically significantly different response rates for their primary reasons for visiting the library (significant at the .001 level). The largest category reported by faculty for library visits was research for a publishable paper or book (21%); for graduate students the largest category was to find and read material required by a course (30%); for undergraduates the largest category was to do homework with their own books (50+%). **(202)**

■ A survey during the 1974-75 academic year at the Queen's University in Kingston (Canada) and Trent University in Peterborough (Canada) of part-time students (survey size: 1,143 students at Trent and 1,408 students at Queen's; responding: 286 or 25.1% students at Trent and 480 or 34.1% students at Queen's) *showed that*, of the 480 respondents to the Queen's University survey, 282 (58.8%) of the students reported obtaining their course readings primarily through the purchase of books. In contrast, 15.8% of the students reported that the university library was the primary source of their readings, while 5.2% reported that the public library was the primary source of their readings. A list of 8 options was provided. **(545)**

■ A study in 1975 of business students (undergraduate and graduate) at the University of Delaware, University of Maryland, and Wright State University *showed that* students felt knowing how to use the library was necessary for academic success but not career success.   **(049)**

Ibid. . . . *showed that* they were infrequent readers of most business periodicals. For example 21% of the undergrads and 8% of the M.B.A.'s reported never having read the *Wall Street Journal*.   **(049)**

Ibid. . . . *showed that* less than 50% of the students rated themselves frequent borrowers of library materials.   **(049)**

Ibid. . . . *showed that* they were infrequent users of almost all the recognized and commonly available sources of marketing information. For example, over 10% of the students reported that they had never heard of *Business Periodical Index*.   **(049)**

■ A 1975 study at the University of Nebraska, Omaha, concerning student perceptions of academic librarians, involving a stratified sample of full-time students (sample size: 700; responding: 362 or 51.7%) *showed that* only 16.1% reported "frequently" or "always" seeking assistance immediately when searching for library materials or information.   **(449)**

■ A 1980 survey of faculty and students at San Jose State University concerning their library use patterns (students—survey size: [not given]; responding: 1,470; faculty—population: 1,753; responding: 443 or 25.3%) *showed that* the reasons given for not using the university library by those students who reported they seldom or never used the library were: "no need" to use the library (38%), poor organization of the library (26%), and greater convenience of another library (11%).   **(519)**

Ibid. . . . *showed that* the reasons given for not using the university library by those faculty who reported they seldom or never used the library were: greater convenience of another library (38%), "no time" (23%), "no need" (21%), and poor organization (15%).   **(519)**

Public

■ A 1966 survey of 21,385 adult (12 years old or older) public library users in the Baltimore-Washington metropolitan region of Maryland conducted during a 6-week period of patrons entering the library (79.1% of patrons approached filled out the survey instrument) *showed that*, of those unsatisified respondents giving reasons for their dissatisfaction, 47.0% wanted a book (or books) that were in circulation, 35.9% wanted a book not in [owned by] the library, 14.4% could not locate material on the necessary subject, 6.4% found the material outdated, 6.1% felt the material they found was too elementary, 2.0% felt the material found was too advanced, and 12.9% reported other reasons. **(301)**

Ibid. . . . *showed that* the top 5 reasons given for visiting the library were (multiple responses allowed): return books (43.4%), obtain materials or information on a subject (33.5%), pick out general reading (33.5%), obtain a specific book (22.1%), and to bring their child (12.9%). **(301)**

Ibid. . . . *showed that*, of the unsatisfied respondents, 5,104 (66%) planned to continue their quest. Of these, 59.3% planned to go to another library, 19.9% put a reserve on the book, 7.7% made arrangements for the library to get the material from another library, and 13.1% planned to use other alternatives (e.g., buying the book or borrowing it from friends). **(301)**

Ibid. . . . *showed that* the top 3 difficulties given by 5,029 respondents in trying to use the library were: getting parking space (9.2%), library too noisy (5.4%), and difficult to figure out the library arrangement (4.7%). **(301)**

■ A survey reported in 1977 based on a stratified random sample of 300 households (response rate: 251 or 83%) in the Piedmont area of North Carolina *showed that* 122 or 49% (67 or 55% of rural respondents; 21 or 36% of small town respondents; and 34 or 49% of urban respondents) of the full sample of respondents reported an interest in bookmobile service; 115 or 46% (53 or 43% of rural respondents; 20 or 34% of small town respondents and 42 or 61% of urban respondents) of the full sample of respondents reported an interest in being able to order library materials over the phone and have them delivered; while 90 or 36% (45 or 37% of rural respondents: 14 or 24% of small town respondents and 31 or 45% of urban respondents) of the full sample of respondents reported an interest in ordering library materials by mail. **(225)**

■ A 1977-78 survey of a random sample of 300 Spanish-surnamed families in the San Bernardino area *showed that* 42% of the sample were unaware that the library's service included books. **(237)**

Ibid. . . . *showed that* 86% of the sample speak some Spanish while 16% of the sample speak only Spanish. If given the choice, 21% of the respondents preferred to conduct their transactions with the library staff in Spanish. **(237)**

School

■ A survey reported in 1964 of 239 12th-grade students from 4 upper socioeconomic level high schools and 4 lower socioeconomic high schools (10% sample from each school) *showed that* students in both groups preferred to use the public library rather than the school library but that students in the lower socioeconomic schools read less and borrowed fewer books than their counterparts in the higher socioeconomic category. **(072)**

Ibid. . . . *showed that* students from the lower socioeconomic schools showed a strong preference for using their own and library materials in the library, while students from the higher socioeconomic schools showed a tendency to borrow materials and study at home. Higher socioeconomic students also tended to use the public library as a social center. **(072)**

Ibid. . . . *showed that*, when asked to indicate books they might like to read, the lower socioeconomic students were more likely to choose that category of books on how to be a more popular or successful person than their higher socioeconomic counterparts. **(072)**

Children's Services

Public

■ A 1962 study of 1,718 fourth graders in Evansville, Indiana, to see whether successful completion of a Summer library reading program improved scores on the California Reading Test (135 completing reading program; 1,583 did not, including 50 who began but did not complete the program) *showed that* the correlation between program membership and fall reading score was .13 with a significance level at .01. The highest correlation (.82) was between Spring reading score and Fall reading score. **(243)**

■ A 1966 survey of 21,385 adult (12 years old or older) public library users in the Baltimore-Washington metropolitan region of Maryland conducted during a 6-week period of patrons entering the library (79.1%

of patrons approached filled out the survey instrument) *showed that* the top 5 reasons given for visiting the library were (multiple responses allowed): return books (43.4%), obtain materials or information on a subject (33.5%), pick out general reading (33.5%), obtain a specific book (22.1%), and to bring their child (12.9%). **(301)**

School

■ A 1980 survey of 310 public library children's specialists in 74 California library systems (all responding) *showed that* the 3 most frequent kinds of programming reported by libraries were: class visits to library (52.9% on weekly or monthly basis), preschool story hour (63.2% on weekly or monthly basis), and film programs (39.7% on weekly or monthly basis). **(163)**

Demographics—General Issues

Public

■ A questionnaire survey of 3,500 public library cardholders in 5 medium-sized Pennsylvania cities in conjunction with interviews of a randomly selected sample of householders in 1 city by the Institute of Public Administration (at Pennsylvania State University) under contract to the Pennsylvania State Library in 1965 *showed that* library cardholders and active library users had the following characteristics: read widely; owned books themselves; purchased paperback books with some regularity; subscribed to a number of magazines/periodicals; read at least 1 newspaper a day; tended to have unsophisticated and unspecialized tastes in reading. **(084)**

■ A 1966 survey of 21,385 adult (12 years old or older) public library users in the Baltimore-Washington metropolitan region of Maryland conducted during a 6-week period of patrons entering the library (79.1% of patrons approached filled out the survey instrument) *showed that* 57.2% of the respondents left home, work, or school only to visit the library, 16% visited the library while shopping, and 24.9% visited the library in connection with some other activity. **(301)**

■ A 1971 survey of North Carolina heads of household or other adult residents (sample size: 1,008), in which 243 (24%) respondents identified themselves as public library users (from once a year to more than once a month) and 765 identified themselves as nonusers, *showed that* marital status of the respondents was as follows: married (users, 73%; nonusers, 74%), widowed (users, 8%; nonusers, 14%), separated/divorced (users, 7%; nonusers 6%), single, never married (users, 12%; nonusers, 6%).

(235)

Ibid. . . . *showed that* the political activity of respondents was as follows: vote always or almost always (users, 64%; nonusers, 47%), often or always talking about politics (users, 62%; nonusers, 32%), work for party or candidate always or often (users, 10%; nonusers, 4%), try to influence voting behavior of others always or often (users, 22%; nonusers, 13%).

(235)

Ibid. . . . *showed that* the political philosophy of respondents was as follows: conservative (users, 34%; nonusers, 28%), liberal (users, 22%; nonusers, 15%), nonaligned (users, 28%; nonusers, 30%), middle of the road (users, 13%; nonusers, 8%). (235)

■ A study based on telephone interviews reported in 1980 of individuals in the Syracuse metropolitan area (sample size: 442; 322 contacted; 202 or 46% participated in the study) *showed that* 6 factors helped predict in a statistically significant way and in descending importance public library use. More specifically, 29% of the variance of the variable "use/nonuse of the public library" could be accounted for by the following 6 independent variables listed in descending order of importance with a cumulative effect as follows (R^2 scores): cultural activities (9%), number of magazines read (12%), sex—female (14%), number of professional sources used in the past year (16%), perceived accessibility of library (28%), and use of nonpublic library (29%). (265)

Ibid. . . . *showed that* of 161 library users 8 factors helped predict in a statistically significant way frequency of library use. More specifically, 36% of the variance of the variable "frequency of contacting the public library" could be accounted for by the following 8 independent variables with a cumulative effect as follows (R^2 scores): adult education activities (13%), number of books read (20%), number of children (negatively correlated) (23%), cultural activities (24%), age (26%), number of books in home (28%), awareness of special programs (34%), and perceived accessibility (36%). (265)

Ibid. . . . *showed that* of 161 library users 2 types of library use were identified. Type 1 use was associated with frequency of visits, use of services, circulation of materials, and importance that the patron placed on use activities. 7 factors helped predict this type of library use. More specifically, 41% of the variance of the variable "type 1 library use" could be accounted for by the following 7 independent variables with a cumulative effect as follows (R2 scores): adult education activities (14%), number of books read (22%), community involvement (26%), sex—female (29%), cultural activities (32%), awareness of special programs (39%), and perceived accessibility (41%). **(265)**

Ibid. . . . *showed that* of 161 library users 2 types of library use were identified. Type 2 use was associated primarily with duration of visit. 6 factors helped predict this type of library use. More specifically, 24% of the variance of the variable "type 2 library use" could be accounted for by the following 6 independent variables with a cumulative effect as follows (R2 scores): adult education activities (8%), sex—female (negatively correlated) (11%), number of children (negatively correlated) (14%), number of books in home (negatively correlated) (17%), age (negatively correlated) (18%), and use of nonpublic library (24%). **(265)**

Demographics—Age

Public

■ A 1966 survey of 21,385 adult (12 years old or older) public library users in the Baltimore-Washington metropolitan region of Maryland conducted during a 6-week period of patrons entering the library (79.1% of patrons approached filled out the survey instrument) *showed that* 22.4% of the respondents were 12-16 years of age, 24.9% were 17-21 years old, 18.1% were 22-34 years old, 25.0% were 35-50 years old, 8.3% were 50+, and 1.3% did not respond. **(301)**

■ A 1971 survey of North Carolina heads of household or other adult residents (sample size: 1,008), in which 243 (24%) respondents identified themselves as public library users (from once a year to more than once a month) and 765 identified themselves as nonusers, *showed that* library users tended to be younger than nonusers. 25% and 28% of the public library users were in their 20s or 30s, respectively, compared to 19% and 15% of the nonusers. While only 12%, 7%, and 5% of public library users were in their 50s, 60s, or 70s+, respectively, 21%, 15%, and 10% of the nonusers were in these age groups. These are statistically significant differences at the .05 level of significance. 21% of the public library users were in their 40s, while 20% of the nonusers were in that age group. This did not constitute a statistically significant difference. **(235)**

Demographics—Automation Experience

Academic

■ A 1981 survey of faculty, students, staff, and community users of the University of Cincinnati Libraries (sample size: 4,074; responding: 912 or 22.4%, including 436 or 39% faculty response and 218 or 11% student response), *showed that* although the University of Cincinnati Libraries operated on manual systems, "approximately 25%" of the students, community users, and university administrators reported experience with computerized library systems, while 33% of the faculty and 37% of the library staff reported experience with automated library systems. **(522)**

Demographics—Distance from Library

Public

■ A study reported in 1963 concerning public library use by 180 (98 black; 82 white) low-income mothers with first-grade children in Chicago *showed that* 42% of the respondents living within 5 blocks of a library had library cards while only 17% of those living further away from a library had cards. (Finding significant at the .001 level.) **(242)**

■ A 1966 survey of 21,385 adult (12 years old or older) public library users in the Baltimore-Washington metropolitan region of Maryland conducted during a 6-week period of patrons entering the library (79.1% of patrons approached filled out the survey instrument) *showed that* 67.9% of the respondents traveled to the library by car, 24.6% walked, and 4.9% traveled by bus. According to self-report, 39.7% of the respondents traveled less than 1 mile, 44.4% between 1 and 5 miles, 9.1% between 5 and 10 miles, 3.5% between 10 and 15 miles, 1.8% over 15 miles, and 1.5% did not respond. **(301)**

Demographics—Education

Public

■ A 1966 survey of 21,385 adult (12 years old or older) public library users in the Baltimore-Washington metropolitan region of Maryland conducted during a 6-week period of patrons entering the library (79.1% of patrons approached filled out the survey instrument) *showed that* the highest level of education attained was elementary school for 8.3% of the respondents, was high school for 28.1% of the respondents, was college for

60.5% of the respondents, with 3.1% of the patrons surveyed not responding to this question. **(301)**

■ A 1971 survey of North Carolina heads of household or other adult residents (sample size: 1,008), in which 243 (24%) respondents identified themselves as public library users (from once a year to more than once a month) and 765 identified themselves as nonusers, *showed that* education of respondents was as follows: less than high school education (users, 16%; nonusers, 62%), high school education (users, 27%; nonusers, 26%), 1-3 years college (users, 25%; nonusers, 8%), B.A. or higher (users, 34%; nonusers, 4%). **(235)**

■ A 1979 telephone survey of 1,046 New Orleans residents over the age of 12 *showed that* library users tend to be more highly educated than library nonusers. 25.5% of users have bachelor's degrees compared to 9.4% of nonusers, and 7.7% have master's degrees compared to 0.8% of nonusers. **(166)**

■ A study reported in 1980-81 comparing level of public library development (a composite factor made up of staff size, expenditures, total books in the collection, and circulation) with 9 community characteristics (e.g., education, per capita income, occupational prestige, etc.) *showed that,* based on 1,441 libraries and communities nationwide, median education (of adults) was most strongly associated with public library development. Specifically, the relationship was positive with an $r2 = .564$. (The relationship was significant at the .05 level.) **(568)**

Demographics—Gender

Public

■ A 1966 survey of 21,385 adult (12 years old or older) public library users in the Baltimore-Washington metropolitan region of Maryland conducted during a 6-week period of patrons entering the library (79.1% of patrons approached filled out the survey instrument) *showed that* 40.1% of the respondents were male. **(301)**

Demographics—General Population, Cardholders

Public

■ A questionnaire survey of 3,500 public library cardholders in 5 medium-sized Pennsylvania cities in conjunction with interviews of a randomly selected sample of householders in 1 city by the Institute of Public Administration (at Pennsylvania State University) under contract to the Pennsylvania State Library in 1965 *showed that* between 20-25% of the adults were registered library users. **(084)**

■ A 1977-78 survey of a random sample of 300 Spanish-surnamed families in the San Bernardino area *showed that* 25% of the respondents had valid library cards and that, of these 25%, 70% had used the library at least once in the past year. **(237)**

Demographics—General Population, Reading

General

■ A 1970 survey of psychiatrists randomly selected from the 1968 membership of the American Psychiatric Association (survey size: 394; responding: 290 or 74%) *showed that* respondents reported an average of 6.7 hours of professional reading per week, with 62% of the reading time devoted to journals and 38% of the reading time devoted to books. Private practitioners read the least (5.6 hours/week), while academicians read the most (9.1 hours/week). **(690)**

Ibid. . . . *showed that* the 4 most frequently reported prime information sources (out of 11) were:

journals	55% respondents	
books and monographs	16% respondents	
colleagues	9% respondents	
no preference indicated	9% respondents	**(690)**

Ibid. . . . *showed that* the average number of journals read regularly was 4.3 while the average number of books read in the previous 12-month period was 9.7. There was considerable variation by type of practice, for example:

academicians	18.9 books/year average
mixed practice psychiatrists	12.6 books/year average
hosptial-clinic	
psychiatrists	9.6 books/year average
administrators	8.7 books/year average
private practitioners	6.4 books/year average **(690)**

Ibid. . . . *showed that* overall, of the books read, 67% were purchased, 28% came from a library, 3% came from colleagues, and 2% from other sources.   **(690)**

Public

■ Self-studies conducted in 1957 in 3 western Kansas counties by public libraries *showed that* respondents gave parallel answers to the question, Where do you and your family get the materials you read? The largest percentage reported getting their reading materials and books through subscription and book clubs; the second largest percentage reported getting their books by borrowing from or exchanging with friends; the third highest percentage was from libraries.   **(064)**

■ A study reported in 1963 concerning public library use by 180 (98 black; 82 white) low-income mothers with first-grade children in Chicago *showed that* 9% of the black women and 45% of the white women reported spending no time reading books or magazines in an average week. **(242)**

■ A 1965 survey of a sample of the U.S. noninstitutional population over 21 years old conducted by the National Opinion Research Center (sample size: 1,469) *showed that* 712 (48%) reported themselves readers by indicating that they had read or started a book within the past 6 months.
(251)

Ibid. . . . *showed that* of the 712 readers the 4 types of books that the most respondents reported reading frequently were (multiple responses were allowed): fiction—classic or current (37%), hobbies, sports, gardening, cookbooks, home repair, home decoration, travel (31%), histories or biographies (26%), and religious books other than the Bible (24%).
(251)

Ibid. . . . *showed that* the 712 readers reported their major source of books to be: stores (30%), libraries (28%), loans from friends and relatives (14%), book clubs (15%), and other (13%).   **(251)**

Ibid. . . . *showed that*, of the total sample (1,468 [sic]), 150 had 4 years of college (89% were readers), 220 had 1-3 years of college (72% readers), 409 had 4 years high school (54% readers), 323 had 1-3 years high school (40% readers), and 366 had 1-8 grades (21% readers).   **(251)**

Ibid. . . . *showed that* the younger part of the population has more readers than the older part. 60% of the 21-24 year olds were readers, 61% of the 25-34 year olds were readers, 54% of the 35-44 year olds were readers, 44% of the 45-54 year olds were readers, 38% of the 55-64 year olds were readers, 25% of the 65-74 year olds were readers, and 30% of those 75+ were readers.   **(251)**

Ibid. . . . *showed that* reading and income seem to be related. 35% of the respondents earning under $5,000 were readers, 50% between $5,000-7,999 were readers, 64% between $8,000-14,999 were readers, and 76% earning $15,000 were readers.   **(251)**

■ A 1968 study of the summer reading of 23 seventh-graders from the Joyce Kilmer School in Chicago during a 5-week period *showed that*, of 191 books reported read, 58.6% came from the public library (involving 73.9% of the students); 24.1% came from siblings, friends, or parents; and 19.3% came from bookstores, were gifts or owned by the student.
                                                                   (247)

Ibid. . . . *showed that*, of the 191 books reported read, the 3 most frequent reasons given for selecting a particular book were: reputation of the book (63.5 or 33.2% of the books), subject of the book (34 or 17.8% of the books), and title of the book (34 or 17.8% of the books). (When 2 reasons were given for selecting a book each was counted as .5.)   **(247)**

Ibid. . . . *showed that* the basis of a book's reputation was largely personal recommendation. Of the 63.5 books so selected, the source of the recommendations was: friend (21.5 books), classmate (10 books), parent (9 books), sibling (8 books), librarian (7 books), and advertisements/book reviews (8 books).   **(247)**

Ibid. . . . *showed that* the sources of magazines reported read by students were: family subscription/purchase (20.5% of magazines read), student purchase (22.1%), read when visiting (11.6%), and old magazine belonging to student (5.8%). **(247)**

■ A survey reported in 1977 of selected seventh-grade students (257 readers, i.e., read 2 books a week or more, and 230 nonreaders, i.e., read 2 books a year or less) in Regina (Canada) concerning the amount of voluntary reading undertaken by these 2 groups *showed that* females were more likely to be readers than males. Specifically, 184 (71.60%) of the readers were female, while 54 (23.48%) of the nonreaders were female. **(547)**

Ibid. . . . *showed that* speaking a second language seemed to have no effect on a student's reading. Specifically, of 254 readers and 230 nonreaders, 47 (18.5%) of the readers spoke a second language, while 42 (18.26%) of the nonreaders spoke a second language. **(547)**

Ibid. . . . *showed that*, in terms of reading preference, nonreaders were more likely to mention nonfiction than readers. Overall, 21% of the nonreaders chose nonfiction compared to 10% of the readers. Further, when first, second, and third choices were combined for nonreaders, 94 (40.9%) chose comics, 55 (23.9%) chose joke books, and 51 (22.2%) chose sports books. When first, second, and third choices were combined for readers, 113 (44.0%) chose mysteries, 73 (28.4%) chose love stories, and 62 (24.1%) chose science fiction. **(547)**

Ibid. . . . *showed that* only 13% of both groups reported never reading comic books, while 87% reported reading them sometimes. 111 (42%) of the readers and 117 (51.1%) of the nonreaders read comic books once a week or more. **(547)**

Ibid. . . . *showed that*, of 254 readers and 226 nonreaders, the format of book preferred by readers was as follows:

paperback	168 (66.14%)	students
hardcover	74 (29.13%)	students
comic	9 (3.54%)	students
magazine	3 (1.18%)	students

While the format of book preferred by nonreaders was as follows:

comic	91 (40.27%)	students
paperback	77 (34.07%)	students

continued

| magazine | 40 (17.70%) students | |
| hardcover | 18 (7.96%) students | **(547)** |

■ A 1977-78 survey of a random sample of 300 Spanish-surnamed families in the San Bernardino area *showed that* 54% of the sample read the local major daily English newspaper, compared to 17% who reported reading the bilingual weekly. **(237)**

School

■ A 1968 study of the summer reading of 23 seventh-graders from the Joyce Kilmer School in Chicago during a 5-week period *showed that,* of 191 books reported read, 58.6% came from the public library (involving 73.9% of the students), 24.1% came from siblings, friends, or parents, and 19.3% came from bookstores, were gifts or owned by the student. **(247)**

Ibid. . . . *showed that,* of the 191 books reported read, the 3 most frequent reasons given for selecting a particular book were: reputation of the book (63.5 or 33.2% of the books), subject of the book (34 or 17.8% of the books), and title of the book (34 or 17.8% of the books). (When 2 reasons were given for selecting a book, each was counted as .5.) **(247)**

Ibid. . . . *showed that* the basis of a book's reputation was largely personal recommendation. Of the 63.5 books so selected, the source of the recommendations was: friend (21.5 books), classmate (10 books), parent (9 books), sibling (8 books), librarian (7 books), and advertisements/book reviews (8 books). **(247)**

Ibid. . . . *showed that* the sources of magazines reported read by students were: family subscription/purchase (20.5% of magazines read), student purchase (22.1%), read when visiting (11.6%), and old magazine belonging to student (5.8%). **(247)**

■ A survey reported in 1977 of selected seventh-grade students (257 readers, i.e., read 2 books a week or more, and 230 nonreaders, i.e., read 2 books a year or less) in Regina (Canada) concerning the amount of voluntary reading undertaken by these 2 groups *showed that* females were more likely to be readers than males. Specifically, 184 (71.60%) of the readers were female, while 54 (23.48%) of the nonreaders were female. **(547)**

Ibid. . . . *showed that* speaking a second language seemed to have no effect on a student's reading. Specifically, of 254 readers and 230 nonreaders, 47 (18.5%) of the readers spoke a second language, while 42 (18.26%) of the nonreaders spoke a second language.   **(547)**

Ibid. . . . *showed that*, in terms of reading preference, nonreaders were more likely to mention nonfiction than readers. Overall, 21% of the nonreaders chose nonfiction compared to 10% of the readers. Further, when first, second, and third choices were combined for nonreaders, 94 (40.9%) chose comics, 55 (23.9%) chose joke books, and 51 (22.2%) chose sports books. When first, second, and third choices were combined for readers, 113 (44.0%) chose mysteries, 73 (28.4%) chose love stories, and 62 (24.1%) chose science fiction.   **(547)**

Ibid. . . . *showed that* only 13% of both groups reported never reading comic books, while 87% reported reading them sometimes. 111 (42%) of the readers and 117 (51.1%) of the nonreaders read comic books once a week or more.   **(547)**

Ibid. . . . *showed that*, of 254 readers and 226 nonreaders, the format of book preferred by readers was as follows:

paperback	168	(66.14%) students
hardcover	74	(29.13%) students
comic	9	(3.54%) students
magazine	3	(1.18%) students

While the format of book preferred by nonreaders was as follows:

comic	91	(40.27%) students
paperback	77	(34.07%) students
magazine	40	(17.70%) students
hardcover	18	(7.96%) students **(547)**

Special

■ A 1970 survey of psychiatrists randomly selected from the 1968 membership of the American Psychiatric Association (survey size: 394; responding: 290 or 74%) *showed that* respondents reported an average of 6.7 hours of professional reading per week, with 62% of the reading time devoted to journals and 38% of the reading time devoted to books. Private practitioners read the least (5.6 hours/week), while academicians read the most (9.1 hours/week).   **(690)**

Ibid. . . . *showed that* the 4 most frequently reported prime information sources (out of 11) were:

journals	55% respondents
books and monographs	16% respondents
colleagues	9% respondents
no preference indicated	9% respondents **(690)**

Ibid. . . . *showed that* the average number of journals read regularly was 4.3 while the average number of books read in the previous 12-month period was 9.7. There was considerable variation by type of practice, for example:

academicians	18.9 books/year average
mixed practice psychiatrists	12.6 books/year average
hosptial-clinic	
psychiatrists	9.6 books/year average
administrators	8.7 books/year average
private practitioners	6.4 books/year average **(690)**

Ibid. . . . *showed that* overall, of the books read, 67% were purchased, 28% came from a library, 3% came from colleagues, and 2% from other sources. **(690)**

■ A 1976 survey of physicians associated with hospitals in a 17-county region of upstate New York (Health Service Area V), based on a systematic sample of "approximately 40%" of the physicians in each county (survey size: 592 physicians; responding: 258 or 45.6%), *showed that* the 3 most frequently used sources of information as reported by the physicians were (in descending order of importance):

1. papers in journals
2. personal contact with colleagues
3. books

As an information source used by physicians "library reference services" ranked 7 out of a list of 19. **(720)**

Ibid. . . . *showed that* there was no statistically significant relationship between the date physicians received their degree and their use of journal papers, library reference services, or books. However, there was a statistically significant relationship between degree date and use of colleagues, with older doctors using colleagues less frequently and younger doctors using colleages more frequently as a source of information (significant at the .05 level). **(720)**

Demographics—Income

Public

■ A questionnaire survey of 3,500 public library cardholders in 5 medium-sized Pennsylvania cities in conjunction with interviews of a randomly selected sample of householders in 1 city by the Institute of Public Administration (at Pennsylvania State University) under contract to the Pennsylvania State Library in 1965 *showed that* people with family incomes higher than the community median were more likely to be cardholders but that frequency of use was not related to income level.

(084)

■ A 1971 survey of North Carolina heads of household or other adult residents (sample size: 1,008), in which 243 (24%) respondents identified themselves as public library users (from once a year to more than once a month) and 765 identified themselves as nonusers, *showed that* income of respondents was as follows: less than $5,000 (users, 1%; nonusers, 37%); $5,000-9,000 (users, 28%; nonusers, 32%); $10,000-24,900 (users, 23%; nonusers, 15%); $25,000+ (users, 21%; nonusers, 8%). 11% of the users and 10% of the nonusers did not respond to the question. **(235)**

■ A study reported in 1980-81 comparing level of public library development (a composite factor made up of staff size, expenditures, total books in the collection, and circulation) with 9 community characteristics (e.g., education, per capita income, occupational prestige, etc.) *showed that*, for the western region of the U.S. based on 278 libraries and communities, income per capita was the factor most strongly associated with public library development. The relationship was positive with an r2 = .537. (The relationship was significant at the .05 level.) **(568)**

Demographics—Low Income

Public

■ A study reported in 1963 concerning public library use by 180 (98 black; 82 white) low-income mothers with first-grade children in Chicago *showed that* white mothers (30%) were more likely than black mothers (17%) to have a library card. However, 26% of the white mothers and 24% of the black mothers reported using the library, with half of each user group reporting library use in excess of 4 times a year.   **(242)**

Ibid. . . . *showed that* holders of library cards, whether white or black, were statistically significantly more likely than nonholders in either group to have read more than 6 books during the past year. (Finding significant at the .05 level.)   **(242)**

Ibid. . . . *showed that* 54% of the respondents who reported using the library regularly had read more than 6 books in the last year, while only 26% of the respondents who used the library occasionally or never had read 6 books. (Finding significant at the .01 level.)   **(242)**

Ibid. . . . *showed that,* while 35% of the respondents who were high school graduates had used the library during the past year, only 15% of the nongraduates reported the same. (Finding significant at the .01 level.)   **(242)**

Ibid. . . . *showed that* the frequency of mother's use of the library and the frequency of the child's use of the library were statistically significantly related beyond the .001 level of significance. Of the 13% of the children who used the library, 7% were taken by parents, 7% by siblings, and 3% by friends and neighbors. (Multiple selection of responses was allowed.)   **(242)**

Ibid. . . . *showed that* 9% of the black women and 45% of the white women reported spending no time reading books or magazines in an average week.   **(242)**

Ibid. . . . *showed that* 42% of the respondents living within 5 blocks of a library had library cards, while only 17% of those living further away from a library had cards. (Finding significant at the .001 level.)   **(242)**

Demographics—Microforms

Academic

■ A 1982 survey of economics and political science faculty members in 9 colleges and universities serving as academic depository institutions in Massachusetts for the Government Printing Office (sample size: 216, including 105 economists and 111 political scientists; responding: 155 or 71.8%, including 86 economists and 69 political scientists) *showed that* 120 (6%) of the 125 respondents who reported using federal government documents reported that they did not have ready access to microform readers in their office, department, or home. Only 5 reported immediate access to viewing equipment outside the central library.   **(316)**

Demographics—Minorities

Public

■ A study reported in 1963 concerning public library use by 180 (98 black; 82 white) low-income mothers with first-grade children in Chicago *showed that* white mothers (30%) were more likely than black mothers (17%) to have a library card. However, 26% of the white mothers and 24% of the black mothers reported using the library, with half of each user group reporting library use in excess of 4 times a year.   **(242)**

Ibid. . . . *showed that* holders of library cards, whether white or black, were statistically significantly more likely than nonholders in either group to have read more than 6 books during the past year. (Finding significant at the .05 level.)   **(242)**

Ibid. . . . *showed that* 54% of the respondents who reported using the library regularly had read more than 6 books in the last year, while only 26% of the respondents who used the library occasionally or never had read 6 books. (Finding significant at the .01 level.)   **(242)**

Ibid. . . . *showed that*, while 35% of the respondents who were high school graduates had used the library during the past year, only 15% of the nongraduates reported the same. (Finding significant at the .01 level.)   **(242)**

Ibid. . . . *showed that* the frequency of mother's use of the library and the frequency of the child's use of the library were statistically significantly

related beyond the .001 level of significance. Of the 13% of the children who used the library, 7% were taken by parents, 7% by siblings, and 3% by friends and neighbors. (Multiple selection of responses was allowed.)
(242)

Ibid. . . . *showed that* 9% of the black women and 45% of the white women reported spending no time reading books or magazines in an average week. **(242)**

Ibid. . . . *showed that* 42% of the respondents living within 5 blocks of a library had library cards, while only 17% of those living further away from a library had cards. (Finding significant at the .001 level.) **(242)**

■ A 1971 survey of North Carolina heads of household or other adult residents (sample size: 1,008), in which 243 (24%) respondents identified themselves as public library users (from once a year to more than once a month) and 765 identified themselves as nonusers, *showed that* sex and race of respondents were as follows: male (users, 37%; nonusers, 46%), female (users, 63%; nonusers 43%); white (users 84%; nonusers 78%); black (users, 13%; nonusers 20%); Indian/other (users, 3; nonusers, 2%). These are statistically significant differences at the .05 level of significance.
(235)

■ A 1977-78 survey of a random sample of 300 Spanish-surnamed families in the San Bernardino area *showed that* 25% of the respondents had valid library cards and that, of these 25%, 70% had used the library at least once in the past year. **(237)**

Ibid. . . . *showed that* 65% of the respondents with library cards lived near a branch library where bilingual service was available, as compared to 11% who lived near the main library. However, 52% of those served by such a branch reported preferring use of the main library and its more adequate resources. **(237)**

Ibid. . . . *showed that* 54% of the sample read the local major daily English newspaper, compared to 17% who reported reading the bilingual weekly. **(237)**

Ibid. . . . *showed that* 86% of the sample speak some Spanish while 16% of the sample speak only Spanish. If given the choice, 21% of the

respondents preferred to conduct their transactions with the library staff in
Spanish.   (237)

Demographics—Occupational Status

Public

■ A questionnaire survey of 3,500 public library cardholders in 5
medium-sized Pennsylvania cities in conjunction with interviews of a
randomly selected sample of householders in 1 city by the Institute of
Public Administration (at Pennsylvania State University) under contract to
the Pennsylvania State Library in 1965 *showed that* business or professional
people and their families were more likely to be library cardholders than
other groups in the community. But while professionals and their family
members who were cardholders were among the most active users of the
library, their use was no higher than that by laborers or working-class
families who were also cardholders.   (084)

■ A 1966 survey of 21,385 adult (12 years old or older) public library
users in the Baltimore-Washington metropolitan region of Maryland
conducted during a 6-week period of patrons entering the library (79.1%
of patrons approached filled out the survey instrument) *showed that* 47.3%
of the patrons were students, 25.9% were employed adults, 16.4% were
housewives, 2.3% were retired, and 8.1% did not respond. Of the student
patrons, 64.5% were high school students, 10.3% were elementary school
students, and 25.2% were in college.   (301)

■ A 1971 survey of North Carolina heads of household or other adult
residents (sample size: 1,008), in which 243 (24%) respondents identified
themselves as public library users (from once a year to more than once a
month) and 765 identified themselves as nonusers, *showed that* occupation
of respondents was as follows: professional (users, 20%; nonusers, 4%);
managers/white collar (users, 25%; nonusers, 20%), skilled/unskilled
(users, 16%; nonusers, 35%), housewives (users, 2%; nonusers, 22%),
retired/unemployed (users, 10%; nonusers, 18%), student (users, 5%;
nonusers, 0%).   (235)

■ A study reported in 1980-81 comparing level of public library development (a composite factor made up of staff size, expenditures, total books in
the collection, and circulation) with 9 community characteristics (e.g.,
education, per capita income, occupational prestige, etc.) *showed that*, for
the western region of the U.S. based on 278 libraries and communities,

income per capita was the factor most strongly associated with public library development. The relationship was positive with an r2 = .537. (The relationship was significant at the .05 level.)   **(568)**

Demographics—Online Bibliographic Searching

General

■ A 12-month study in 1977-78 of online bibliographic literature searching of MINET (Kansas City Libraries Metropolitan Information Network, which includes 4 public libraries, 3 medical libraries, and 1 academic medical library), involving 403 paid search sessions and searches of 544 files or data bases, *showed that*, of the 544 data bases searched, 231 (42.0%) were requested by graduate or advanced professional students; 108 (19.7%) were requested by college or university faculty; 67 (12.2%) were requested by the business community; and 26 (4.7%) were requested by undergraduate students.   **(234)**

Academic

■ A 14-month study during 1972-73 at the Yale Medical Library (serving the Yale University School of Medicine, the Yale University School of Nursing, and the Yale-New Haven Hospital), involving 1,466 online search requests (MEDLINE) from 455 different individuals for the faculty and professional staff of the Yale-New Haven Medical Center, *showed that* there were substantial differences in the number of individuals (455) requesting online searches by professorial rank. The number of individuals requesting online searches and their percentage of the faculty at that rank were as follows:

professor (112 faculty)	32 (28.6%) individuals
associate professor (160 faculty)	70 (43.8%) individuals
assistant professor (215 faculty)	81 (37.7%) individuals
instructor (94 faculty)	29 (30.9%) individuals
lecturer (134 faculty)	2 (1.5%) individuals
postdoctoral fellow (319 faculty)	102 (32.0%) individuals
research associate (192 faculty)	28 (14.9%) individuals

Clinical faculty and staff:

clinical professor (23 faculty)	1 (4.4%) individuals
associate clinical professor (105 faculty)	8 (7.6%) individuals

continued

assistant clinical professor
(291 faculty)   11 (3.8%) individuals
clinical professor [sic,
lecturer?] (105 faculty)   1 (1.0%) individuals
clinical instructor (85 faculty)   4 (4.9%) individuals
resident (257 staff)   79 (30.7%) individuals
intern (25 staff)   7 (28.0%) individuals   **(714)**

Ibid. . . . *showed that* there was generally little difference in per capita use
by faculty/staff rank for those who used online searches. Specifically, the
per capita number of searches requested by those who requested searches
in terms of faculty or staff rank was as follows:

professor	2.7 searches each
associate professor	2.8 searches each
assistant professor	3.2 searches each
instructor	2.6 searches each
lecturer	2.5 searches each
postdoctoral fellow	3.4 searches each
research associate	5.9 searches each

Clinical faculty and staff:

clinical professor	3.0 searches each
associate clinical professor	2.5 searches each
assistant clinical professor	5.3 searches each
clinical professor [sic, lecturer?]	2.0 searches each
clinical instructor	4.8 searches each
resident	2.7 searches each
intern	2.0 searches each **(714)**

■ A 1975-76 study at the University of Utah Marriott Library of online
bibliographic data base searching *showed that* a survey of 26 patrons using
the online searching service revealed that (multiple responses allowed): 10
(36%) were faculty, 9 (33%) were doctoral students, 2 (8%) were master's
students, 2 (8%) were undergraduate students, and 4 (15%) were professional researchers.   **(329)**

■ A study of the University of Delaware during the 1976-77 academic
year *showed that* the percentage of undergraduates among users of online
searching increased greatly when the library subsidized 50% of the total
search costs.   **(001)**

■ A study reported in 1982 at the University of Iowa Health Sciences Library concerning the effect of the patron's presence during MEDLINE searches, based on searches for 100 different patrons (each search was conducted twice by different staff members, once with and once without the patron) and subsequent survey (100% responding) of those patrons, *showed that* there were no statistically significant differences among undergraduate, graduate, or faculty search requesters for precision, recall, or satisfaction rates. **(743)**

■ A study reported in 1982 at Nazareth College of Rochester concerning online bibliographic searching and involving 183 patrons during the period May 1980-June 1981 *showed that* distribution of users was as follows:

undergraduates	40	(21.9% of total)
graduates	105	(57.4% of total)
faculty	28	(15.3% of total)
library	6	(3.3% of total)
administration	4	(2.2% of total) **(300)**

Special

■ A 14-month study during 1972-73 at the Yale Medical Library (serving the Yale University School of Medicine, the Yale University School of Nursing, and the Yale-New Haven Hospital), involving 1,466 online search requests (MEDLINE) from 455 different individuals for the faculty and professional staff of the Yale-New Haven Medical Center, *showed that* there were substantial differences in the number of individuals (455) requesting online searches by professorial rank. The number of individuals requesting online searches and their percentage of the faculty at that rank were as follows:

professor (112 faculty)	32 (28.6%) individuals
associate professor (160 faculty)	70 (43.8%) individuals
assistant professor (215 faculty)	81 (37.7%) individuals
instructor (94 faculty)	29 (30.9%) individuals
lecturer (134 faculty)	2 (1.5%) individuals
postdoctoral fellow (319 faculty)	102 (32.0%) individuals
research associate (192 faculty)	28 (14.9%) individuals

Clinical faculty and staff:

clinical professor (23 faculty)	1 (4.4%) individuals
associate clinical professor (105 faculty)	8 (7.6%) individuals
assistant clinical professor (291 faculty)	11 (3.8%) individuals

continued

clinical professor [sic,
   lecturer?] (105 faculty)   1 (1.0%) individuals
clinical instructor (85 faculty)   4 (4.9%) individuals
resident (257 staff)   79 (30.7%) individuals
intern (25 staff)   7 (28.0%) individuals   **(714)**

Ibid. . . . *showed that* there was generally little difference in per capita use by faculty/staff rank for those who used online searches. Specifically, the per capita number of searches requested by those who requested searches in terms of faculty or staff rank was as follows:

professor	2.7 searches each
associate professor	2.8 searches each
assistant professor	3.2 searches each
instructor	2.6 searches each
lecturer	2.5 searches each
postdoctoral fellow	3.4 searches each
research associate	5.9 searches each

Clinical faculty and staff:

clinical professor	3.0 searches each
associate clinical professor	2.5 searches each
assistant clinical professor	5.3 searches each
clinical professor [sic, lecturer?]	2.0 searches each
clinical instructor	4.8 searches each
resident	2.7 searches each
intern	2.0 searches each **(714)**

■ A 1978 survey of North American health sciences libraries that were users of the National Library of Medicine search services in November 1977 (survey size: 708 libraries; responding: 376; usable: 345 or 48.7%) *showed that*, based on replies from 251 respondents, 16.3% of all MED-LINE searches in 1966-67 were for outside users. **(724)**

■ A study reported in 1982 at the University of Iowa Health Sciences Library concerning the effect of the patron's presence during MEDLINE searches, based on searches for 100 different patrons (each search was conducted twice by different staff members, once with and once without the patron) and subsequent survey (100% responding) of those patrons, *showed that* there were no statistically significant differences among undergraduate, graduate, or faculty search requesters for precision, recall, or satisfaction rates. **(743)**

Demographics—Personal Subscriptions

Academic

■ A 1973 survey of physicists in 6 universities of the greater Boston area (Boston University, Brandeis, Brown, Harvard, MIT, and Northeastern) to determine how they meet their information needs (sample size: 339; responding: 179 or 52.8%) *showed that* 42% of the physicists subscribed to 1 or 2 journals, with the overall average 2.2 journals. The 2 most common journal subscriptions were: *Physics Review Letters* (55 respondents) and *Physics Review* (41 respondents). No number of respondents given.
(404)

■ A study reported in 1978 at Indiana University, Bloomington, of materials requested through a delivery service to faculty in the political science and economics departments during a 32-month period (October 1972-June 1975), involving 39 political scientists and 14 economists (40-50% of the faculty in the departments) and 5,478 articles from 620 different journals and newspapers, *showed that*, of 29 respondents from the 2 departments, faculty members personally subscribed to an average of 4.5 periodicals each. **(421)**

Special

■ A 1976 survey of physicians associated with hospitals in a 17-county region of upstate New York (Health Service Area V), based on a systematic sample of "approximately 40%" of the physicians in each county (survey size: 592 physicians; responding: 258 or 45.6%), *showed that* respondents personally subscribed to an average of 4.1 professional journals, with "nearly 40% claiming five or more subscriptions." The 4 most frequently reported journals were (multiple responses allowed):

Journal of the American Medical Association	26.0% physicians	
New England Journal of Medicine	24.4% physicians	
Annals of Internal Medicine	13.6% physicians	
New York State Journal of Medicine	12.8% physicians	**(720)**

Demographics—Reading Habits

Academic

■ A study in 1975 of business students (undergraduate and graduate) at the University of Delaware, University of Maryland, and Wright State University *showed that* they were infrequent readers of most business periodicals. For example 21% of the undergrads and 8% of the M.B.A.'s reported never having read the *Wall Street Journal*.   **(049)**

Handicapped

Academic

■ A 1976 study at Ohio State University of visually impaired students (population: 38; surveyed, i.e., who could be reached: 26, including 6 blind students and 20 partially sighted students) concerning their special equipment needs *showed that* 9 (45.0%) of the partially sighted students and 1 (16.7%) of the blind students reported using none of the available library equipment for the visually impaired.   **(462)**

Public

■ A report published in 1979 by the National Library Service for the Blind and Physically Handicapped of the Library of Congress *showed that* the number of circulating braille materials remained relatively stable between 1969 (500,000) and 1978 (600,000), while the number of circulating recorded books almost tripled between 1969 (5 million) and 1978 (14 million).   **(164)**

■ A 1971 survey of Canadian public libraries serving communities with populations of more than 8,000 people conducted by the Adult Services Section of the Canadian Library Association concerning service to the physically handicapped (survey size: 222; responding: 111 or 50%) *showed that* the number of libraries providing various special materials was as follows:

large-print books	90 (81.1%) libraries
films	64 (57.7%) libraries
cassettes	23 (20.7%) libraries
cassette players	16 (14.4%) libraries

continued

opaque projectors	9 (8.1%) libraries	
overhead projectors	7 (6.3%) libraries	
talking books	4 (3.6%) libraries	
talking book machines	3 (2.7%) libraries	**(540)**

Ibid. . . . *showed that* the following number of libraries provided the following types of services or facilities for handicapped patrons:

home delivery service	46 (41.4%) libraries	
wheel chair ramps, elevators	31 (27.9%) libraries	
books or other material by mail	24 (21.6%) libraries	
programs for the handicapped	13 (11.7%) libraries	
television/radio programs	3 (2.7%) libraries	
deposit collections:		
senior citizen homes	60 (54.1%) libraries	
nursing homes	32 (28.8%) libraries	
hospitals	28 (25.2%) libraries	
senior citizen centers	22 (19.8%) libraries	
drop-in centers	4 (3.6%) libraries	
other	14 (12.6%) libraries	**(540)**

Ibid. . . . *showed that* 52 (46.8%) libraries reported promoting services to the physically handicapped.   **(540)**

Minorities

Academic

■ A 1980 survey of faculty and students at San Jose State University concerning their library use patterns (students—survey size: [not given]; responding: 1,470; faculty—population: 1,753; responding: 443 or 25.3%) *showed that* there were statistically significant differences in the frequency of university library use by ethnic background. For example, 21.9% of the Asian students reported seldom or never using the library (i.e., less than once a month), compared to 27.8% of the Chicano students, 38.7% of the black students, and 40.5% of the white students so reporting (significant at the .0001 level).   **(519)**

Public

■ A study reported in 1963 concerning public library use by 180 (98 black; 82 white) low-income mothers with first-grade children in Chicago *showed that* white mothers (30%) were more likely than black mothers (17%) to have a library card. However, 26% of the white mothers and 24% of the black mothers reported using the library, with half of each user group reporting library use in excess of 4 times a year.   **(242)**

Ibid. . . . *showed that* holders of library cards, whether white or black, were statistically significantly more likely than nonholders in either group to have read more than 6 books during the past year. (Finding significant at the .05 level.)   **(242)**

Ibid. . . . *showed that* 54% of the respondents who reported using the library regularly had read more than 6 books in the last year, while only 26% of the respondents who used the library occasionally or never had read 6 books. (Finding significant at the .01 level.)   **(242)**

Ibid. . . . *showed that*, while 35% of the respondents who were high school graduates had used the library during the past year, only 15% of the nongraduates reported the same. (Finding significant at the .01 level.)   **(242)**

Ibid. . . . *showed that* the frequency of mother's use of the library and the frequency of the child's use of the library were statistically significantly related beyond the .001 level of significance. Of the 13% of the children who used the library, 7% were taken by parents, 7% by siblings, and 3% by friends and neighbors. (Multiple selection of responses was allowed.)   **(242)**

Ibid. . . . *showed that* 9% of the black women and 45% of the white women reported spending no time reading books or magazines in an average week.   **(242)**

Ibid. . . . *showed that* 42% of the respondents living within 5 blocks of a library had library cards, while only 17% of those living further away from a library had cards. (Finding significant at the .001 level.)   **(242)**

■ A 1977-78 survey of a random sample of 300 Spanish-surnamed families in the San Bernardino area *showed that* 25% of the respondents had valid library cards and that, of these 25%, 70% had used the library at least once in the past year.   **(237)**

Ibid. . . . *showed that* 65% of the respondents with library cards lived near a branch library where bilingual service was available, as compared to 11% who lived near the main library. However, 52% of those served by such a branch reported preferring use of the main library and its more adequate resources. **(237)**

Ibid. . . . *showed that* 42% of the sample were unaware that the library's service included books. **(237)**

Ibid. . . . *showed that* 54% of the sample read the local major daily English newspaper, compared to 17% who reported reading the bilingual weekly. **(237)**

Ibid. . . . *showed that* 86% of the sample speak some Spanish while 16% of the sample speak only Spanish. If given the choice, 21% of the respondents preferred to conduct their transactions with the library staff in Spanish. **(237)**

School

■ A 1971-72 study of the effect of microfiche copies of children's trade books on fourth-graders' attitudes toward reading and on reading achievement conducted in the Oglethorpe County Elementary School (near Athens, Georgia), involving 142 pupils divided into control (no access to microfiche materials) and experimental groups (access to microfiche materials and readers), *showed that*, although there was no statistically significant difference between the full control and experimental groups in vocabulary and reading comprehension, there was a statistically significant difference for the black subgroups between the control and experimental groups, with an increase in vocabulary and reading comprehension for the black experimental subgroup using the microfiche materials and readers (significant at the .05 level.) **(319)**

Use Patterns—General Issues

General

■ A 1970 survey of psychiatrists randomly selected from the 1968 membership of the American Psychiatric Association (survey size: 394; responding: 290 or 74%) *showed that* overall, of the books read, 67% were purchased, 28% came from a library, 3% came from colleagues, and 2% from other sources.   **(690)**

Public

■ A 1966 survey of 21,385 adult (12 years old or older) public library users in the Baltimore-Washington metropolitan region of Maryland conducted during a 6-week period of patrons entering the library (79.1% of patrons approached filled out the survey instrument) *showed that*, of the unsatisfied respondents, 5,104 (66%) planned to continue their quest. Of these, 59.3% planned to go to another library, 19.9% put a reserve on the book, 7.7% made arrangements for the library to get the material from another library, and 13.1% planned to use other alternatives (e.g., buying the book or borrowing it from friends).   **(301)**

Ibid. . . . *showed that* 57.2% of the respondents left home, work, or school only to visit the library, 16% visited the library while shopping, and 24.9% visited the library in connection with some other activity.   **(301)**

Ibid. . . . *showed that* the top 5 reasons given for visiting the library were (multiple responses allowed): return books (43.4%), obtain materials or information on a subject (33.5%), pick out general reading (33.5%), obtain a specific book (22.1%), and to bring their child (12.9%).   **(301)**

Ibid. . . . *showed that* the reasons given for visiting the library were as follows (multiple responses allowed): personal reading (49.3%), school-work (41.7%), for another person (9.1%), for one's job (6.5%), for club activity (2.0%), for other reasons (2.6%), and no answer (5.8%).   **(301)**

■ A 1973 study in the Burnaby Public Library (British Columbia) involving patron use of the card catalog (survey size: 367 patrons) *showed that* 152 (42%) were looking for a specific publication (about which they knew something), 208 (57%) were looking for information on a topic or something to read but without a specific item in mind, 6 (1%) were using the catalog to find something out about a book rather than looking for a book, and none were using the catalog to find out something about an author.   **(542)**

■ A 1979 telephone survey of 1,046 New Orleans residents over the age of 12 *showed that* the Central Library was used more for reference and research, while the branches were used more for recreational reading.

43.7% of Central's use was for information other than school, 34% for school, and 19.3% for pleasure, while the branches were used 26.9% for information other than school, 38.7% for school, and 33.4% for pleasure. **(166)**

■ A study based on telephone interviews reported in 1980 of individuals in the Syracuse metropolitan area (sample size: 442; 322 contracted; 202 or 46% participated in the study) *showed that* of 161 library users 2 types of library use were identified. Type 1 use was associated with frequency of visits, use of services, circulation of materials, and importance that the patron placed on use activities. 7 factors helped predict this type of library use. More specifially, 41% of the variance of the variable "type 1 library use" could be accounted for by the following 7 independent variables with a cumulative effect as follows (R^2 scores): adult education activities (14%), number of books read (22%), community involvement (26%), sex—female (29%), cultural activities (32%), awareness of special programs (39%), and perceived accessibility (41%). **(265)**

Ibid. . . . *showed that* of 161 library users 2 types of library use were identified. Type 2 use was associated primarily with duration of visit. 6 factors helped predict this type of library use. More specifically, 24% of the variance of the variable "type 2 library use" could be accounted for by the following 6 independent variables with a cumulative effect as follows (R^2 scores): adult education activities (8%), sex—female (negatively correlated) (11%), number of children (negatively correlated) (14%), number of books in home (negatively correlated) (17%), age (negatively correlated) (18%), and use of nonpublic library (24%). **(265)**

■ A 1980 survey of 523 adult patrons using the Ramsey County (Minnesota) Public Library during a 5-day period in November *showed that* there is no statistically significant relationship between measures of library use and either patrons' evaluation of the library (library grade scale) or patrons' satisfaction with the library (user satisfaction score). The measures of library use involved were: frequency of visits, number of services used during the visit, duration of visit, fiction circulation, nonfiction circulation and combined circulation. This replicated earlier findings. **(270)**

■ An attempt reported in 1982 to establish 4 input measures and 4 output measures for public libraries, based on published statistical reports for 301 New Jersey public libraries over a 6-year period (1974-79) and survey data for 96 public libraries in New Jersey, *showed that* (per capita based on population in library's service area):

INPUT MEASURES

The proportion of budget spent on materials averaged 19.9% with a standard deviation of .081 (based on 301 libraries).

The new volumes per capita averaged .181 with a standard deviation of .097 (based on 301 libraries).

The periodical titles per capita averaged .0094 with a standard deviation of .0054 (based on 301 libraries).

The circulation per volume averaged 1.79 with a standard deviation of .77 (based on 301 libraries).

OUTPUT MEASURES

The circulation per capita averaged 5.04 with a standard deviation of 3.07 (based on 301 libraries).

The patron visits per capita averaged 2.82 with a standard deviation of 1.82 (based on 96 libraries).

The reference questions per capita averaged 1.12 with a standard deviation of .79 (based on 96 libraries).

The in-library uses of materials per capita averaged 2.29 with a standard deviation of 2.02 (based on 96 libraries).   **(576)**

■ A survey reported in 1982 by the New York Library Association's Film and Video Roundtable of 63 administrators of large- and medium-sized public library film collections both in and outside of New York state (38 or 60% responding) *showed that* the following community groups were identified as heavy or moderate film users: nursing homes (100%), senior citizen centers (93%), day care centers (92%), adult clubs and organizations (89%), children's clubs and organizations (86%), hospitals (82%), and social service agencies (79%).   **(162)**

Special

■ A 1970 survey of psychiatrists randomly selected from the 1968 membership of the American Psychiatric Association (survey size: 394; responding: 290 or 74%) *showed that* overall, of the books read, 67% were purchased, 28% came from a library, 3% came from colleagues, and 2% from other sources.   **(690)**

■ A 1974 user survey of the Bristol Laboratory library (Syracuse, New York) involving 32 individuals (14% sample size) from 21 departments, including 18 directors and 14 nondirectors, *showed that* the main differences between directors and nondirectors were:

12 (66%) of the directors used the library frequently, compared to 7 (50%) of the nondirectors;

7 (39%) of the directors usually visit the library personally, compared to 10 (70%) of the nondirectors;

8 (44%) of the directors use the library for keeping up to date, compared to 3 (21%) of the nondirectors. **(407)**

■ A 1976 survey of physicians associated with hospitals in a 17-county region of upstate New York (Health Service Area V), based on a systematic sample of "approximately 40%" of the physicians in each county (survey size: 592 physicians; responding: 258 or 45.6%), *showed that* physicians reported that the speed with which their information needs had to be met was as follows: 24 hours (39% physicians, including 5% who reported "immediately"), up to a week (54% physicians), and longer than a week (7% physicians). **(720)**

■ A survey reported in 1983 of U.S. dental school libraries concerning their service to dental practitioners (population: 60 dental school libraries; responding: 53 or 88%) *showed that* 40 respondents estimated the following monthly use of their library by dental practitioners:

0-10 requests	31 (73.8%) libraries	
11-20 requests	7 (16.6%) libraries	
21-30 requests	2 (4.8%) libraries	
31-40 requests	0 (0.0%) libraries	
41-50 requests	2 (4.8%) libraries	**(752)**

Use Patterns—General Issues, Faculty

Academic

■ A 1973 survey of physicists in 6 universities of the greater Boston area (Boston University, Brandeis, Brown, Harvard, MIT, and Northeastern) to determine how they meet their information needs (sample size: 339; responding: 179 or 52.8%) *showed that* at all universities physicists rated formal publications (i.e., journals primarily) their most important source of information and reference materials their least important source of information, with semiformal publications, meetings and conferences, and informal oral communication in between. **(404)**

Ibid. . . . *showed that* the reasons for library use (Harvard chemistry faculty respondents included) were (multiple responses allowed): specific information (160 respondents), keeping up (122 respondents), browsing

(88 respondents), and other (6 respondents). No number of respondents given.   **(404)**

■ A survey in 1979 of faculty members and graduate students at the School of Management at Purdue and the School of Commerce at the University of Illinois, Urbana (sample size: 567; responding: 213) *showed that* 85.5% used working papers from institutions other than their own.
                                                                                    (120)

■ A 1980 survey of faculty and students at San Jose State University concerning their library use patterns (students—survey size: [not given]; responding: 1,470; faculty—population: 1,753; responding: 443 or 25.3%) *showed that* 62.2% of the faculty reported they relied on purchased books and periodicals as their primary source of information for teaching and research while 29.1% reported relying on the library as their primary source of information. [The remaining percent is not identified.]   **(519)**

Ibid. . . . *showed that* 57.5% of the students and 70.2% of the faculty reported that they used other libraries in connection with San Jose State course work, whether teaching, study, or research.   **(519)**

Use Patterns—General Issues, Students

Academic

■ A sample in 1960 of 4,977 patrons of the Newark Public Library during the Christmas/New Year's holiday period *showed that* 64.1% of the patrons were students (high school or college) as compared to 28.8% nonstudents, 39.8% were nonresident college students as compared to 28.9% resident college students, 11.5% nonresident high school students and 18.4% resident high school students.   **(066)**

■ An hourly room count at the University of Denver's late study area in 1972 at the beginning, middle, and end of Winter quarter (January 1, January 30, and March 8) *showed that* use is heaviest during exam periods. Total headcounts on the 3 dates for the period from midnight to 8 a.m. totaled 26, 48, and 254, respectively.   **(095)**

■ A survey during the 1974-75 academic year at the Queen's University in Kingston (Canada) and Trent University in Peterborough (Canada) of part-time students (survey size: 1,143 students at Trent and 1,408 students at Queen's; responding: 286 or 25.1% students at Trent and 480 or 34.1%

students at Queen's) *showed that*, of the 480 respondents to the Queen's University survey, 282 (58.8%) of the students reported obtaining their course readings primarily through the purchase of books. In contrast, 15.8% of the students reported that the university library was the primary source of their readings, while 5.2% reported that the public library was the primary source of their readings. A list of 8 options was provided.

(545)

Ibid. . . . *showed that* taking courses on campus and university library use seemed related. For example, of the Queen's students, of 231 respondents who took their courses on campus, 78.8% reported using the university library at least once, while of 242 respondents who took their courses off campus, 32.6% used the library at least once.   **(545)**

■ A 1975 study at the University of Nebraska, Omaha, concerning student perceptions of academic librarians and involving a stratified sample of full-time students (sample size: 700; responding: 362 or 51.7%) *showed that* only 16.1% reported "frequently" or "always" seeking assistance immediately when searching for library materials or information.   **(449)**

■ A survey in 1979 of faculty members and graduate students at the School of Management at Purdue and the School of Commerce at the University of Illinois, Urbana (sample size: 567; responding: 213) *showed that* 85.5% used working papers from institutions other than their own.

(120)

Public

■ A sample in 1960 of 4,977 patrons of the Newark Public Library during the Christmas/New Year's holiday period *showed that* 64.1% of the patrons were students (high school or college) as compared to 28.8% nonstudents, 39.8% were nonresident college students as compared to 28.9% resident college students, 11.5% nonresident high school students and 18.4% resident high school students.   **(066)**

Use Patterns—Browsing

General

■ A 1970 survey of psychiatrists randomly selected from the 1968 membership of the American Psychiatric Association (survey size: 394; responding: 290 or 74%) *showed that* the 4 most frequently mentioned prime methods of searching the literature (out of 11) were:

> library reference services   23% respondents
> abstracts and indexes   17% respondents
> bibliographies   17% respondents
> review articles   16% respondents

Use of the card catalog as a prime method of searching the literature was reported by 5% of the respondents, while browsing as a prime method was reported by 4% of the respondents.   **(690)**

Academic

■ A 1973 survey of physicists in 6 universities of the greater Boston area (Boston University, Brandeis, Brown, Harvard, MIT, and Northeastern) to determine how they meet their information needs (sample size: 339; responding: 179 or 52.8%) *showed that* the reasons for library use (Harvard chemistry faculty respondents included) were (multiple responses allowed): specific information (160 respondents), keeping up (122 respondents), browsing (88 respondents), and other (6 respondents). No number of respondents given.   **(404)**

Public

■ A 1966 survey of 21,385 adult (12 years old or older) public library users in the Baltimore-Washington metropolitan region of Maryland conducted during a 6-week period of patrons entering the library (79.1% of patrons approached filled out the survey instrument) *showed that* the use made of the library was as follows (multiple responses allowed): browsing (43.1%), reference books (22.1%), library catalogs (19.0%), help from a librarian (16.0%), consulting books or magazines (12.4%), read new magazines or newspapers (8.7%), periodical indexes (5.7%), recordings (2.7%), films (0.7%), other (2.0%), and no response (11.1%).   **(301)**

Special

■ A 1970 survey of psychiatrists randomly selected from the 1968 membership of the American Psychiatric Association (survey size: 394; responding: 290 or 74%) *showed that* the 4 most frequently mentioned prime methods of searching the literature (out of 11) were:

> library reference services   23% respondents
> abstracts and indexes   17% respondents
> bibliographies   17% respondents
> review articles   16% respondents

Use of the card catalog as a prime method of searching the literature was reported by 5% of the respondents, while browsing as a prime method was reported by 4% of the respondents.   **(690)**

Use Patterns—Catalogs, Card

General

■   A 1970 survey of psychiatrists randomly selected from the 1968 membership of the American Psychiatric Association (survey size: 394; responding: 290 or 74%) *showed that* the 4 most frequently mentioned prime methods of searching the literature (out of 11) were:

library reference services	23% respondents
abstracts and indexes	17% respondents
bibliographies	17% respondents
review articles	16% respondents

Use of the card catalog as a prime method of searching the literature was reported by 5% of the respondents, while browsing as a prime method was reported by 4% of the respondents.   **(690)**

Academic

■   A 1967-70 study in the Main Library at Yale University involving 2,100 interviews at the card catalog during a 1-year period *showed that* known-item searches to determine if the library held the item and, if so, where, accounted for 73% of the catalog use, subject searches accounted for 16%, author searches (to determine what works are available for a known author or publishing body) accounted for 6%, and bibliographic searches (to make use of data on the catalog card rather than locate a book) accounted for 5%. Follow-up questioning about known-item searches suggested that many of these are really subject searches using a known item to identify an appropriate call number or subject heading. The real or "underlying" percentage of known-item and subject searches in the card catalog may be more like 56 and 33, respectively.   **(248)**

Ibid. . . . *showed that* the 4 most popular approaches to searching the card catalog were: author name (personal or corporate) 62.0%, title 28.5%, subject (4.5%), and editor (4.0%).   **(248)**

Ibid. . . . *showed that* use of the card catalog during the academic year was as follows: Yale freshmen (8.3% of catalog use), other Yale undergraduates (27.7%), graduate/postgraduate students (35.6%), Yale faculty (7.3%), Yale staff (2.9%), and other (18.1%).   **(248)**

Ibid. . . . *showed that* weekly charting of card catalog use and book circulation revealed by inspection that card catalog use and book borrowing always remained in the same proportion.   **(248)**

Ibid. . . . *showed that* 84% of the card catalog searches were successful, that 5% of the searches were unsuccessful for the patron even though library staff later located the document in the card catalog, that 10% of the searches were for documents that probably exist but which were not in the card catalog at the time, and that 1% of the searches were for documents too vaguely or inaccurately described to follow up on. **(248)**

■ A survey in 1976 of 999 library users at San Jose State University Library *showed that* of 288 card catalog users only 74 (26%) asked for help, and of individuals who had only partial or no success in locating materials in the catalog only 34% had requested help. **(010)**

■ A 1979 study at Iowa State University concerning queuing at the public card catalog during a month and a half period, involving 2,327 sample counts of patrons at the catalog, *showed that* the correlation between card catalog use and exit counts, books circulated, and number of individuals checking out books, while statistically significant at the .001 level or better in all 3 cases, was so low as to be negligible. The highest R2 (exit count with card catalog use), for example, was .075. With a 1-hour differential between card catalog use counts and number of books circulated, the correlation began to be substantial with an R2 of 22%. (No significance level given.) **(497)**

Ibid. . . . *showed that*, when the Friday and Sunday counts (there were no Saturday counts) of card catalog patrons were ignored, there was no statistically significant difference among the daily means during Monday through Thursday. For example, the average number of arrivals at the card catalog during a 10-minute period during any of these 4 days ranged from 11.9 patrons (Wednesday) to 12.9 patrons (Monday). **(497)**

Ibid. . . . *showed that* there were statistically significant differences between patron counts at the card catalog by hour of the day, especially when Friday and Sunday (there were no Saturday counts) were excluded. Arrivals at the card catalog during 10-minute periods averaged 9.7 patrons at 10:00 a.m. and rose regularly until a high of 18.0 patrons was reached at 2:00 p.m. and then fell to 8.8 patrons at 4:00 p.m. (No significance level was given.) **(497)**

■ A 1980 study of patron use of the serial card catalog at the University of Illinois, Urbana (sample size: 452 patrons; usable responses: 445 patrons) involving faculty, students, and staff *showed that* 94% of the materials sought were English-language materials, with 27 (6%) in other languages. **(505)**

Ibid. . . . *showed that* the top 2 sources of 192 serial citations that patrons obtained through use of an index, abstract, or bibliography were *Readers' Guide* (accounting for 54 or 28% of the citations) and *Business Periodicals Index* (accounting for 17 or 9% of the citations). **(505)**

Ibid. . . . *showed that* the sources of the 445 serial citations that patrons brought to the serial card catalog were as follows:

class reading list	42 (9%)	citations
index, abstract or bibliography	192 (43%)	citations
bibliography or footnote in book or journal	127 (29%)	citations
online literature search	40 (9%)	citations
other/no answer	44 (10%)	citations **(505)**

Ibid. . . . *showed that* 366 (83%) of the searches undertaken by patrons in the serial card catalog were successful, i.e., a citation was matched to a catalog entry. Further, the success rate of the frequent catalog user (daily or once/twice per week) was not statistically significantly better than the success rate of the infrequent catalog user. Specifically, 167 (46%) of the frequent catalog users and 199 (54%) of the infrequent catalog users were successful in their searches. **(505)**

Ibid. . . . *showed that* of 427 searches there was no statistically significant difference in success rates between patrons who wrote their citation down (or Xeroxed them) and those who did not. For example, 246 (70%) of the patrons who found their citations in the card catalog had written them down, compared to 52 (69%) of the patrons who did not find their citations in the card catalog but who had written them down. Conversely, 93 (26%) of the patrons found their citations in the card catalog without writing them down, compared to 20 (27%) of the patrons who did not find their citations in the card catalog but also did not write the citation down. **(505)**

Ibid. . . . *showed that* of the 79 (18%) unsuccessful searches in the serial card catalog the reasons for failure were as follows:

not owned by the library	24 (5%)	citations
patron missed the entry	22 (5%)	citations
patron had incomplete entry	5 (1%)	citations
serial record failures	28 (6%)	citations

Of those not owned by the library, 20 of the 24 titles were verified as correct in spelling and existing in print, i.e., not simply incorrect citations. **(505)**

■ A 1981 survey of faculty, students, staff, and community users of the University of Cincinnati Libraries (sample size: 4,074; responding: 912 or 22.4%, including 436 or 39% faculty response and 218 or 11% student response) *showed that*, when asked their most frequent access point used in the public card catalog, faculty and library staff reported "author," while community users, university administrators, and students reported "subject." Further, subgroups among the faculty reported differently from the 57% overall report of author access. For example, 74% of the Arts and Sciences faculty reported "author" as the most frequent point of access, while 60% of the faculty in the College of Business Administration and College of Education reported "subject" as the most frequent point of access.   **(522)**

Special

■ A 1970 survey of psychiatrists randomly selected from the 1968 membership of the American Psychiatric Association (survey size: 394; responding: 290 or 74%) *showed that* the 4 most frequently mentioned prime methods of searching the literature (out of 11) were:

library reference services	23% respondents
abstracts and indexes	17% respondents
bibliographies	17% respondents
review articles	16% respondents

Use of the card catalog as a prime method of searching the literature was reported by 5% of the respondents, while browsing as a prime method was reported by 4% of the respondents.   **(690)**

Use Patterns—Catalogs, Online

Academic

■ A 1978 study at Ohio State University Library involving 2 full days' transactions in the OCLC data base for each of the OSU terminals (1,153 searches of the data base) *showed that* of 158 searches by the public the 2 most frequent types of searches were by name/title (77 or 48.7% of the searches by the public, of which 22 or 28.6% were successful) and by title (44 or 27.8% of the searches by the public, of which 20 or 45.4% were successful).   **(336)**

■ A 1982 online survey of MELVYL patrons from all 9 UC campuses conducted over a 2-month period for each 25th user of the system (1,259 questionnaires collected; 72.2 questionnaires complete and usable) *showed that* respondents' university affiliations were:

freshman/sophomore	23.2% respondents
junior/senior	39.0% respondents
graduate-master's level	6.4% respondents
graduate-doctoral level	7.6% respondents
graduate-professional school	1.9% respondents
faculty	3.2% respondents
staff	2.6% respondents
other	16.1% respondents **(349)**

Ibid. . . . *showed that* respondents' academic areas were:

art/humanities	24.2% respondents
physical/biological sciences	22.7% respondents
social sciences	19.3% respondents
engineering	14.1% respondents
medical and health sciences	5.8% respondents
business management	4.7% respondents
major undeclared	4.0% respondents
law	2.9% respondents
education	2.0% respondents
interdisciplinary	0.2% respondents **(349)**

Ibid. . . . *showed that* the average length of time a patron spent at the terminal was 8 minutes 41 seconds, while the average number of commands issued during a session was 22.297.   **(349)**

Ibid. . . . *showed that* the patrons conducted an average of 5.66 searches per session.   **(349)**

Ibid. . . . *showed that* the help facilities were used in 14.28% of the sessions, with those patrons who did use the help facilities averaging 1.59 unqualified help requests and 2.63 help requests with a specific glossary term. Only 2.6% of the patrons made the same error 3 times in a row.
                                                                                           (349)

Ibid. . . . *showed that* 75.22% of the patrons made no errors at all during their sessions (this includes command syntax errors, logical errors, and unrecognizable commands). The remaining 24.77% of the patrons made an average of 2.85 errors during their sessions.   **(349)**

Ibid. . . . *showed that* the 3 most frequently used searches in the COM-MAND mode were subject (51.6%), personal author (21.5%), and title (18.8%), while the 3 most frequently used searches in the LOOKUP mode were subject/title (63.4%), personal author/corporate author (15.4%), and title/personal author/corporate author (13.2%).   **(349)**

Use Patterns—Circulation, General Issues

Public

■ A questionnaire survey of 3,500 public library cardholders in 5 medium-sized Pennsylvania cities in conjunction with interviews of a randomly selected sample of householders in 1 city by the Institute of Public Administration (at Pennsylvania State University) under contract to the Pennsylvania State Library in 1965 *showed that* the major service provided by the library was book borrowing (60% of respondents), while reference/information was the next most important use made of the library (26% of respondents).   **(084)**

Use Patterns—Circulation, Faculty

Academic

■ A study of all library books (2,898) checked out by the faculty (441) of a midwestern university during Spring semester 1962 *showed that* the checkout rate did not vary greatly from rank to rank, with full professors having the lowest checkout rate (5.6 books per individual) and associate professors having the highest checkout rate (7.9%). The overall average number of books checked out per faculty member was 6.6.   **(130)**

Ibid. . . . *showed that* the highest per capita faculty book checkout rates were in physics (21.7), library science (20.5), and English (17.0), whereas in the departments of sociology/anthropology, chemistry, library science, and philosophy every faculty member checked out at least 1 book during the semester.   **(130)**

■ A 1-year study during 1964-65 at the Yale Medical School Library concerning patron use patterns of library materials (based on 34,825 book/journal circulations) *showed that* 20,563 journal circulations were distributed among members of the medical school as follows (accounting for 74.6% of the journal use):

full-time faculty	32.0% journal uses	
students	27.2% journal uses	
house officers	11.6% journal uses	
part-time faculty	3.8% journal uses	**(675)**

Ibid. . . . *showed that* the per capita book and journal use (over 1 year's time) was as follows:

students	10.0 journals; 6.3 books	
full-time faculty	11.9 journals; 4.6 books	
house officers	7.9 journals; 3.1 books	
part-time faculty	1.6 journals; 0.8 books	**(675)**

Ibid. . . . *showed that* 14,262 book circulations were distributed among members of the medical school as follows (accounting for 51.7% of the book use):

students	24.6% book uses	
full-time faculty	17.6% book uses	
house officers	6.5% book uses	
part-time faculty	3.0% book uses	**(675)**

■ A study during the 1981-82 academic year in the main library at Purdue concerning books that undergraduates selected to read (involving interviews with 240 undergraduate borrowers and analysis of 598 of the mongraphic titles borrowed by both students and nonstudents) *showed that* undergraduates (and surprisingly) graduate students tended to use a core of heavily used titles, while faculty tended to use materials that had never before circulated. For example, of 67 items circulated to faculty, 18 (26.9%) had circulated 6 or more times, while of 131 items circulated to graduate students, 77 (58.8%) had been circulated 6 or more times, and of 364 items circulated to undergraduates, 253 (69.5%) had been circulated 6 or more times. (There were 36 missing cases.) **(530)**

Special

■ A 1-year study during 1964-65 at the Yale Medical School Library concerning patron use patterns of library materials (based on 34,825 book/journal circulations) *showed that* 20,563 journal circulations were distributed among members of the medical school as follows (accounting for 74.6% of the journal use):

full-time faculty	32.0% journal uses	
students	27.2% journal uses	
house officers	11.6% journal uses	
part-time faculty	3.8% journal uses	**(675)**

Ibid. . . . *showed that* 14,262 book circulations were distributed among members of the medical school as follows (accounting for 51.7% of the book use):

students	24.6% book uses	
full-time faculty	17.6% book uses	
house officers	6.5% book uses	
part-time faculty	3.0% book uses	**(675)**

Ibid. . . . *showed that* the per capita book and journal use (over 1 year's time) was as follows:

students	10.0 journals; 6.3 books	
full-time faculty	11.9 journals; 4.6 books	
house officers	7.9 journals; 3.1 books	
part-time faculty	1.6 journals; 0.8 books	**(675)**

Use Patterns—Circulation, Students

Academic

■   A 1962 study repeated the following year of all book charges in a 1-month period in the middle of the semester at Eastern Illinois University *showed that* during the month 63% (1,849) of the students borrowed no books from the library in 1962 and 62% (2,318) borrowed no books in 1963.   **(172)**

Ibid. . . . *showed that* a higher percentage of freshmen checked out books than upperclassmen, with 44% (451) of the freshmen checking books out during this 1-month period in 1962, 35% (238) of the sophomores, 36% (226) of the juniors, 35% (15) of the seniors, and 28% (42) of the graduate students. The per capita number of books checked out in each group was 1.8, 1.2, 1.6, 1.4, 1.7, respectively.   **(172)**

■   A study in academic 1963-64 at the Grand Canyon College (Phoenix, Arizona; 1963 enrollment: 479) of circulation records for 9 weeks *showed that* 468 students checked out a total of 3,181 books. Median per capita = 3 books; average per capita = 6.7 books. Half of the student borrowers—the most active half—accounted for 3,024 circulations (95.1% of the total).

(179)

■ A 1-year study during 1964-65 at the Yale Medical School Library concerning patron use patterns of library materials (based on 34,825 book/journal circulations) *showed that* 20,563 journal circulations were distributed among members of the medical school as follows (accounting for 74.6% of the journal use):

full-time faculty	32.0%	journal uses
students	27.2%	journal uses
house officers	11.6%	journal uses
part-time faculty	3.8%	journal uses

(675)

Ibid. . . . *showed that* 14,262 book circulations were distributed among members of the medical school as follows (accounting for 51.7% of the book use):

students	24.6%	book uses
full-time faculty	17.6%	book uses
house officers	6.5%	book uses
part-time faculty	3.0%	book uses

(675)

Ibid. . . . *showed that* the per capita book and journal use (over 1 year's time) was as follows:

students	10.0 journals; 6.3 books
full-time faculty	11.9 journals; 4.6 books
house officers	7.9 journals; 3.1 books
part-time faculty	1.6 journals; 0.8 books

(675)

■ A study during the 1981-82 academic year in the main library at Purdue concerning books that undergraduates selected to read (involving interviews with 240 undergraduate borrowers and analysis of 598 of the monographic titles borrowed by both students and nonstudents) *showed that* undergraduates (and surprisingly) graduate students tended to use a core of heavily used titles, while faculty tended to use materials that had never before circulated. For example, of 67 items circulated to faculty, 18 (26.9%) had circulated 6 or more times, while of 131 items circulated to graduate students, 77 (58.8%) had been circulated 6 or more times, and of 364 items circulated to undergraduates, 253 (69.5%) had been circulated 6 or more times. (There were 36 missing cases.)

(530)

Ibid. . . . *showed that*, based on 364 items circulated to undergraduates, only 15.9% of the titles selected by undergraduates were based on instructor recommendation (direct recommendation or reading lists) while the remaining titles were selected without instructor direction. 86.6% were selected for subject matter relating to a specific course, 11.6% were selected for leisure reading, and 1.8% were selected for research in the student's major with no specific course in mind.   **(530)**

Ibid. . . . *showed that* titles recommended by instructors and checked out by undergraduates were no more likely to fall within the core of highly circulating materials than outside it. For example, of 111 titles that circulated less than 6 times, 16 or 14.4% had been recommended by faculty, while of 253 titles that had circulated 6 times or more, 42 (16.6%) had been recommended by faculty.   **(530)**

Ibid. . . . *showed that* the "best and most critically acclaimed" books do not make up the majority of undergraduate reading. For example, of 252 books checked out by undergraduates that had been published before 1973, only 61 (24.2%) were listed in *Books for College Libraries*, while of 246 books published after 1963, only 74 (30.1%) were reviewed in *Choice* and of these, only 35% were given top recommendations.   **(530)**

Special

■ A 1-year study during 1964-65 at the Yale Medical School Library concerning patron use patterns of library materials (based on 34,825 book/journal circulations) *showed that* 20,563 journal circulations were distributed among members of the medical school as follows (accounting for 74.6% of the journal use):

full-time faculty	32.0% journal uses
students	27.2% journal uses
house officers	11.6% journal uses
part-time faculty	3.8% journal uses **(675)**

Ibid. . . . *showed that* 14,262 book circulations were distributed among members of the medical school as follows (accounting for 51.7% of the book use):

students	24.6% book uses
full-time faculty	17.6% book uses
house officers	6.5% book uses
part-time faculty	3.0% book uses **(675)**

Ibid. . . . *showed that* the per capita book and journal use (over 1 year's time) was as follows:

students	10.0 journals; 6.3 books
full-time faculty	11.9 journals; 4.6 books
house officers	7.9 journals; 3.1 books
part-time faculty	1.6 journals; 0.8 books	**(675)**

Use Patterns—Circulation, Other

Academic

■ A 1-year study during 1964-65 at the Yale Medical School Library concerning patron use patterns of library materials (based on 34,825 book/journal circulations) *showed that* 20,563 journal circulations were distributed among members of the medical school as follows (accounting for 74.6% of the journal use):

full-time faculty	32.0% journal uses
students	27.2% journal uses
house officers	11.6% journal uses
part-time faculty	3.8% journal uses	**(675)**

Ibid. . . . *showed that* 14,262 book circulations were distributed among members of the medical school as follows (accounting for 51.7% of the book use):

students	24.6% book uses
full-time faculty	17.6% book uses
house officers	6.5% book uses
part-time faculty	3.0% book uses	**(675)**

Ibid. . . . *showed that* the per capita book and journal use (over 1 year's time) was as follows:

students	10.0 journals; 6.3 books
full-time faculty	11.9 journals; 4.6 books
house officers	7.9 journals; 3.1 books
part-time faculty	1.6 journals; 0.8 books	**(675)**

Special

■ A 1-year study during 1964-65 at the Yale Medical School Library concerning patron use patterns of library materials (based on 34,825 book/journal circulations) *showed that* 20,563 journal circulations were distributed among members of the medical school as follows (accounting for 74.6% of the journal use):

full-time faculty	32.0% journal uses
students	27.2% journal uses
house officers	11.6% journal uses
part-time faculty	3.8% journal uses **(675)**

Ibid. . . . *showed that* 14,262 book circulations were distributed among members of the medical school as follows (accounting for 51.7% of the book use):

students	24.6% book uses
full-time faculty	17.6% book uses
house officers	6.5% book uses
part-time faculty	3.0% book uses **(675)**

Ibid. . . . *showed that* the per capita book and journal use (over 1 year's time) was as follows:

students	10.0 journals; 6.3 books
full-time faculty	11.9 journals; 4.6 books
house officers	7.9 journals; 3.1 books
part-time faculty	1.6 journals; 0.8 books **(675)**

Use Patterns—Class Preparation, Faculty

Academic

■ A survey in 1959 of 8,660 library patrons during 1 week at the 4 largest MIT libraries (General and Humanities, Science, Engineering, and Dewey) during selected hours *showed that* 46.0% of all patrons were undergraduates who reported spending 71.9% of their time for class preparation and 14.9% time on research; 35.4% were graduate students who spent 52.4% time in class preparation and 37.2% time in research; and 11.8% were faculty/staff who spent 17.1% time in class preparation and 56.4% time in research.   **(115)**

■ A 1964 study at the Yale Medical Library involving faculty use of books (survey size: 831 borrowers; responding: 430) during a 5-month period *showed that* 11% of the books were reported used in lecture preparation, while 89% appeared to be "associated with research activites." Further,

28% of the books were reported used to "acquire general information to keep up with the field."   **(672)**

Special

■ A 1964 study at the Yale Medical Library involving faculty use of books (survey size: 831 borrowers; responding: 430) during a 5-month period *showed that* 11% of the books were reported used in lecture preparation while 89% appeared to be "associated with research activites." Further, 28% of the books were reported used to "acquire general information to keep up with the field."   **(672)**

Use Patterns—Class Preparation, Students

Academic

■ A survey in 1959 of 8,660 library patrons during 1 week at the 4 largest MIT libraries (General and Humanities, Science, Engineering, and Dewey) during selected hours *showed that* 46.0% of all patrons were undergraduates who reported spending 71.9% of their time for class preparation and 14.9% time on research; 35.4% were graduate students who spent 52.4% time in class preparation and 37.2% time in research; and 11.8% were faculty/staff who spent 17.1% time in class preparation and 56.4% time in research.   **(115)**

■ A survey reported in 1970 of library patrons at Purdue University (6,568 sampled; 6,323 usable responses) and statistically analyzed by Chi Square tests *showed that* the 3 patron groupings (faculty, graduate, and undergraduate) gave statistically significantly different response rates for their primary reasons for visiting the library (significant at the .001 level). The largest category reported by faculty for library visits was research for a publishable paper or book (21%); for graduate students the largest category was to find and read material required by a course (30%); for undergraduates the largest category was to do homework with their own books (50+%).   **(202)**

Use Patterns—Competing/Complementary Libraries

General

■ A survey reported in 1980 of 4 public and 2 private schools involving 13 high school classes and 234 students researching independent study papers selected as a purposeful, not random, sample *showed that* 7% of the students used 1 library, 20% used 2 libraries, 32% used 3 libraries, 26% used 4 libraries, and 15% used 5 or more libraries.   **(281)**

Ibid. . . . *showed that* (multiple responses allowed) 86% of the students used a school library, 70% used a neighborhood public library, 54% used a regional public library, 56% used a home library, 37% used a college or university library, 4% used a community college library, and 19% used various other libraries (private and/or special).   **(281)**

Ibid. . . . *showed that* (multiple responses allowed) 75% of the students using a school library found information used in their paper, 40% reported receiving staff help, and 4% reported help from friends/family; 69% of the students using a neighborhood public library found information used in their paper, 25% received staff help, and 10% reported help from friends/family; 100% of the students using a regional public library found information used in their paper, 50% reported receiving staff help, and 16% reported help from friends/family; 67% of the students using a community college library found information used in their paper, 22% received staff help, and 0% reported help from friends/family; 84% of the students using a college/university library found information used in their paper, 50% received help from the staff, and 27% received help from friends/family; 85% of the students who used home libraries found information used in their paper, 0% received staff help, and 13% reported help from friends/family; 100% of the students who used other (private/special) libraries found information used in their paper, 18% received staff help, and 18% received help from friends/family.   **(281)**

Academic

■ A survey during the 1974-75 academic year at the Queen's University in Kingston (Canada) and Trent University in Peterborough (Canada) of part-time students (survey size: 1,143 students at Trent and 1,408 students at Queen's; responding: 286 or 25.1% students at Trent and 480 or 34.1% students at Queen's) *showed that*, of the 480 respondents to the Queen's University survey, 282 (58.8%) of the students reported obtaining their course readings primarily through the purchase of books. In contrast, 15.8% of the students reported that the university library was the primary source of their readings, while 5.2% reported that the public library was the primary source of their readings. A list of 8 options was provided.

(545)

■ A 1980 survey of faculty and students at San Jose State University concerning their library use patterns (students—survey size: [not given]; responding: 1,470; faculty—population: 1,753; responding: 443 or 25.3%) *showed that* 57.5% of the students and 70.2% of the faculty reported that they used other libraries in connection with San Jose State course work, whether teaching, study, or research. **(519)**

Ibid. . . . *showed that* the reasons given for not using the university library by those students who reported they seldom or never used the library were: "no need" to use the library (38%), poor organization of the library (26%), and greater convenience of another library (11%).

(519)

Ibid. . . . *showed that* the reasons given for not using the university library by those faculty who reported they seldom or never used the library were: greater convenience of another library (38%), "no time" (23%), "no need" (21%), and poor organization (15%). **(519)**

■ A 1981 study of 53 ninth-grade honors students in science in a suburban Philadelphia public high school *showed that* 98% of the students used school libraries (92% of these found information), 87% used public libraries (83% of these found information), 74% used home libraries (74% of these found information), 11% used college or university libraries (100% of these found information), 8% used private or special libraries (99% of these found information), and 6% used other institutions (67% of these found information). **(222)**

Public

■ A questionnaire survey of 3,500 public library cardholders in 5 medium-sized Pennsylvania cities in conjunction with interviews of a randomly selected sample of householders in 1 city by the Institute of Public Administration (at Pennsylvania State University) under contract to the Pennsylvania State Library in 1965 *showed that* students as a group, regardless of family background, were more frequent library users than any other group.   **(084)**

Ibid. . . . *showed that*, where competing or complementary library facilities existed, such as branch, school, college, law, or business libraries, a majority of the library cardholders actively used these other services as well.   **(084)**

■ A survey reported in 1980 of 1,178 high school students (representing a sample from 73 classes, 15 schools, and 5 school districts) including a study of their bibliographic citations to periodical articles *showed that* only 14% of the students reported using only 1 library. Overall, 84% reported using the school library media center, 75% reported using a public library, and 59% reported using home collections.   **(219)**

■ A 1981 study of 53 ninth-grade honors students in science in a suburban Philadelphia public high school *showed that* 98% of the students used school libraries (92% of these found information), 87% used public libraries (83% of these found information), 74% used home libraries (74% of these found information), 11% used college or university libraries (100% of these found information), 8% used private or special libraries (99% of these found information), and 6% used other institutions (67% of these found information).   **(222)**

School

■ A 1960 survey of 298 high school participants in the Annual Central New Jersey Science Fair (265 responding) *showed that* the sources of intellectual materials for the science project were as follows (multiple responses possible): home, including friends and relatives 103 (39%) respondents, public library 96 (36%), school library 66 (25%), special library 53 (20%), magazine 20 (8%), college library 18 (7%).   **(276)**

■ A survey in 1964 of 239 12th-grade students from 4 upper socioeconomic level high schools and 4 lower socioeconomic high schools (10% sample from each school) *showed that* students in both groups preferred to use the public library rather than the school library but that

students in the lower socioeconomic schools read less and borrowed fewer books than their counterparts in the higher socioeconomic category.
(072)

■ A study reported in 1979 of term paper bibliographies of high school students (270 students/papers from 6 high schools, involving 3,165 identifiable references) *showed that* only 7% of the students reported using only a single library, while "nearly three-quarters" of the students used 3 or more libraries. Further, the types of libraries reported used by students were as follows (multiple responses allowed):

school libraries	86%	students
1 or more public libraries	89%	students
home libraries	56%	students
college/university libraries	37%	students
special libraries	19%	students **(564)**

■ A survey reported in 1980 of 1,178 high school students (representing a sample from 73 classes, 15 schools, and 5 school districts) including a study of their bibliographic citations to periodical articles *showed that* only 460 students (39%) cited at least 1 periodical article. Overall, 62% of the total citations were to books, 19% to periodicals, and the rest to newspapers, encyclopedias, etc. **(219)**

Ibid. . . . *showed that* only 14% of the students reported using only 1 library. Overall, 84% reported using the school library media center, 75% reported using a public library, and 59% reported using home collections. **(219)**

■ A survey reported in 1980 of 4 public and 2 private schools involving 13 high school classes and 234 students researching independent study papers selected as a purposeful, not random, sample *showed that* 7% of the students used 1 library, 20% used 2 libraries, 32% used 3 libraries, 26% used 4 libraries, and 15% used 5 or more libraries. **(281)**

Ibid. . . . *showed that* (multiple responses allowed) 86% of the students used a school library, 70% used a neighborhood public library, 54% used a regional public library, 56% used a home library, 37% used a college or university library, 4% used a community college library, and 19% used various other libraries (private and/or special). **(281)**

Ibid. . . . *showed that* (multiple responses allowed) 75% of the students using a school library found information used in their paper, 40% reported receiving staff help, and 4% reported help from friends/family; 69% of the students using a neighborhood public library found information used in their paper, 25% received staff help, and 10% reported help from friends/family; 100% of the students using a regional public library found information used in their paper, 50% reported receiving staff help, and 16% reported help from friends/family; 67% of the students using a community college library found information used in their paper, 22% received staff help, and 0% reported help from friends/family; 84% of the students using a college/university library found information used in their paper, 50% received help from the staff, and 27% received help from friends/family; 85% of the students who used home libraries found information used in their paper, 0% received staff help, and 13% reported help from friends/family; 100% of the students who used other (private/special) libraries found information used in their paper, 18% received staff help, and 18% received help from friends/family.   **(281)**

■ A 1981 study of 53 ninth-grade honors students in science in a suburban Philadelphia public high school *showed that* 98% of the students used school libraries (92% of these found information), 87% used public libraries (83% of these found information), 74% used home libraries (74% of these found information), 11% used college or university libraries (100% of these found information), 8% used private or special libraries (99% of these found information), and 6% used other institutions (67% of these found information).   **(222)**

Use Patterns—Distance from Library

Academic

■ A survey during the 1974-75 academic year at the Queen's University in Kingston (Canada) and Trent University in Peterborough (Canada) of part-time students (survey size: 1,143 students at Trent and 1,408 students at Queen's; responding: 286 or 25.1% students at Trent and 480 or 34.1% students at Queen's) *showed that* the distance students lived from the university and university library use seemed related. For example, of the Trent students, 81.5% of the university library users lived 40 miles away or less, while "an almost equal proportion of non-users lived 40 miles or more from the library."   **(545)**

Public

■ A questionnaire survey of 3,500 public library cardholders in 5 medium-sized Pennsylvania cities in conjunction with interviews of a randomly selected sample of householders in 1 city by the Institute of Public Administration (at Pennsylvania State University) under contract to the Pennsylvania State Library in 1965 *showed that* only when the distance between the cardholder's home and the library went beyond 10 miles was there any appreciable decline in the rate of library use. The most active library users tended to live within 5 blocks of the library. **(084)**

Use Patterns—Document Delivery

Academic

■ A survey in 1970 of the users of a library book delivery system for the campus of the University of Colorado (survey population: 377; responding: 208 or 55% [of whom 89% were resident teaching faculty]) *showed that* 33% of the faculty had used it during the first 18 months of its operation, with 68% of the respondents rating the service as excellent and 23% rating the service as good. **(123)**

Ibid. . . . *showed that* of those responding 46% were in the humanities and social sciences; 36% were in the pure and applied sciences; 13% were in interdisciplinary institutes; and 4% were administrators or no answer. **(123)**

Ibid. . . . *showed that* 54% of the respondents reported that the campus book delivery system had changed their pattern of library use. The main reasons given were saved time, library easier to use, and library more convenient to use. **(123)**

Use Patterns—Education

Public

■ A questionnaire survey of 3,500 public library cardholders in 5 medium-sized Pennsylvania cities in conjunction with interviews of a randomly selected sample of householders in 1 city by the Institute of Public Administration (at Pennsylvania State University) under contract to the Pennsylvania State Library in 1965 *showed that* a larger proportion of high school graduates, college attenders, and graduates of colleges and professional schools held library cards than less-educated groups. However, the frequency of library use among cardholders was not related to formal education except possibly inversely.   **(084)**

■ A 1979 telephone survey of 1,046 New Orleans residents over the age of 12 *showed that* library users tend to be more highly educated than library nonusers. 25.5% of users have bachelor's degrees compared to 9.4% of nonusers, and 7.7% have master's degrees compared to 0.8% of nonusers.   **(166)**

Use Patterns—Foreign-Language Materials

Public

■ A 1969 survey of Canadian public libraries serving populations of more than 10,000 people as well as all county and regional libraries belonging to the Canadian Library Association concerning holdings and use of non-English collections (survey size: 203; responding: 83 or 41%) *showed that* the demand for non-English material did not come from predominately French-speaking Canadians. Specifically, 37 (44%) of the libraries reported that their non-English material was primarily used by new Canadians,while only 19 (23%) libraries reported that their non-English material was used primarily by native Canadians.   **(534)**

Use Patterns—Frequency

General

■ A 1970 survey of psychiatrists randomly selected from the 1968 membership of the American Psychiatric Association (survey size: 394; responding: 290 or 74%) *showed that* overall 27% of the respondents used medical libraries weekly, 69% used them at least monthly, 92% used them at least yearly, and 8% reported never using them. There was considerable variation by practice. For example, 70% of the academicians used medical libraries weekly, compared to 11% of the private practitioners.   **(690)**

Special

■ A 1970 survey of psychiatrists randomly selected from the 1968 membership of the American Psychiatric Association (survey size: 394; responding: 290 or 74%) *showed that* overall 27% of the respondents used medical libraries weekly, 69% used them at least monthly, 92% used them at least yearly, and 8% reported never using them. There was considerable variation by practice. For example, 70% of the academicians used medical libraries weekly, compared to 11% of the private practitioners. **(690)**

Use Patterns—Frequency, Faculty

Academic

■ A 1970 survey of psychiatrists randomly selected from the 1968 membership of the American Psychiatric Association (survey size: 394; responding: 290 or 74%) *showed that* overall 27% of the respondents used medical libraries weekly, 69% used them at least monthly, 92% used them at least yearly, and 8% reported never using them. There was considerable variation by practice. For example, 70% of the academicians used medical libraries weekly, compared to 11% of the private practitioners. **(690)**

■ A 1973 survey of physicists in 6 universities of the greater Boston area (Boston University, Brandeis, Brown, Harvard, MIT, and Northeastern) to determine how they meet their information needs (sample size: 339; responding: 179 or 52.8%) *showed that* frequency of library use for 190 respondents (Harvard chemistry faculty respondents included) was as follows:

daily	18 (9.47%)	respondents
several times per week	65 (34.22%)	respondents
once per week	51 (26.84%)	respondents
several times per month	32 (16.84%)	respondents
once a month or less	24 (12.63%)	respondents **(404)**

■ A 1980 survey of faculty and students at San Jose State University concerning their library use patterns (students—survey size: [not given]; responding: 1,470; faculty—population: 1,753; responding: 443 or 25.3%) *showed that* overall 12.2% of the students reported they never use the library, while only 29.6% reported using the library once a week or more. Of the faculty, 5.2% of the respondents reported never using the library, while 31.9% reported using the library once a week or more. **(519)**

Ibid. . . . *showed that* teachers of evening classes made statistically significantly less use of the university library than teachers of day classes. For example, 34.3% of the evening teachers reported seldom or never using the library (i.e., less than once a month) compared to 21.7% of the day teachers so reporting (significant at the .0001 level). **(519)**

Ibid. . . . *showed that* part-time teachers made statistically significantly less use of the university library than full-time teachers. For example, 42.7% of the part-time teachers reported seldom or never making use of the library (i.e., less than once a month) compared to 19.8% of the full-time teachers so reporting (significant at the .0001 level). **(519)**

Ibid. . . . *showed that* female teachers made statistically significantly less use of the university library than male teachers. For example, 29.6% of the female teachers reported seldom or never using the library (i.e., less than once a month) compared to 21.5% of the male teachers so reporting (significant at the .0001 level). **(519)**

Ibid. . . . *showed that* there were statistically significant differences of reported library use among tenured, tenure track, and temporary faculty. For example, 45.4% of the temporary faculty reported seldom or never using the library (i.e., less than once a month) compared to 20.9% of the tenure track faculty and 15.6% of the tenured faculty. Further, 21.3% of the temporary faculty reported frequent use of the library (i.e., once a week or more) compared to 44.2% of the tenure track faculty and 34.4% of the tenured faculty so reporting. (Significant at the .0001 level.) **(519)**

Ibid. . . . *showed that* there were statistically significant differences in reported frequency of university library use by faculty in different broad subject areas. The number of faculty in each area reporting they seldom or never used the library (i.e., less than once a month) was as follows:

social science	12.0% faculty	
humanities	17.6% faculty	
science	20.2% faculty	
education	27.5% faculty	
applied arts	32.8% faculty	
engineering	37.2% faculty	
business	45.8% faculty	**(519)**

■ A study reported in 1981 at Southern Illinois University, Carbondale, investigating teaching faculty perception of librarians (survey size: 507; responding: 386; usable: 384 or 75.7%) *showed that* faculty reported the following use of the library:

daily use	6% of the faculty
several times a week	26% of the faculty

continued

once a week   31% of the faculty
once a month or less   36% of the faculty   **(493)**

Use Patterns—Frequency, Students

Academic

■ A 1968 study of graduate students at the University of Michigan concerning their use of periodical literature (sample size: 399; responding: 338 or 85%) *showed that* approximately 78% of the students used the library about once a week, while 61% reported using the periodical literature about once a week. **(195)**

■ A study reported in 1972 of 79 graduate business students at a large, accredited southeastern business school *showed that* 67% of the graduate buiness students reported library use of more than 6 times a month; 18% reported library use from 1-5 times a month; and 15% reported no library use at all. **(297)**

■ A survey during the 1974-75 academic year at the Queen's University in Kingston (Canada) and Trent University in Peterborough (Canada) of part-time students (survey size: 1,143 students at Trent and 1,408 students at Queen's; responding: 286 or 25.1% students at Trent and 480 or 34.1% students at Queen's) *showed that* use of the university library by respondents was reported as follows:

Trent students: 29.7% of the students did not use the university library, 30.4% used the library less than once per week, 12.9% used the library once per week, and 26.9% used the library more than once per week;

Queen's students: 25.4% of the students did not use the university library, 30.6% used the library 1-5 times "during their courses," 12.9% used the library 6-10 times "during their courses," 11.5% used the library more than 11 times, and 19.6% did not respond. **(545)**

■ A 1980 survey of faculty and students at San Jose State University concerning their library use patterns (students—survey size: [not given]; responding: 1,470; faculty—population: 1,753; responding: 443 or 25.3%) *showed that* overall 12.2% of the students reported they never use the library, while only 29.6% reported using the library once a week or more.

Of the faculty, 5.2% of the respondents reported never using the library, while 31.9% reported using the library once a week or more. **(519)**

Ibid. . . . *showed that* there were statistically significant differences in frequency of university library use among day students, evening students, and those taking both day and evening classes. For example, 49.6% of the evening students reported seldom or never using the library (i.e., less than once a month) compared to 38.2% of the day students and 27.0% of the day/evening students so reporting (significant at the .0001 level). **(519)**

Ibid. . . . *showed that* there was a statistically significant difference in the frequency of university library use between full-time and part-time students. For example, 45.8% of the part-time students reported seldom or never using the library (i.e., less than once a month) compared to 34.7% of the full-time students so reporting (significant at the .001 level). **(519)**

Ibid. . . . *showed that* female students made statistically significantly less frequent use of the university library than male students. For example, 42.1% of the females reported seldom or never using the library (i.e., less than once a month) compared to 30.6% of the male students so reporting (significant at the .0001 level). **(519)**

Ibid. . . . *showed that* there were statistically significant differences in the frequency of university library use by ethnic background. For example, 21.9% of the Asian students reported seldom or never using the library (i.e., less than once a month) compared to 27.8% of the Chicano students, 38.7% of the black students, and 40.5% of the white students so reporting (significant at the .0001 level). **(519)**

Ibid. . . . *showed that* there were statistically significant differences in reported frequency of university library use by students in different broad subject areas. The number of students in each area reporting they seldom or never used the library (i.e., less than once a month) was as follows:

humanities	27.5%	students
social science	31.1%	students
science	31.1%	students
engineering	31.8%	students
education	32.5%	students
applied arts	39.9%	students
business	40.9%	students **(519)**

Public

■ A questionnaire survey of 3,500 public library cardholders in 5 medium-sized Pennsylvania cities in conjunction with interviews of a randomly selected sample of householders in 1 city by the Institute of Public Administration (at Pennsylvania State University) under contract to the Pennsylvania State Library in 1965 *showed that* students as a group, regardless of family background, were more frequent library users than any other group.   **(084)**

Use Patterns—Gender

Academic

■ A 1980 survey of faculty and students at San Jose State University concerning their library use patterns (students—survey size: [not given]; responding: 1,470; faculty—population: 1,753; responding: 443 or 25.3%) *showed that* female students made statistically significantly less frequent use of the university library than male students. For example, 42.1% of the females reported seldom or never using the library (i.e., less than once a month) compared to 30.6% of the male students so reporting (significant at the .0001 level).   **(519)**

Ibid. . . . *showed that* female teachers made statistically significantly less use of the university library than male teachers. For example, 29.6% of the female teachers reported seldom or never using the library (i.e., less than once a month) compared to 21.5% of the male teachers so reporting (significant at the .0001 level).   **(519)**

Public

■ A study reported in 1963 concerning public library use by 180 (98 black; 82 white) low-income mothers with first-grade children in Chicago *showed that* white mothers (30%) were more likely than black mothers (17%) to have a library card. However, 26% of the white mothers and 24% of the black mothers reported using the library, with half of each user group reporting library use in excess of 4 times a year.   **(242)**

Ibid. . . . *showed that* the frequency of mother's use of the library and the frequency of the child's use of the library were statistically significantly related beyond the .001 level of significance. Of the 13% of the children who used the library, 7% were taken by parents, 7% by siblings, and 3% by friends and neighbors. (Multiple selection of responses was allowed.)   **(242)**

■ A questionnaire survey of 3,500 public library cardholders in 5 medium-sized Pennsylvania cities in conjunction with interviews of a randomly selected sample of householders in 1 city by the Institute of Public Administration (at Pennsylvania State University) under contract to the Pennsylvania State Library in 1965 *showed that* women were more likely to hold library cards than were men but that men used the library more frequently than women.   **(084)**

Use Patterns—Government Documents

Academic

■ A survey reported in 1972 of one-third of the social science and humanities faculty at Case Western Reserve University (sample size: 116; responding: 103 or 89%) concerning government document use *showed that* 62% (64) never used documents, 23% (24) used documents 1-2 times a year, 14% (14) used documents 1-2 times a semester, and 1% (1) used documents 2-3 times a month.   **(209)**

Ibid. . . . *showed that* of 87 faculty respondents the 2 main reasons for nonuse of the document department reported by faculty respondents were lack of need of government documents (46%) and obtaining their own copies (32%).   **(209)**

Ibid. . . . *showed that* of 39 users of the government document collection the frequency with which respondents reported needing assistance from the staff was as follows: more than 50% of the time, 28% (11); 25-50% of the time, 10% (4); less than 25% of the time, 36% (14); never, 23% (9); no answer, 3% (1).   **(209)**

■ A 1982 survey of economics and political science faculty members in 9 colleges and universities serving as academic depository institutions in Massachusetts for the Government Printing Office (sample size: 216, including 105 economists and 111 political scientists; responding: 155 or 71.8%, including 86 economists and 69 political scientists) *showed that* 125 (80.6%) had made some use of federal government documents during the past year, while 53 (42.2%) reported citing a federal government publication in 1 or more of their scholarly writings in the past 3 years.   **(316)**

Ibid. . . . *showed that* the 125 faculty respondents who used documents reported using U.S. govenment publications as follows (multiple responses allowed): for research or scholarly writing (117 respondents), for teaching (95 respondents), for consulting activities (33 respondents), and for recreational reading or statistical data necessary for presentations before community groups (6 respondents). **(316)**

Ibid. . . . *showed that* the top 3 kinds of federal documents sought by the 125 respondents who used documents were: statistical data (82 respondents), research and technical reports (77 respondents), and resources that may be of value to students (74 respondents). The difference between the responses given by economists and political scientists was not great, with a Spearman rank correlation coefficient showing a strong relationship between the responses of the 2 groups (rho = .87). **(316)**

Ibid. . . . *showed that* the top 6 methods used by the 125 respondents who used documents to locate federal documents were (multiple responses allowed): finding citations in the general literature of the subject discipline (97 respondents), receiving assistance from librarians (84 respondents), being on the mailing lists of federal agencies (70 respondents), finding citations in indexes, abstracts, and subject bibliographies (68), receiving citations from colleagues (53 respondents), and contacting federal agencies (46 respondents). The difference between the responses given by economists and political scientists was not great, with a Spearman rank correlation coefficient showing a strong relationship between the responses of the 2 groups (rho = .97). **(316)**

Ibid. . . . *showed that* of the 125 respondents who used federal documents, in addition to use of federal documents in paper copy format, 24 (19.2%) respondents also used federal documents in microformat, 21 (16.8%) used machine-readable federal government information, and 13 (10.4%) used audiovisual federal government information. Of these responses, economists accounted for 70.8% of the reported use of microform and 90.5% of the use of machine-readable formats. **(316)**

Ibid. . . . *showed that*, for the 125 respondents who used federal documents, the top 3 kinds of federal documents used frequently by economists were (multiple responses allowed): statistical reports (47 respondents), annual reports (21 respondents), and reports of investigation and research (19 respondents), while the top 3 kinds of federal documents used frequently by political scientists were (multiple responses allowed): statistical reports (13 respondents), decisions and opinions, e.g., from the Supreme Court (12 respondents), and journals and proceedings, e.g., from the *Congressional Record* (11 respondents). **(316)**

Use Patterns—ILL

Academic

■ A study reported in 1970 at the medical school library of the University of New Mexico (also serving as the library of the local county medical society) of interlibrary loans lent to practicing physicians during fiscal 1965-67 *showed that*, of 180 physicians belonging to the local medical society, 65 (36.1%) borrowed 1 or more books, journals, or pamphlets from the library during the 2-year period. 23 of the 65 borrowed 10 or more items from the library during that period.   **(685)**

■ A 1971 survey of owners (primarily academics) of personal library collections (sample selected from authors of 300 single-author articles published during 1969-70 in one of 3 broad areas: humanities, social science, and science; 178 authors responding, of which 175 owned personal collections) *showed that* cited material received through interlibrary loan accounted for only 38 (0.7%) items.   **(258)**

Special

■ A study reported in 1970 at the medical school library of the University of New Mexico (also serving as the library of the local county medical society) of interlibrary loans lent to practicing physicians during fiscal 1965-67 *showed that*, of 180 physicians belonging to the local medical society, 65 (36.1%) borrowed 1 or more books, journals, or pamphlets from the library during the 2-year period. 23 of the 65 borrowed 10 or more items from the library during that period.   **(685)**

Use Patterns—Income Level

Public

■ A study reported in 1963 concerning public library use by 180 (98 black; 82 white) low-income mothers with first-grade children in Chicago *showed that* white mothers (30%) were more likely than black mothers (17%) to have a library card. However, 26% of the white mothers and 24% of the black mothers reported using the library, with half of each user group reporting library use in excess of 4 times a year.   **(242)**

Ibid. . . . *showed that* the frequency of mother's use of the library and the frequency of the child's use of the library were statistically significantly

related beyond the .001 level of significance. Of the 13% of the children who used the library, 7% were taken by parents, 7% by siblings, and 3% by friends and neighbors. (Multiple selection of responses was allowed.)
(242)

■ A questionnaire survey of 3,500 public library cardholders in 5 medium-sized Pennsylvania cities in conjunction with interviews of a randomly selected sample of householders in 1 city by the Institute of Public Administration (at Pennsylvania State University) under contract to the Pennsylvania State Library in 1965 *showed that* people with family incomes higher than the community median were more likely to be cardholders but that frequency of use was not related to income level.
(084)

School

■ A survey in 1964 of 239 12th-grade students from 4 upper socioeconomic level high schools and 4 lower socioeconomic high schools (10% sample from each school) *showed that* students in both groups preferred to use the public library rather than the school library but that students in the lower socioeconomic schools read less and borrowed fewer books than their counterparts in the higher socioeconomic category.
(072)

Ibid. . . . *showed that* students from the lower socioeconomic schools showed a strong preference for using their own and library materials in the library, while students from the higher socioeconomic schools showed a tendency to borrow materials and study at home. Higher socioeconomic students also tended to use the public library as a social center.
(072)

Ibid. . . . *showed that,* when asked to indicate books they might like to read, the lower socioeconomic students were more likely to choose that category of books on how to be a more popular or successful person than their higher socioeconomic counterparts.
(072)

Use Patterns—Main versus Branches

Public

■ A 1977-78 survey of a random sample of 300 Spanish-surnamed families in the San Bernardino area *showed that* 65% of the respondents with library cards lived near a branch library where bilingual service was available as compared to 11% who lived near the main library. However, 52% of those served by such a branch reported preferring use of the main library and its more adequate resources.   **(237)**

■ A 1979 telephone survey of 1,046 New Orleans residents over the age of 12 *showed that* 37.6% report having visited the public library in the past 12 months. Of these, 28.2% visited the Central Library, and 71.8% visited the branches. The 1978 circulation figures indicated that the Central Library accounted for 28% of the overall circulation and the branches for 72% of the overall circulation.   **(166)**

Ibid. . . . *showed that* the Central Library was used more for reference and research while the branches were used more for recreational reading. 43.7% of Central's use was for information other than school, 34% for school, and 19.3% for pleasure, while the branches were used 26.9% for information, 38.7% for school, and 33.5% for pleasure.   **(166)**

Use Patterns—Maps

Academic

■ A 1972 study of Map Room use at Southern Illinois University during Summer and Fall quarters, involving the circulation of 2,721 maps and aerial photos to 223 borrowers, *showed that* borrowers were: undergraduates (44%), graduate students (32%), and faculty (19%). However, graduate students accounted for 72% of the loans, undergraduates for 16%, and faculty for 10%.   **(403)**

Ibid. . . . *showed that* the stated purpose of 60% of the loans was research.
                                                                        (403)

Ibid. . . . *showed that* borrowers were "widely scattered in approximately 40 departments." The largest number of borrowers came from the Forestry Department and involved 23 individuals or 10% of the borrowing population.   **(403)**

Ibid. . . . *showed that*, in terms of broad areas, 58 (26%) borrowers came from the social sciences, 52 (23%) from the sciences, 37 (17%) from the applied sciences, 24 (11%) from education, and 22 (10%) from humanities.
                                                                        (403)

Ibid. . . . *showed that*, of the items borrowed, 1,869 (68%) were maps and aerial photos of Illinois areas, 253 (9%) were maps and aerial photos of nearby states, 430 (16%) were U.S. areas except for Illinois and nearby states, 77 (3%) were Canadian and Latin American areas, and 70 (3%) were areas in the Eastern Hemisphere. **(403)**

Ibid. . . . *showed that* the 2 most common types of maps borrowed were aerial photos (1,641 items or 60% of the total) and topographic maps (639 maps or 23% of the total). **(403)**

■ A 1972-75 study at Southern Illinois University, Carbondale, of map and aerial photograph circulation from the Map Room *showed that* for all 3 years (1972-73, 1973-74, and 1974-75) undergraduate circulation consistently increased with academic status. Freshmen borrowed less than sophomores, sophomores less than juniors, and juniors less than seniors. **(420)**

Ibid. . . . *showed that* the main general trend over the 3-year period was a decrease in social science use (from 26% of the borrowers and 22% of the borrowing in 1972-73 to 16% of the borrowers and 8% of the borrowing in 1974-75) and an increase in science use (from 22% of the borrowers and 39% of the borrowing in 1972-73 to 25% of the borrowers and 46% of the borrowing in 1974-75). **(420)**

Ibid. . . . *showed that* for 2,699 loans in 1972-73 the purpose of borrowing the material was as follows:

class use	741 (27%) items	
research	544 (20%) items	
recreation	512 (19%) items	
travel	460 (17%) items	
theses and dissertations	271 (10%) items	
other	170 (06%) items	**(420)**

Ibid. . . . *showed that* over the 3-year period the region covered by the maps and photos borrowed was: southern Illinois (37-53% of the borrowing), northern and central Illinois (3-5% of the borrowing), nearby states (10-20% of the borrowing), U.S. (24-31% of the borrowing), and other including space maps (6-13% of the borrowing). **(420)**

Ibid. . . . *showed that* over the 3-year period undergraduates made up 49-52% of the borrowers in any given year, graduate students made up of 25-28% of the borrowers, faculty made up 12-15% of the borrowers, and "other" made up 8-11% of the borrowers. **(420)**

Ibid. . . . *showed that* over the 3-year period undergraduates accounted for 34-38% of the borrowing in any given year, graduates accounted for 30-38% of the borrowing, faculty accounted for 14-22% of the borrowing, and "other" accounted for 8-14% of the borrowing. **(420)**

Ibid. . . . *showed that* over the 3-year period 5 departments accounted for 33-37% of the borrowers and 45-50% of the borrowing. These were: forestry, geology, geography, zoology, and botany. The other borrowers were scattered throughout 80 other departments. **(420)**

Ibid. . . . *showed that* each year the proportion of male to female borrowers was "about 80% male, 20% female, although university enrollment was 36-38% female during this period." **(420)**

Use Patterns—Media

Public

■ A 1966 survey of 21,385 adult (12 years old or older) public library users in the Baltimore-Washington metropolitan region of Maryland conducted during a 6-week period of patrons entering the library (79.1% of patrons approached filled out the survey instrument) *showed that* the use made of the library was as follows (multiple responses allowed): browsing (43.1%), reference books (22.1%), library catalogs (19.0%), help from a librarian (16.0%), consulting books or magazines (12.4%), read new magazines or newspapers (8.7%), periodical indexes (5.7%), recordings (2.7%), films (0.7%), other (2.0%), and no response (11.1%). **(301)**

■ A survey reported in 1982 by the New York Library Association's Film and Video Roundtable of 63 administrators of large- and medium-sized public library film collections both in and outside of New York state (38 or 60% responding) *showed that* the following community groups were identified as heavy or moderate film users: nursing homes (100%), senior citizen centers (93%), day care centers (92%), adult clubs and organizations (89%), children's clubs and organizations (86%), hospitals (82%), and social service agencies (79%). **(162)**

Use Patterns—Microforms

Academic

■ A comparison of circulation statistics at the Georgia Tech library for Spring quarter 1971 and Spring quarter 1972, before and after they had installed microfiche catalogs for the collection in 35 academic and research departments and an accompanying twice-daily book delivery service, *showed that* faculty book circulation as a percentage of total book circulation increased from 13% to 16%, a statistically significant difference. **(106)**

Ibid. . . . *showed that* the new system changed the way faculty retrieved books from the library. Phone requests increased from 0 to 21.6% of total checkouts, books obtained by going to the library decreased from 88% to 71.6% of total checkouts, and books obtained by sending someone else to the library decreased from 10.5% to 2.7%. **(106)**

Ibid. . . . *showed that*, in a survey of 50 faculty patrons who had not used the new system which was reported in 1975, the following were the reasons for not using the new system:

	NUMBER
inertia	13
I like to go to the library.	14
I have not had occasion to use the new system.	9
It is more convenient for me to go to the library.	15
I like to browse or look at the books I select.	8
I do not fully understand the (new system).	6

(Some faculty gave more than 1 response.)   **(106)**

■ A survey reported in 1976 of 120 randomly selected patrons of the Bobst Library Microform Center of New York University *showed that* there was a user population of 4 faculty, 9 visitors, 63 graduates, and 44 undergraduates. **(224)**

Ibid. . . . *showed that* 55 (46%) used the center either seldom or occasionally, while 65 (54%) used it often (at least once a month) or frequently (at least once a week). 15 (35%) reported spending 30 minutes or less per session; 24 (20%) spent 30 minutes to 1 hour; 39 (33%) spent 1-2 hours; 28 (23%) spent 2-4 hours; and 14 (12%) spent more than 4 hours.   **(224)**

Use Patterns—Minorities

Public

■ A study reported in 1963 concerning public library use by 180 (98 black; 82 white) low-income mothers with first-grade children in Chicago *showed that* white mothers (30%) were more likely than black mothers (17%) to have a library card. However, 26% of the white mothers and 24% of the black mothers reported using the library, with half of each user group reporting library use in excess of 4 times a year.   **(242)**

Ibid. . . . *showed that* 54% of the respondents who reported using the library regularly had read more than 6 books in the last year, while only 26% of the respondents who used the library occasionally or never had read 6 books. (Finding significant at the .01 level.)   **(242)**

Ibid. . . . *showed that* the frequency of mother's use of the library and the frequency of the child's use of the library were statistically significantly related beyond the .001 level of significance. Of the 13% of the children who used the library, 7% were taken by parents, 7% by siblings, and 3% by friends and neighbors. (Multiple selection of responses was allowed.)
   (242)

■ A 1969 survey of Canadian public libraries serving populations of more than 10,000 people as well as all county and regional libraries belonging to the Canadian Library Association concerning holdings and use of non-English collections (survey size: 203; responding: 83 or 41%) *showed that* the demand for non-English material did not come from predominately French-speaking Canadians. Specifically, 37 (44%) of the libraries reported that their non-English material was primarily used by new Canadians, while only 19 (23%) libraries reported that their non-English material was used primarily by native Canadians.
   (534)

■ A 1977-78 survey of a random sample of 300 Spanish-surnamed families in the San Bernardino area *showed that* 25% of the respondents had valid library cards and that, of these 25%, 70% had used the library at least once in the past year.   **(237)**

Ibid. . . . *showed that* 65% of the respondents with library cards lived near a branch library where bilingual service was available as compared to 11% who lived near the main library. However, 52% of those served by such a branch reported preferring use of the main library and its more adequate resources. **(237)**

Ibid. . . . *showed that* 54% of the sample read the local major daily English newspaper, compared to 17% who reported reading the bilingual weekly. **(237)**

Use Patterns—Nonresident Fees

Public

■ A study reported in 1980 of monthly library circulation data for the 12-year period 1965-76 for the Dallas public library system (main library and 14 branches) comparing circulation before and after the institution of the Nonresident Fee Card Program *showed that* analysis by a series of statistical tests indicated strong evidence for statistically significant circulation declines in 3 libraries, moderate evidence for statistically significant declines in 2 libraries, weak evidence for declines in 4 libraries, and no evidence of statistically significant declines in 6 libraries. (Significance at the .05 level for all tests.) **(266)**

Use Patterns—Occupational Status

Public

■ A questionnaire survey of 3,500 public library cardholders in 5 medium-sized Pennsylvania cities in conjunction with interviews of a randomly selected sample of householders in 1 city by the Institute of Public Administration (at Pennsylvania State University) under contract to the Pennsylvania State Library in 1965 *showed that* business or professional people and their families were more likely to be library cardholders than other groups in the community. But while professionals and their family members who were cardholders were among the most active users of the library, their use was no higher than that by laborers or working-class families who were also cardholders. **(084)**

Use Patterns—Online Bibliographic Searching

General

■ A 12-month study in 1977-78 of online bibliographic literature search-ing of MINET (Kansas City Libraries Metropolitan Information Network, which includes 4 public libraries, 3 medical libraries, and 1 academic medical library) involving 403 paid search sessions and searches of 544 files or data bases *showed that* of the 544 data bases searched 231 (42.0%) were requested by graduate or advanced professional students; 108 (19.7%) were requested by college or university faculty; 67 (12.2%) were requested by the business community; and 26 (4.7%) were requested by undergradu-ate students.   **(234)**

Ibid. . . . *showed that* the 4 most used data bases were ERIC with 181 (33.1%) searches, PYSCHOLOGICAL ABSTRACTS with 77 (14.1%) searches, SOCIAL SCISEARCH with 51 (9.3%) searches, and MEDLARS/MEDLINE with 32 (5.8%) searches.   **(234)**

Ibid. . . . *showed that* of the 544 data bases searched the vendors most used were: Lockheed, 296 uses of its files (54.3% of total data base use); BRS, 182 uses of its files (33.5% of total data base use); and National Library of Medicine, 34 uses (6.2% of total data base use).   **(234)**

Ibid. . . . *showed that*, of the 403 search sessions, 296 (73.6%) searched 1 data base; 77 (19.1%) searched 2 data bases; 22 (5.4%) searched 3 data bases; and 7 (1.7%) searched 4 data bases.   **(234)**

Ibid. . . . *showed that* of the 544 data bases searched 229 (42%) had all citations printed online, while 315 (58%) had at least some citations printed offline.   **(234)**

Academic

■ A 14-month study during 1972-73 at the Yale Medical Library (serving the Yale University School of Medicine, the Yale University School of Nursing, and the Yale-New Haven Hospital) involving 1,466 online search requests (MEDLINE) from 455 different individuals for the faculty and professional staff of the Yale-New Haven Medical Center *showed that* the purposes of the requests were as follows:

research   1,140 (77.8%) search requests
patient care   221 (15.0%) search requests
education   105 (7.2%) search requests   **(714)**

Ibid. . . . *showed that* there were substantial differences in the number of individuals (455) requesting online searches by professorial rank. The number of individuals requesting online searches and their percentage of the faculty at that rank were as follows:

professor (112 faculty)   32 (28.6%) individuals
associate professor (160 faculty)   70 (43.8%) individuals
assistant professor (215 faculty)   81 (37.7%) individuals
instructor (94 faculty)   29 (30.9%) individuals
lecturer (134 faculty)   2 (1.5%) individuals
postdoctoral fellow (319 faculty) 102 (32.0%) individuals
research associate (192 faculty)   28 (14.9%) individuals

Clinical faculty and staff:

clinical professor (23 faculty)   1 (4.4%) individuals
associate clinical professor
   (105 faculty)   8 (7.6%) individuals
assistant clinical professor
   (291 faculty)   11 (3.8%) individuals
clinical professor [sic,
   lecturer?] (105 faculty)   1 (1.0%) individuals
clinical instructor (85 faculty)   4 (4.9%) individuals
resident (257 staff)   79 (30.7%) individuals
intern (25 staff)   7 (28.0%) individuals **(714)**

Ibid. . . . *showed that* there was generally little difference in per capita use by faculty/staff rank for those who used online searches. Specifically, the per capita number of searches requested by those who requested searches in terms of faculty or staff rank was as follows:

professor   2.7 searches each
associate professor   2.8 searches each
assistant professor   3.2 searches each
instructor   2.6 searches each
lecturer   2.5 searches each
postdoctoral fellow   3.4 searches each
research associate   5.9 searches each

Clinical faculty and staff:

clinical professor   3.0 searches each
associate clinical professor 2.5 searches each

continued

assistant clinical professor	5.3 searches each
clinical professor [sic,	
lecturer?]	2.0 searches each
clinical instructor	4.8 searches each
resident	2.7 searches each
intern	2.0 searches each (714)

■ A 1975-76 study at the University of Utah Marriottt Library of online bibliographic data base searching *showed that*, for a sample of 50
searches each in each of 4 major data bases, the patron chose to be present in 49 cases during ERIC searches, in 48 cases during PSYCHO-
LOGICAL ABSTRACTS searches, in 18 cases during NTIS searches,
and in 12 cases during CHEMICAL ABSTRACTS CONDENSATES
searches.   (329)

Ibid. . . . *showed that* a survey of 26 patrons using the online searching
service revealed that (multiple responses allowed): 10 (36%) were faculty,
9 (33%) were doctoral students, 2 (8%) were master's students, 2 (8%)
were undergraduate students, and 4 (15%) were professional researchers.
                                                                             (329)

■ A survey reported in 1976 of 10 academic and public libraries using the
New York Times Information Bank *showed that* the areas in which the
most requests for information were made were: politics (9 libraries), news
reports (7 libraries), and biography (6 libraries).   (149)

■ A study of the University of Delaware during the 1976-77 academic
year *showed that* the percentage of undergraduates among users of online
searching increased greatly when the library subsidized 50% of the total
search costs.   (001)

■ An analysis of records of online bibliographic data base searching at
Florida State University Chemistry Department and Monsanto Textiles Company in Pensacola, Florida (353 searches conducted at FSU
and 345 conducted at Monsanto) reported in 1978 *showed that* the type of
approach to the online search differed in a statistically significant way between FSU and Monsanto (significance level .001) in that 50% of the
FSU searches were exhaustive (i.e., wanted everything available) compared to 33% at Monsanto, while 14% of the FSU searches wished
specific facts or procedures, compared to 39% of the Monsanto searches.
                                                                             (155)

Ibid. . . . *showed that* anticipated use of the search results between FSU and Monsanto differed in some statistically significant ways. 53% of the FSU searches compared to 41% of the Monsanto searches were to keep current in the researcher's own field (significance level .002); 17% of the FSU searches compared to 10% of the Monsanto searches were to keep current in fields related to the researcher's field (significance level .02); 25% of the FSU searches compared to 53% of the Monsanto searches were concerned with procedures, apparatus, or methodology to support ongoing project (significance level .001), and 33% of the FSU searches compared to 5% of the Monsanto searches were for papers for external dissemination (significance level .001). **(155)**

■ A study reported in 1982 at the University of Iowa Health Sciences Library concerning the effect of the patron's presence during MEDLINE searches, based on searches for 100 different patrons (each search was conducted twice by different staff members, once with and once without the patron) and subsequent survey (100% responding) of those patrons, *showed that* there were no statistically significant differences among undergraduate, graduate, or faculty search requesters for precision, recall, or satisfaction rates. **(743)**

■ A study reported in 1982 at Nazareth College of Rochester concerning online bibliographic searching and involving 183 patrons during the period May 1980-June 1981 *showed that* distribution of users was as follows:

undergraduates	40	(21.9% of total)
graduates	105	(57.4% of total)
faculty	28	(15.3% of total)
library	6	(3.3% of total)
administration	4	(2.2% of total)

(300)

Public

■ A 1975-76 study of 359 online searches over a 7-month period using DIALOG in 4 public libraries in the San Francisco Bay area where patrons were charged half the connect costs (in contrast to a study the year before in the same libraries when searches were free) *showed that* the 3 most frequently used data bases were: ERIC (159 or 22.78% searches), NTIS (119 or 17.05% searches), and PSYCHOLOGICAL ABSTRACTS (107 or 15.33% searches). (See 326 for earlier study.) **(332)**

Ibid. . . . *showed that* the number of data bases used per search dropped from an average of 2.3 reported in an earlier study when the searches were

free to an average of 1.9 in the present study when the patron was charged
half the connect costs.   (332)

■ A survey reported in 1976 of 10 academic and public libraries using the
New York Times Information Bank *showed that* the areas in which the
most requests for information were made were: politics (9 libraries), news
reports (7 libraries), and biography (6 libraries).   (149)

School

■ A 1981 study of 53 ninth-grade honors students in science in a suburban
Philadelphia public high school *showed that*, although all the students were
required to undertake online bibliographic searches, 81% did not cite any
materials so retrieved in their bibliographies. The 21 citations that were
from online bibliographic searches accounted for less than 5% of all
bibliographic citations.   (222)

Special

■ A 14-month study during 1972-73 at the Yale Medical Library (serving
the Yale University School of Medicine, the Yale University School of
Nursing, and the Yale-New Haven Hospital) involving 1,466 online search
requests (MEDLINE) from 455 different individuals for the faculty and
professional staff of the Yale-New Haven Medical Center *showed that* the
purposes of the requests were as follows:

research	1,140 (77.8%)	search requests
patient care	221 (15.0%)	search requests
education	105 (7.2%)	search requests	**(714)**

Ibid. . . . *showed that* there were substantial differences in the number of
individuals (455) requesting online searches by professorial rank. The
number of individuals requesting online searches and their percentage of
the faculty at that rank were as follows:

professor (112 faculty)	32 (28.6%) individuals
associate professor (160 faculty)	70 (43.8%) individuals
assistant professor (215 faculty)	81 (37.7%) individuals
instructor (94 faculty)	29 (30.9%) individuals
lecturer (134 faculty)	2 (1.5%) individuals
postdoctoral fellow (319 faculty)	102 (32.0%) individuals
research associate (192 faculty)	28 (14.9%) individuals

Clinical faculty and staff:

clinical professor (23 faculty)	1 (4.4%) individuals
associate clinical professor (105 faculty)	8 (7.6%) individuals
assistant clinical professor (291 faculty)	11 (3.8%) individuals
clinical professor [sic, lecturer?] (105 faculty)	1 (1.0%) individuals
clinical instructor (85 faculty)	4 (4.9%) individuals
resident (257 staff)	79 (30.7%) individuals
intern (25 staff)	7 (28.0%) individuals **(714)**

Ibid. . . . *showed that* there was generally little difference in per capita use by faculty/staff rank for those who used online searches. Specifically, the per capita number of searches requested by those who requested searches in terms of faculty or staff rank was as follows:

professor	2.7 searches each
associate professor	2.8 searches each
assistant professor	3.2 searches each
instructor	2.6 searches each
lecturer	2.5 searches each
postdoctoral fellow	3.4 searches each
research associate	5.9 searches each

Clinical faculty and staff:

clinical professor	3.0 searches each
associate clinical professor	2.5 searches each
assistant clinical professor	5.3 searches each
clinical professor [sic, lecturer?]	2.0 searches each
clinical instructor	4.8 searches each
resident	2.7 searches each
intern	2.0 searches each **(714)**

■ A 1976 survey of physicians associated with hospitals in a 17-county region of upstate New York (Health Service Area V), based on a systematic sample of "approximately 40%" of the physicians in each county (survey size: 592 physicians; responding: 258 or 45.6%), *showed that* physicians working on a medical research project, engaged in medical education programs (as teachers), or with a hospital-based medical practice reported statistically significant greater use of library reference services (including requests for information from the medical librarian) and MEDLARS searches. (All significant at the .05 level or greater.) For example, 69% of the physicians engaged in medical research, 47% of the teachers, and 41% of the hospital-based physicians reported using MEDLARS at least once, compared to 27% of all respondents. Further, 82% of the teachers and 76% of the hospital-based physicians requested information from a medical librarian at least once in the past year, compared to 61% of all respondents.   **(720)**

■ An analysis of records of online bibliographic data base searching at Florida State University Chemistry Department and Monsanto Textiles Company in Pensacola, Florida (353 searches conducted at FSU and 345 conducted at Monsanto) reported in 1978 *showed that* the type of approach to the online search differed in a statistically significant way between FSU and Monsanto (significance level .001) in that 50% of the FSU searches were exhaustive (i.e., wanted everything available) compared to 33% at Monsanto, while 14% of the FSU searches wished specific facts or procedures, compared to 39% of the Monsanto searches.   **(155)**

Ibid. . . . *showed that* anticipated use of the search results between FSU and Monsanto differed in some statistically significant ways. 53% of the FSU searches compared to 41% of the Monsanto searches were to keep current in the researcher's own field (significance level .002); 17% of the FSU searches compared to 10% of the Monsanto searches were to keep current in fields related to the researcher's field (significance level .02); 25% of the FSU searches compared to 53% of the Monsanto searches were concerned with procedures, apparatus, or methodology to support ongoing project (significance level .001) and 33% of the FSU searches compared to 5% of the Monsanto searches were for papers for external dissemination (significance level .001).   **(155)**

■ A 1978 survey of North American health sciences libraries that were users of the National Library of Medicine search services in November 1977 (survey size: 708 libraries; responding: 376; usable: 345 or 48.7%) *showed that*, based on replies from 251 respondents, 16.3% of all MED-LINE searches in 1966-67 were for outside users.   **(724)**

■ A study reported in 1982 at the University of Iowa Health Sciences Library concerning the effect of the patron's presence during MEDLINE searches, based on searches for 100 different patrons (each search was conducted twice by different staff members, once with and once without the patron) and subsequent survey (100% responding) of those patrons, *showed that* there were no statistically significant differences among undergraduate, graduate, or faculty search requesters for precision, recall, or satisfaction rates.   **(743)**

Use Patterns—Outreach and Extension

Academic

■ A 1971-72 study of the articles supplied by the University of Oklahoma Health Sciences Center Library to state health professionals and institutions during a 4-month period, involving 1,756 articles (from 373 journals) sent to individual health professionals and 1,620 articles (from 527 journals) sent to health institutions, *showed that* 69% of the articles sent to individual health professionals went to physicans.   **(409)**

■ A survey reported in 1973 of medical researchers (75% time or more in research) and clinicians (75% time or more in patient care) in 6 area Chicago hospitals who were each offered the medical information services of a professional medical librarian stationed at the John Crerar Library for 7 weeks *showed that* the following was the breakdown of the 141 information requests made:

copies of specific articles	85
reprints of compilations of bibliographies	50
literature searches/answers to specific	
questions	6 **(089)**

■ A survey reported in 1973 of medical researchers (75% or more time in research) and clinicians (75% or more time in patient care) in 6 Chicago area hospitals (sample size: 88) *showed that* 70% of the researchers and 74% of the clinicians used the services of the associated medical librarian less than once a month. In comparison both groups made frequent use of written sources and libraries.   **(089)**

Ibid. . . . *showed that*, while researchers' use of written sources and libraries was significantly greater than that of the clinicians, a Chi Square test of significance showed no significant difference between researchers and clinicians in the frequency with which they used the services of the associated medical librarian.   **(089)**

Ibid. . . . *showed that* the percentages of medical researchers and clinicians using the following sources of information more than 4 times a week were:

	RESEARCHERS	CLINICIANS
textbooks	35	9
scientific books	43	22

continued

	RESEARCHERS	CLINICIANS	
handbooks	32	16	
professional journals	55	56	
technical publications	24	13	
colleagues	54	63	
subordinates	20	36	
superiors	21	31	
librarians	6	0	
libraries	26	10	(089)

Ibid. . . . *showed that* the percentages of medical researchers and clinicians reporting the following 4 sources as the most important factors in forming their information-seeking style were:

	RESEARCHERS	CLINICIANS	
personal (colleagues)	33	50	
written sources	31	17	
general education	23	31	
specific education in the use of information services	13	2	(089)

■ A study reported in 1977 by the University of Oklahoma Health Sciences Center Library of the literature searches performed during a 3-year period (1973-75) for physicians and fourth-year medical students serving a 5-week "preceptorship" with a rural physician (1,775 searches) *showed that* for both the physicians and students the subject category of most requests was "Diseases" (66% of the physicians' searches; 84% of the students' searches) while the subject category of the next most requests for both groups was "Chemicals and Drugs" (27.2% of the physicians' searches; 27.6% of the students' searches).   (716)

■ A survey reported in 1983 of U.S. dental school libraries concerning their service to dental practitioners (population: 60 dental school libraries; responding: 53 or 88%) *showed that* 40 respondents estimated the following monthly use of their library by dental practitioners:

0-10 requests	31 (73.8%) libraries
11-20 requests	7 (16.6%) libraries
21-30 requests	2 (4.8%) libraries

continued

31-40 requests　　0 (0.0%) libraries
41-50 requests　　2 (4.8%) libraries　　　　　(752)

Special

■ A 1971-72 study of the articles supplied by the University of Oklahoma Health Sciences Center Library to state health professionals and institutions during a 4-month period, involving 1,756 articles (from 373 journals) sent to individual health professionals and 1,620 articles (from 527 journals) sent to health institutions, *showed that* 69% of the articles sent to individual health professionals went to physicans. **(409)**

■ A survey reported in 1973 of medical researchers (75% time or more in research) and clinicians (75% time or more in patient care) in 6 area Chicago hospitals who were each offered the medical information services of a professional medical librarian stationed at the John Crerar Library for 7 weeks *showed that* the following was the breakdown of the 141 information requests made:

copies of specific articles	85
reprints of compilations of bibliographies	50
literature searches/answers to specific questions	6

　　　　　　　　　　　　　　　　　　　　　　　　　　(089)

■ A survey reported in 1973 of medical researchers (75% or more time in research) and clinicians (75% or more time in patient care) in 6 Chicago area hospitals (sample size: 88) *showed that* 70% of the researchers and 74% of the clinicians used the services of the associated medical librarian less than once a month. In comparison both groups made frequent use of written sources and libraries. **(089)**

Ibid. . . . *showed that*, while researchers' use of written sources and libraries was significantly greater than that of the clinicians, a Chi Square test of significance showed no significant difference between researchers and clinicians in the frequency with which they used the services of the associated medical librarian. **(089)**

Ibid. . . . *showed that* the percentages of medical researchers and clinicians using the following sources of information more than 4 times a week were:

	RESEARCHERS	CLINICIANS	
textbooks	35	9	
scientific books	43	22	
handbooks	32	16	
professional journals	55	56	
technical publications	24	13	
colleagues	54	63	
subordinates	20	36	
superiors	21	31	
librarians	6	0	
libraries	26	10	(089)

Ibid. . . . *showed that* the percentages of medical researchers and clinicians reporting the following 4 sources as the most important factors in forming their information-seeking style were:

	RESEARCHERS	CLINICIANS	
personal (colleagues)	33	50	
written sources	31	17	
general education	23	31	
specific education in the use of information services	13	2	(089)

■ A study reported in 1977 by the University of Oklahoma Health Sciences Center Library of the literature searches performed during a 3-year period (1973-75) for physicians and fourth-year medical students serving a 5-week "preceptorship" with a rural physician (1,775 searches) *showed that* for both the physicians and students the subject category of most requests was "Diseases" (66% of the physicians' searches; 84% of the students' searches) while the subject category of the next most requests for both groups was "Chemicals and Drugs" (27.2% of the physicians' searches; 27.6% of the students' searches).   **(716)**

■ A survey reported in 1983 of U.S. dental school libraries concerning their service to dental practitioners (population: 60 dental school libraries; responding: 53 or 88%) *showed that* 40 respondents estimated the following monthly use of their library by dental practitioners:

0-10 requests	31 (73.8%) libraries
11-20 requests	7 (16.6%) libraries
21-30 requests	2 (4.8%) libraries
31-40 requests	0 (0.0%) libraries
41-50 requests	2 (4.8%) libraries **(752)**

Use Patterns—Outside Users

Academic

■ A 1968 survey of junior colleges by ACRL's Committee on Community Use of Academic Libraries (sample size: 689; responding: 308 or 45%) *showed that*, on a typical day, 1/3 of the libraries responded that they estimated that they had either no outside users or not more than 1; another 1/3 estimated that 1-4 outsiders visited them on a typical day; 14% estimated the number between 5 and 9; and 10% estimated that more than 10 outsiders a day visited the library.   **(197)**

■ A 1970 survey of psychiatrists randomly selected from the 1968 membership of the American Psychiatric Association (survey size: 394; responding: 290 or 74%) *showed that* overall 27% of the respondents used medical libraries weekly, 69% used them at least monthly, 92% used them at least yearly, and 8% reported never using them. There was considerable variation by practice. For example, 70% of the academicians used medical libraries weekly, compared to 11% of the private practitioners.   **(690)**

Use Patterns—Personal Collections

Academic

■ A 1971 survey of owners (primarily academics) of personal library collections (sample selected from authors of 300 single-author articles published during 1969-70 in 1 of 3 broad areas: humanities, social science, and science; 178 authors responding, of which 175 owned personal collections) *showed that*, of the 5,175 citations made in the 178 articles, 3,055 (59%) came from materials in the authors' personal libraries, 1,320 (25.5%) came from materials in either the departmental or main library, 530 (10.2%) came from materials in libraries in other cities or countries, and 270 (5.2%) came from other sources.   **(258)**

Ibid. . . . *showed that* a physical check of the libraries reported used by 45 (25%) of the respondents indicated that the 244 (21%) of the cited materials that they reported as in the library were indeed actually in the library as well as 592 (88%) of the personal collection works cited by this group.   **(258)**

Ibid. . . . *showed that* the location of cited materials was statistically significantly different for science and social science materials as compared

to humanities materials (significant at the .001 level). Personal collections accounted for 983 (73.9%) of the science materials, 1,366 (73.3%) of the social science materials, and 3,055 (59.0%) of the humanities materials; departmental/main libraries accounted for 278 (20.6%) of the science, 366 (19.6%) of the social science, and 676 (34.2%) of the humanities materials; libraries in other cities and countries accounted for 17 (1.3%) of the science, 33 (1.8%) of the social science, and 480 (24.3%) of the humanities materials; while "other" accounted for 57 (4.2%) of the science, 100 (5.2%) of the social science, and 113 (5.6%) of the humanities materials.
(258)

Use Patterns—Predicted

Public

■ A study based on telephone interviews reported in 1980 of individuals in the Syracuse metropolitan area (sample size: 442; 322 contacted; 202 or 46% participated in the study) *showed that* 6 factors helped predict in a statistically significant way and in descending order of importance public library use. More specifically, 29% of the variance of the variable "use/nonuse of the public library" could be accounted for by the following 6 independent variables, listed in descending order of importance with a cumulative effect as follows (R2 scores): cultural activities (9%), number of magazines read (12%), sex—female (14%), number of professional sources used in the past year (16%), perceived accessibility of library (28%), and use of nonpublic library (29%).   (265)

Ibid. . . . *showed that* of 161 library users 8 factors helped predict in a statistically significant way frequency of library use. More specifically, 36% of the variance of the variable "frequency of contacting the public library" could be accounted for by the following 8 independent variables with a cumulative effect as follows (R2 scores): adult education activities (13%), number of books read (20%), number of children (negatively correlated) (23%), cultural activities (24%), age (26%), number of books in home (28%), awareness of special programs (34%), and perceived accessibility (36%).   (265)

Ibid. . . . *showed that* of 161 library users 2 types of library use were identified. Type 1 use was associated with frequency of visits, use of services, circulation of materials, and importance that the patron placed on use activities. 7 factors helped predict this type of library use. More specifically, 41% of the variance of the variable "type 1 library use" could be accounted for by the following 7 independent variables with a cumulative effect as follows (R2 scores): adult education activities (14%), number of books read (22%), community involvement (26%), sex—female (29%), cultural activities (32%), awareness of special programs (39%), and perceived accessibility (41%). **(265)**

Ibid. . . . *showed that* of 161 library users 2 types of library use were identified. Type 2 use was associated primarily with duration of visit. 6 factors helped predict this type of library use. More specifically, 24% of the variance of the variable "type 2 library use" could be accounted for by the following 6 independent variables with a cumulative effect as follows (R2 scores): adult education activities (8%), sex—female (negatively correlated) (11%), number of children (negatively correlated) (14%), number of books in home (negatively correlated) (17%), age (negatively correlated) (18%), and use of nonpublic library (24%). **(265)**

■ A 1980 survey of 623 adult patrons using the Ramsey County (Minnesota) Public Library during a 5-day period in November *showed that* 4 demographic variables were statistically important factors in accounting for patron evaluation of the library. More specifically, the 4 factors account for 23% of the variance of the library grade scale scores and each had a cumulative effect as follows (R2 scores): age (13%), educational level (inversely correlated) (17%), importance of visit (22%), and style of use—book borrowing in contrast to in-house use (23%). (Significant at the .001 level.) **(270)**

Use Patterns—Reading, General Issues

Public

■ A 1966 survey of 21,385 adult (12 years old or older) public library users in the Baltimore-Washington metropolitan region of Maryland conducted during a 6-week period of patrons entering the library (79.1% of patrons approached filled out the survey instrument) *showed that* the top 5 reasons given for visiting the library were (multiple responses allowed): return books (43.4%), obtain materials or information on a subject (33.5%), pick out general reading (33.5%), obtain a specific book (22.1%), and to bring their child (12.9%). **(301)**

Ibid. . . . *showed that* the reasons given for visiting the library were as follows (multiple responses allowed): personal reading (49.3%), schoolwork (41.7%), for another person (9.1%), for one's job (6.5%), for club activity (2.0%), for other reasons (2.6%), and no answer (5.8%). **(301)**

Ibid. . . . *showed that* the use made of the library was as follows (multiple responses allowed): browsing (43.1%), reference books (22.1%), library catalogs (19.0%), help from a librarian (16.0%), consulting books or magazines (12.4%), read new magazines or newspapers (8.7%), periodical indexes (5.7%), recordings (2.7%), films (0.7%), other (2.0%), and no response (11.1%).   **(301)**

Use Patterns—Reading, Faculty

Academic

■ A 1964 study at the Yale Medical Library involving faculty use of books (survey size: 831 borrowers; responding: 430) during a 5-month period *showed that* 11% of the books were reported used in lecture preparation while 89% appeared to be "associated with research activites." Further, 28% of the books were reported used to "acquire general information to keep up with the field."   **(672)**

Use Patterns—Reading, Students

Academic

■ A 1968 study of graduate students at the University of Michigan concerning their use of periodical literature (sample size: 399; responding: 338 or 85%) *showed that*, of those reporting use of the periodical literature during the term (284), 20% were interested in general/professional reading, 65% were interested in research reading, 7% were interested in both, and 8% did not respond.   **(195)**

Public

■ A sample in 1960 of 4,977 patrons of the Newark Public Library during the Christmas/New Year's holiday period *showed that* the combined total of those using the library for school-related and business-related purposes was about 3 times the number of those coming for general information and recreational reading.   **(066)**

Use Patterns—Reference, General Issues

General

■ A 1970 survey of psychiatrists randomly selected from the 1968 membership of the American Psychiatric Association (survey size: 394;

responding: 290 or 74%) *showed that* library reference services were used as follows (multiple responses allowed):

guidance by the librarian	40% respondents	
recent acquisitions lists	38% respondents	
requested bibliographies	35% respondents	
MEDLARS	11% respondents	
other	11% respondents	**(690)**

Ibid. . . . *showed that* the 4 most frequently mentioned prime methods of searching the literature (out of 11) were:

library reference services	23% respondents
abstracts and indexes	17% respondents
bibliographies	17% respondents
review articles	16% respondents

Use of the card catalog as a prime method of searching the literature was reported by 5% of the respondents, while browsing as a prime method was reported by 4% of the respondents. **(690)**

Academic

■ An analysis of reference questions asked during fiscal year 1977-78 at the Engineering, Mathematics and Science Library at the University of Waterloo (Ontario), using step categories where each step represents a "distinct and definable judgment leading to a decision, action or recommendation" and where roughly 1 step corresponds to directional questions, 2 steps corresponds to ready reference questions, and multistep corresponds to reference questions, *showed that* of 5,761 questions that it was possible to code out of 5,969 asked: 1,800 (31%) were 1-step, 2,714 (47%) were 2-step, and 1,247 (22%) were multistep. **(154)**

Ibid. . . . *showed that* the proportion of 1-step, 2-step, and multistep questions asked by undergraduates was 37%, 42%, and 21%, respectively, that of graduates was 28%, 52%, and 20%, respectively, and that of faculty was 24%, 51%, and 25%, respectively. **(154)**

■ An analysis of reference questions asked during selected periods throughout the major part of the academic year 1967-77 at Albion College Library, using step categories where each step represents a "distinct and definable judgment leading to a decision, action or recommendation" and where roughly 1 step corresponds to directional questions, 2 steps corresponds to ready reference questions, and multistep corresponds to reference questions, *showed that* of 1,245 questions 753 (60%) were 1-step, 271

(22%) were 2-step, and 221 (18%) were multistep.   **(154)**

■ A study reported in 1982 of 14,026 reference questions asked during randomly selected periods over 40 weeks at Virginia Polytechnic Institute and State University *showed that* 6,374 (45.5%) were locational, 3,387 (24.1%) were instructional, 2,879 (20.5%) were reference, and 1,386 (9.9%) were miscellaneous (how to operate equipment, special permissions, etc.).   **(160)**

Ibid. . . . *showed that*, of the locational questions, the location of publications (54.6%) was the most frequent type of question, followed by finding items not in the stacks (20.6%) and seeking directions to facilities (rest rooms, drinking fountains) (16.4%).   **(160)**

Ibid. . . . *showed that*, of the instructional questions, the most frequent category was how to use bibliographic tools (48.8%), followed by how to find journals in the library (33.3%)   **(160)**

Ibid. . . . *showed that* the 20.5% reference questions consisted of 11.3% ready reference questions, 8.5% regular reference, and 0.7% in-depth reference questions.   **(160)**

Public

■ A questionnaire survey of 3,500 public library cardholders in 5 medium-sized Pennsylvania cities in conjunction with interviews of a randomly selected sample of householders in 1 city by the Institute of Public Administration (at Pennsylvania State University) under contract to the Pennsylvania State Library in 1965 *showed that* the major service provided by the library was book borrowing (60% of respondents), while reference/information was the next most important use made of the library (26% of respondents).   **(084)**

■ A 1966 survey of 21,385 adult (12 years old or older) public library users in the Baltimore-Washington metropolitan region of Maryland conducted during a 6-week period of patrons entering the library (79.1% of patrons approached filled out the survey instrument) *showed that* the top 5 reasons given for visiting the library were (multiple responses allowed): return books (43.4%), obtain materials or information on a subject (33.5%), pick out general reading (33.5%), obtain a specific book (22.1%), and to bring their child (12.9%).   **(301)**

Ibid. . . . *showed that* the use made of the library was as follows (multiple responses allowed): browsing (43.1%), reference books (22.1%), library catalogs (19.0%), help from a librarian (16.0%), consulting books or magazines (12.4%), read new magazines or newspapers (8.7%), periodical indexes (5.7%), recordings (2.7%), films (0.7%), other (2.0%), and no response (11.1%). **(301)**

■ A 1979 telephone survey of 1,046 New Orleans residents over the age of 12 *showed that* the Central Library was used more for reference and research, while the branches were used more for recreational reading. 43.7% of Central's use was for information other than school, 34% for school, and 19.3% for pleasure, while the branches were used 26.9% for information other than school, 38.7% for school, and 33.4% for pleasure. **(166)**

■ An attempt reported in 1982 to establish 4 input measures and 4 output measures for public libraries, based on published statistical reports for 301 New Jersey public libraries over a 6-year period (1974-79) and survey data for 96 public libraries in New Jersey, *showed that* (per capita based on population in library's service area):

INPUT MEASURES

The proportion of budget spent on materials averaged 19.9% with a standard deviation of .081 (based on 301 libraries).

The new volumes per capita averaged .181 with a standard deviation of .097 (based on 301 libraries).

The periodical titles per capita averaged .0094 with a standard deviation of .0054 (based on 301 libraries).

The circulation per volume averaged 1.79 with a standard deviation of .77 (based on 301 libraries).

OUTPUT MEASURES

The circulation per capita averaged 5.04 with a standard deviation of 3.07 (based on 301 libraries).

The patron visits per capita averaged 2.82 with a standard deviation of 1.82 (based on 96 libraries).

The reference questions per capita averaged 1.12 with a standard deviation of .79 (based on 96 libraries).

The in-library uses of materials per capita averaged 2.29 with a standard deviation of 2.02 (based on 96 libraries). **(576)**

Special

■ A 1970 survey of psychiatrists randomly selected from the 1968 membership of the American Psychiatric Association (survey size: 394; responding: 290 or 74%) *showed that* library reference services were used as follows (multiple responses allowed):

guidance by the librarian	40% respondents	
recent acquisitions lists	38% respondents	
requested bibliographies	35% respondents	
MEDLARS	11% respondents	
other	11% respondents	(690)

Ibid. . . . *showed that* the 4 most frequently mentioned prime methods of searching the literature (out of 11) were:

library reference services	23% respondents
abstracts and indexes	17% respondents
bibliographies	17% respondents
review articles	16% respondents

Use of the card catalog as a prime method of searching the literature was reported by 5% of the respondents, while browsing as a prime method was reported by 4% of the respondents. **(690)**

■ A 1976 survey of physicians associated with hospitals in a 17-county region of upstate New York (Health Service Area V), based on a systematic sample of "approximately 40%" of the physicians in each county (survey size: 592 physicians; responding: 258 or 45.6%), *showed that* the 3 most frequently used sources of information as reported by the physicians were (in descending order of importance):

1. papers in journals
2. personal contact with colleagues
3. books

As an information source used by physicians, "library reference services" ranked 7 out of a list of 19. **(720)**

Ibid. . . . *showed that,* of the 61% physicians who had asked a medical librarian for work-related information within the past year, 61.8% rated the information received as "adequate," 28.9% as "more than adequate," and 9.2% as "less than adequate." Further, 84.9% of the physicians had requested the information themselves, while 15.1% had used an intermediary (e.g., secretary). **(720)**

■ A 1975-77 study of the use of a drug information service (including closed-circuit TV capability for sending answers) originating from the Health Sciences Library at the University of Cincinnati to provide information about drugs, chemicals, and poisons to health professionals in 14 local hospitals (2,294 questions researched; TV used to help provide the answer in 460 instances) *showed that* types of users were as follows:

pharmacists accounted for 31.3% of the total queries and 29.3% of the queries with a TV response;

physicians accounted for 25.8% of the total queries and 22.6% of the queries with a TV response;

nurses accounted for 21.2% of the total queries and 24.8% of the queries with a TV response;

medical students accounted for 2.4% of the total queries and 3.5% of the queries with a TV response;

"other" accounted for 22.0% of the total queries and 24.1% of the queries with a TV response. **(422)**

Ibid. . . . *showed that* the 3 main uses of the drug information system were to: select patient treatment approach (50.0% of all cases; 57.6% of the cases where TV response was used), explain observations in a patient (15.2% of all cases; 15.7% of the cases where TV response was used), and add to personal knowledge (13.0% of all cases; 9.2% of the cases where TV response was used). **(422)**

Use Patterns—Reference, Faculty

Academic

■ A survey reported in 1973 of the faculty of 6 institutions of higher education in the California system of state colleges and universities involving 955 full-time faculty of the colleges (694 or 73% responding) *showed that* faculty from the humanities and education had a higher level of awareness of specific library reference services than other teaching areas, although only in relation to the science faculty was the difference statistically significant. **(663)**

Ibid. . . . *showed that* the 3 reference services with which the most faculty were acquainted were:

advice & assistance in use of library 95%
interlibrary borrowing 85%
library instruction for classes 65%

while the 3 references services with which the least faculty were acquainted were:

> lists of reference sources for specific classes   17%
> answer requiring a search (i.e., answering
> questions that required a librarian to spend
> some time searching for the answer)   22%
> answer to a factual question by phone   36%   **(663)**

Ibid. . . . *showed that* the reference services that teaching faculty valued most highly (top 5) were:

	# REPORTING FAVORABL ATTITUDE
advice & assistance in use of the library	89%
interlibrary borrowing	89%
library bulletins and handbooks	87%
library instruction for classes	81%
answer to a factual question	81%

while the 2 reference services that the faculty valued least were:

> lists of reference sources for classes   54%
> answer requiring a search (i.e., answering
> questions that required a librarian to
> spend some time searching for the answer)   60%   **(663)**

Ibid. . . . *showed that* the average teaching faculty member responding to the questionnaire was aware of only 50% of the reference services available to him from his college library.   **(663)**

■ An analysis of reference questions asked during fiscal year 1977-78 at the Engineering, Mathematics and Science Library at the University of Waterloo (Ontario), using step categories where each step represents a "distinct and definable judgment leading to a decision, action or recommendation" and where roughly 1 step corresponds to directional questions, 2 steps corresponds to ready reference questions, and multistep corresponds to reference questions, *showed that* the proportion of 1-step, 2-step, and multistep questions asked by undergraduates was 37%, 42%, and 21%, respectively, that of graduates was 28%, 52%, and 20%, respectively, and that of faculty was 24%, 51%, and 25%, respectively.   **(154)**

■ An analysis of reference questions asked during selected periods throughout the major part of the academic year 1967-77 at Albion College

Library, using step categories where each step represents a "distinct and definable judgment leading to a decision, action or recommendation" and where roughly 1 step corresponds to directional questions, 2 steps corresponds to ready reference questions, and multistep corresponds to reference questions, *showed that* the proportion of 1-step, 2-step, and multistep questions asked by undergraduates was 62%, 22%, and 16%, respectively, while that of faculty was 41%, 25%, and 34%, respectively.

(154)

Use Patterns—Reference, Students

Academic

■ A 1975 telephone survey of a random stratified sample of undergraduates, graduates, and professional students at the University of Chicago to determine awareness of reference services (population: 7,940; sample size: 124; responding: 98) *showed that*, although 100% of the respondents had used the Regenstein Library, 22 (22.4%) reported that they did not know what the reference department did and 33 (34%) reported that they had never used reference services there.   **(151)**

Ibid. . . . *showed that* 75 (75.5%) of the respondents had not used Regenstein reference services in the previous month (October/November), that 10 (10.2%) had used reference services there once in the previous month, and 8 (8.2%) reported using the reference services twice in the previous month.   **(151)**

Ibid. . . . *showed that* out of the 12 reference services that were available in Regenstein, only 7 were known by 50% or more of the respondents.
(151)

■ An analysis of reference questions asked during fiscal year 1977-78 at the Engineering, Mathematics and Science Library at the University of Waterloo (Ontario), using step categories where each step represents a "distinct and definable judgment leading to a decision, action or recommendation" and where roughly 1 step corresponds to directional questions, 2 steps corresponds to ready reference questions, and multistep corresponds to reference questions, *showed that* the proportion of 1-step, 2-step, and multistep questions asked by undergraduates was 37%, 42%, and 21%, respectively, that of graduates was 28%, 52%, and 20%,

respectively, and that of faculty was 24%, 51%, and 25%, respectively.
(154)

■ An analysis of reference questions asked during selected periods
throughout the major part of the academic year 1967-77 at Albion College
Library, using step categories where each step represents a "distinct and
definable judgment leading to a decision, action or recommendation" and
where roughly 1 step corresponds to directional questions, 2 steps corresponds to ready reference questions, and multistep corresponds to reference questions, *showed that* the proportion of 1-step, 2-step, and multistep
questions asked by undergraduates was 62%, 22%, and 16%, respectively,
while that of faculty was 41%, 25%, and 34%, respectively.   (154)

Use Patterns—Reference Tools

Academic

■ A survey reported in 1969 of a representative sample of agricultural
economists in universities and the USDA (sample size: 590; response rate:
379 or 64%) *showed that* 23.9% reported that they never use the
Bibliography of Agriculture, 40.8% report never using *Index of Economic
Journals*, 41.1% report never using *Journal of Economic Abstracts*, 50.0%
report never using *Biological and Agricultural Index*, 58.0% report never
using *World Agricultural Economics and Rural Sociology Abstracts*, 72.7%
report never using *International Bibliography of Economics*, 76.2% report
never using *Biological Abstracts*, and 79.8% report never using *PAIS
Bulletin*.   (245)

■ A 1973 survey of physicists in 6 universities of the greater Boston area
(Boston University, Brandeis, Brown, Harvard, MIT, and Northeastern)
to determine how they meet their information needs (sample size: 339;
responding: 179 or 52.8%) *showed that* at all universities physicists rated
formal publications (i.e., journals primarily) their most important source
of information and reference materials their least important source of
information, with semiformal publications, meetings and conferences, and
informal oral communication in between.   (404)

■ A study in 1975 of business students (undergraduate and graduate) at
the University of Delaware, University of Maryland, and Wright State
University *showed that* they were infrequent readers of most business
periodicals. For example, 21% of the undergrads and 8% of the M.B.A.'s

reported never having read the *Wall Street Journal*. **(049)**

Ibid. . . . *showed that* the students felt knowing how to use the library was necessary for academic success but not career success. **(049)**

Ibid. . . . *showed that* they were infrequent users of almost all the recognized and commonly available sources of marketing information. For example, over 10% of the students reported that they had never heard of *Business Periodical Index*. **(049)**

Special

■ A 1970 study of physicians in 14 hospitals and medical institutions in the Toronto metropolitan area concerning self-education (survey size: 1,050 physicians; responding: 390 or 37.1%) *showed that* the following numbers were *not* acquainted with the following tools:

Index Medicus	6.0% of total	
Excerpta Medica	21.0% of total	
Science Citation Index	84.0% of total	
Pandex	91.5% of total	**(634)**

Use Patterns—Research, Faculty

Academic

■ A survey in 1959 of 8,660 library patrons during 1 week at the 4 largest MIT libraries (General and Humanities, Science, Engineering, and Dewey) during selected hours *showed that* 46.0% of all patrons were undergraduates who reported spending 71.9% of their time for class preparation and 14.9% time on research; 35.4% were graduate students who spent 52.4% time in class preparation and 37.2% time in research; and 11.8% were faculty/staff who spent 17.1% time in class preparation and 56.4% time in research. **(115)**

■ A 1964 study at the Yale Medical Library involving faculty use of books (survey size: 831 borrowers; responding: 430) during a 5-month period *showed that* 11% of the books were reported used in lecture preparation, while 89% appeared to be "associated with research activites." Further, 28% of the books were reported used to "acquire general information to keep up with the field." **(672)**

■ A survey reported in 1970 of library patrons at Purdue University (6,568 sampled; 6,323 usable responses) and statistically analyzed by Chi Square tests *showed that* the 3 patron groupings (faculty, graduate, and undergraduate) gave statistically significantly different response rates for their primary reasons for visiting the library (significant at the .001 level). The largest category reported by faculty for library visits was research for a publishable paper or book (21%); for graduate students the largest category was to find and read material required by a course (30%); for undergraduates the largest category was to do homework with their own books (50+%).   **(202)**

Special

■ A 1964 study at the Yale Medical Library involving faculty use of books (survey size: 831 borrowers; responding: 430) during a 5-month period *showed that* 11% of the books were reported used in lecture preparation, while 89% appeared to be "associated with research activites." Further, 28% of the books were reported used to "acquire general information to keep up with the field."   **(672)**

Use Patterns—Research, Students

Academic

■ A survey in 1959 of 8,660 library patrons during 1 week at the 4 largest MIT libraries (General and Humanities, Science, Engineering, and Dewey) during selected hours *showed that* 46.0% of all patrons were undergraduates who reported spending 71.9% of their time for class preparation and 14.9% time on research; 35.4% were graduate students who spent 52.4% time in class preparation and 37.2% time in research; and 11.8% were faculty/staff who spent 17.1% time in class preparation and 56.4% time in research.   **(115)**

■ A 1968 study of graduate students at the University of Michigan concerning their use of periodical literature (sample size: 399; responding: 338 or 85%) *showed that* approximately 78% of the students use the library about once a week, while 61% reported using the periodical literature about once a week.   **(195)**

Ibid. . . . *showed that*, of those reporting use of the periodical literature during the term (284), 20% were interested in general/professional reading, 65% were interested in research reading, 7% were interested in both, and 8% did not respond.   **(195)**

Use Patterns—SDI Services

General

■ A 1970 survey by the Canadian National Science Library of users of its nationwide SDI system, involving bibliographies produced from the Chemical Abstracts Service, the Institute for Scientific Information, and the British Institution of Electrical Engineers (survey size: 604; responding: 406 or 67.2%) *showed that* the numbers of colleagues with whom 377 respondents reported sharing the results of the SDI searches were as follows: no sharing (118 or 29.1%), share with 1 to 5 colleagues (248 or 61.1%), share with over 5 colleagues (34 or 8.4%).   **(536)**

■ A 1970 survey of psychiatrists randomly selected from the 1968 membership of the American Psychiatric Association (survey size: 394; responding: 290 or 74%) *showed that* library reference services were used as follows (multiple responses allowed):

guidance by the librarian	40% respondents	
recent acquisitions lists	38% respondents	
requested bibliographies	35% respondents	
MEDLARS	11% respondents	
other	11% respondents	**(690)**

Academic

■ A comparison in 1962 at a midwestern university of the book titles that faculty had checked out with the monthly list of new acquisitions that those faculty had elected to receive *showed that* within 30 days 7 titles out of 232 were charged out from 1 monthly list and 15 titles out of 280 were charged out from a second monthly list.   **(130)**

■ A 1974 study of current awareness methods used by Canadian academic chemists in 34 institutions (survey size: 170; responding: 134 or 80%) *showed that* only 19% of the respondents subscribed to a selective dissemination of information service. Among the reasons given for not subscribing were ignorance of the existence of such services (15% respondents), not needed because of the nature of their work (15%), cost (25%), and personal preference (45%).   **(636)**

Ibid. . . . *showed that* the time spent on current awareness activities averaged 2-5 hours per week, with a distribution as follows:

0-1 hours per week	7 (5.2%)	respondents	
1-2 hours per week	30 (22.4%)	respondents	
2-5 hours per week	53 (39.6%)	respondents	
5-10 hours per week	38 (28.4%)	respondents	
10-20 hours per week	6 (4.5%)	respondents	**(636)**

■ A survey reported in 1974 at the Hershey Medical Center Library of Pennsylvania State University comparing medical faculty views of a manually generated selective dissemination of information service with SDILINE (Selective Dissemination of Information Online, from the National Library of Medicine) *showed that* SDILINE was not used as the only source of current awareness. Of the 13 faculty users of SDILINE, 55.5% reported use of *Current Contents* as well, and of the 8 faculty users who had used both systems, 66.7% reported that SDILINE was used as a backup to other forms of current awareness. **(705)**

■ A study reported in 1975 of a pilot SDI program at the University of Arkansas, Little Rock, involving 9 faculty members who had received grants for 7 different research studies *showed that*, of 1,188 citations sent to the faculty members, 717 (60.4%) were directly used in the research projects, while an additional 255 citations (21%) were of general interest to the researchers but not incorporated into the research projects. **(145)**

■ A study reported in 1978 at Indiana University, Bloomington, of materials requested through a delivery service to faculty in the political science and economics departments during a 32-month period (October 1972-June 1975), involving 39 political scientists and 14 economists (40-50% of the faculty in the departments) and 5,478 articles from 620 different journals and newspapers, *showed that*, when the delivery service supplied copies of contents pages, this current awareness service and was used by 40 (64%) of the faculty, while materials listed in the contents pages accounted for 30.3% of all materials requested on the delivery service. **(421)**

Public

■ A 1973 experimental project with SDI service in the Mideastern Michigan Library Cooperative (a random sample of 2,498 were invited to participate; 96 responded) *showed that* the most popular SDI topics were fiction with the following headings: fiction with a twentieth-century setting (50%), mystery-suspense (43%), historical fiction (38%). The 3 most popular nonfiction categories were: drawing and decorative arts (35%), recreation (30%), and psychology (30%). **(144)**

■ A 1973 study of an experimental SDI service in the Mideastern Michigan Library Cooperative (sample size: 96; responding: 42 or 44%) *showed that* 43% of the respondents indicated they found the service "very useful," while an additional 45% reported that they found the service "of some use." 52% indicated that they thought that at least half of the books suggested fit their interests. **(144)**

Special

■ A survey reported in 1974 at the Hershey Medical Center Library of Pennsylvania State University comparing medical faculty views of a manually generated selective dissemination of information service with SDILINE (Selective Dissemination of Information Online, from the National Library of Medicine) *showed that* SDILINE was not used as the only source of current awareness. Of the 13 faculty users of SDILINE, 55.5% reported use of *Current Contents* as well, and of the 8 faculty users who had used both systems, 66.7% reported that SDILINE was used as a backup to other forms of current awareness. **(705)**

■ A survey reported in 1978 of the current awareness service provided at the General Electric Corporate Research and Development library (Schenectady, New York), involving the Chemical Abstracts CONDENSATES data base (sample size: 65; responding: 60.0% [no raw number given]) and the Engineering Index COMPENDEX data base (sample size: 68; responding: 38.2% [no raw number given]), *showed that* 59.0% of the CONDENSATES users and 50.0% of the COMPENDEX users reported their literature searching time decreased, 20.5% of the CONDENSATES users and 38.5% of the COMPENDEX users reported no change in literature searching time, and 10.3% of the CONDENSATES users and none of the COMPENDEX users reported that their literature search time had increased. The remainder did not reply to the question. Further, 46.2% of both groups reported that they were reading more articles. **(424)**

Ibid. . . . *showed that* 76.9% of the CONDENSATES users and 41.0% of the COMPENDEX users shared their profile with colleagues, 61.5% of the CONDENSATES users and 69.2% of the COMPENDEX users told others about the service, and 12.8% of the CONDENSATES users and 7.7% of the COMPENDEX users suggested names of potential users. **(424)**

Use Patterns—Studying, General Issues

Public

■ A 1966 survey of 21,385 adult (12 years old or older) public library users in the Baltimore-Washington metropolitan region of Maryland conducted during a 6-week period of patrons entering the library (79.1% of patrons approached filled out the survey instrument) *showed that* the reasons given for visiting the library were as follows (multiple responses allowed): personal reading (49.3%), schoolwork (41.7%), for another person (9.1%), for one's job (6.5%), for club activity (2.0%), for other reasons (2.6%), and no answer (5.8%).   **(301)**

Use Patterns—Studying, Students

Academic

■ A survey reported in 1970 of library patrons at Purdue University (6,568 sampled; 6,323 usable responses) and statistically analyzed by Chi Square tests *showed that* the 3 patron groupings (faculty, graduate, and undergraduate) gave statistically significantly different response rates for their primary reasons for visiting the library (significant at the .001 level). The largest category reported by faculty for library visits was research for a publishable paper or book (21%); for graduate students the largest category was to find and read material required by a course (30%); for undergraduates the largest category was to do homework with their own books (50+%).   **(202)**

Use Patterns—Subject Areas

Public

■ A 1966 survey of 21,385 adult (12 years old or older) public library users in the Baltimore-Washington metropolitan region of Maryland conducted during a 6-week period of patrons entering the library (79.1% of patrons approached filled out the survey instrument) *showed that*, of the 6,212 respondents who were seeking materials or information on a subject and who named a subject, 45.2% reported a social science subject, 30.6% reported a humanities subject, and 24.2% reported a science/technology subject. The 2 main social science subjects were history (40.7%) and business/economics (14.8%); the 2 main humanities subjects were literature (53.8%) and art (24.8%); and the 2 main science and technology subjects were engineering (17.5%) and medicine (12.2%).   **(301)**

4.

Collection Maintenance

Binding

Academic

■ An investigation reported in 1960 into the comparative differences between microfilm and bound periodical volumes at Colby Junior College (New London, New Hampshire) and Abraham Baldwin College (Tifton, Georgia) *showed that* the comparative cost of microfilm purchase vs. binding costs for a sample of 5 journals was almost exactly equal, $40.37 in binding costs and $41.00 for microfilm purchase.   **(107)**

■ A study reported in 1976 at Southern Illinois University, Carbondale, of science/technology periodicals (population: 3,948 titles; sample size: 1,519 titles or 38%) for the period 1968-72 *showed that* the "typical" science/technology journal was issued once each 51 days and generated "about" 1.5 bound volumes each year.   **(415)**

■ A study reported in 1978 at the undergraduate library of the University of Tennessee, Knoxville, of patron success rate in finding books over a 5-week period (sample size: 1,010 patrons; responding: 503 or 49.5%, involving 2,375 titles) *showed that* the 828 titles not available involved 1,025 volumes. The 2 main reasons for unavailability were: volumes checked out (729 or 71.1%) and volumes unaccounted for (208 or 20.3%). Binding accounted for 22 (2.1%) volumes, while interlibrary loan accounted for 2 (0.2%) volumes.   **(466)**

■ A 1978 survey of major biomedical libraries (primarily those serving accredited medical schools) (survey size: 120 libraries; responding: 88 or 73%) *showed that* using microform copy in lieu of binding hard copy volumes of abstracts and indexes was not common practice. Only 1 (1%) library reported using microforms in lieu of binding all volumes of abstracts and indexes, 7 (8%) libraries reported using microforms in lieu of binding some abstracts and indexes, while 78 (89%) libraries reported using no microforms in lieu of binding abstracts or indexes. 2 (2%) libraries did not reply.   **(726)**

■ A 1980 survey of law school libraries with collections in excess of 175,000 volumes (sample size: 50; responding: 37 or 70%) *showed that* the degree to which periodical titles were bound was as follows:

40-60% bound	2 libraries
80-89% bound	6 libraries
90-95% bound	13 libraries

continued

96-100% bound	14 libraries	
no answer	2 libraries	**(369)**

Special

■ A 1978 survey of major biomedical libraries (primarily those serving accredited medical schools) (survey size: 120 libraries; responding: 88 or 73%) *showed that* using microform copy in lieu of binding hard copy volumes of abstracts and indexes was not common practice. Only 1 (1%) library reported using microforms in lieu of binding all volumes of abstracts and indexes, 7 (8%) libraries reported using microforms in lieu of binding some abstracts and indexes, while 78 (89%) libraries reported using no microforms in lieu of binding abstracts or indexes. 2 (2%) libraries did not reply.   **(726)**

■ A 1980 survey of law school libraries with collections in excess of 175,000 volumes (sample size: 50; responding: 37 or 70%) *showed that* the degree to which periodical titles were bound was as follows:

40-60% bound	2 libraries	
80-89% bound	6 libraries	
90-95% bound	13 libraries	
96-100% bound	14 libraries	
no answer	2 libraries	**(369)**

Copyright

Academic

■ A 1979 survey of 3 types of health sciences libraries (U.S. academic medical libraries, special health science libraries, and hospital libraries) concerning compliance with the copyright law (survey size: 273 libraries; responding: 157 or 57%) *showed that* the number of libraries by library type that reported that the copyright law had had no effect on collection maintenance was as follows:

academic libraries	73 (82%) libraries
hospital libraries	35 (83%) libraries
special libraries	13 (87%) libraries

while the number of libraries by library type that reported that the copyright law had had no effect on library service was as follows:

academic libraries	58 (65%) libraries	
hospital libraries	28 (65%) libraries	
special libraries	12 (80%) libraries	**(736)**

Special

■ A 1979 survey of 3 types of health sciences libraries (U.S. academic medical libraries, special health science libraries, and hospital libraries) concerning compliance with the copyright law (survey size: 273 libraries; responding: 157 or 57%) *showed that* that the number of libraries by library type that reported that the copyright law had had no effect on collection maintenance was as follows:

academic libraries   73 (82%) libraries
hospital libraries   35 (83%) libraries
special libraries   13 (87%) libraries

while the number of libraries by library type that reported that the copyright law had had no effect on library service was as follows:

academic libraries   58 (65%) libraries
hospital libraries   28 (65%) libraries
special libraries   12 (80%) libraries   **(736)**

Inventory Procedures

Academic

■ A 1973 study in the Art and Architecture library at Washington University involving a collection of 50,202 volumes and lacking any exit control (sample size: 594 volumes) *showed that* 153 or 25.5% of the collection was missing. Additional searches during a subsequent 8-month period reduced the loss rate to 55 (9.2%), while by the end of a 2-year period the loss rate had dropped to 33 (5.5%) volumes. At the 95% confidence level, this adjusted loss rate ranged between 8% and 4% of the collection.   **(444)**

■ A study reported in 1976 at Washington University's central library (Olin Library) involving book loss in a collection of 850,000 volumes protected by a manual check of exiting patrons (sample size: 2,949 volumes) *showed that* additional searches during a subsequent 10-month period located almost half of the missing volumes, leaving only 86 (2.91%) of the collection missing. At the 95% confidence level, this adjusted loss rate ranged between 2.7% and 1.7% of the collection.
(444)

Ibid. . . . *showed that* 161 (5.45%) volumes could not be found. With a 95% confidence level, the loss rate ranged between 6.3% and 4.7% of the collection.   **(444)**

■ A study reported in 1977 of book loss at Northwestern University *showed that* sampling to determine book loss may provide an artifically high loss figure. An inventory of 110,000 high-use books at Northwestern University revealed a loss figure of 1.8%; a sample of the same collection indicated a loss rate between 2.2 and 4.0% with a 95% confidence interval. **(004)**

■ A study reported in 1982 at Washington State University of a relatively homogeneous book collection (a recent social science collection of 100,000 volumes) *showed that* patron reports of missing items in a collection subject area were the strongest single predictor of the actual number of missing items in that area with an r2 = .4049 (significant at the .01 level). **(062)**

Ibid. . . . *showed that* circulation rate of a collection subject area was the second strongest predictor of the actual number of missing items in that area with an r2 = .3187 (significant at the .01 level). **(062)**

Ibid. . . . *showed that* combining patron reports of missing items in a collection subject area with the circulation rate of that subject area produced a combined predictor of the actual number of missing items in that area that was a more powerful predictor than either of the 2 factors singly with an r2 = .4892 (significant at the .01 level). **(062)**

Public

■ The experience of the Huston Public Library in inventorying its collection (236,519 titles) *showed that* a 2-man team comparing the shelflist card to item on the shelf could check 42 volumes per man per minute. **(097)**

Ibid. . . . *showed that* catalog cards could be pulled from the catalog at the rate of 40 cards per hour per person. **(097)**

■ A full inventory of the Main Library of the Huston Public Library after a sample had been used to re-estimate missing volumes in a collection of 236,519 titles *showed that* the sample overestimated volume losses by 10% (sample projected losses = 41% vols.; actual losses = 31% vols.) and title losses by 15% (sample projected losses = 35%; actual losses = 20%). The discrepancy was felt to be due to using many individuals unfamiliar with the shelflist to take the sample rather than using a single knowledgeable invidideual. **(097)**

Loss Rates—General Issues

Academic

■ Studies undertaken in the 1971-73 period at Washington University in various libraries (none with exit control) concerning loss rates *showed that*:

the biology collection (27,218 volumes) had a loss rate over a 2-year period of 0.70% per year;

the Chemistry Library (16,719 volumes) had an annual loss rate in 1973 of 0.13%;

the earth sciences collection (19,632 volumes) had an annual loss rate between 1972-73 of 0.54%;

and the East Asian collection (60,108 volumes) showed an annual loss rate of 0.19%.   **(444)**

■ A 1973 study in the Art and Architecture library at Washington University involving a collection of 50,202 volumes and lacking any exit control (sample size: 594 volumes) *showed that* 153 or 25.5% of the collection was missing. Additional searches during a subsequent 8-month period reduced the loss rate to 55 (9.2%), while by the end of a 2-year period the loss rate had dropped to 33 (5.5%) volumes. At the 95% confidence level, this adjusted loss rate ranged between 8% and 4% of the collection.   **(444)**

■ A study reported in 1976 at Washington University's central library (Olin Library) involving book loss in a collection of 850,000 volumes protected by a manual check of exiting patrons (sample size: 2,949 volumes) *showed that* additional searches during a subsequent 10-month period located almost half of the missing volumes, leaving only 86 (2.91%) of the collection missing. At the 95% confidence level, this adjusted loss rate ranged between 2.7% and 1.7% of the collection.   **(444)**

■ A study at the University of Rhode Island reported in 1977, after the installation of an electronic security system in 1973, *showed that* the number of interlibrary loan requests for missing pages in mutilated items increased from 55 in 1973-74, to 91 in 1974-75, to 60 in the first half of 1975-76.   **(003)**

■ A 1977 study at the Lee Library of Brigham Young University concerning the collection loss rate in a collection of over 1 million volumes (sample size: 384 items selected from the shelflist) *showed that* "over the years of its operation" its loss rate based on a single search of the collection totaled 4.95% (19 items). (Sample results correct ±.05 with a confidence interval of .95.)   **(529)**

■ A 1977 study of the language and linguistics collection (Dewey 400's) of the Lee Library of Brigham Young University concerning the collection loss rate (sample size: 384 items selected from a shelflist of "approximately 19,000" cards) *showed that* its loss rate based on a single search of the collection totaled 5.73% (22 items). (Sample results correct ±.05 with a confidence interval of .95.)   **(529)**

■ A study reported in 1977 at the State University of New York, Stony Brook, involving an inventory of 320,000 volumes over a 3-year period (1973-76) *showed that* over a 13-year period 19,253 volumes (16,467 titles) or "approximately 6%" were missing.   **(450)**

■ A study reported in 1978 at the Van Pelt Library of the University of Pennsylvania comparing collection loss rates before and after installation of an electronic security system, based on a sample size of 1,391 items in the first case and a sample size of 849 in the second case, *showed that* the overall annual loss rate in the circulating collection dropped from .79% in 1971, before installation of the security system, to .48% in 1976, 2 years after installation of the security system. This was a drop in the overall annual loss rate of 39% during a period when the circulation rate increased by 320%.   **(464)**

■ A study reported in 1980 over a 6-year period (1973-78) at West Virginia University main library concerning the effect of switching from closed to open stacks in 1976 with a collection of just under 1 million volumes of primarily humanities and social science materials *showed that* loss rate and disorder did not appear to increase under the open stack system. Specifically, for books requested on the delivery system, the number that could not be accounted for during the closed stack system (1974, no number of requests given) was 15.0%, while 2 studies of books requested on the delivery system after the stacks were opened showed 11.2% unavailable in 1977 and 12.2% unavailable in 1978 (no number of requests given).   **(484)**

Public

■ A report published in 1974 of a full inventory of the Main Library of the Huston Public Library to re-estimate missing volumes in a collection of 236,519 titles after a sample had been previously used *showed that* the sample overestimated volume losses by 10% (sample projected losses = 41% vols.; actual losses = 31% vols.) and title losses by 15% (sample projected losses = 35%; actual losses = 20%). The discrepancy was felt to be due to using many individuals unfamiliar with the shelflist to take the sample rather than using a single knowledgeable invididual. **(097)**

Loss Rates—Books

Academic

■ A sample of the total library holdings at Ohio State University libraries in May 1967 (sample size: 5,742 or 1% of titles, not volumes, in collection) of a collection uninventoried in decades, *showed that* overall 4.37% of the books were missing. **(085)**

■ A 1968-69 study at Loretto Heights College (a women's college with an enrollment of 900 located in Denver, Colorado) comparing a traditional charge-out system operated by staff with a patron self-charge system *showed that* fewer students reported taking books out of the library without charging them and fewer books were taken out of the library without charging them out under the self-charge system of circulation. During a comparable 1-month period 32.1% (1,183) of the books returned to the library had not been charged out under the self-serve system, compared to 51.0% (2,324) under the traditional system. Further, 32.2% (176) of a sample of 546 students reported taking library materials out of the library without charging them under the self-serve system, compared to 40.6% (103) of a sample of 254 students reporting similarly under the traditional system. Both changes in books returned and student reports of behavior are statistically significant according to Chi Square tests at the .001 significance level. **(206)**

■ A study reported in 1976 at Washington University's central library (Olin Library) involving book loss in a collection of 850,000 volumes protected by a manual check of exiting patrons (sample size: 2,949 volumes) *showed that* 161 (5.45%) volumes could not be found. With a 95% confidence level, the loss rate ranged between 6.3% and 4.7% of the collection. **(444)**

Ibid. . . . *showed that* additional searches during a subsequent 10-month period located almost half of the missing volumes, leaving only 86 (2.91%) of the collection missing. At the 95% confidence level, this adjusted loss rate ranged between 2.7% and 1.7% of the collection. **(444)**

■ A study reported in 1977 of book loss at Northwestern University, *showed that* sampling to determine book loss may provide an artifically high loss figure. An inventory of 110,000 high-use books at Northwestern University revealed a loss figure of 1.8%; a sample of the same collection indicated a loss rate between 2.2 and 4.0% with a 95% confidence interval.

(004)

■ A study reported in 1977 of book loss at Northwestern University based on a sample of 740,000 books in the humanities and social sciences *showed that* the loss rate over a 3 1/2-year period was between 2.8-4.8%.

(004)

■ A study reported in 1982 at Washington State University of a relatively homogeneous book collection (a recent social science collection of 100,000) *showed that* the percentage of lost items by the subject subgroups within the collection varied greatly, ranging from 1.1 to 9.7%.

(062)

Ibid. . . . *showed that* patron reports of missing items in a collection subject area were the strongest single predictor of the actual number of missing items in that area with an r2 = .4049.

(062)

Ibid. . . . *showed that* circulation rate of a collection subject area was the second strongest predictor of the actual number of missing items in that area with an r2 = .3187.

(062)

Ibid. . . . *showed that* combining patron reports of missing items in a collection subject area with the circulation rate of that subject area produces a combined predictor of the actual number of missing items in that area that is a more powerful predictor than either of the 2 factors singly with an r2 = .4892.

(062)

Public

■ A sample inventory of the Main Library of the Huston Public Library reported in 1974 (population: 236,519 titles; sample size: 600 titles) of a collection last fully inventoried in 1924 and only partially inventoried in 1934 and 1943 *showed that* 41% (±3.5%) of the volumes and approximately 35% of the titles in the shelflist for the Main Library were missing.

(097)

School

■ A 1977 study at an Edmonton high school (Canada) concerning book loss before and after installation of an electronic security system *showed that*, based on a sample inventory of "approximately 10% of the main collection," book loss decreased by 87%. Specifically, book loss in a 10% sample decreased from 62 books in Fall semester before the installation of the security system to 8 books in Spring semester after the installation of the security system.   **(548)**

Loss Rates—Periodicals

Academic

■ A study reported in 1982 at Brock University Library (Canada) concerning periodical losses and mutilation during the period 1972 through 1981 based on a sample of 106 titles *showed that* in the 10 years prior to installation of an electronic security system (although a manual check of bags and briefcases at the exit was in force) the library lost 5.73% of the issues received (718 issues out of 12,536 issues received). In the 2 years subsequent to the installation of an electronic security system, the periodical loss rate dropped to 2.54% and 3.90% of the periodical issues received each year. However, if the temporarily missing issues are included, the figures rose to 4.77% and 5.46% each year.   **(559)**

Misshelving

Academic

■ A study in 1976 at Princeton University Library *showed that* out-of-order materials in high-use areas tended to cluster on shelves at eye level, whereas out-of-order materials in low-use areas tended to cluster on the top and bottom shelves.   **(014)**

Ibid. . . . *showed that* 5.83% of the collection (last shelf read during the period 1970 to 1974) out of order; 96.6% of the out-of-order materials were within 2 shelves of their correct location.   **(014)**

■ A study reported in 1980 over a 6-year period (1973-78) at West Virginia University main library concerning the effect of switching from closed to open stacks in 1976 with a collection of just under 1 million volumes of primarily humanities and social science materials *showed that* loss rate and disorder did not appear to increase under the open stack system. Specifically, for books requested on the delivery system, the number that could not be accounted for during the closed stack system (1974, no number of requests given) was 15.0%, while 2 studies of books requested on the delivery system after the stacks were opened showed 11.2% unavailable in 1977 and 12.2% unavailable in 1978 (no number of requests given).   **(484)**

Mutilation

Academic

■ A study reported in 1969 of a staged book mutilation episode in 2 libraries at Miami University, involving 82 students either singly or in groups, *showed that* 9 (11%) of the student bystanders responded to stop or report the incident. 38 (46%) reported that they had noticed the mutilation but chose to do nothing about it, while 35 (43%) reported that they had not noticed the obvious, nearby student tearing pages out of a book.   **(194)**

Ibid. . . . *showed that*, of those who admitted witnessing the book mutilation but who had chosen not to do anything about it, the reasons given for inaction were primarily: desire for noninvolvement (30%), vacillation (27%), and irrelevant, i.e., "I thought he had permission," "I thought it wasn't a library book" (24%).   **(194)**

■ A survey in 1973 of 168 students in introductory psychology and social psychology at Kent State University *showed that* 154 (91.7%) reported they had not cut or torn an article from a magazine at Kent State University, while 14 students (8.3%) reported they had. Of the 14, 5 were males (7.9% of all males in the survey) and 9 females (8.5% of all females in the survey).   **(099)**

Ibid. . . . *showed that* the great majority of students were unconcerned about getting caught cutting or tearing articles from journals. 100% of the mutilators were totally unconcerned about getting caught; 68.8% of the nonmutilators were totally unconcerned about getting caught; and only 43.4% of the nonmutilators and 21.4% of the mutilators rated tearing or cutting articles from journals as "definitely wrong."
                                                                                      (099)

Ibid. . . . *showed that* 36.6% of the nonmutilators who saw someone tearing an article out of a journal would ask them to stop or would report the action. **(099)**

Ibid. . . . *showed that* while there was a statistically significant difference between mutilators and nonmutilators at the .002 level, student perceptions of replacement costs and time were grossly inaccurate for both groups. 58.4% of the mutilators and 26.8% of the nonmutilators thought it would take 3 days to a week to replace a torn-out article, while 84.6% of the mutilators and 55.7% of the nonmutilators thought it would cost $1 or less to replace the article. **(099)**

Ibid. . . . *showed that* student estimates of the percentage of students who tore or cut articles from journals were high. 92.9% of the mutilators and 78.5% of the nonmutilators judged that 21% or higher of the student body tore or cut articles from library journals. **(099)**

Ibid. . . . *showed that* mutilators and nonmutilators alike generally had positive attitudes toward the library. 100% of the mutilators and 92.9% of the nonmutilators reported positive or neutral feelings toward the library; 57.2% of mutilators and 64.7% of nonmutilators disagreed with the statement that the library was a cold and anonymous place; and 92.9% of the mutilators and 90.8% of the nonmutilators found the library staff to be "quite friendly and helpful." **(099)**

Ibid. . . . *showed that* mutilators seem to be aware of the inconvenience their action causes others. Only 7.1% of the mutilators agreed that no harm was done by tearing or cutting articles from journals since no one else was likely to need that article, while 71.5% disagreed with the statement. However, the perception of inconvenience was statistically significantly higher among nonmutilators. **(099)**

Ibid. . . . *showed that* according to the students the greatest deterrent to having articles torn or cut from journals would be:

	MUTILATORS	NONMUTILATORS
free copying	85.7%	83.9%
2-week periodical checkout	71.4%	71.8%
warning sign ($500 fine or 30 days in jail)	64.3%	61.5% **(099)**

■   Interviews reported in 1974 with 3 students at Kent State University who admitted cutting or tearing articles from library journals in 1973 *showed that* all 3 went to the library with no prior intention of mutilating journals, that 2 of the 3 cut or tore the articles because the library was closing (and journals could not be checked out), that all 3 used carrels for cutting or tearing the articles from the journals, that all 3 had been previously angered or upset to find articles gone from journals and that they would not cut or tear material from books because they were much more expensive.   **(099)**

■   An interview reported in 1975 with 3 Kent State University students who had mutilated periodicals *showed that* study carrels and penknives are the favorable place and instrument of mutilation, that bound volumes are less likely to be vandalized than unbound issues, and that dramatic attitude change may occur when the students know the full costs of mutilation.
                                                                    (059)

■   A survey of student attitudes toward mutilation of library materials conducted in 1976 at the University of Rhode Island *showed that* 12% felt they could do nothing about the problem; 15.9% stated they would report mutilators; just over 30% indicated they would report mutilated items; 43.7% said they would encourage others to refrain from mutilating materials; and 58.1% responded that they would personally be more careful with library materials.   **(003)**

■   A 1977 study of periodical mutilation in a major university library involving bound volumes of 7 "popular education titles" (132 issues, dated 1969-72) as a follow-up to an identical, prior mutilation study in 1973 of the same issues *showed that*, while in the 1973 study 20 issues (15%) had been found mutilated after 1 to 1.5 years on the shelf, the 1977 study showed an additional 39 issues (30%) mutilated in the subsequent 3.5 years. This was a reduction of the annual mutilation rate from 15% to 9% as the age of the material increased.   **(239)**

Ibid. . . . *showed that* mutilation appeared to encourage mutilation. By the 1977 study 87% of previously mutilated volumes had been further mutilated, while only 67% of the previously unmutilated volumes had been mutilated.   **(239)**

■   A 1978 survey of 201 undergraduate students in a large urban university concerning book theft and mutilation *showed that* 17 (8%) students reported "sneaking" books out of the library while 18 (9%)

students reported mutilating books or periodicals. Only 2 students were in
both groups. **(499)**

Ibid. . . . *showed that* a statistically significantly greater number of students who reported doing well academically also reported stealing or
mutilating library materials. 37 (22%) of the nonviolators reported doing
"very well" academically, while 14 (42%) of the violators reported doing
"very well" (significant at the .05 level). **(499)**

Ibid. . . . *showed that* neither feeling poorly served by the library nor
lack of access to a copy machine appeared to be related to the theft
or mutilation of library materials. Specifically, 61 (37%) of the nonviolators and 11 (33%) of the violators felt "served well" by the library.
Further, 111 (67%) of the nonviolators and 21 (70%) of the violators
reported that the cost of the copy machine was "never too expensive,"
while 30 (21%) of the nonviolators and 6 (19%) of the violators reported that they were "never inconvenienced" by a broken copy machine.
(499)

Ibid. . . . *showed that* there was a statistically significant difference between violators and nonviolators in their perception of the ease of ripping
out pages of library material. 103 (61%) of the nonviolators and 25 (76%)
of the violators reported it was "very easy" to rip pages out of library
material (significant at the .05 level). **(499)**

Ibid. . . . *showed that* the reasons given for stealing or mutilating library
materials were as follows (multiple responses allowed):

Do not consider the needs of others	45%	violators
Need the photographs or charts in books and cannot photocopy them	36%	violators
Do not think about the act but steal and mutilate casually and thoughtlessly	30%	violators
Are not aware of the cost of theft and mutilation to the library	27%	violators
Cannot afford the copy machine or price of a book but want to own a copy	24%	violators
Steal and mutilate books as an expression of hostility toward the library and the university	18%	violators **(499)**

■ A study reported in 1982 at Brock University Library (Canada) concerning periodical losses and mutilation during the period 1972 through 1981 based on a sample of 106 titles *showed that* installation of an electronic security system seemed to be related to a rise in periodical mutilation. Between 1972 and June 1979 (the electronic security system was installed in December 1978) the average number of periodical pages mutilated per year was 359, compared to 529 pages mutilated per year during academic years 1979-80 and 1980-81.   **(559)**

Special

■ A survey reported in 1975 of 110 U.S. law libraries with collections of 50,000 volumes or more (responding: 70 libraries) concerning theft and mutilation control *showed that* the 3 most popular approaches respondents favored in dealing with the problem of theft and multilation of law library material were (multiple responses allowed):

egress limitations	59 (84.3%) respondents
increase reference and photocopy services	43 (61.4%) respondents
denial of privileges	40 (57.1%) respondents **(395)**

Ibid. . . . *showed that* the 3 most disliked approaches respondents reported in dealing with the problem of theft and mutilation of law library material were (multiple responses allowed):

closed stacks	43 (61.4%)
stack pass	37 (52.9%)
uniformed guards	33 (47.1%) **(395)**

Organization of Materials

Academic

■ A survey of 31 members of the Association for Research Libraries in 1958 (23 or 75% responding) dealing with the treatment of government documents collections *showed that* 15 (65%) thought that housing government documents as a separate collection provided higher quality bibliographic service by the library, 1 (4%) thought a separate collection for government documents provided lower quality bibliographic service, 4 (17%) thought it made no difference, and 3 (13%) reported that they did not know.   **(108)**

Ibid. . . . *showed that* 8 libraries housed their government documents collections completely separately, 4 housed them predominately separately, 6 housed government documents like any other publications, and 5 libraries reported quite mixed systems. **(108)**

Ibid. . . . *showed that* of 16 (out of a possible total of 17) libraries housing their government documents separately to some degree, the following opinions were reported:

	YES	NO	
Favor state and local documents in separate collections	12	4	
Favor foreign documents in separate collection	12	4	
Favor United Nations documents in separate collections	15	1	**(108)**

Ibid. . . . *showed that* of 16 (out of a possible total of 17) libraries housing their government documents separately to some degree, the most common single pattern of arranging nonfederal document collections was alphabetically by area, agency, and title. For state document collections over half of the 16 libraries used an alphabetical arrangement either in whole or in part, with 2 using the Swank system and 2 others switching to it; for foreign document collections the practice was fairly evenly divided between alphabetical as opposed to either LC or Dewey; with UN documents the leading arrangement was the UN classification scheme. **(108)**

■ A study reported in 1961 at Cornell University Library comparing shelving books by size rather than by LC class number in a storage area, based on a book count in 1 6-section area in both the compact shelving and the regular shelving, *showed that*, while 930 volumes were housed in the regular area (by LC class number), 1,235 volumes were housed in the compact area (by volume size). This represented an increase of 32.8% in the number of volumes housed. **(579)**

■ A study reported in 1974 investigating the materials used by master's and doctoral candidates completing theses after 1966 in public health at 5 universities (Yale; Harvard; University of California, Los Angeles; University of California, Berkeley; and California State University, Northridge), involving 3,456 citations taken from 44 theses, *showed that* the most efficient journal collection did not keep all its journals for the same length of time. For example, the most efficient journal collection of

1,500 volumes to cover the materials cited in this study was based on 60 journal titles with backfiles ranging from 37 years (*American Journal of Public Health*) to 8 years (*Journal of Experimental Medicine*). This would cover 48% of the citations needed.   **(698)**

■ A survey reported in 1977 of moderate-sized (120,000-500,000 volumes) U.S. academic libraries listed in the 1972-73 *American Library Directory* (survey size: 200; responding: 147 or 74%) *showed that* 92 (63%) libraries arranged bound volumes alphabetically by title, 33% arranged bound volumes in call number order, and 3% use some "other" arrangement.   **(454)**

Ibid. . . . *showed that* smaller bound volume collections tended to be arranged alphabetically, while larger bound volume collections tended to be arranged in call number order. Of 99 libraries reporting 70,000 bound volumes or less, 75% arranged their volumes alphabetically by title (22% arranged by call number), while of 18 libraries with more than 70,000 bound volumes, 72% arranged their bound volumes in call number order (28% arranged alphabetically by title).   **(454)**

■ A 1977 study of biomedical journal use in the Lane Medical Library at Stanford University Medical Center during the month of November involving the bound volumes of 334 journal titles for a 10-year period (1967-76) *showed that* the higher use of newer volumes was not due to their containing more articles. For example, for the 10-year period of holdings there was an exponential decrease in use but only a linear decrease in shelf space occupied. Specifically, 24.35% of the journal use involved bound volumes 1 year old, while volumes 10 years old received only 3.12% of the total use; bound volumes 1 year old occupied 10.63% of the shelf space, while volumes 10 years old occupied 9.26% of the shelf space.   **(567)**

■ A study reported in 1980 over a 6-year period (1973-78) at West Virginia University main library concerning the effect of switching from closed to open stacks in 1976 with a collection of just under 1 million volumes of primarily humanities and social science materials *showed that* building use increased after the switch to open stacks. Specifically, in 1973 the annual building use was 431,285 patrons, while in 1978 the annual building use was 500,178 patrons even though circulation decreased during this period.   **(484)**

■ A 1980 survey of law school libraries with collections in excess of 175,000 volumes (sample size: 50; responding: 37 or 70%) *showed that* 15 libraries reported arranging their legal materials by form, 14 reported arranging their legal materials by jurisdiction, 3 reported arranging most materials by jurisdiction but Shepard's by form, "two or three" reported varying the arrangement with the type of materials, 1 reported they anticipated organizing all materials by LC class number, and no information was provided on the remaining library.   **(369)**

Public

■ A 1969 survey of Canadian public libraries serving populations of more than 10,000 people as well as all county and regional libraries belonging to the Canadian Library Association concerning holdings and use of non-English collections (survey size: 203; responding: 83 or 41%) *showed that* 59 (71.1%) libraries reported they had a special section for non-English language books. Further, non-English language books were handled as follows:

books clearly marked	61 (73.5%) respondents
shelves labelled	52 (62.7%) respondents
special catalog	24 (29.8%) respondents
special booklists	20 (24.1%) respondents
linguist staff	21 (25.3%) respondents **(534)**

Special

■ A 1977 study of biomedical journal use in the Lane Medical Library at Stanford University Medical Center during the month of November involving the bound volumes of 334 journal titles for a 10-year period (1967-76) *showed that* the higher use of newer volumes was not due to their containing more articles. For example, for the 10-year period of holdings there was an exponential decrease in use but only a linear decrease in shelf space occupied. Specifically, 24.35% of the journal use involved bound volumes 1 year old, while volumes 10 years old received only 3.12% of the total use; bound volumes 1 year old occupied 10.63% of the shelf space, while volumes 10 years old occupied 9.26% of the shelf space.   **(567)**

■ A 1977 study at the Treadwell Library of the Massachusetts General Hospital comparing raw-use ranking of journal use (frequency of use per title) with density-of-use ranking (raw-use frequency/linear shelf space occupied by a title) involving 647 titles studied over a year's time *showed that* density-of-use ranking of periodicals had substantial advantages over raw-use ranking in terms of using shelf space most efficiently. Specifically, although 240 titles were required to provide 80% of the periodical use in the density-of-use ranking (compared to 136 titles in the raw-use ranking), the amount of shelf space required to hold the 240 titles was less than the amount required to hold the 136 titles. Conversely, when shelf space was held constant (2 different points were examined) the higher number of titles allowed under the density-of-use ranking provided greater user satisfaction (the smaller number of raw-use titles provided 19% less potential uses).   **(649)**

■ A 1980 survey of law school libraries with collections in excess of 175,000 volumes (sample size: 50; responding: 37 or 70%) *showed that* 15 libraries reported arranging their legal materials by form, 14 reported arranging their legal materials by jurisdiction, 3 reported arranging most materials by jurisdiction but Shepard's by form, "two or three" reported varying the arrangement with the type of materials, 1 reported they anticipated organizing all materials by LC class number, and no information was provided on the remaining library.   **(369)**

■ A survey reported in 1983 of Medical Library Association institutional members concerning their use of audiovisual materials (survey size: 300; responding: 201; usable: 198 or 66%) *showed that*, of 143 respondents (91 hospital, 29 medical school, and 13 "other" libraries) that did provide AV services, the favored method of shelving AV materials were as follows:

   hospital libraries: formats shelved separately and in accession order (45% used this method);

   medical school libraries: all formats shelved together in classified order (41% used this method);

   other libraries: formats shelved separately in classified order (45% used this method).

Further, repackaging of AV programs for storage or circulation is practiced in 43% of the hospital libraries, 68% of the medical school libraries, and 60% of other libraries.   **(750)**

Preservation

General

■ A sample of books drawn from the *National Union Catalog* (735 titles) for analysis in terms of imprint date, reported in 1962, *showed that* 73.05% of all titles (7,665,800) and 57.34% of the pages of those titles (1,720,570,000) were printed after 1869, when the "poorer paper" era began and so will not likely last into the twenty-first century.   **(118)**

Academic

■ A survey undertaken in 1972 of preservation efforts in academic libraries with collections of 500,000 volumes or more (sample size: 115;

responding: 86 [75%]) *showed that* 62 of responding libraries (72%) reported some preservation procedures. **(102)**

Ibid. . . . *showed that* 40 responding libraries use stack checks to discover items needing preservation attention, 20 libraries use inventories, and 25 rely upon staff reports. **(102)**

Ibid. . . . *showed that* 32 responding libraries reported treating less than 300 volumes a year for preservation purposes, 4 libraries treated more than 1,000 volumes annually, and 1 library processed more than 1% of the collection annually. **(102)**

■ A survey reported in 1976 of large (over 500,000 volumes) U.S. academic libraries *showed that* 72% have an independent preservation department or specific mechanism to deal with library materials. **(057)**

■ A study reported in 1980 of a systematic sample of English, German, French, Italian, and Spanish literary materials at the University of Michigan investigating deterioration (sample size: 2,000 volumes; available for inspection: 1,731 volumes) *showed that*:

> 44.9% of the materials were rated 2 or less (where "a typical 2 might be a book with original hard binding firmly attached but with brittle paper that was either discolored or had inadequate margins");

> 24.5% of the materials were rated 1 or less (where "a book rated '1' might be securely paperbound, with fair paper and inadequate margins, or it might have a hard binding, insecurely attached, and brittle paper. If that last book also had discoloration or inadequate margins, it rated '0'"). **(759)**

■ A study reported in 1983 at the University of North Carolina investigating the quality of paper in French books dealing with French literature and criticism and history that were published during the period 1860-1914 (1,349 imprints held in the Wilson Library of the University of North Carolina examined) *showed that* for 5-year periods on the basis of the paper in the book, the number of books in "good" condition declined from 94% in 1860 to 56% in 1894, while the books in "bad" condition increased from 4% in 1860 to 17% in 1894. Thereafter, the number of books in "good" condition generally ran about 40% up to 1914, while the books in "bad" condition generally ran between 22-28% up to 1914. **(775)**

Ibid. . . . *showed that* for the period 1895-1914 the number of books in "good" or "bad" condition (based on their paper) by major publishers of the period were as follows:

Calmann-Levy	51% good; 12% bad
Champion	36% good; 23% bad
Charpentier	19% good; 72% bad
Hachette	16% good; 39% bad
Mercure de France	24% good; 5% bad
Perrin	31% good; 26% bad
Plon	61% good; 13% bad

For all publishers sampled (77) the overall average of "good" books for this time period was 39%, while the overall average of "bad" books was 24%.   **(775)**

Ibid. . . . *showed that* between 1860 and 1914 the paper in the history had generally held up better than the paper in the literature books. Specifically, 66% of the history books were in "good" condition, compared to 55% of the literature books, while 12% of the history books were in "bad" condition, compared to 20% of the literature books.   **(775)**

Replacement

Academic

■ A survey reported in 1977 of moderate-sized (120,000-500,000 volumes) U.S. academic libraries listed in the 1972-73 *American Library Directory* (survey size: 200; responding: 147 or 74%) *showed that*, of 89 responding libraries, 39 (43.8%) reported that they reordered current issues less than 1 month after they were reported missing, while 13 (14.6%) reported that they wait 6 months or longer before reordering current issues. On the other hand, 19 (21.3%) libraries reported reordering bound volumes less than 1 month after they were reported missing, while 45 (50.4%) libraries reported that they wait 6 months or more before reordering bound volumes.   **(454)**

Ibid. . . . *showed that*, in order to fill a gap, 45% of responding libraries reported they would purchase microform, 26% reported they would purchase paper, and 29% reported they might do either.   **(454)**

Special

■ A 1978 survey of major biomedical libraries (primarily those serving accredited medical schools) (survey size: 120 libraries; responding: 88 or

73%) *showed that* using microform copy in lieu of binding hard copy volumes of abstracts and indexes was not common practice. Only 1 (1%) library reported using microforms in lieu of binding all volumes of abstracts and indexes, 7 (8%) libraries reported using microforms in lieu of binding some abstracts and indexes, while 78 (89%) libraries reported using no microforms in lieu of binding abstracts or indexes. 2 (2%) libraries did not reply.   **(726)**

Security Systems and Procedures

Academic

■ A 1968-69 study at Loretto Heights College (a women's college with an enrollment of 900 located in Denver, Colorado) comparing a traditional charge-out system operated by staff with a patron self-charge system *showed that* fewer students reported taking books out of the library without charging them and fewer books were taken out of the library without charging them out under the self-charge system of circulation. During a comparable 1-month period 32.1% (1,183) of the books returned to the library had not been charged out under the self-serve system, compared to 51.0% (2,324) under the traditional system. Further, 32.2% (176) of a sample of 546 students reported taking library materials out of the library without charging them under the self-serve system, compared to 40.6% (103) of a sample of 254 students reporting similarly under the traditional system. Both changes in books returned and student reports of behavior are statistically significant according to Chi Square tests at the .001 significance level.   **(206)**

■ A 1968 survey of 254 students at Loretto Heights College (a women's college with an enrollment of 900 located in Denver, Colorado) investigating reasons for taking materials out of the library without charging them *showed that* responses were: need book beyond time limit (39%), in a hurry (36%), no one at the desk (12%), and other (13%).   **(206)**

■ A study at the University of Rhode Island reported in 1977, after the installation of an electronic security system in 1973, *showed that* the number of interlibrary loan requests for missing pages in mutilated items increased from 55 in 1973-74, to 91 in 1974-75, to 60 in the first half of 1975-76.   **(003)**

■ A study reported in 1976 at Washington University's central library (Olin Library) involving book loss in a collection of 850,000 volumes protected by a manual check of exiting patrons (sample size: 2,949 volumes) *showed that* 161 (5.45%) volumes could not be found. With a 95% confidence level, the loss rate ranged between 6.3% and 4.7% of the collection. **(444)**

Ibid. . . . *showed that* additional searches during a subsequent 10-month period located almost half of the missing volumes, leaving only 86 (2.91%) of the collection missing. At the 95% confidence level, this adjusted loss rate ranged between 2.7% and 1.7% of the collection. **(444)**

■ A survey reported in 1977 of moderate-sized (120,000-500,000 volumes) U.S. academic libraries listed in the 1972-73 *American Library Directory* (survey size: 200; responding: 147 or 74%), *showed that*, of 36 libraries with electronic security systems, 14% sensitize current issues of all periodicals, 53% sensitize current issues of frequently used periodicals, 58% sensitize bound volumes of all periodicals, 22% sensitize bound volumes of frequently used periodicals, and 6% sensitize no current issues and no bound issues. **(454)**

■ A study reported in 1978 at the Van Pelt Library of the University of Pennsylvania comparing collection loss rates before and after installation of an electronic security system, based on a sample size of 1,391 items in the first case and a sample size of 849 in the second case, *showed that* the overall annual loss rate in the circulating collection dropped from .79% in 1971, before installation of the security system, to .48% in 1976, 2 years after installation of the security system. This was a drop in the overall annual loss rate of 39% during a period when the circulation rate increased by 320%. **(464)**

■ A survey reported in 1979 of 100 academic librarians (81 responding) *showed that* there was no pattern or formula for dealing with the theft of library materials, with 22 responding that there had never been a case of proven book theft during their tenure. **(025)**

■ A study reported in 1980 over a 6-year period (1973-78) at West Virginia University main library concerning the effect of switching from closed to open stacks in 1976 with a collection of just under 1 million volumes of primarily humanities and social science materials *showed that* loss rate and disorder did not appear to increase under the open stack system. Specifically, for books requested on the delivery system, the number that could not be accounted for during the closed stack system (1,974 books, no number of requests given) was 15.0%, while 2 studies of books requested on the delivery system after the stacks were opened showed 11.2% unavailable in 1977 and 12.2% unavailable in 1978 (no number of requests given). **(484)**

■ A study reported in 1982 at Brock University Library (Canada) concerning periodical losses and mutilation during the period 1972 through 1981, based on a sample of 106 titles, *showed that* in the 10 years prior to installation of an electronic security system (although a manual check of bags and briefcases at the exit was in force) the library lost 5.73% of the issues received (718 issues out of 12,536 issues received). In the 2 years subsequent to the installation of an electronic security system, the periodical loss rate dropped to 2.54% and 3.90% of the periodical issues received each year. However, if the temporarily missing issues are included, the figures rise to 4.77% and 5.46% each year. **(559)**

Ibid. . . . *showed that* installation of an electronic security system seemed to be related to a rise in periodical mutilation. Between 1972 and June 1979 (the electronic security system was installed in December 1978) the average number of periodical pages mutilated per year was 359, compared to 529 pages mutilated per year during academic years 1979-80 and 1980-81. **(559)**

School

■ A 1977 study at an Edmonton high school (Canada) concerning book loss before and after installation of an electronic security system *showed that,* based on a sample inventory of "approximately 10% of the main collection," book loss decreased by 87%. Specifically, book loss in a 10% sample decreased from 62 books in Fall semester before the installation of the security system to 8 books in Spring semester after the installation of the security system. **(548)**

Shelfreading

Academic

■ A study in 1976 at the Princeton University Library *showed that* student assistants could shelfread an average of 950 books per hour per student with a supervisory commitment of 12 minutes an hour per student. Students worked 3 100-minute sessions with 1/2-hour breaks between. **(014)**

■ A study reported in 1981 at Purdue University of the degree to which books in 5 different subject areas as determined by reviews and bibliographies in the disciplines were actually classed in those areas by Dewey and LC cataloging [source of cataloging not given] (anthropology: 254 books; history: 352 books; political science: 534 books; sociology: 602 books; and philosophy: 265 books) *showed that* a shelflist count [based on class numbers] would have missed between 30-80% of the titles in the 5 disciplines.   **(574)**

Theft

Academic

■ A 1978 survey of 201 undergraduate students in a large urban university concerning book theft and mutilation *showed that* 17 (8%) students reported "sneaking" books out of the library, while 18 (9%) students reported mutilating books or periodicals. Only 2 students were in both groups.   **(499)**

Ibid. . . . *showed that* a statistically significantly greater number of students who reported doing well academically also reported stealing or mutilating library materials. 37 (22%) of the nonviolators reported doing "very well" academically while 14 (42%) of the violators reported doing "very well" (significant at the .05 level).   **(499)**

Ibid. . . . *showed that* neither feeling poorly served by the library nor lack of access to a copy machine appeared to be related to the theft or mutilation of library materials. Specifically, 61 (37%) of the nonviolators and 11 (33%) of the violators felt "served well" by the library. Further, 111 (67%) of the nonviolators and 21 (70%) of the violators reported that the cost of the copy machine was "never too expensive," while 30 (21%) of the nonviolators and 6 (19%) of the violators reported that they were "never inconvenienced" by a broken copy machine.   **(499)**

Ibid. . . . *showed that* there was a statistically significant difference between violators and nonviolators in their perception of the ease of ripping out pages of library material. 103 (61%) of the nonviolators and 25 (76%) of the violators reported it was "very easy" to rip pages out of library material (significant at the .05 level).   **(499)**

Ibid. . . . *showed that* there was a statistically significant difference between violators and nonviolators in their perception of the odds of getting caught "sneaking" a book out of the library. 126 (71%) of the non-violators and 7 (44%) of the violators (only those who reported "sneaking" books out of the library) reported the odds of getting caught as 1 in 10, while 52 (29%) of the nonviolators and 9 (56%) of the violators reported the odds of getting caught as 1 in 100 (significant at the .05 level).

(499)

Ibid. . . . *showed that* there was a statistically significant difference between violators and nonviolators in their perception of whether their friends steal books. None of the nonviolators reported that their friends steal books, while 3 (9%) of the violators reported that their friends steal books (significant at the .05 level). **(499)**

Ibid. . . . *showed that* 82 (53%) of the nonviolators and 15 (52%) of the violators reported the perception that 10% or less of the student body stole books, while 72 (47%) of the nonviolators and 15 (48%) of the violators reported the perception that 25% or more of the student body stole books. **(499)**

Ibid. . . . *showed that* the reasons given for stealing or mutilating library materials were as follows (multiple responses allowed):

Do not consider the needs of others	45% violators
Need the photographs or charts in books and cannot photocopy them	36% violators
Do not think about the act but steal and mutilate casually and thoughtlessly	30% violators
Are not aware of the cost of theft and mutilation to the library	27% violators
Cannot afford the copy machine or price of a book but want to own a copy	24% violators
Steal and mutilate books as an expression of hostility toward the library and the university	18% violators **(499)**

■ A survey reported in 1979 of 100 academic librarians (81 responding) *showed that* there was no pattern or formula for dealing with the theft of library materials, with 22 responding that there had never been a case of proven book theft during their tenure. **(025)**

Special

■ A survey reported in 1975 of 110 U.S. law libraries with collections of 50,000 volumes or more (responding: 70 libraries) concerning theft and mutilation control *showed that* the 3 most popular approaches respondents favored in dealing with the problem of theft and multilation of law library material were (multiple responses allowed):

egress limitations	59 (84.3%) respondents
increase reference and photocopy services	43 (61.4%) respondents
denial of privileges	40 (57.1%) respondents **(395)**

Ibid. . . . *showed that* the 3 most disliked approaches respondents reported in dealing with the problem of theft and mutilation of law library material were (multiple responses allowed):

closed stacks	43 (61.4%)
stack pass	37 (52.9%)
uniformed guards	33 (47.1%) **(395)**

Weeding

Academic

■ A study reported in 1974 investigating the materials used by master's and doctoral candidates completing theses after 1966 in public health at 5 universities (Yale; Harvard; University of California, Los Angeles; University of California, Berkeley; and California State University, Northridge), involving 3,456 citations taken from 44 theses, *showed that* the most efficient journal collection did not keep all its journals for the same length of time. For example, the most efficient journal collection of 1,500 volumes to cover the materials cited in this study was based on 60 journal titles with backfiles ranging from 37 years (*American Journal of Public Health*) to 8 years (*Journal of Experimental Medicine*). This would cover 48% of the citations needed. **(698)**

■ A 1977 study of biomedical journal use in the Lane Medical Library at Stanford University Medical Center during the month of November involving the bound volumes of 334 journal titles for a 10-year period (1967-76) *showed that* the higher use of newer volumes was not due to their containing more articles. For example, for the 10-year period of holdings there was an exponential decrease in use but only a linear decrease in shelf space occupied. Specifically, 24.35% of the journal use involved bound volumes 1 year old, while volumes 10 years old received only 3.12% of the total use; bound volumes 1 year old occupied 10.63% of the shelf space, while volumes 10 years old occupied 9.26% of the shelf space. **(567)**

■ A 1977 study at the Music Library of the University of California, Berkeley, to investigate weeding criteria (based on a sample of 116 circulated volumes and a sample of 515 volumes from the shelf) *showed that*, to satisfy the needs of 97% of the borrowers over a year's time by weeding by publication date alone, the library would have to keep on the shelves all books published since "about 1900." **(756)**

Ibid. . . . *showed that* weeding on the basis of language alone was not a feasible idea. For example, during the period 1950-77, while 84.8% of the English-language books in the sample circulated, 79.3% of the French-language books and 71.8% of the German-language books circulated as well. Overall, during the 1950-77 period, 45.6% of the materials circulated were non-English language materials. **(756)**

Ibid. . . . *showed that* weeding on the basis of circulation activity in distinct subject areas was the most feasible idea. For example, the number of books that had never been charged out ranged from 5.6% of the books in "performance practice" to 35.0% of the books in "history." **(756)**

■ A survey reported in 1981 of 11 TALON resource libraries [100% response rate] concerning weeding policies *showed that* 3 libraries had written policies for discarding books, 4 had informal (i.e., nonwritten) procedures, and 4 did not weed materials and hence had no need for policies. Further, of the 7 respondents who did weed materials, the 2 most common practices were discarding multiple copies (4 respondents) and keeping only the latest edition of specified types of materials (4 respondents). **(739)**

Public

■ A study reported in 1979 at the Washington State Library, based on 5 days' circulation information (1,878 items) and a shelflist sample of 159 titles concerning the issue of selecting materials for remote storage, *showed that*:

90% of the user needs for monographs could be satisfied with
monographs that had circulated within the past 35 months
(these constituted 50% of the collection);

95% of the user needs for monographs could be satisfied with
monographs that had circulated within the past 58 months
(these constituted 60% of the collection);

and 99% of the user needs for monographs could be satisfied
with monographs that had circulated within the past 131
months (these constituted 85% of the collection).

Data accurate to ±1.55 months at the .99 confidence level.   **(527)**

Special

■ A 1964 study at the Air Force Cambridge Research Laboratories
(Bedford, Massachusetts) over a 6-month period, involving use of 4,579
articles from 552 journal titles by 382 patrons, *showed that* even low-use
journals were an important part of the collection for a substantial number
of patrons. Specifically, while 281 (51%) titles had only 1 patron using
them during this period and accounted for only 598 (13%) of the total
articles requested, this group of titles was nevertheless requested by 144
(38% of the total) different patrons.   **(586)**

■ A study reported in 1974 investigating the materials used by master's
and doctoral candidates completing theses after 1966 in public health at 5
universities (Yale; Harvard; University of California, Los Angeles; University of California, Berkeley; and California State University, Northridge), involving 3,456 citations taken from 44 theses, *showed that* the most
efficient journal collection did not keep all its journals for the same length
of time. For example, the most efficient journal collection of 1,500 volumes
to cover the materials cited in this study was based on 60 journal titles with
backfiles ranging from 37 years (*American Journal of Public Health*) to 8
years (*Journal of Experimental Medicine*). This would cover 48% of the
citations needed.   **(698)**

■ A 1977 study of biomedical journal use in the Lane Medical Library at
Stanford University Medical Center during the month of November,
involving the bound volumes of 334 journal titles for a 10-year period
(1967-76) *showed that* the higher use of newer volumes was not due to their
containing more articles. For example, for the 10-year period of holdings
there was an exponential decrease in use but only a linear decrease in shelf
space occupied. Specifically, 24.35% of the journal use involved bound

volumes 1 year old, while volumes 10 years old received only 3.12% of the total use; bound volumes 1 year old occupied 10.63% of the shelf space, while volumes 10 years old occupied 9.26% of the shelf space. **(567)**

■ A 1977 study at the Treadwell Library of the Massachusetts General Hospital comparing raw-use ranking of journal use (frequency of use per title) with density-of-use ranking (raw-use frequency/linear shelf space occupied by a title), involving 647 titles studied over a year's time, *showed that* density-of-use ranking of periodicals had substantial advantages over raw-use ranking in terms of using shelf space most efficiently. Specifically, although 240 titles were required to provide 80% of the periodical use in the density-of-use ranking (compared to 136 titles in the raw-use ranking), the amount of shelf space required to hold the 240 titles was less than the amount required to hold the 136 titles. Conversely, when shelf space was held constant (2 different points were examined) the higher number of titles allowed under the density-of-use ranking provided greater user satisfaction (the smaller number of raw-use titles provided 19% less potential uses). **(649)**

■ A 1977 study at the Music Library of the University of California, Berkeley, to investigate weeding criteria (based on a sample of 116 circulated volumes and a sample of 515 volumes from the shelf) *showed that*, to satisfy the needs of 97% of the borrowers over a year's time by weeding by publication date alone, the library would have to keep on the shelves all books published since "about 1900." **(756)**

Ibid. . . . *showed that* weeding on the basis of language alone was not a feasible idea. For example, during the period 1950-77, while 84.8% of the English-language books in the sample circulated, 79.3% of the French-language books and 71.8% of the German-language books circulated as well. Overall, during the 1950-77 period, 45.6% of the materials circulated were non-English language materials. **(756)**

Ibid. . . . *showed that* weeding on the basis of circulation activity in distinct subject areas was the most feasible idea. For example, the number of books that had never been charged out ranged from 5.6% of the books in "performance practice" to 35.0% of the books in "history." **(756)**

■ A survey reported in 1981 of 11 TALON resource libraries [100% response rate] concerning weeding policies *showed that* 3 libraries had written policies for discarding books, 4 had informal (i.e., nonwritten) procedures, and 4 did not weed materials and hence had no need for policies. Further, of the 7 respondents who did weed materials, the 2 most common practices were discarding multiple copies (4 respondents) and keeping only the latest edition of specified types of materials (4 respondents). **(739)**

BIBLIOGRAPHY OF ARTICLES

Note: This Bibliography cites all articles summarized in the six-volume set of *Handbooks.* Entries in the Bibliography are sequentially arranged by the citation reference numbers that correspond to the numbers appearing at the end of each research summary throughout the six volumes. The numbers in boldface located at the end of some citations refer only to those research summaries contained in this volume. Alphabetic access to the Bibliography is provided through the Author Index.

1   Pamela Kobelski and Jean Trumbore. "Student Use of On-line Bibliographic Services," *Journal of Academic Librarianship* 4:1 (March 1978), 14-18.**(186, 238)**

2   John V. Richardson, Jr. "Readability and Readership of Journals in Library Science," *Journal of Academic Librarianship* 3:1 (March 1977), 20-22.

3   Elizabeth Gates Kesler. "A Campaign against Mutilation," *Journal of Academic Librarianship* 3:1 (March 1977), 29-30. **(3, 271, 278, 287)**

4   Bruce Miller and Marilyn Sorum. "A Two Stage Sampling Procedure for Estimating the Proportion of Lost Books in a Library," *Journal of Academic Librarianship* 3:2 (May 1977), 74-80. **(270, 274)**

5   Jeffrey St. Clair and Rao Aluri. "Staffing the Reference Desk: Professionals or Nonprofessionals," *Journal of Academic Librarianship* 3:3 (July 1977), 149-153.

6   Valentine DeBruin. "Sometimes Dirty Things Are Seen on the Screen," *Journal of Academic Librarianship* 3:5 (November 1977), 256-266.

7   Herbert S. White. "The View from the Library School," *Journal of Academic Librarianship* 3:6 (January 1970), 321.

8   Stella Bentley. "Collective Bargaining and Faculty Status," *Journal of Academic Librarianship* 4:2 (May 1978), 75-81.

9   Steven Seokho Chwe. "A Comparative Study of Job Satisfaction: Catalogers and Reference Librarians in University Libraries," *Journal of Academic Librarianship* 4:3 (July 1978), 139-143.

10 Jo Bell Whitlatch and Karen Kieffer. "Service at San Jose State University: Survey of Document Availability," *Journal of Academic Librarianship* 4:4 (September 1978), 196-199. **(202)**

11 Joan Grant and Susan Perelmuter. "Vendor Performance Evaluation," *Journal of Academic Librarianship* 4:5 (November 1978), 366-367.

12   Robert Goehlert. "Book Availability and Delivery Service," *Journal of Academic Librarianship* 4:5 (November 1978), 368-371. **(56)**

13   Linda L. Phillips and Ann E. Raup. "Comparing Methods for Teaching Use of Periodical Indexes," *Journal of Academic Librarianship* 4:6 (January 1979), 420-423.

14   Margaret Johnson Bennett, David T. Buxton and Ella Capriotti. "Shelf Reading in a Large, Open Stack Library," *Journal of Academic Librarianship* 5:1 (March 1979), 4-8. **(275, 289)**

15   Sarah D. Knapp and C. James Schmidt. "Budgeting To Provide Computer-Based Reference Services: A Case Study," *Journal of Academic Librarianship* 5:1 (March 1979), 9-13.

16   Herbert S. White. "Library Materials Prices and Academic Library Practices: Between Scylla and Charybdis," *Journal of Academic Librarianship* 5:1 (March 1979), 20-23.

17   Dorothy P. Wells. "Coping with Schedules for Extended Hours: A Survey of Attitudes and Practices," *Journal of Academic Librarianship* 5:1 (March 1979), 24-27.

18   Johanna E. Tallman. "One Year's Experience with CONTU Guidelines for Interlibrary Loan Photocopies," *Journal of Academic Librarianship* 5:2 (May 1979), 71-74. **(80, 93)**

19   Robert Goehlert. "The Effect of Loan Policies on Circulation Recalls," *Journal of Academic Librarianship* 5:2 (May 1979), 79-82. **(23, 41, 56, 57)**

20   James R. Dwyer. "Public Response to an Academic Library Microcatalog," *Journal of Academic Librarianship* 5:3 (July 1979), 132-141.

21   Paul Metz. "The Role of the Academic Library Director," *Journal of Academic Librarianship* 5:3 (July 1979), 148-152.

22   Anne B. Piternick. "Problems of Resource Sharing with the Community: A Case Study," *Journal of Academic Librarianship* 5:3 (July 1979), 153-158.

23   Shelley Phipps and Ruth Dickstein. "The Library Skills Program at the University of Arizona: Testing, Evaluation and Critique," *Journal of Academic Librarianship* 5:4 (September 1979), 205-214.

24   Michael Stuart Freeman. "Published Study Guides: What They Say about Libraries," *Journal of Academic Librarianship* 5:5 (November 1979), 252-255.

25   James H. Richards, Jr. "Missing Inaction," *Journal of Academic Librarianship* 5:5 (November 1979), 266-269. **(288, 291)**

26   Philip H. Kitchens. "Engineers Meet the Library," *Journal of Academic Librarianship* 5:5 (November 1979), 277-282.

27 Michael Rouchton. "OCLC Serials Records: Errors, Omissions, and Dependability," *Journal of Academic Librarianship* 5:6 (January 1980), 316-321.

28 Charles R. McClure. "Academic Librarians, Information Sources, and Shared Decision Making," *Journal of Academic Librarianship* 6:1 (March 1980), 9-15.

29 Marjorie E. Murfin. "The Myth of Accessibility: Frustration and Failure in Retrieving Periodicals," *Journal of Academic Librarianship* 6:1 (March 1980), 16-19.

30 Anthony W. Ferguson and John R. Taylor. "What Are You Doing? An Analysis of Activities of Public Service Librarians at a Medium-sized Research Library," *Journal of Academic Librarianship* 6:1 (March 1980), 24-29.

31 Regina Shelton. "Adaption: A One-Year Survey of Reserve Photocopying," *Journal of Academic Librarianship* 6:2 (May 1980), 74-76.

32 Dorothea M. Thompson. "The Correct Uses of Library Data Bases Can Improve Interlibrary Loan Efficiency," *Journal of Academic Librarianship* 6:2 (May 1980), 83-86. **(82, 85, 91)**

33 Joan Repp and Julia A. Woods. "Student Appraisal Study and Allocation Formula: Priorities and Equitable Funding in a University Setting," *Journal of Academic Librarianship* 6:2 (May 1980), 87-90.

34 Elaine S. Friedman. "Patron Access to Online Cataloging Systems: OCLC in the Public Service Environment," *Journal of Academic Librarianship* 6:3 (July 1980), 132-139.

35 Edward C. Jestes. "Manual vs. Automated Circulation: A Comparison of Operating Costs in a University Library," *Journal of Academic Librarianship* 6:3 (July 1980), 144-150. **(5, 6)**

36 Kathleen A. Johnson and Barbara S. Plake. "Evaluation of PLATO Library Instructional Lessons: Another View," *Journal of Academic Librarianship* 6:3 (July 1980), 154-158.

37 Priscilla C. Yu. "International Gift and Exchange: The Asian Experience," *Journal of Academic Librarianship* 6:6 (January 1981), 333-338.

38 George W. Black, Jr. "Estimating Collection Size Using the Shelf List in a Science Library," *Journal of Academic Librarianship* (January 1981), 339-341.

39 Beth Macleod. "*Library Journal* and *Choice*: A Review of Reviews," *Journal of Academic Librarianship* 7:1 (March 1981), 23-28.

40 Frank Wm. Goudy. "HEA, Title II-C Grant Awards: A Financial Overview from FY 1978-79 through FY 1981-82," *Journal of Academic Librarianship* 8:5 (November 1982), 264-269.

41 Larry Hardesty and John Wright. "Student Library Skills and Attitudes and Their Change: Relationships to Other Selected Variables," *Journal of Academic Librarianship* 8:4 (September 1982), 216-220.

42 Penelope Pearson and Virginia Teufel. "Evaluating Undergraduate Library Instruction at the Ohio State University," *Journal of Academic Librarianship* 7:6 (January 1982), 351-357.

43 David S. Ferrioro. "ARL Directors as Proteges and Mentors," *Journal of Academic Librarianship* 7:6 (January 1982), 358-365.

44 Albert F. Maag. "So You Want to be a Director...," *Journal of Academic Librarianship* 7:4 (September 1981), 213-217.

45 Mary Noel Gouke and Sue Pease. "Title Searches in an Online Catalog and a Card Catalog: A Comparative Study of Patron Success in Two Libraries," *Journal of Academic Librarianship* 8:3 (July 1982), 137-143.

46 John K. Mayeski and Marilyn T. Sharrow. "Recruitment of Academic Library Managers: A Survey," *Journal of Academic Librarianship* 8:3 (July 1982), 151-154.

47 Linda K. Rambler. "Syllabus Study: Key to a Responsive Academic Library," *Journal of Academic Librarianship* 8:3 (July 1982), 155-159.

48 Marion T. Reid. "Effectiveness of the OCLC Data Base for Acquisitions Verification," *Journal of Academic Librarianship* 2:6 (January 1977), 303-326.

49 James D. Culley, Denis F. Healy and Kermit G. Cudd. "Business Students and the University Library: An Overlooked Element in the Business Curriculum," *Journal of Academic Librarianship* 2:6 (January 1977), 293-296. **(49, 50, 165, 190, 258, 259)**

50 Edward Kazlauskas. "An Exploratory Study: A Kenesic Analysis of Academic Library Service Points," *Journal of Academic Librarianship* 2:3 (July 1976), 130-134. **(69, 128, 148)**

51 Helen Gothberg. "Immediacy: A Study of Communication Effect on the Reference Process," *Journal of Academic Librarianship* 2:3 (July 1976), 126-129.

52 John Vasi. "Building Libraries for the Handicapped: A Second Look," *Journal of Academic Librarianship* 2:2 (May 1976), 82-83.

53 Elliot S. Palais. "The Significance of Subject Dispersion for the Indexing of Political Science Journals," *Journal of Academic Librarianship* 2:2 (May 1976), 72-76.

54 Ruth Carol Cushman. "Lease Plans—A New Lease on Life for Libraries," *Journal of Academic Librarianship* 2:1 (March 1976), 15-19.

55   Charles R. McClure. "Subject and Added Entries as Access to Information," *Journal of Academic Librarianship* 2:1 (March 1976), 9-14.

56   Marilyn L. Miller and Barbara B. Moran. "Expenditures for Resources in School Library Media Centers FY '82-'83," *School Library Journal* 30:2 (October 1983), 105-114.

57   Karen Lee Shelley. "The Future of Conservation in Research Libraries," *Journal of Academic Librarianship* 1:6 (January 1976), 15-18. **(285)**

58   Maryan E. Reynolds. "Challenges of Modern Network Development," *Journal of Academic Librarianship* 1:2 (May 1975), 19-22.

59   Marjorie E. Martin and Clyde Hendrick. "Ripoffs Tell Their Story: Interviews with Mutilators in a University Library," *Journal of Academic Librarianship* 1:2 (May 1975), 8-12. **(278)**

60   Audrey Tobias. "The Yule Curve Describing Periodical Citations by Freshmen: Essential Tool or Abstract Frill?" *Journal of Academic Librarianship* 1:1 (March 1975), 14-16.

61   Allan J. Dyson. "Organizing Undergraduate Library Instruction," *Journal of Academic Librarianship* 1:1 (March 1975), 9-13.

62   David F. Kohl. "High Efficiency Inventorying through Predictive Data," *Journal of Academic Librarianship* 8:2 (May 1982), 82-84. **(26, 27, 270, 274)**

63   Eleanor Phinney. "Trends in Public Library Adult Services," *ALA Bulletin* 57:3 (March 1963), 262-266.

64   Zelia J. French. "Library-Community Self-studies in Kansas," *ALA Bulletin* 56:1 (January 1962), 37-41. **(159, 174)**

65   Guy Garrison. "Nonresident Library Fees in Suburban Chicago," *ALA Bulletin* 55:6 (June 1961), 1013-1017.

66   James E. Bryan. "The Christmas Holiday Jam," *ALA Bulletin* 55:6 (June 1961), 526-530. **(198, 199, 250)**

67   Joint Libraries Committee on Fair Use in Photocopying, American Library Association. "Fair Use in Photocopying, Report on Single Copies," *ALA Bulletin* 55:6 (June 1961), 571-573. **(75, 79, 80, 81, 92, 93, 94, 103)**

68   Henry J. Dubester. "Stack Use of a Research Library," *ALA Bulletin* 55:10 (November 1961), 891-893.

69   Mary Virginia Gaver. "Teacher Education and School Libraries," *ALA Bulletin* 60:1 (January 1966), 63-72.

70   Richard Waters. "Free Space: Can Public Libraries Receive It?" *ALA Bulletin* 58:3 (March 1964), 232-234.

71 Frank L. Schick. "Professional Library Manpower," *ALA Bulletin* 58:4 (April 1964), 315-317.

72 Milbrey Jones. "Socio-Economic Factors in Library Service to Students," *ALA Bulletin* 58:11 (December 1964), 1003-1006. (146, 167, 216, 217, 229)

73 Elizabeth W. Stone. "Administrators Fiddle while Employees Burn or Flee," *ALA Bulletin* 63:2 (February 1969), 181-187.

74 Staff Organizations Round Table, American Library Association. "Opinions on Collective Bargaining," *ALA Bulletin* 63:6 (June 1969), 803-808.

75 Library Administration Division, American Library Association. "Library Employment of Minority Group Personnel," *ALA Bulletin* 63:7 (July-August 1969), 985-987.

76 Eli M. Oboler. "The Case for ALA Regional Annual Conferences," *ALA Bulletin* 63:8 (September 1969), 1099-1101.

77 Edward N. Howard. "Breaking the Fine Barrier," *ALA Bulletin* 63:11 (December 1969), 1541-1545. (19, 23, 24, 41, 42, 125)

78 Elin B. Christianson. "Variation of Editorial Material in Periodicals Indexed in *Reader's Guide*," *ALA Bulletin* 62:2 (February 1968), 173-182.

79 Insurance for Libraries Committee, American Library Association. "The Makings of a Nationwide Scandal," *ALA Bulletin* 62:4 (April 1968), 384-386.

80 George L. Gardiner. "Collective Bargaining: Some Questions Asked," *ALA Bulletin* 62:8 (September 1968), 973-976.

81 Barbara M. Conant. "Trials and Tribulations of Textbook Price Indexing," *ALA Bulletin* 61:2 (February 1967), 197-199.

82 Henry T. Drennan and Sarah R. Reed. "Library Manpower," *ALA Bulletin* 61:8 (September 1967), 957-965.

83 Jerry L. Walker. "Changing Attitudes toward the Library and the Librarian," *ALA Bulletin* 61:8 (September 1967), 977-981.

84 William R. Monat. "The Community Library: Its Search for a Vital Purpose," *ALA Bulletin* 61:11 (December 1967), 1301-1310. (27, 132, 168, 173, 180, 184, 206, 216, 219, 220, 225, 226, 229, 235, 252)

85 Irene A. Braden. "Pilot Inventory of Library Holdings," *ALA Bulletin* 62:9 (October 1968), 1129-1131. (273)

86 Genevieve Casey. "Library Manpower in the Detroit Metropolitan Region," *American Libraries* 1:8 (September 1970), 787-789.

87 Nora Cambier, Barton Clark, Robert Daugherty and Mike Gabriel. "Books in Print 1969: An Analysis of Errors," *American Libraries* 1:9 (October 1970), 901-902.

88 Tom Childers and Beth Krevitt. "Municipal Funding of Library Services," *American Libraries* 3:1 (January 1972), 53-57.

89 Albert H. Rubenstein, David J. Werner, Gustave Rath, John A. Kernaghan, and Robert D. O'Keefe. "Search versus Experiment—the Role of the Research Librarian," *College and Research Libraries* 34:4 (July 1973), 280-286. (**243, 244, 245, 246**)

90 Frank F. Kuo. "A Comparison of Six Versions of Science Library Instruction," *College and Research Libraries* 34:4 (July 1973), 287-290.

91 Laurence Miller. "The role of Circulation Services in the Major University Library," *College and Research Libraries* 34:6 (November 1973), 463-471.

92 Ruth Hyman and Gail Schlachter. "Academic Status: Who Wants It?" *College and Research Libraries* 34:6 (November 1973), 472-478.

93 Larry E. Harrelson. "Large Libraries and Information Desks," *College and Research Libraries* 35:1 (January 1974), 21-27.

94 Robert B. Downs. "Library Resources in the United States," *College and Research Libraries* 35:2 (March 1974), 97-108.

95 Richard J. Beeler. "Late-Study Areas: A Means of Extending Library Hours," *College and Research Libraries* 35:3 (May 1974), 200-203. (**198**)

96 Rolland E. Stevens. "A Study of Interlibrary Loan," *College and Research Libraries* 35:5 (September 1974), 336-343. (**75, 87, 88, 105, 110**)

97 Jay B. Clark. "An Approach to Collection Inventory," *College and Research Libraries* 35:5 (September 1974), 354-359. (**270, 272, 273, 274**)

98 Jan Baaske, Don Tolliver and Judy Westerberg. "Overdue Policies: A Comparison of Alternatives," *College and Research Libraries* 35:5 (September 1974), 354-359. (**23, 41**)

99 Clyde Hendrick and Marjorie E. Murfin. "Project Library Ripoff: A Study of Periodical Mutilation in a University Library," *College and Research Libraries* 35:6 (November 1974), 402-411. (**137, 276, 277, 278**)

100 Peter Marshall. "How Much, How Often?" *College and Research Libraries* 35:6 (November 1974), 453-456. (**60**)

101 Robert Balay and Christine Andres. "Use of the Reference Service in a Large Academic Library," *College and Research Libraries* 36:1 (January 1975), 9-26.

102 Guy Walker. "Preservation Efforts in Larger U.S. Academic Libraries," *College and Research Libraries* 36:1 (January 1975), 39-44.(**284, 285**)

103 Susanne Patterson Wahba. "Job Satisfaction of Librarians: A Comparison between Men and Women," *College and Research Libraries* 36:1 (January 1975), 45-51.

104 Grant T. Skelley. "Characteristics of Collections Added to American Research Libraries 1940-1970: A Preliminary Investigation," *College and Reseach Libraries* 36:1 (January 1975), 52-60.

105 Laura M. Boyer and William C. Theimer, Jr. "The Use and Training of Nonprofessional Personnel at Reference Desks in Selected College and University Libraries," *College and Research Libraries* 36:3 (May 1975), 193-200.

106 Robert J. Greene. "LENDS: An Approach to the Centralization/Decentralization Dilemma," *College and Research Libraries* 36:3 (May 1975), 201-207. (**16, 17, 21, 233**)

107 Frances L. Meals and Walter T. Johnson. "We Chose Microfilm," *College and Research Libraries* 21:3 (May 1960), 223-228. (**267**)

108 George Caldwell. "University Libraries and Government Publications: A Survey," *College and Research Libraries* 22:1 (January 1961), 30-34. (**280, 281**)

109 Allen Story. "Leo in Libraryland," *American Libraries* 7:9 (October 1976), 569-571.

110 Leslie R. Morris. "The Rise and Fall of the Library Job Market," *American Libraries* 12:9 (October 1981), 557-558.

111 Richard De Gennaro. "Escalating Journal Prices: Time To Fight Back," *American Libraries* 8:1 (January 1977), 69-74.

112 Joe A. Hewitt. "The Impact of OCLC," *American Libaries* 7:5 (May 1976), 268-275.(**86, 88, 89, 95, 101**)

113 Fritz Veit. "Book Order Procedures in the Publicly Controlled Colleges and Universities of the Midwest," *College and Research Libraries* 23:1 (January 1962), 33-40.

114 Keyes D. Metcalf. "Compact Shelving," *College and Research Libraries* 23:2 (March 1962), 103-111.

115 Natalie N. Nicholson and Eleanor Bartlett. "Who Uses University Libraries," *College and Research Libraries* 23:3 (May 1962), 217-259. (**212, 213, 259, 260**)

116 H. William Axford. "Rider Revisited," *College and Research Libraries* 23:4 (July 1962), 345-347.

117 E.J. Josey. "The Role of the College Library Staff in Instruction in the Use of the Library," *College and Research Libraries* 23:6 (November 1962), 492-498.

118 Edwin E. Williams. "Magnitude of the Paper-Deterioration Problems as Measured by a National Union Catalog Sample," *College and Research Libraries* 23:6 (November 1962), 499. (**284**)

119 Stella Frank Mosborg. "Measuring Circulation Desk Activities Using a Random Alarm Mechanism," *College and Research Libraries* 41:5 (September 1980), 437-444. (**69**)

120 Jean E. Koch and Judith M. Pask. "Working Papers in Academic Business Libraries," *College and Research Libraries* 41:6 (November 1980), 517-523. (**198, 199**)

121 Paul Metz. "Administrative Succession in the Academic Library," *College and Research Libraries* 39:5 (September 1978), 358-364.

122 Libby Trudell and James Wolper. "Interlibrary Loan in New England," *College and Research Libraries* 39:5 (September 1978), 365-371. (**82, 89, 95, 101, 105, 106, 107**)

123 Richard M. Dougherty. "The Evaluation of Campus Library Document Delivery Service," *College and Research Libraries* 34:1 (January 1973), 29-39. (**20, 21, 123, 219**)

124 Ung Chon Kim. "A Comparison of Two Out-of-Print Book Buying Methods," *College and Research Libraries* 34:5 (September 1973), 258-264.

125 Ann Gwyn, Anne McArthur and Karen Furlow. "Friends of the Library," *College and Research Libraries* 36:4 (July 1975), 272-282.

126 John J. Knightly. "Library Collections and Academic Curricula: Quantitative Relationships," *College and Research Libraries* 36:4 (July 1975), 295-301.

127 Alice S. Clark and Rita Hirschman. "Using the 'Guidelines': A Study of the State-Supported Two-Year College Libraries in Ohio," *College and Research Libraries* 36:5 (September 1975), 364-370.

128 Virginia E. Yagello and Gerry Gutherie. "The Effect of Reduced Loan Periods on High Use Items," *College and Research Libraries* 36:5 (September 1975), 411-414. (**16, 17, 37**)

129 George Piternick. "Library Growth and Academic Quality," *College and Research Libraries* 24:3 (May 1963), 223-229.

130 Robert N. Broadus. "An Analysis of Faculty Circulation in a University Library," *College and Research Libraries* 24:4 (July 1963), 323-325. (**25, 44, 45, 206, 261**)

131 Perry D. Morrison. "The Personality of the Academic Librarian," *College and Research Libraries* 24:5 (September 1963), 365-368.

132 W.J. Bonk. "What is Basic Reference?" *College and Research Libraries* 25:3 (May 1964), 5-8.

133 Jean Legg "The Periodical Scene," *RQ* 7:3 (Spring 1968), 129-132. (55, 63)

134 Richard H. Perrine. "Catalog Use Difficulties," *RQ* 7:4 (Summer 1968), 169-174.

135 Thelma E. Larson. "A Survey of User Orientation Methods," *RQ* 8:3 (Spring 1969), 182-187.

136 Phil Hoehn and Jean Hudson. "Academic Library Staffing Patterns," *RQ* 8:4 (Summer 1969), 242-244.

137 T.H. Milby. "Two Approaches to Biology," *RQ* 11:3 (Spring 1972), 231-235.

138 James B. Way. "Loose Leaf Business Services," *RQ* 9:2 (Winter 1969), 128-133.

139 Mary Jane Swope and Jeffrey Katzer. "Why Don't They Ask Questions?" *RQ* 12:2 (Winter 1972), 161-165. (127, 147)

140 Robert M. Simmons. "Finding That Government Document," *RQ* 12:2 (Winter 1972), 167-171.

141 Lee Regan. "Status of Reader's Advisory Service," *RQ* 12:3 (Spring 1973), 227-233.

142 Bruce Cossar. "Interlibrary Loan Costs," *RQ* 12:3 (Spring 1973), 243-246. (82, 84, 96, 97, 108)

143 Mary R. Turtle and William C. Robinson. "The Relationship between Time Lag and Place of Publication in *Library and Information Science Abstracts* and *Library Literature*," *RQ* 14:1 (Fall 1974), 28-31.

144 Rosemary Magrill and Charles H. Davis. "Public Library SDI; A Pilot Study," *RQ* 14:2 (Winter 1974), 131-137. (152, 262, 263)

145 Steve Parker and Kathy Essary. "A Manual SDI System for Academic Libraries," *RQ* 15:1 (Fall 1975), 47-54. (262)

146 Carl F. Orgren and Barbara J. Olson. "Statewide Teletype Reference Service," *RQ* 15:3 (Spring 1976), 203-209.

147 Anne S. Mavor, Jose Orlando Toro and Ernest R. Deprospo. "An Overview of the National Adult Independent Learning Project," *RQ* 15:4 (Summer 1976), 293-308. (121, 122)

148 Danuta A. Nitecki. "Attitudes toward Automated Information Retrieval Services among RASD Members," *RQ* 16:2 (Winter 1976), 133-141.

149 Rhoda Garoogian. "Library Use of the New York Times Information Bank: A Preliminary Survey," *RQ* 16:1 (Fall 1976), 59-64. (238, 240)

150 Marcella Ciucki. "Recording of Reference/Information Service Activities: A Study of Forms Currently Used," *RQ* 16:4 (Summer 1977), 273-283.

151 Mollie Sandock. "A Study of University Students' Awareness of Reference Services," *RQ* 16:4 (Summer 1977), 284-296. **(257)**

152 Kathleen Imhoff and Larry Brandwein. "Labor Collections and Services in Public Libraries throughout the United States, 1976," *RQ* 17:2 (Winter 1977), 149-158.

153 Cynthia Swenk and Wendy Robinson. "A Comparison of the Guides to Abstracting and Indexing Services Provided by Katz, Chicorel and Ulrich," *RQ* (Summer 1978), 317-319.

154 John P. Wilkinson and William Miller. "The Step Approach to Reference Service," *RQ* (Summer 1978), 293-299. **(251, 252, 256, 257, 258)**

155 Gerald Johoda, Alan Bayer and William L. Needham. "A Comparison of On-Line Bibliographic Searches in One Academic and One Industrial Organization," *RQ* 18:1 (Fall 1978), 42-49. **(140, 142, 238, 239, 242)**

156 Stephen P. Harter and Mary Alice S. Fields. "Circulation, Reference and the Evaluation of Public Library Service," *RQ* 18:2 (Winter 1978), 147-152. **(59)**

157 Daniel Rearn. "An Evaluation of Four Book Review Journals," *RQ* 19:2 (Winter 1979), 149-153.

158 Joseph W. Palmer. "Review Citations for Best-Selling Books," *RQ* 19:2 (Winter 1979), 154-158.

159 "An Evaluation of References to Indexes and Abstracts in Ulrich's 17th Edition," *RQ* 20:2 (Winter 1980), 155-159.

160 Victoria T. Kok and Anton R. Pierce. "The Reference Desk Survey: A Management Tool in an Academic Research Library," *RQ* 22:2 (Winter 1982), 181-187. **(252)**

161 Sheila S. Intner. "Equality of Cataloging in the Age of AACR2," *American Libraries* 14:2 (February 1983), 102-103.

162 Joseph W. Palmer. "The Future of Public Library Film Service," *American Libraries* 13:2 (February 1982), 140-142. **(196, 232)**

163 Robert Grover and Mary Kevin Moore. "Print Dominates Library Service to Children," *American Libraries* 13:4 (April 1982), 268-269. **(168)**

164 Richard H. Evensen and Mary Berghaus Levering. "Services Are 500% Better," *American Libraries* 10:6 (June 1979), 373. **(190)**

165 Judith Schick. "Job Mobility of Men and Women Librarians and How It Affects Career Advancement," *American Libraries* 10:11 (December 1979), 643-647.

166   Elizabeth Rountree. "Users and Nonusers Disclose Their Needs," *American Libraries* 10:8 (September 1979), 486-487. **(27, 132, 172, 194, 195, 220, 230, 253)**

167   George Bobinski. "A Survey of Faculty Loan Policies," *College and Research Libraries* 24:6 (November 1963), 483-486. add **(23, 37, 41)**

168   L. Miles Raisig and Frederick G. Kilgour. "The Use of Medical Theses as Demonstrated by Journal Citations, 1850-1960," *College and Research Libraries* 25:2 (March 1964), 93-102.

169   George H. Fadenrecht. "Library Facilities and Practices in Colleges of Veterinary Medicine," *College and Research Libraries* 25:4 (July 1964), 308-335.

170   Donald Thompson. "Working Conditions in Selected Private College Libraries," *College and Research Libraries* 25:4 (July 1964), 261-294.

171   Benedict Brooks and Frederick G. Kilgour. "Catalog Subject Searches in the Yale Medical Library," *College and Research Libraries* 25:6 (November 1964), 483-487.

172   Patrick Barkey. "Patterns of Student Use of a College Library," *College and Research Libraries* 26:2 (March 1965), 115-118. **(47, 58, 208)**

173   Genevieve Porterfield. "Staffing of Interlibrary Loan Service," *College and Research Libraries* 26:4 (July 1965), 318-320. **(92)**

174   Harold Mathis. "Professional or Clerical: A Cross-Validation Study," *College and Research Libraries* 26:6 (November 1965), 525-531.

175   David H. Doerrer. 'Overtime' and the Academic Librarian," *College and Research Libraries* 27:3 (May 1966), 194-239.

176   Lois L. Luesing. "Church Historical Collections in Liberal Arts Colleges," *College and Research Libraries* 27:5 (July 1966), 291-317.

177   W.C. Blankenship. "Head Librarians: How Many Men? How Many Women?" *College and Research Libraries* 28:1 (January 1967), 41-48.

178   Morrison C. Haviland. "Loans to Faculty Members in University Libraries," *College and Research Libraries* 28:3 (May 1967), 171-174. **(22, 37, 53)**

179   R. Vernon Ritter. "An Investigation of Classroom-Library Relationships on a College Campus as Seen in Recorded Circulation and GPA's," *College and Research Libraries* 29:1 (January 1968), 3-4. **(48, 58, 59, 208, 209)**

180   Peter Spyers-Duran. "Faculty Studies: A Survey of Their Use in Selected Libraries," *College and Research Libraries* 29:1 (January 1968), 55-61. **(53)**

181   Raymond Kilpela. "The University Library Committee," *College and Research Libraries* 29:2 (March 1968), 141-143.

182 W. Porter Kellam and Dale L. Barker. "Activities and Opportunities of University Librarians for Full Participation in the Educational Enterprise," *College and Research Libraries* 29:5 (May 1968), 195-199.

183 Lloyd A. Kramer and Martha B. Kramer. "The College Library and the Drop-Out," *College and Research Libraries* 29:4 (July 1968), 310-312.(**48, 59**)

184 Carl Hintz. "Criteria for Appointment to and Promotion in Academic Rank," *College and Research Libraries* 29:5 (September 1968), 341-346.

185 Desmond Taylor. "Classification Trends in Junior College Libraries," *College and Research Libraries* 29:6 (September 1968), 351-356.

186 Raj Madan, Eliese Hetler and Marilyn Strong. "The Status of Librarians in Four-Year State Colleges and Universities," *College and Research Libraries* 29:5 (September 1968), 381-386.

187 Victor Novak. "The Librarian in Catholic Institutions," *College and Research Libraries* 29:5 (September 1968), 403-410.

188 Barbara H. Phipps. "Library Instruction for the Undergraduate," *College and Research Libraries* 29:5 (September 1968), 411-423.

189 Ashby J. Fristoe. "Paperbound Books: Many Problems, No Solutions," *College and Research Libraries* 29:5 (September 1968), 437-442.

190 Sidney Forman. "Innovative Practices in College Libraries," *College and Research Libraries* 29:6 (November 1968), 486-492. (**3**)

191 Richard W. Trueswell. "Some Circulation Data from a Research Library," *College and Research Libraries* 29:6 (November 1968), 493-495. (**28**)

192 Jane P. Kleiner. "The Information Desk: The Library's Gateway to Service," *College and Research Libraries* 29:6 (November 1968), 496-501.

193 J.E.G. Craig, Jr. "Characteristics of Use of Geology Literature," *College and Research Libraries* 3:3 (May 1969), 230-236.

194 Ronald A. Hoppe and Edward C. Simmel. "Book Tearing: The Bystander in the University Library," *College and Research Libraries* 3:3 (May 1969), 247-251.(**136, 276**)

195 Stephen L. Peterson. "Patterns of Use of Periodical Literature," *College and Research Libraries* 30:5 (September 1969), 422-430. (**223, 250, 260, 261**)

196 Mary B. Cassata. "Teach-in: The Academic Librarian's Key to Status," *College and Research Libraries* 31:1 (January 1970), 22-27.

197 E.J. Josey. "Community Use of Junior College Libraries—A Symposium," *College and Research Libraries* 31:3 (May 1970), 185-198.(**44, 50, 51, 53, 247**)

198 Virgil F. Massman. "Academic Library Salaries in a Seven-State Area," *College and Research Libraries* 3:6 (November 1969), 477-482.

199 James Krikelas. "Subject Searches Using Two Catalogs: A Comparative Evaluation," *College and Research Libraries* 30:6 (November 1969), 506-517.

200 James Wright. "Fringe Benefits for Academic Library Personnel," *College and Research Libraries* 31:1 (January 1970), 18-21.

201 Howard Clayton. "Femininity and Job Satisfaction among Male Library Students at One Midwestern University," *College and Research Libraries* 31:6 (November 1970), 388-398.

202 Philip V. Rzasa and John H. Moriarty. "The Types and Needs of Academic Library Users: A Case Study of 6,568 Responses," *College and Research Libraries* 31:6 (November 1970),403-409. (164, 213, 260, 264)

203 Bob Carmack and Trudi Loeber. "The Library Reserve System—Another Look," *College and Research Libraries* 32:2 (March 1971), 105-109.(59, 60)

204 C. James Schmidt and Kay Shaffer. "A Cooperative Interlibrary Loan Service for the State-Assisted University Libraries in Ohio," *College and Research Libraries* 32:3 (May 1971), 197-204. (77, 78, 79, 80, 84, 93, 98, 104)

205 Edward S. Warner. "A Tentative Analytical Approach to the Determination of Interlibrary Loan Network Effectiveness," *College and Research Libraries* 32:3 (May 1971), 217-221. (84)

206 Irving Zelkind and Joseph Sprug. "Increased Control through Decreased Controls: A Motivational Approach to a Library Circulation Problem," *College and Research Libraries* 32:3 (May 1971), 222-226.(63, 64, 273, 287)

207 William E. McGrath. "Correlating the Subjects of Books Taken Out Of and Books Used Within an Open-Stack Library," *College and Research Libraries* 32:4 (July 1971), 280-285.(15)

208 Thomas Kirk. "A Comparison of Two Methods of Library Instruction for Students in Introductory Biology," *College and Research Libraries* 32:6 (November 1971), 465-474. (130)

209 Dawn McCaghy and Gary Purcell. "Faculty Use of Government Publications," *College and Research Libraries* 33:1 (January 1972), 7-12. (226)

210 Joe A. Hewitt. "Sample Audit of Cards from a University Library Catalog," *College and Research Libraries* 33:1 (January 1972), 24-27.

211 William E. McGrath. "The Significance of Books Used According to a Classified Profile of Academic Departments," *College and Research Libraries* 33:3 (May 1972), 212-219. (25)

212 Carlos A. Cuadra and Ruth J. Patrick. "Survey of Academic Library Consortia in the U.S.," *College and Research Libraries* 33:4 (July 1972), 271-283. (86)

213 Marjorie Johnson. "Performance Appraisal of Librarians—A Survey," *College and Research Libraries* 33:5 (September 1972), 359-367.

214 Marvin E. Wiggins. "The Development of Library Use Instruction Programs," *College and Research Libraries* 33:6 (November 1972), 473-479.

215 Margaret E. Monroe. "Community Development as a Mode of Community Analysis," *Library Trends* 24:3 (January 1976), 497-514.

216 Janet K. Rudd and Larry G. Carver. "Topographic Map Acquisition in U.S. Academic Libraries," *Library Trends* 29:3 Winter 1981), 375-390.

217 John Belland. "Factors Influencing Selection of Materials," *School Media Quarterly* 6:2 (Winter 1978), 112-119.

218 Virginia Witucke. "A Comparative Analysis of Juvenile Book Review Media," *School Media Quarterly* 8:3 (Spring 1980), 153-160.

219 M. Carl Drott and Jacqueline C. Mancall. "Magazines as Information Sources: Patterns of Student Use," *School Media Quarterly* 8:4 (Summer 1980), 240-250. **(216, 217)**

220 Jerry J. Watson and Bill C. Snider. "Book Selection Pressure on School Library Media Specialists and Teachers," *School Media Quarterly* 9:2 (Winter 1981), 95-101.

221 Jerry J. Watson and Bill C. Snider. "Educating the Potential Self-Censor," *School Media Quarterly* 9:4 (Summer 1981), 272-276.

222 Lucy Anne Wozny. "Online Bibliographic Searching and Student Use of Information: An Innovative Teaching Approach," *School Library Media Quarterly* 11:1 (Fall 1982), 35-42. **(215, 216, 218, 240)**

223 Carol A. Doll. "School and Public Library Collection Overlap and the Implications for Networking," *School Library Media Quarterly* 11:3 (Spring 1983), 193-199.

224 Arthur Tannenbaum and Eva Sidhom. "User Environment and Attitudes in an Academic Microform Center," *Library Journal* 101:18 (October 15, 1976), 2139-2143. **(134, 135, 233, 234)**

225 Timothy Hays, Kenneth D. Shearer and Concepcion Wilson. "The Patron Is Not the Public," *Library Journal* 102:16 (September 15, 1977), 1813-1818. **(124, 143, 159, 166)**

226 Wilma Lee Woolard. "The Combined School and Public Library: Can It Work?" *Library Journal* 103:4 (February 15, 1978), 435-438.

227 David C. Genaway. "Bar Coding and the Librarian Supermarket: An Analysis of Advertised Library Vacancies," *Library Journal* 103:3 (February 1, 1978), 322-325.

228 Hoyt Galvin. "Public Library Parking Needs," *Library Journal* 103:2 (November 15, 1978), 2310-2313.

229 Harold J. Ettelt. "Book Use at a Small (Very) Community College Library," *Library Journal* 103:2 (November 15, 1978), 2314-2315. **(10, 17)**

230 Frederick G. Kilgour. "Interlibrary Loans On-Line," *Library Journal* 104:4 (February 15, 1979), 460-463.

231 Paul Little. "The Effectiveness of Paperbacks," *Library Journal* 104:2 (November 15, 1979), 2411-2416. **(13, 14, 70, 71)**

232 Ken Kister. "Encyclopedias and the Public Library: A National Survey," *Library Journal* 104:8 (April 15, 1979), 890-893.

233 Arlene T. Dowell. "Discrepancies in CIP: How Serious Is the Problem," *Library Journal* 104:19 (November 1, 1979), 2281-2287.

234 Gary D. Byrd, Mary Kay Smith and Norene McDonald. "MINET in K.C.," *Library Journal* 104:17 (October 1, 1979), 2044-2047. **(185, 236)**

235 Ray L. Carpenter. "The Public Library Patron," *Library Journal* 104:3 (February 1, 1979), 347-351.**(168, 169, 170, 172, 180, 183, 184)**

236 Cathy Schell. "Preventive Medicine: The Library Prescription," *Library Journal* 105:8 (April 15, 1980), 929-931. **(115)**

237 Michael Gonzalez, Bill Greeley and Stephen Whitney. "Assessing the Library Needs of the Spanish-speaking," *Library Journal* 105:7 (April 1, 1980), 786-789. **(166, 167, 173, 177, 183, 184, 192, 193, 229, 230, 234, 235)**

238 Thomas Childers. "The Test of Reference," *Library Journal* 105:8 (April 15, 1980), 924-928.

239 Mary Noel Gouke and Marjorie Murfin. "Periodical Mutilization: The Insidious Disease," *Library Journal* 105:16 (September 15, 1980), 1795-1797. **(278)**

240 Sheila Creth and Faith Harders. "Requirements for the Entry Level Librarian," *Library Journal* 105:18 (October 15, 1980), 2168-2169.

241 Kathleen M. Heim and Leigh S. Estabrook. "Career Patterns of Librarians," *Drexel Library Quarterly* 17:3 (Summer 1981), 35-51.

242 Margaret Peil. "Library Use by Low-Income Chicago Families," *Library Quarterly* 33:4 (October 1963), 329-333.**(171, 174, 181, 182, 183, 192, 225, 228, 229, 234)**

243 Herbert Goldhor and John McCrossan. "An Exploratory Study of the Effect of a Public Library Summer Reading Club on Reading Skills," *Library Quarterly* 36:1 (June 1966), 14-24. **(167)**

244 Robert Sommer. "Reading Areas in College Libraries," *Library Quarterly* 38:3 (July 1968), 249-260. **(163, 164)**

245 Isaac T. Littleton. "The Literature of Agricultural Economics: Its Bibliographic Organization and Use," *Library Quarterly* 39:2 (April 1969), 140-152. **(156, 258)**

246 G. Edward Evans. "Book Selection and Book Collection Usage in Academic Libraries," *Library Quarterly* 40:3 (July 1970), 297-308.

247 Marilyn Werstein Greenberg. "A Study of Reading Motivation of Twenty-Three Seventh-Grade Students," *Library Quarterly* 40:3 (July 1970), 309-317. **(175, 176, 177)**

248 Ben-Ami Lipetz. "Catalog Use in a Large Research Library," *Library Quarterly* 42:1 (January 1972), 129-130. **(57, 201, 202)**

249 John Aubry. "A Timing Study of the Manual Searching of Catalogs," *Library Quarterly* 42:4 (October 1972), 399-415.

250 Kenneth H. Plate and Elizabeth W. Stone. "Factors Affecting Librarians' Job Satisfaction: A Report of Two Studies," *Library Quarterly* 44:2 (April 1974), 97-109.

251 Elizabeth Warner McElroy. "Subject Variety in Adult Reading: I. Factors Related to Variety in Reading," *Library Quarterly* 38:1 (April 1968), 154-167. **(174, 175)**

252 James C. Baughman. "A Structural Analysis of the Literature of Sociology," *Library Quarterly* 44:4 (October 1974), 293-308.

253 Edd E. Wheeler. "The Bottom Lines: Fifty Years of Legal Footnoting in Review," *Law Library Journal* 72:2 (Spring 1979), 245-259.

254 Daniel O'Connor and Phyllis Van Orden. "Getting into Print," *College and Research Libraries* 39:5 (September 1978), 389-396.

255 Howard Fosdick. "Library Education in Information Science: Present Trends," *Special Libraries* 69:3 (March 1978), 100-108.

256 Paula de Simone Watson. "Publication Activity among Academic Librarians," *College and Research Libraries* 38:5 (September 1977), 375-384.

257 Susan Andriette Ariew. "The Failure of the Open Access Residence Hall Library," *College and Research Libraries* 39:5 (September 1978), 372-380.

258 Mary Ellen Soper. "Characteristics and Use of Personal Collections," *Library Quarterly* (October 1976), 397-415. **(108, 247, 248)**

259 Ronald R. Powell. "An Investigation of the Relationships Between Quantifiable Reference Service Variables and Reference Performance in Public Libraries," *Library Quarterly* 48:1 (January 1978), 1-19.

260 Mary Jo Lynch. "Reference Interviews in Public Libraries," *Library Quarterly* 48:2 (April 1978), 119-142.

261 William A. Satariano. "Journal Use in Sociology: Citation Analysis versus Readership Patterns," *Library Quarterly* 48:3 (July 1978), 293-300.

262 Paul Metz. "The Use of the General Collection in the Library of Congress," *Library Quarterly* 49:4 (October 1979), 415-434.

263 Michael Halperin and Maureen Strazdon. "Measuring Students' Preferences for Reference Service: A Conjoint Analysis," *Library Quarterly* 50:2 (April 1980), 208-224. (148, 149)

264 Herbert S. White. "Factors in the Decisions by Individuals and Libraries To Place or Cancel Subscriptions to Scholarly and Research Journals," *Library Quarterly* 50:3 (July 1980), 287-309. (145, 157)

265 George D'Elia. "The Development and Testing of a Conceptual Model of Public Library User Behavior," *Library Quarterly* 50:4 (October 1980), 410-430. (169, 170, 195, 248, 249)

266 Donald A. Hicks. "Diversifying Fiscal Support by Pricing Public Library Services: A Policy Impact Analysis," *Library Quarterly* 50:4 (October 1980), 453-474. (27, 235)

267 Theodora Hodges and Uri Block. "Fiche or Film for COM Catalogs: Two Use Tests," *Library Quarterly* 52:2 (April 1982), 131-144. (116)

268 Terry L. Weech and Herbert Goldhor. "Obtrusive versus Unobtrusive Evaluation of Reference Service in Five Illinois Public Libraries: A Pilot Study," *Library Quarterly* 52:4 (October 1982), 305-324.

269 Stephen E. Wiberley, Jr. "Journal Rankings From Citation Studies: A Comparison of National and Local Data From Social Work," *Library Quarterly* 52:4 (October 1982), 348-359.

270 George D'Elia and Sandra Walsh. "User Satisfaction with Library Service— A Measure of Public Library Performance?" *Library Quarterly* 53:2 (April 1983), 109-133. (132, 133, 195, 249)

271 Edward A. Dyl. "A Note on Price Discrimination by Academic Journals," *Library Quarterly* 53:2 (April 1983), 161-168.

272 Michael R. Kronenfeld and James A. Thompson. "The Impact of Inflation on Journal Costs," *Library Journal* 106:7 (April 1,1981), 714-717.

273 George D'Elia and Mary K. Chelton. "Paperback Books," *Library Journal* 107:16 (September 15, 1982), 1718-1721. (14)

274 Patsy Hansel and Robert Burgin. "Hard Facts about Overdues," *Library Journal* 108:4 (February 15,1983), 349-352. (24, 25, 38, 39, 42, 43, 44, 55, 56)

275 Robert Dale Karr. "Becoming a Library Director," *Library Journal* 108:4 (February 15, 1983), 343-346.

276 Mary V. Gaver. "The Science Collection—New Evidence To Consider," *Junior Libraries* (later *School Library Journal*) 7:6 (February 1961), 4-7. (216)

277 Dorothy G. Petersen. "Teachers' Professional Reading," *School Library Journal* 9:8 (April 1963), 24-27.

278 Linda Kraft. "Lost Herstory: The Treatment of Women in Children's Encyclopedias," *School Library Journal* 19:5 (January 1973), 26-35.

279 John Stewig and Margaret Higgs. "Girls Grow Up: A Study of Sexism in Children's Literature," *School Library Journal* 19:5 (January 1973), 44-49.

280 W. Bernard Lukenbill. "Fathers in Adolescent Novels," *School Library Journal* 20:6 (February 1974), 26-30.

281 Jacqueline C. Mancall and M. Carl Drott. "Tomorrow's Scholars: Patterns of Facilities Use," *School Library Journal* 20:7 (March 1980), 99-103. (**214, 217, 218**)

282 John McCrossan. "Education of Librarians Employed in Small Public Libraries," *Journal of Education for Librarianship* 7:4 (Spring 1967), 237-245.

283 Gail Schlachter and Dennis Thomison. "The Library Science Doctorate: A Quantitative Analysis of Dissertations and Recipients," *Journal of Education for Librarianship* 15:2 (Fall 1974), 95-111.

284 Constance Rinehart and Rose Mary Magrill. "Characteristics of Applicants for Library Science Teaching Positions," *Journal of Education for Librarianship* 16:3 (Winter 1976), 173-182.

285 George W. Whitbeck. "Grade Inflation in the Library School—Myth or Reality," *Journal of Education for Librarianship* 17:4 (Spring 1977), 214-237. (**228**)

286 Charles H. Davis. "Computer Programming for Librarians," *Journal of Education for Librarianship* 18:1 (Summer 1977), 41-52.

287 Helen M. Gothberg. "A Study of the Audio-Tutorial Approach to Teaching Basic Reference," *Journal of Education for Librarianship* 18:3 (Winter 1978), 193-202.

288 J. Periam Danton. "British and American Library School Teaching Staffs: A Comparative Inquiry," *Journal of Education for Librarianship* 19:2 (Fall 1978), 97-129.

289 Lucille Whalen. "The Role of the Assistant Dean in Library Schools," *Journal of Education for Librarianship* 20:1 (Summer 1979), 44-54.

290 A. Neil Yerkey. "Values of Library School Students, Faculty and Librarians: Premises for Understanding," *Journal of Education for Librarianship* 21:2 (Fall 1980), 122-134.

291 Judith B. Katz. "Indicators of Success: Queens College Department of Library Science," *Journal of Education for Librarianship* 19:2 (Fall 1978), 130-139.

292 Lawrence Auld, Kathleen H. Heim and Jerome Miller. "Market Receptivity for an Extended M.L.S.," *Journal of Education for Librarianship* 21:3 (Winter 1981), 235-245.

293   John Richardson, Jr. and Peter Hernon. "Theory vs. Practice: Student Preferences," *Journal of Education for Librarianship* 21:4 (Spring 1981), 287-300,

294   Richard I. Blue and James L. Divilbiss. "Optimizing Selection of Library School Students," *Journal of Education for Librarianship* 21:4 (Spring 1981), 301-312.

295   David H. Jonassen and Gerald G. Hodges. "Student Cognitive Styles: Implications for Library Educators," *Journal of Education for Librarianship* 22:3 (Winter 1982), 143-153.

296   Mary Kingsbury. "How Library Schools Evaluate Faculty Performance," *Journal of Education for Librarianship* 22:4 (Spring 1982), 219-238.

297   John W. Lee and Raymond L. Read. "The Graduate Business Student and the Library," *College and Research Libraries* 33:5 (September 1972), 403-407. **(223)**

298   Carol Steer. "Authors Are Studied," *Canadian Library Journal* 39:3 (June 1982), 151-155.

299   Rashid Tayyeb. "Implementing AACR 2—A National Survey," *Canadian Library Journal* 39:6 (December 1982), 373-376.

300   Dick Matzek and Scott Smith. "Online Searching in the Small College Library—The Economics and the Results," *Online* (March 1982), 21-29. **(187, 239)**

301   Mary Lee Bundy. "Metropolitan Public Library Use," *Wilson Library Bulletin* 41:9 (May 1967), 950-961. **(57, 109, 165, 166, 167, 168, 170, 171, 172, 184, 194, 200, 232, 249, 250, 252, 253, 264)**

302   John Shipman. "Signifying Renewal as Well as Change: One Library's Experience with the Center for Research Libraries," *Library Acquisitions: Practice and Theory* 2:5 (1978), 243-248. **(77, 85, 101, 102, 109)**

303   Nathan R. Einhorn. "The Inclusion of the Products of Reprography in the International Exchange of Publications," *Library Acquisitions: Practice and Theory* 2:5 (1978), 227-236

304   Nancy J. Williamson. "Education for Acquisitions Librarians: A State of the Art Review," *Library Acquisitions: Practice and Theory* 2:3-4 (1978), 199-208.

305   Janet L. Flowers. "Time Logs for Searchers: How Useful?" *Library Acquisitions: Practice and Theory* 2:2 (1978), 77-83.

306   D.N. Wood. "Current Exchange of Serials at the British Library Lending Division," *Library Acquisitions: Practice and Theory* 3:2 (1979), 107-113.

307   Robert Goehlert. "Journal Use Per Monetary Unit: A Reanalysis of Use Data," *Library Acquisitions: Practice and Theory* 3:2 (1979), 91-98. **(70)**

308 Margaret Landesman and Christopher Gates. "Performance of American Inprint Vendors: A Comparison at the University of Utah," *Library Acquisitions: Practice and Theory* 4:3-4 (1980), 187-192.

309 Kenton Pattie and Mary Ernst. "Chapter II Grants: Libraries Gain," *School Library Journal* 29:5 (January 1983), 17-19.

310 John Erlandson and Yvonne Boyer. "Acquistions of State Documents," *Library Acquisitions: Practice and Theory* 4:2 (1980), 117-127.

311 George V. Hodowanec. "Analysis of Variables Which Help To Predict Book and Periodical Use," *Library Acquisitions: Practice and Theory* 4:1 (1980), 75-85. **(8, 15, 30, 36, 46, 50)**

312 Darrell L. Jenkins. "Acquiring Acquisitions Librarians," *Library Acquisitions: Practice and Theory* 5:2 (1981), 81-87.

313 Steven E. Maffeo. "Invoice Payment by Library Acquisitions: A Controlled Time Study," *Library Acquisitions: Practice and Theory* 5:2 (1981), 67-71.

314 Joyce G. McDonough, Carol Alf O'Connor and Thomas A. O'Connor. "Moving the Backlog: An Optimum Cycle for Searching OCLC," *Library Acquisitions: Practice and Theory* 6:3 (1982), 265-270.

315 Paul B. Wiener. "Recreational Reading Services in Academic Libraries: An Overview," *Library Acquisitions: Practice and Theory* 6:1 (1982), 59-70. **(30, 54, 62)**

316 Peter Hernon. "Use of Microformatted Government Publications," *Microform Review* 11:4 (Fall 1982), 237-252. **(126, 127, 135, 136, 182, 226, 227)**

317 Charles R. McClure. "Online Government Documents Data Base Searching and the Use of Microfiche Documents Online by Academic and Public Depository Librarians," *Microfilm Review* 10:4 (Fall 1981), 245-259.

318 Peter Hernon and George W. Whitbeck. "Government Publications and Commercial Microform Publishers: A Survey of Federal Depository Libraries," *Microform Review* 6:5 (September 1977), 272-284.

319 Robert F. Jennings and Hathia Hayes. "The Use of Microfiche Copies of Children's Trade Books in Selected Fourth-Grade Classrooms," *Microform Review* 3:3 (July 1974), 189-193. **(193)**

320 E.R. Norten. "New Books in Microform: A Survey," *Microform Review* 1:4 (October 1972), 284-288.

321 Renata Tagliacozzo, Manfred Kochen and Lawrence Rosenberg. "Orthographic Error Patterns of Author Names in Catalog Searches," *Journal of Library Automation* 3:2 (June 1970), 93-101.

322 Lorne R. Buhr. "Selective Dissemination of MARC: A User Evaluation," *Journal of Library Automation* 5:1 (March 1972), 39-50. **(151)**

323 Gerry D. Guthrie and Steven D. Slifko. "Analysis of Search Key Retrieval on a Large Bibliographic File," *Journal of Library Automation* 6:2 (June 1972), 96-100.

324 Alan L. Landgraf and Frederick G. Kilgour. "Catalog Records Retrieved by Personal Author Using Derived Search Keys," *Journal of Library Automation* 6:2 (June 1973), 103-108.

325 Martha E. Williams. "Data Element Statistics for the MARC II Data Base," *Journal of Library Automation* 6:2 (June 1976), 89-100.

326 Michael D. Cooper and Nancy A. DeWath. "The Cost of On-Line Bibliographic Searching," *Journal of Library Automation* 9:3 (September 1976), 195-209.

327 Edward John Kazlauskas. "The Application of the Instrumental Development Process to a Module on Flowcharting," *Journal of Library Automation* 9:3 (September 1976), 234-244.

328 Lawrence K. Legard and Charles P. Bourne. "An Improved Title Word Search Key for Large Catalog Files," *Journal of Library Automation* 9:4 (December 1976), 318-327.

329 Ryan E. Hoover. "Patron Appraisal of Computer-Aided On-Line Bibliographic Retrieval Services," *Journal of Library Automation* 9:4 (December 1976), 335-350. (186, 238)

330 T.D.C. Kuch. "Analysis of the Literature of Library Automation through Citations in the *Annual Review of Information Science and Technology*," *Journal of Library Automation* 10:1 (March 1977), 82-84.

331 Isobel Jean Mosley. "Cost-Effectiveness Analysis of the Automation of a Circulation System," *Journal of Library Automation* 10:3 (September 1977), 240-254. (5, 6, 70)

332 Michael D. Cooper and Nancy A. DeWath. "The Effect of User Fees on the Cost of On-Line Searching in Libraries," *Journal of Library Automation* 10:4 (December 1977), 304-319. (239, 240)

333 James W. Bourg, Douglas Lacy, James Llinas and Edward T. O'Neill. "Developing Corporate Author Search Keys," *Journal of Library Automation* 11:2 (June 1978), 106-125.

334 Cynthia C. Ryans. "A Study of Errors Found in Non-MARC Cataloging in a Machine-Assisted System," *Journal of Library Automation* 11:2 (June 1978), 125-132.

335 Joselyn Druschel. "Cost Analysis of an Automated and Manual Cataloging and Book Processing System," *Journal of Library Automation* 14:1 (March 1981), 24-49.

336 Kunj B. Bastogi and Ichiko T. Morita. "OCLC Search Key Usage Patterns in a Large Research Library," *Journal of Library Automation* 14:2 (June 1981), 90-99. **(204)**

337 Georgia L. Brown. "AACR 2: OCLC's Implementation and Database Conversion," *Journal of Library Automation* 14:3 (September 1981), 161-173.

338 James R. Martin. "Automation and the Service Attitudes of ARL Circulation Managers," *Journal of Library Automation* 14:3 (September 1981), 190-194. **(4, 5, 6, 7, 64, 65, 69, 70, 118, 119)**

339 University of Oregon Library. "A Comparison of OCLC, RLG/RLIN and WLN," *Journal of Library Automation* 14:3 (September 1981), 215-217.

340 Terence Crowley. "Comparing Fiche and Film: A Test of Speed," *Journal of Library Automation* 14:4 (December 1981), 292-294.

341 Public Service Satellite Consortium. "Cable Library Survey Results," *Journal of Library Automation* 14:4 (December 1981), 304-313.

342 Dennis Reynolds. "Entry of Local Data on OCLC: The Options and Their Impact on the Processing of Archival Tapes," *Information Technology and Libraries* 1:1 (March 1982), 5-14. **(90, 91, 95, 96)**

343 Joseph Ford. "Network Service Centers and Their Expanding Role," *Information Technology and Libraries* 1:1 (March 1982), 28-35. **(3, 86, 90)**

344 Carolyn A. Johnson. "Retrospective Conversion of Three Library Collections," *Information Technology and Libraries* 1:2 (June 1982), 133-139.

345 Lynn L. Magrath. "Computers in the Library: The Human Element," *Information Technology and Libraries* 1:3 (September 1982), 266-270. **(117)**

346 Izabella Taler. "Automated and Manual ILL: Time Effectiveness and Success Rate," *Information Technology and Libraries* 1:3 (September 1982), 277-280. **(85, 91, 92, 102, 103)**

347 Martha E. Williams, Stephen W. Barth and Scott E. Preece. "Summary of Statistics for Five Years of the MARC Data Base," *Journal of Library Automation* 12:4 (December 1979), 314-337.

348 Susan U. Golden and Gary A. Golden. "Access to Periodicals: Search Key versus Keyword," *Information Technology and Libraries* 2:1 (March 1983), 26-32.

349 Ray R. Larson and Vicki Graham. "Monitoring and Evaluating MELVYL," *Information Technology and Libraries* 2:1 (March 1983), 93-104. **(117, 204, 205, 206)**

350   Barbara E. Carr. "Improving the Periodicals Collection through an Index Correlation Study," *Reference Services Review* 9:4 (October/December 1981), 27-31.

351   I.N. Sengupta. "Impact of Scientific Serials on the Advancement of Medical Knowledge: An Objective Method of Analysis," *International Library Review* 4:2 (April 1972), 169-195.

352   June L. Stewart. "The Literature of Politics: A Citation Analysis," *International Library Review* 2:3 (July 1970), 329-353.

353   I.N. Sengupta. "The Literature of Microbiology," *International Library Review* 6:3 (July 1974), 353-369.

354   I.N. Sengupta. "The Literature of Pharmacology," *International Library Review* 6:4 (October 1974), 483-504.

355   A.W. Hafner. "Citation Characteristics of Physiology Literature, 1970-72," *International Library Review* 8:1 (January 1976), 85-115.

356   Hans Hanan Wellisch. "Script Conversion Practices in the World's Libraries," *International Library Review* 8:1 (January 1976), 55-84.

357   Christine Anderson Brock and Gayle Smith Edelman. "Teaching Practices of Academic Law Librarians," *Law Library Journal* 71:1 (February 1978), 96-107.

358   Charles B. Wolfe. "Current Problems Facing State Law Libraries," *Law Library Journal* 71:1 (February 1978), 108-114).

359   Mindy J. Myers. "The Impact of Lexis on the Law Firm Library: A Survey," *Law Library Journal* 71:1 (February 1978), 158-169. **(99, 100, 111)**

360   Nancy P. Johnson. "Legal Periodical Usage Survey: Method and Application," *Law Library Journal* 71:1 (February 1978), 177-186.

361   Ann M. Carter. "Budgeting in Private Law Firm Libraries," *Law Library Journal* 71:1 (February 1978), 187-194. **(133)**

362   James F. Bailey, III and Oscar M. Trelles, II. "Autonomy, Librarian Status, and Librarian Tenure in Law School Libraries: The State of the Art, 1978," *Law Library Journal* 71:3 (August 1978), 425-462.

363   Frank Wm. Goudy. "Funding Local Public Libraries: FY 1966 to FY 1980," *Public Libraries* 21:2 (Summer 1982), 52-54.

364   Guy Garrison. "A Look At Research on Public Library Problems in the 1970's," *Public Libraries* 19:1 (Spring 1980), 4-8.

365   Terry L. Weech. "School and Public Library Cooperation—What We Would Like To Do, What We Do," *Public Libraries* 18:2 (Summer 1979), 33-34.

366 Patricia L. Piper and Cecilia Hing Ling Kwan. "Cataloging and Classification Practices in Law Libraries: Results of a Questionnaire," *Law Library Journal* 71:3 (August 1978), 481-483.

367 Christian M. Boissonnas. "The Quality of OCLC Bibliographic Records: The Cornell Law Library Experience," *Law Library Journal* 72:1 (Winter 1979), 80-85.

368 Kent Schrieffer and Linnea Christiani. "Ballots at Boalt," *Law Library Journal* 72:3 (Summer 1979), 497-512.

369 Ermina Hahn. "Survey of Technical Services Practices at Fifty Large Law School Libraries," *Law Library Journal* 73:3 (Summer 1980), 715-725. (**268, 282, 283**)

370 Lana Caswell Garcia. "Legal Services Law Librarianship—An Investigation of Salary and Benefits in a Pioneer Field," *Law Library Journal* 73:3 (Summer 1980), 731-733.

371 Reynold J. Kosek. "Faculty Status and Tenure for Nondirector, Academic Law Librarians" a section within "Status of Academic Law Librarians," *Law Library Journal* 73:4 (Fall 1980), 892-905.

372 Martha C. Adamson and Gloria J. Zamora. "Authorship Characteristics in *Law Library Journal*: A Comparative Study," *Law Library Journal* 74:3 (Summer 1981), 527-533.

373 David G. Badertscher. "An Examination of the Dynamics of Change in Information Technology as Viewed from Law Libraries and Information Centers," *Law Library Journal* 75:2 (Spring 1982), 198-211.

374 Donald J. Dunn. "The Law Librarian's Obligation To Publish," *Law Library Journal* 75:2 (Spring 1982), 225-231.

375 Audio-Visual Committee, American Association of Law Libraries. "Summary of Audio-Visual Materials Used in Legal Education: Audio-Visual Committee Report—June 1967," *Law Library Journal* 60:3 (August 1967), 272-276.

376 Cameron Allen. "Duplicate Holding Practices of Approved American Law School Libraries." *Law Library Journal* 62:2 (May 1969), 191-200.

377 Margaret Shediac. "Private Law Libraries Special Interest Section 1980 Salary Survey," *Law Library Journal* 74:2 (Spring 1981), 444-457.

378 Bettie H. Scott. "Price Index for Legal Publications," *Law Library Journal* 75:1 (Winter 1982), 171-174.

379 Silvia A. Gonzalez. "County Law Library Survey," *Law Library Journal* 74:3 (Summer 1981), 654-691. (**103, 104**)

380 Silvia A. Gonzalez. "Survey of State Law Libraries," *Law Library Journal* 74:1 (Winter 1981), 160-201.

381 Silvia A. Gonzalez. "Survey of Court Law Libraries," *Law Library Journal* 74:2 (Spring 1981), 458-494.

382 David A. Thomas. "1980 Statistical Survey of Law School Libraries and Librarians," *Law Library Journal* 74:2 (Spring 1981), 359-443.

383 Marija Hughes. "Sex-Based Discrimination in Law Libraries," *Law Library Journal* 64:1 (February 1971), 13-22.

384 Oscar M. Trelles. "Law Libraries and Unions," *Law Library Journal* 65:2 (May 1972), 158-180.

385 Claudia Sumler, Kristine Barone and Art Goetz. "Getting Books Faster and Cheaper: A Jobber Acquisitions Study," *Public Libraries* 19:4 (Winter 1980), 103-105.

386 Vernon A. Rayford. "A Black Librarian Takes a Look at Discrimination: by a Law School Library Survey," *Law Library Journal* 65:2 (May 1972), 183-189.

387 Audio-Visual Committee, American Association of Law Libraries. "The Use of Audio-Visual Teaching Aids and Library Microforms in American Legal Education," *Law Library Journal* 66:1 (February 1973), 84-87.

388 Cameron Allen. "Whom We Shall Serve: Secondary Patrons of the University Law School Library," *Law Library Journal* 66:2 (May 1973), 160-171.

389 O. James Werner. "The Present Legal Status and Conditions of Prison Law Libraries," *Law Library Journal* 66:3 (August 1973), 259-269.

390 George S. Grossman. "Clinical Legal Education and the Law Library," *Law Library Journal* 67:1 (February 1974), 60-78.

391 Kurt Schwerin and Igor I. Kavass. "Foreign Legal Periodicals in American Law Libraries 1973 Union List," *Law Library Journal* 67:1 (February 1974), 120-126.

392 Bethany J. Ochal. "County Law Libraries," *Law Library Journal* 67:2 (May 1974), 177-234.

393 Peter Enyingi. "Subject Cataloging Practices in American Law Libraries: A Survey," *Law Library Journal* 68:1 (February 1975), 11-17.

394 Sandra Sadow and Benjamin R. Beede. "Library Instruction in American Law Schools," *Law Library Journal* 68:1 (February 1975), 27-32.

395 Michael L. Richmond. "Attitudes of Law Librarians to Theft and Mutilation Control Methods," *Law Library Journal* 68:1 (February 1975), 60-81. **(280, 292)**

396 Ellin B. Christianson. "Mergers in the Publishing Industry, 1958-1970," *Journal of Library History, Philosophy and Comparative Librarianship* 7:1 (January 1972), 5-32.

397 Eugene E. Graziano. "Interlibrary Loan Analysis: Diagnostic for Scientific Serials Backfile Acquisitions," *Special Libraries* 53:5 (May/June 1962), 251-257. **(108)**

398 John E. James. "Library Technician Program: The Library Technician Graduates' Point of View," *Special Libraries* 62:6 (July/August 1971), 268-278.

399 James M. Matarazzo. "Scientific Journals: Page or Price Explosion?" *Special Libraries* 63:2 (February 1972), 53-58.

400 Julie L. Moore. "Bibliographic Control of American Doctoral Dissertations," *Special Libraries* 63:7 (July 1972), 285-291.

401 Robert T. Bottle and William W. Chase. "Some Characteristics of the Literature on Music and Musicology," *Special Libraries* 63:10 (October 1972), 469-476.

402 William P. Koughan and John A. Timour. "Are Hospital Libraries Meeting Physicians' Information Needs?" *Special Libraries* 64:5/6 (May/June 1972), 222-227. **(122, 145, 147)**

403 Jean M. Ray. "Who Borrows Maps from a University Library Map Collection —And Why?" *Special Libraries* 65:3 (March 1974), 104-109. **(39, 45, 46, 49, 230, 231)**

404 Ching-Chih Chen. "How Do Scientists Meet Their Information Needs?" *Special Libraries* 65:7 (July 1974), 272-280. **(127, 147, 156, 189, 197, 200, 221, 258)**

405 Katherine C. Owen. "Productive Journal Titles in the Pharmaceutical Industry," *Special Libraries* 65:10/11 (October/November 1974), 430-439.

406 Stanley A. Elman. "Cost Comparison of Manual and On-Line Computerized Literature Searching," *Special Libraries* 66:1 (January 1975), 12-18.

407 Jerome P. Fatcheric. "Survey of Users of a Medium-Sized Technical Library," *Special Libraries* 66:5/6 (May/June 1975), 245-251. **(153, 196, 197, 198)**

408 Bahaa El-Hadidy. "Bibliographic Control among Geoscience Abstracting and Indexing Services," *Special Libraries* 66:5/6 (May/June 1975), 260-265.

409 Ruth W. Wender. "Hospital Journal Title Usage Study," *Special Libraries* 66:11 (November 1975), 532-537. **(243, 245)**

410 Thelma Freides. "Bibliographic Gaps in the Social Science Literature," *Special Libraries* 67:2 (February 1976), 68-75.

411 Eileen E. Hitchingham. "MEDLINE Use in a University without a School of Medicine," *Special Libraries* 67:4 (April 1976), 188-194. **(99, 100, 109, 110, 140)**

412 David Hull and Henry D. Fearnley. "The Museum Library in the United States: A Sample," *Special Libraries* 67:7 (July 1976), 289-298.(56, 63)

413 Amelia Breiting, Marcia Dorey and Deirdre Sockbeson. "Staff Development in College and University Libraries," *Special Libraries* 67:7 (July 1976), 305-309.

414 Arley L. Ripin and Dorothy Kasman. "Education for Special Librarianship: A Survey of Courses Offered in Accredited Programs," *Special Libraries* 67:11 (November 1976), 504-509.

415 George W. Black, Jr. "Selected Annaul Bound Volume Production," *Special Libraries* 67:11 (November 1976), 534-536.(267)

416 Howard Fosdick. "An SDC-Based On-Line Search Service: A Patron Evaluation Survey and Implications," *Special Libraries* 68:9 (September 1977), 305-312. (99, 100, 153)

417 Diane M. Nelson. "Methods of Citation Analysis in the Fine Arts," *Special Libraries* 68:11 (November 1977), 390-395.

418 Annette Corth. "Coverage of Marine Biology Citations,"*Special Libraries* 68:12 (December 1977), 439-446.

419 Jean K. Martin. "Computer-Based Literature Searching: Impact on Interlibrary Loan Service," *Special Libaries* 69:1 (January 1978), 1-6. (100)

420 Jean M. Ray. "Who Borrows Maps from a University Library Map Collection —and Why? Report II," *Special Libraries* 69:1 (January 1978), 13-20. (39, 40, 41, 46, 49, 231, 232)

421 Robert Goehlert. "Periodical Use in an Academic Library: A Study of Economists and Political Scientists," *Special Libraries* 69:2 (February 1978), 51-60.(21, 22, 31, 32, 33, 35, 54, 61, 189, 262)

422 Sandra J. Springer, Robert A. Yokel, Nancy M. Lorenzi, Leonard T. Sigell and E. Don Nelson. "Drug Information to Patient Care Areas via Television: Preliminary Evaluation of Two Years' Experience," *Special Libraries* 69:4 (April 1978), 155-163. (150, 151, 157, 161, 255)

423 Martha J. Bailey. "Requirement for Middle Managerial Positions," *Special Libraries* 69:9 (September 1978), 323-331.

424 Carolyn L. Warden. "An Industrial Current Awareness Service: A User Evaluation Study," *Special Libraries* 69:12 (December 1978), 459-467. (153, 154, 263)

425 Charles H. Davis. "Programming Aptitude as a Function of Undergraduate Major," *Special Libraries* 69:12 (December 1978), 482-485.

426 Jean Mace Schmidt. "Translation of Periodical Literature in Plant Pathology," *Special Libraries* 70:1 (January 1979), 12-17. (125)

427 Susan Dingle-Cliff and Charles H. Davis. "Collection Overlap in Canadian Addictions Libraries," *Special Libraries* 70:2 (February 1979), 76-81.

428 John J. Knightly. "Overcoming the Cirterion Problem in the Evaluation of Library Performance," *Special Libraries* 70:4 (April 1979), 173-178.

429 Ruth W. Wender. "Counting Journal Title Usage in the Health Sciences," *Special Libraries* 70:5/6 (May/June 1975), 219-226.

430 John Steuben. "Interlibrary Loan of Photocopies of Articles under the New Copyright Law," *Special Libraries* 70:5/6 (May/June 1979), 227-232.

431 John Kok and Edward G. Strable. "Moving Up: Librarians Who Have Become Officers of Their Organization," *Special Libraries* 71:1 (January 1980), 5-12.

432 Rebecca J. Jensen, Herbert D. Asbury and Radford G. King. "Costs and Benefits to Industry of Online Literature Searches," *Special Libraries* 71:7 (July 1980), 291-299.

433 C. Margaret Bell. "The Applicability of OCLC and Inforonics in Special Libraries," *Special Libraries* 71:9 (September 1980), 398-404.

434 A. Neil Yerkey. "The Psychological Climate of Librarianship: Values of Special Librarians," *Special Libraries* 72:3 (July 1981), 195-200.

435 Virgil P. Diodato. "Author Indexing," *Special Libraries* 72:4 (October 1981), 361-369.

436 Judith M. Pask. "Bibliographic Instruction in Business Libraries," *Special Libraries* 72:4 (October 1981), 370-378.

437 Ann T. Dodson, Paul P. Philbin and Kunj B. Rastogi. "Electronic Interlibrary Loan in the OCLC Library: A Study of its Effectiveness," *Special Libraries* 73:1 (January 1982), 12-20. (**83, 90, 97, 102**)

438 Gloria J. Zamora and Martha C. Adamson. "Authorship Characteristics in *Special Libraries*: A Comparative Study," *Special Libraries* 73:2 (April 1982), 100-107.

439 Robert K. Poyer. "Time Lag in Four Indexing Services," *Special Libraries* 73:2 (April 1982), 142-146.

440 Pauline R. Hodges. "Keyword in Title Indexes: Effectiveness of Retrieval in Computer Searches," *Special Libraries* 74:1 (January 1983), 56-60.

441 D.K. Varma. "Increased Subscription Costs and Problems of Resource Allocation," *Special Libraries* 74:1 (January 1983), 61-66.

442 Michael Halperin and Ruth A. Pagell. "Searchers' Perceptions of Online Database Vendors," *Special Libraries* 74:2 (April 1973), 119-126.

443   Michael E.D. Koenig. "Education for Special Librarianship," *Special Libraries* 74:2 (April 1983), 182-196.

444   Powell Niland and William H. Kurth. "Estimating Lost Volumes in a University Library Collection," *College and Research Libraries* 37:2 (March 1976), 128-136. (**269, 271, 273, 287, 288**)

445   Rush G. Miller. "The Influx of Ph.D.s into Librarianship: Intrusion or Transfusion?" *College and Research Libraries* 37:2 (March 1976), 158-165.

446   Steven Leach. "The Growth Rates of Major Academic Libraries: Rider and Purdue Reviewed," *College and Research Libraries* 37:6 (November 1976), 531-542.

447   T. Saracevic, W.M. Shaw, Jr. and P.B. Kantor. "Causes and Dynamics of User Frustration in an Academic Library," *College and Research Libraries* 38:1 (January 1977), 7-18. (**12, 38**)

448   R.W. Meyer and Rebecca Panetta. "Two Shared Cataloging Data Bases: A Comparison," *College and Research Libraries* 38:1 (January 1977), 19-24.

449   Peter Hernon and Maureen Pastine. "Student Perceptions of Academic Librarians," *College and Research Libraries* 38:2 (March 1977), 129-139. (**127, 128, 148, 156, 157, 165, 199**)

450   Catherine V. Von Schon. "Inventory 'By Computer'," *College and Research Libraries* 38:2 (March 1977), 147-152. (**272**)

451   David C. Genaway and Edward B. Stanford. "Quasi-Departmental Libraries," *College and Research Libraries* 38:3 (May 1977), 187-194. (**21, 122, 123, 124**)

452   Elizabeth W. Matthews. "Trends Affecting Community College Library Administrators," *College and Research Libraries* 38:3 (May 1977), 210-217.

453   Lawrence J. Perk. "Secondary Publications in Education: A Study of Duplication," *College and Research Libraries* 38:3 (May 1977), 221-226.

454   Geraldine Murphy Wright. "Current Trends in Periodical Collections," *College and Research Libraries* 38:3 (May 1977), 234-240. (**53, 62, 282, 286, 288**)

455   Lawrence J. Perk and Noelle Van Pulis. "Periodical Usage in an Education-Psychology Library," *College and Research Libraries* 38:4 (July 1977), 304-308. (**29, 30, 31**)

456   Egill A. Halldorsson and Marjorie E. Murfin. "The Performance of Professionals and Nonprofessionals in the Reference Interview," *College and Research Libraries* 38:5 (September 1977), 385-395.

457   Susan A. Lee. "Conflict and Ambiguity in the Role of the Academic Library Director," *College and Research Libraries* 38:5 (September 1977), 396-403.

458 Glenn R. Wittig. "Dual Pricing of Periodicals," *College and Research Libraries* 38:5 (September 1977), 412-418.

459 Miriam A. Drake. "Attribution of Library Costs," *College and Research Libraries* 38:6 (November 1977), 514-519. (**36**)

460 Harry M. Kriz. "Subscriptions vs. Books in a Constant Dollar Budget," *College and Research Libraries* 39:2 (March 1978), 105-109.

461 Charles J. Popovich. "The Characteristics of a Collection for Research in Business/Management," *College and Research Libraries* 39:2 (March 1978), 117.

462 Jean A. Major. "The Visually Impaired Reader in the Academic Library," *College and Research Libraries* 39:3 (May 1978), 191-196. (**190**)

463 Herbert S. White and Karen Momenee. "Impact of the Increase in Library Doctorates," *College and Research Libraries* 39:3 (May 1978), 207-214.

464 James Michalko and Toby Heidtmann. "Evaluating the Effectiveness of an Electronic Security System," *College and Research Libraries* 39:4 (July 1978), 263-267. (**272, 288**)

465 William M. McClellan. "Judging Music Libraries," *College and Research Libraries* 39:4 (July 1978), 281-286.

466 Rita Hoyt Smith and Warner Granade. "User and Library Failures in an Undergraduate Library," *College and Research Libraries* 39:6 (November 1978), 467-473. (**12, 60, 61, 98, 267**)

467 Linda Ann Hulbert and David Stewart Curry. "Evaluation of an Approval Plan," *College and Research Libraries* 39:6 (November 1978), 485-491.

468 Julia F. Baldwin and Robert S. Rudolph. "The Comparative Effectiveness of a Slide/Tape Show and a Library Tour," *College and Research Libraries* 40:1 (January 1979), 31-35.

469 Melissa D. Trevvett. "Characteristics of Interlibrary Loan Requests at the Library of Congress," *College and Research Libraries* 40:1 (January 1979), 36-43. (**75, 77, 82, 97, 98, 106, 107**)

470 Elaine Zaremba Jennerich and Bessie Hess Smith. "A Bibliographic Instruction Program in Music," *College and Research Libraries* 40:3 (May 1979), 226-233.

471 William J. Maher and Benjamin F. Shearer. "Undergraduate Use Patterns of Newspapers on Microfilm," *College and Research Libraries* 40:3 (May 1979), 254-260.

472 Larry Hardesty, Nicholas P. Lovrich, Jr. and James Mannon. "Evaluating Library-Use Instruction," *College and Research Libraries* 40:4 (July 1979), 309-317.

473 Seymour H. Sargent. "The Uses and Limitations of Trueswell," *College and Research Libraries* 40:5 (September 1979), 416-425. **(8, 10)**

474 Patricia Stenstrom and Ruth B. McBride." Serial Use by Social Science Faculty: A Survey," *College and Research Libraries* 40:5 (September 1979), 426-431.

475 Elaine C. Clever. "Using Indexes as 'Memory Assists'," *College and Research Libraries* 40:5 (September 1979), 444-449.

476 William E. McGrath, Donald J. Simon and Evelyn Bullard. "Ethnocentricity and Cross-Disciplinary Circulation," *College and Research Libraries* 40:6 (November 1979), 511-518.

477 Michael Gorman and Jami Hotsinpiller. "ISBD: Aid or Barrier to Understanding," *College and Research Libraries* 40:6 (November 1979), 519-526.

478 Jinnie Y. Davis and Stella Bentley. "Factors Affecting Faculty Perceptions of Academic Libraries," *College and Research Libraries* 40:6 (November 1979), 527-532. **(130, 131)**

479 Dennis J. Reynolds. "Regional Alternatives for Interlibrary Loan: Access to Unreported Holdings," *College and Research Libraries* 41:1 (January 1980), 33-42. **(83, 89, 90, 101, 102)**

480 Ronald Rayman and Frank William Goudy. "Research and Publication Requirements in University Libraries," *College and Research Libraries* 41:1 (January 1980), 43-48.

481 John N. Olsgaard and Jane Kinch Olsgaard. "Authorship in Five Library Periodicals," *College and Research Libraries* 41:1 (January 1980), 49-53.

482 Albert F. Maag. "Design of the Library Director Interview: The Candidate's Perspective," *College and Research Libraries* 41:2 (March 1980), 112-121.

483 Thomas M. Gaughan. "Resume Essentials for the Academic Librarian," *College and Research Libraries* 41:2 (March 1980), 122-127.

484 Harold B. Shill. "Open Stacks and Library Performance," *College and Research Libraries* 41:3 (May 1980), 220-225. **(17, 272, 276, 282, 288, 289)**

485 Robert L. Turner, Jr. "Femininity and the Librarian—Another Test," *College and Research Libraries* 41:3 (May 1980), 235-241.

486 Ray L. Carpenter. "College Libraries: A Comparative Analysis in Terms of the ACRL Standards," *College and Research Libraries* 42:1 (January 1981), 7-18. **(17)**

487 George V. Hodowanec. "An Acquisition Rate Model for Academic Libraries," *College and Research Libraries* 39:6 (September 1978), 439-442. **(17)**

488 Roland Person. "Long-Term Evaluation of Bibliographic Instruction: Lasting Encouragement," *College and Research Libraries* 42:1 (January 1981), 19-25.

489 Laslo A. Nagy and Martha Lou Thomas. "An Evaluation of the Teaching Effectiveness of Two Library Instructional Videotapes," *College and Research Libraries* 42:1 (January 1981), 26-30.

490 David N. King and John C. Ory. "Effects of Library Instruction on Student Research: A Case Study," *College and Research Libraries* 42:1 (January 1981), 31-41.

491 Herbert S. White. "Perceptions by Educators and Administrators of the Ranking of Library School Programs," *College and Research Libraries* 42:3 (May 1981), 191-202.

492 Russ Davidson, Connie Capers Thorson and Margo C. Trumpeter. "Faculty Status for Librarians in the Rocky Mountain Region: A Review and Analysis," *College and Research Libraries* 42:3 (May 1981), 203-213.

493 M. Kathy Cook. "Rank, Status, and Contribution of Academic Librarians as Perceived by the Teaching Faculty at Southern Illinois University, Carbondale," *College and Research Libraries* 42:3 (May 1981), 214-223. (**129, 130, 149, 150, 222, 223**)

494 John N. Olsgaard and Jane Kinch Olsgaard. "Post-MLS Educational Requirements for Academic Librarians," *College and Research Libraries* 42:3 (May 1981), 224-228.

495 Ronald Rayman. "Employment Opportunities for Academic Librarians in the 1970's: An Analysis of the Past Decade," *College and Research Libraries* 42:3 (May 1981), 229-234.

496 Martha C. Adamson and Gloria J. Zamora. "Publishing in Library Science Journals: A Test of the Olsgaard Profile," *College and Research Libraries* 42:3 (May 1981), 235-241.

497 Charles Sage, Janet Klass, Helen H. Spalding and Tracey Robinson. "A Queueing Study of Public Catalog Use," *College and Research Libraries* 42:4 (July 1981), 317-325. (**58, 202**)

498 Doris Cruger Dale. "Cataloging and Classification Practices in Community College Libraries," *College and Research Libraries* 42:4 (July 1981), 333-339.

499 Dana Weiss. "Book Theft and Book Mutilation in a Large Urban University Library," *College and Research Libraries* 42:4 (July 1981), 341-347. (**138, 139, 162, 163, 278, 279, 290, 291**)

500 Raymond L. Carpenter. "Two-Year College Libraries: A Comparative Analysis in Terms of the ACRL Standards," *College and Research Libraries* 42:5 (September 1981), 407-415. (**18**)

501 Paul D. Luyben, Leonard Cohen, Rebecca Conger and Selby U. Gration. "Reducing Noise in a College Library," *College and Research Libraries* 42:5 (September 1981), 470-481.

502 Prabha Sharma. "A Survey of Academic Librarians and Their Opinions Related to Nine-Month Contracts and Academic Status Configurations in Alabama, Georgia and Mississippi," *College and Research Libraries* 42:6 (November 1981), 561-570.

503 Priscilla Geahigan, Harriet Nelson, Stewart Saunders and Lawrence Woods. "Acceptability of Non-Library/Information Science Publications in the Promotion and Tenure of Academic Librarians," *College and Research Libraries* 42:6 (November 1981), 571-575.

504 Barbara Moore, Tamara J. Miller and Don L. Tolliver. "Title Overlap: A Study of Duplication in the University of Wisconsin System Libraries," *College and Research Libraries* 43:1 (January 1982), 14-21.

505 Gary A. Golden, Susan U. Golden and Rebecca T. Lenzini. "Patron Approaches to Serials: A User Study," *College and Research Libraries* 43:1 (January 1982), 22-30. (**202, 203**)

506 Thomas T. Surprenant. "Learning Theory, Lecture, and Programmed Instruction Text: An Experiment in Bibliographic Instruction," *College and Research Libraries* 43:1 (January 1982), 31-37.

507 Larry Hardesty, Nicholas P. Lovrich, Jr. and James Mannon. "Library-Use Instruction: Assessment of the Long-Term Effects," *College and Research Libraries* 43:1 (January 1982), 38-46.

508 Robert Swisher and Peggy C. Smith. "Journals Read by ACRL Academic Librarians, 1973 and 1978," *College and Research Libraries* 43:1 (January 1982), 51-58.

509 William Caynon. "Collective Bargaining and Professional Development of Academic Librarians," *College and Research Libraries* 43:2 (March 1982), 133-139.

510 Barbara J. Smith. "Background Characteristics and Education Needs of a Group of Instruction Librarians in Pennsylvania," *College and Research Libraries* 43:3 (May 1982), 199-207.

511 Gloria S. Cline. "*College and Research Libraries*: Its First Forty Years," *College and Research Libraries* 43:3 (May 1982), 208-232.

512 John B. Harer and C. Edward Huber. "Copyright Policies in Virginia Academic Library Reserve Rooms," *College and Research Libraries* 43:3 (May 1982), 233-241.

513 Laurie S. Linsley. "Academic Libraries in an Interlibrary Loan Network," *College and Research Libraries* 43:4 (July 1982), 292-299. (**81, 82, 83, 96, 107**)

514 Timothy D. Jewell. "Student Reactions to a Self-Paced Library Skills Workbook Program: Survey Evidence," *College and Research Libraries* 43:5 (September 1982), 371-378.

515 Mary Baier Wells. "Requirements and Benefits for Academic Librarians: 1959-1979," *College and Research Libraries* 43:6 (November 1982), 450-458.

516 Marjorie A. Benedict, Jacquelyn A. Gavryck and Hanan C. Selvin. "Status of Academic Librarians in New York State," *College and Research Libraries* 44:1 (January 1983), 12-19.

517 Carol Truett. "Services to Developmental Education Students in the Community College: Does the Library Have a Role?" *College and Research Libraries* 44:1 (January 1983), 20-28.

518 Gene K. Rinkel and Patricia McCandless. "Application of a Methodology Analyzing User Frustration," *College and Research Libraries* 44:1 (January 1983), 29-37.

519 Jo Bell Whitlatch. "Library Use Patterns Among Full- and Part-Time Faculty and Students," *College and Research Libraries* 44:2 (March 1983), 141-152. **(165, 191, 198, 215, 221, 222, 223, 224, 225)**

520 Madeleine Stern. "Characteristics of the Literature of Literary Scholarship," *College and Research Libraries* 44:4 (July 1983), 199-209.

521 Philip Schwarz. "Demand-Adjusted Shelf Availability Parameters: A Second Look," *College and Research Libraries* 44:4 (July 1983), 210-219. **(12, 33)**

522 Paul M. Anderson and Ellen G. Miller. "Participative Planning for Library Automation: The Role of the User Opinion Survey," *College and Research Libraries* 44:4 (July 1983), 245-254. **(4, 116, 171, 204)**

523 Raymond W. Barber and Jacqueline C. Mancall. "The Application of Bibliometric Techniques to the Analysis of Materials for Young Adults," *Collection Management* 2:3 (Fall 1978), 229-245.

524 Kenneth C. Kirsch and Albert H. Rubenstein. "Converting from Hard Copy to Microfilm: An Administrative Experiment," *Collection Management* 2:4 (Winter 1978), 279-302. **(136)**

525 Herbert Goldhor. "U.S. Public Library Adult Non-Fiction Book Collections in the Humanities," *Collection Management* 3:1 (Spring 1979), 31-43.

526 Sally F. Williams. "Construction and Application of a Periodical Price Index," *Collection Management* 2:4 (Winter 1978), 329-344.

527 Mary Jane Pobst Reed. "Identification of Storage Candidates among Monographs," *Collection Management* 3:2/3 (Summer/Fall 1979), 203-214. **(11, 293, 294)**

528 Ung Chon Kim. "Participation of Teaching Faculty in Library Book Selection," *Collection Management* 3:4 (Winter 1979), 333-352.

529 Glenn R. Lowry. "A Heuristic Collection Loss Rate Determination Methodology: An Alternative to Shelf-Reading," *Collection Management* 4:1/2 (Spring/Summer 1982), 73-83. **(271, 272)**

530 Stewart Saunders. "Student Reliance on Faculty Guidance in the Selection of Reading Materials: The Use of Core Collections," *Collection Management* 4:4 (Winter 1982), 9-23.**(207, 209, 210)**

531 Ralph M. Daehn. "The Measurement and Projection of Shelf Space," *Collection Management* 4:4 (Winter 1982), 25-39.

532 Igor I. Kavass. "Foreign and International Law Collections in Selected Law Libraries of the United States: Survey, 1972-73," *International Journal of Law Libraries* 1:3 (November 1973), 117-133.

533 Robert J. Garen. "Library Orientation on Television," *Canadian Library Journal* 24:2 (September 1967), 124-126.

534 D.W. Miller. "Non-English Books in Canadian Public Libraries," *Canadian Library Journal* 27:2 (March/April 1970), 123-129. **(220, 234, 283)**

535 Robert H. Blackburn. "Canadian Content in a Sample of Photocopying," *Canadian Library Journal* 27:5 (September/October 1970), 332-340.

536 Peter H. Wolters and Jack E. Brown. "CAN/SDI System: User Reaction to a Computer Information Retrieval System for Canadian Scientists and Technologists," *Canadian Library Journal* 28:1 (January/ February), 20-23.**(261)**

537 M. Jamil Qureshi. "Academic Status, Salaries and Fringe Benefits in Community College Libraries of Canada," *Canadian Library Journal* 28:1 (January/February 1971), 41-45.

538 George J. Snowball. "Survey of Social Sciences and Humanities Monograph Circulation by Random Sampling of the Stack," *Canadian Library Journal* 28:5 (September/October 1971), 352-361. **(16)**

539 Roop K. Sandhu and Harjit Sandhu. "Job Perception of University Librarians and Library Students," *Canadian Library Journal* 28:6 (November/ December 1971), 438-445.

540 Brian Dale and Patricia Dewdney. "Canadian Public Libraries and the Physically Handicapped," *Canadian Library Journal* 29:3 (May/June 1972), 231-236. **(190, 191)**

541 R.G. Wilson. "Interlibrary Loan Experiments at the University of Calgary," *Canadian Library Journal* 30:1 (January/February 1973), 38-40. **(84, 88, 102)**

542 Peter Simmons. "Studies in the Use of the Card Catalogue in a Public Library," *Canadian Library Journal* 31:4 (August 1974), 323-337.**(194)**

543 L.J. Amey and R.J. Smith. "Combination School and Public Libraries: An Attitudinal Study," *Canadian Library Journal* 33:3 (June 1976), 251-261.

544 John Wilkinson. "The Library Market for Canadian Juvenile Fiction: A Further Analysis," *Canadian Library Journal* 34:1 (February 1977), 5-15.

545 Larry Orten and John Wiseman. "Library Service to Part-time Students," *Canadian Library Journal* 34:1 (February 1977), 23-27. **(121, 156, 164, 199, 214, 215, 218, 223)**

546 Esther L. Sleep. "Whither the ISSN? A Practical Experience," *Canadian Library Journal* 34:4 (August 1977), 265-270.

547 Sarah Landy. "Why Johnny Can Read...but Doesn't," *Canadian Library Journal* 34:5 (October 1977), 379-387. **(146, 147, 176, 177, 178)**

548 Sharon Mott. "An Edmonton High School Reduces Book Losses," *Canadian Library Journal* 35:1 (February 1978), 45-49. **(275, 289)**

549 Fotoula Pantazis. "Library Technicians in Ontario Academic Libraries," *Canadian Library Journal* 35:2 (April 1978), 77-91.

550 Dorothy Ryder. "Canadian Reference Sources—A 10 Year Overview," *Canadian Library Journal* 35:4 (August 1978), 289-293.

551 Laurent-G. Denis. "Full-time Faculty Survey Describes Educators," *Canadian Library Journal* 36:3 (June 1979), 107-121.

552 Marie Foster. "Philosophy of Librarianship," *Canadian Library Journal* 36:3 (June 1979), 131-137.

553 Kenneth H. Plate and Jacob P. Seigel. "Career Patterns of Ontario Librarians," *Canadian Library Journal* 36:3 (June 1979), 143-148.

554 Mavis Cariou. "Liaison Where Field and Faculty Meet," *Canadian Library Journal* 36:3 (June 1979), 155-163.

555 Norman Horrocks. "Encyclopedias and Public Libraries: A Canadian Survey," *Canadian Library Journal* 38:2 (April 1981), 79-83.

556 Stephen B. Lawton. "Diffusion of Automation in Post-Secondary Institutions," *Canadian Library Journal* 38:2 (April 1980), 93-97. **(4)**

557 Mary Ann Wasylycia-Coe. "Profile: Canadian Chief Librarians by Sex," *Canadian Library Journal* 38:3 (June 1981), 159-163.

558 Margaret Currie, Elaine Goettler and Sandra McCaskill. "Evaluating the Relationship between Library Skills and Library Instruction," *Canadian Library Journal* 39:1 (February 1982), 35-37.

559 Esther L. Sleep. "Periodical Vandalism: A Chronic Condition," *Canadian Library Journal* 39:1 (February 1982), 39-42. **(275, 280, 289)**

560 Kenneth Setterington. "The Ph.D. in Library Administration: A Report of Research," *Library Research* (after Spring 1983 called *Library and Information Science Research*) 5:2 (Summer 1983), 177-194.

561 Robert F. Rose. "Identifying a Core Collection of Business Periodicals for Academic Libraries," *Collection Management* 5:1/2 (Spring/Summer 1983), 73-87.

562 Raymond Kilpela. "A Profile of Library School Deans, 1960-81," *Journal of Education for Librarianship* 23:3 (Winter 1983), 173-191.

563 Charlene Renner and Barton M. Clark. "Professional and Nonprofessional Staffing Patterns in Departmental Libraries," *Library Research* 1 (1979), 153-170.

564 Jacqueline C. Mancall and M. Carl Drott. "Materials Used by High School Students in Preparing Independent Study Projects: A Bibliometric Approach," *Library Research* 1 (1979), 223-236. (217)

565 Alan R. Samuels. "Assessing Organizational Climate in Public Libraries," *Library Research* 1 (1979), 237-254.

566 Diane Mittermeyer and Lloyd J. Houser. "The Knowledge Base for the Administration of Libraries," *Library Research* 1 (1979), 255-276.

567 Michael V. Sullivan, Betty Vadeboncoeur, Nancy Shiotani and Peter Stangl. "Obsolescence in Biomedical Journals: Not an Artifact of Literature Growth," *Library Research* 2 (1980-81), 29-46. (282, 283, 292, 293, 294, 295)

568 Robert V. Williams. "Sources of the Variability in Level of Public Library Development in the United States: A Comparative Analysis," *Library Research* 2 (1980-81), 157-176. (172, 180, 184, 185)

569 Bluma C. Peritz. "The Methods of Library Science Research: Some Results from a Bibliometric Survey," *Library Research* 2 (1980-81), 251-268.

570 Nancy Van House DeWath. "Fees for Online Bibliographic Search Services in Publicly-Supported Libraries," *Library Research* 3 (1981), 29-45.

571 Bluma C. Peritz. "Citation Characteristics in Library Science: Some Further Results from a Bibliometric Survey," *Library Research* 3 (1981), 47-65.

572 Gary Moore. "Library Long-Range Planning: A Survey of Current Practices," *Library Research* 3 (1981), 155-165.

573 Larry Hardesty. "Use of Library Materials at a Small Liberal Arts College," *Library Research* 3 (1981), 261-282. (8, 9, 11)

574 Stewart Saunders, Harriet Nelson and Priscilla Geahigan. "Alternatives to the Shelflist Measure for Determining the Size of a Subject Collection," *Library Research* 3 (1981), 383-391. (290)

575 P. Robert Paustian. "Collection Size and Interlibrary Loan in Large Academic Libraries," *Library Research* 3 (1981), 393-400. (79)

576 Daniel O. O'Connor. "Evaluating Public Libraries Using Standard Scores: The Library Quotient," *Library Research* 4 (1982), 51-70. (19, 27, 28, 195, 196, 253)

577 Snunith Shoham. "A Cost-Preference Study of the Decentralization of Academic Library Services," *Library Research* 4 (1982), 175-194.

578 A.S. Pickett. "San Franscisco State College Library Technical Services Time Study," *Library Resources and Technical Services* 4:1 (Winter 1960), 45-46.

579 Rosamond H. Danielson. "Cornell's Area Classification: A Space-Saving Device for Less-Used Books," *Library Resources and Technical Services* 5:2 (Spring 1961), 139-141. **(281)**

580 Miriam C. Maloy. "Reclassification for the Divisional Plan," Library Resources and Technical Services 6:3 (Summer 1962), 239-242.

581 Andre Nitecki. "Costs of a Divided Catalog," *Library Resources and Technical Services* 6:4 (Fall 1962), 351-355.

582 Donald V. Black. "Automatic Classification and Indexing, for Libraries?" *Library Resources and Technical Services* 9:1 (Winter 1965), 35-52.

583 Perry D. Morrison. "Use of Library of Congress Classsification Decisions in Academic Libraries—An Empirical Study," *Library Resources and Technical Services* 9:2 (Spring 1965), 235-242.

584 Manuel D. Lopez. "Subject Catalogers Equal to the Future?" *Library Resources and Technical Services* 9:3 (Summer 1965), 371-375.

585 Ashby J. Fristoe. "The Bitter End," *Library Resources and Technical Services* 10:1 (Winter 1966), 91-95.

586 Ole V. Groos. "Less-Used Titles and Volumes of Science Journals: Two Preliminary Notes," *Library Resources and Technical Services* 10:3 (Summer 1966), 289-290. **(294)**

587 Paula M. Strain. "A Study of the Usage and Retention of Technical Periodicals," *Library Resources and Technical Services* 10:3 (Summer 1966), 295-304.

588 William R. Nugent. "Statistics of Collection Overlap at the Libraries of the Six New England State Universities," *Library Resources and Technical Services* 12:1 (Winter 1968), 31-36.

589 Walter R. Stubbs and Robert N. Broadus. "The Value of the Kirkus Service for College Libraries," *Library Resources and Technical Services* 13:2 (Spring 1969), 203-205.

590 Barton R. Burkhalter and LaVerne Hoag. "Another Look at Manual Sorting and Filing: Backwards and Forwards," *Library Resources and Technical Services* 14:3 (Summer 1970), 445-454.

591 "More on DC Numbers on LC Cards: Quantity and Quality," *Library Resources and Technical Services* 14:4 (Fall 1970), 517-527.

592   Carol A. Nemeyer. "Scholarly Reprint Publishing in the United States: Selected Findings from a Recent Survey of the Industry," *Library Resources and Technical Services* 15:1 (Winter 1971), 35-48.

593   Betty J. Mitchell and Carol Bedoian. "A Systematic Approach to Performance Evaluation of Out-of-Print Book Dealers: The San Fernando Valley State College Experience," *Library Resources and Technical Services* 15:2 (Spring 1971), 215-222.

594   Barbara Schrader and Elaine Orsini. "British, French and Australian Publications in the National Union Catalog: A Study of NPAC's Effectiveness," *Library Resources and Technical Services* 15:3 (Summer 1971), 345-353.

595   Joel Levis. "Canadian Publications in the English Language: CBI vs. *Canadiana*," *Library Resources and Technical Services* 15:3 (Summer 1971), 354-358.

596   Zubaidah Isa. "The Entry-Word in Indonesian Names and Titles," *Library Resources and Technical Services* 15:3 (Summer 1971), 393-398.

597   Richard J. Hyman. "Access to Library Collections: Summary of a Documentary and Opinion Survey on the Direct Shelf Approach and Browsing," *Library Resources and Technical Services* 15:4 (Fall 1971), 479-491.

598   Robert L. Mowery. "The Cryptic Other," *Library Resources and Technical Services* 16:1 (Winter 1972), 74-78.

599   Ann Craig Turner. "Comparative Card Production Methods," *Library Resources and Technical Services* 16:3 (Summer 1972), pp. 347-358.

600   Edmund G. Hamann. "Expansion of the Public Card Catalog in a Large Library," *Library Resources and Technical Services* 16:4 (Fall 1972), 488-496.

601   Ernest R. Perez. "Acquisitions of Out-of-Print Materials," *Library Resources and Technical Services* 17:1 (Winter 1973), 42-59.

602   E. Dale Cluff and Karen Anderson. "LC Card Order Experiment Conducted at University of Utah Marriott Library," *Library Resources and Technical Services* 17:1 (Winter 1973), 70-72.

603   Betty J. Mitchell. "Methods Used in Out-of-Print Acquisition; A Survey of Out-of-Print Book Dealers," *Library Resources and Technical Services* 17:2 (Spring 1973), 211-215.

604   George Piternick. "University Library Arrearages," *Library Resources and Technical Services* 13:1 (Winter 1969), 102-114.

605   Nancy E. Brodie. "Evaluation of a KWIC Index for *Library Literature*," *Journal of the American Society for Information Science* 21:1 (January-February 1970), 22-28.

606 William S. Cooper. "The Potential Usefulness of Catalog Access Points Other than Author, Title and Subject," *Journal of the American Society for Information Science* 21:2 (March-April 1970), 112-127.

607 Barbara F. Frick and John M. Ginski. "Cardiovascular Serial Literature: Characteristics, Productive Journals, and Abstracting/Indexing Coverage," *Journal of the American Society for Information Science* 21:5 (September-October 1970), 338-344.

608 Ching-Chih Chen. "The Use Patterns of Physics Journals in a Large Academic Research Library," *Journal of the American Society for Information Science* 23:4 (July-August 1972), 254-265.

609 Janet Friedlander. "Clinician Search for Information," *Journal of the American Society for Information Science* 24:1 (January-February 1973), 65-69. **(155, 160, 161)**

610 Tefko Saracevic and Lawrence J. Perk. "Ascertaining Activities in a Subject Area through Bibliometric Analysis," *Journal of the American Society for Information Science* 24:3 (March-April 1973), 120-134.

611 Ruth Kay Maloney. "Title versus Title/Abstract Text Searching in SDI Systems," *Journal of the American Society for Information Science* 25:6 (November-December 1974), 370-373.

612 Gladys B. Dronberger and Gerald T. Kowitz. "Abstract Readability as a Factor in Information Systems," *Journal of the American Society for Information Science* 26:2 (March-April 1975), 108-111.

613 Jerry R. Byrne. "Relative Effectiveness of Titles, Abstracts and Subject Headings for Machine Retrieval from the COMPENDEX Services," *Journal of the American Society for Information Science* 26:4 (July-August 1975), 223-229.

614 Joseph D. Smith and James E. Rush. "The Relationship between Author Names and Author Entries in a Large On-Line Union Catalog as Retrieved Using Truncated Keys," *Journal of the American Society for Information Science* 28:2 (March 1977), 115-120.

615 Marcia J. Bates. "Factors Affecting Subject Catalog Search Success," *Journal of the American Society for Information Science* 28:3 (May 1977), 161-169.

616 Terry Noreault, Matthew Koll and Michael J. McGill. "Automatic Ranked Output from Boolean Searches in SIRE," *Journal of the American Society for Information Science* 28:6 (November 1977), 333-339.

617 Chai Kim and Eui Hang Shin. "Sociodemographic Correlates of Intercounty Variations in the Public Library Output," *Journal of the American Society for Information Science* 28:6 (November 1977), 359-365. **(37)**

618 Harold E. Bamford, Jr. "Assessing the Effect of Computer Augmentation on Staff Productivity," *Journal of the American Society for Information Science* 30:3 (May 1979), 136-142.

619   Charles H. Davis and Deborah Shaw. "Collection Overlap as a Function of Library Size: A Comparison of American and Canadian Public Libraries," *Journal of the American Society for Information Science* 30:1 (January 1979), 19-24.

620   M. Carl Drott and Belver C. Griffith. "An Empirical Examination of Bradford's Law and the Scattering of Scientific Literature," *Journal of the American Society for Information Science* 29:5 (September 1978), 238-246.

621   James D. Anderson. "*Ad hoc* and Selective Translations of Scientific and Technical Journal Articles: Their Characteristicsand Possible Predictability," *Journal of the American Societyfor Information Science* 29:3 (May 1978), 130-135.

622   Richard C. Anderson, Francis Narin and Paul McAllister. "Publication Ratings versus Peer Ratings of Universities," *Journal of the American Society for Information Science* 29:2 (March 1978), 91-103.

623   Dennis R. Eichesen. "Cost-Effectiveness Comparison of Manual and On-line Retrospective Bibliographic Searching," *Journal of the American Society for Information Science* 29:2 (March 1978), 56-66.

624   Topsy N. Smalley. "Comparing *Psychological Abstracts* and *Index Medicus* for Coverage of the Journal Literature in a Subject Area in Psychology," *Journal of the American Society for Information Science* 31:3 (May 1980), 144-146.

625   Paul R. McAllister, Richard C. Anderson and Francis Narin. "Comparison of Peer and Citation Assessment of the Influence of Scientific Journals," *Journal of the American Society for Information Science* 31:3 (May 1980), 148-152.

626   Jerry Specht. "Patron Use of an Online Circulation System in Known-Item Searching," *Journal of the American Society for Information Science* 31:5 (September 1980), 335-346.

627   Guilbert C. Hentschke and Ellen Kehoe. "Serial Acquisition as a Capital Budgeting Problem," *Journal of the American Society for Information Science* 31:5 (September 1980), 357-362.

628   G. Edward Evans and Claudia White Argyres. "Approval Plans and Collection Development in Academic Libraries," *Library Resources and Technical Services* 18:1 (Winter 1974), 35-50. **(25, 26)**

629   Doris E. New and Retha Zane Ott. "Interlibrary Loan Analysis as a Collection Development Tool," *Library Resources and Technical Services* 18:3 (Summer 1974), 275-283. **(80, 104)**

630   H. William Axford. "The Validity of Book Price Indexes for Budgetary Projections," *Library Resources and Technical Services* 19:1 (Winter 1975), 5-12.

631 Geza A. Kosa. "Book Selection Tools for Subject Specialists in a Large Research Library: An Analysis," *Library Resources and Technical Services* 19:1 (Winter 1975), 13-18.

632 George P. D'Elia. "The Determinants of Job Satisfaction among Beginning Librarians," *Library Quarterly* 49:3 (July 1979), 283-302.

633 Tim LaBorie and Michael Halperin. "Citation Patterns in Library Science Dissertations," *Journal of Education for Librarianship* 16:4 (Spring 1976), 271-283.

634 Anne Woodsworth and Victor R. Neufeld. "A Survey of Physician Self-education Patterns in Toronto. Part 1: Use of Libraries," *Canadian Library Journal* 29:1 (January-February 1972), 38-44. **(259)**

635 Richard Eggleton. "The ALA Duplicates Exchange Union—A Study and Evaluation," *Library Resources and Technical Services* 19:2 (Spring 1975), 148-163.

636 Katherine H. Packer and Dagobert Soergel. "The Importance of SDI for Current Awareness in Fields with Severe Scatter of Information," *Journal of the American Society for Information Science* 30:3 (May 1979), 125-135. **(152, 261)**

637 Doris M. Carson. "The Act of Cataloging," *Library Resources and Technical Services* 20:2 (Spring 1976), 149-153.

638 Robert L. Mowery. "The Cutter Classification: Still at Work," *Library Resources and Technical Services* 20:2 (Spring 1976), 154-156.

639 Kelly Patterson, Carol White and Martha Whittaker. "Thesis Handling in University Libraries," *Library Resources and Technical Services* 21:3 (Summer 1977), 274-285.

640 Sandra L. Stokley and Marion T. Reid. "A Study of Performance of Five Book Dealers Used by Louisiana State University Library," *Library Resources and Technical Services* 22:2 (Spring 1978), 117-125.

641 Hans H. Wellisch. "Multiscript and Multilingual Bibliographic Control: Alternatives to Romanization," *Library Resources and Technical Services* 22:2 (Spring 1978), 179-190.

642 Bert R. Boyce and Mark Funk. "Bradford's Law and the Selection of High Quality Papers," *Library Resources and Technical Services* 22:4 (Fall 1978), 390-401.

643 Susan Dingle-Cliff and Charles H. Davis. "Comparison of Recent Acquisitions and OCLC Find Rates for Three Canadian Special Libraries," *Journal of the American Society for Information Science* 32:1 (January 1981), 65-69. **(92, 97)**

644 Rose Mary Juliano Longo and Ubaldino Dantas Machado. "Characterization of Databases in the Agricultural Sciences," *Journal of the American Society for Information Science* 32:2 (March 1981), 83-91.

645 Edward S. Warner. "The Impact of Interlibrary Access to Periodicals on Subscription Continuation/Cancellation Decision Making," *Journal of the American Society for Information Science* 32:2 (March 1981), 93-95. **(87)**

646 Charles T. Payne and Robert S. McGee. "Comparisons of LC Proofslip and MARC Tape Arrival Dates at the University of Chicago Library," *Journal of Library Automation* 3:2 (June 1970), 115-121.

647 Wanda V. Dole and David Allerton. "University Collections: A Survey of Costs," *Library Acquistions: Practice and Theory* 6:2(1982), 25-32. **(54, 62, 63)**

648 Silvia A. Gonzalez. "1976 Statistical Survey of Law Libraries Serving a Local Bar," *Law Library Journal* 70:2 (May 1977), 222-237.

649 Carole J. Mankin and Jacqueline D. Bastille. "An Analysis of the Differences between Density-of-Use Ranking and Raw-Use Ranking of Library Journal Use," *Journal of the American Society for Information Science* 32:3 (May 1981), 224-228. **(283, 284, 295)**

650 Katherine W. McCain and James E. Bobick. "Patterns of Journal Use in a Departmental Library: A Citation Analysis," *Journal of the American Society for Information Science* 32:4 (July 1981), 257-267.

651 Manfred Kochen, Victoria Reich and Lee Cohen. "Influence on [sic] Online Bibliographic Services on Student Behavior," *Journal of the American Society for Information Science* 32:6 (November 1981), 412-420.

652 Mark P. Carpenter and Francis Narin. "The Adequacy of the *Science Citation Index* (SCI) as an Indicator of International Scientific Activity," *Journal of the American Society for Information Science* 32:6 (November 1981), 430-439.

653 Chai Kim. "Retrieval Languages of Social Sciences and Natural Sciences: A Statistical Investigation," *Journal of the American Society for Information Science* 33:1 (January 1982), 3-7.

654 Ann H. Schabas. "Postcoordinate Retrieval: A Comparison of Two Indexing Languages," *Journal of the American Society for Information Science* 33:1 (January 1982), 32-37.

655 Miranda Lee Pao. "Collaboration in Computational Musicology," *Journal of the American Society for Information Science* 33:1 (January 1982), 38-43.

656 Robert K. Poyer. "*Science Citation Index*'s Coverage of the Preclinical Science Literature," *Journal of the American Society for Information Science* 33:5 (September 1982), 333-337.

657 Stephen M. Lawani and Alan E. Bayer. "Validity of Citation Criteria for Assessing the Influence of Scientific Publications: New Evidence with Peer Assessment," *Journal of the American Society for Information Science* 34:1 (January 1983), 59-66.

658 Edward G. Summers, Joyce Matheson and Robert Conry. "The Effect of Personal, Professional and Psychological Attributes, and Information Seeking Behavior on the Use of Information Sources by Educators," *Journal of the American Society for Information Science* 34:1 (January 1983), 75-85. **(160)**

659 Bluma C. Peritz. "A Note on 'Scholarliness' and 'Impact,'" *Journal of the American Society for Information Science* 34:5 (September 1983), 360-362.

660 Michael D. Cooper. "Response Time Variations in an Online Search System," *Journal of the American Society for Information Science* 34:6 (November 1983), 374-380.

661 Richard S. Marcus. "An Experimental Comparison of the Effectiveness of Computers and Humans as Search Intermediaries," *Journal of the American Society for Information Science* 34:6 (November 1983), 381-404.

662 Michael J. Simonds. "Work Attitudes and Union Membership," *College and Research Libraries* 36:2 (March 1975), 136-142.

663 Jerold Nelson. "Faculty Awareness and Attitudes toward Academic Library Reference Services: A Measure of Communication," *College and Research Libraries* 34:5 (September 1973), 268-275. **(255, 256)**

664 Andre Nitecki, "Polish Books in America and the Farmington Plan," *College and Research Libraries* 27:6 (November 1966), 439-449.

665 Leslie R. Morris. "Projections of the Number of Library School Graduates," *Journal of Education for Librarianship* 22:4 (Spring 1982), 283-291.

666 Thomas J. Galvin and Allen Kent. "Use of a University Library Collection," *Library Journal* 102:20 (November 1977), 2317-2320. [For further and more complete information see Allen Kent, et al. *Use of Library Materials: The University of Pittsburgh Study.* New York: Marcel Dekker, 1979.] **(7, 8, 9, 10, 26, 60, 98)**

667 Allen Kent. "Library Resource Sharing Networks: How To Make a Choice," *Library Acquisitions: Practice and Theory* 2 (1978), 69-76. [For further and more complete information see Allen Kent, et al. *Use of Library Materials: The University of Pittsburgh Study.* New York: Marcel Dekker, 1979.] **(10, 46, 50, 52, 81, 94, 104, 105)**

668 Leigh S. Estabrook and Kathleen M. Heim. "A Profile of ALA Personal Members," *American Libraries* 11:11 (December 1980), 654-659. [For a fuller and more complete description of this study see Kathleen M. Heim and Leigh S. Estabrook. *Career Profiles and Sex Discrimination in the Library Profession.* Chicago: American Library Association, 1983.]

669 Mary Lee DeVilbiss. "The Approval-Built Collection in the Medium-Sized Academic Library," *College and Research Libraries* 36:6 (November 1975), 487-492.

670 Thomas P. Fleming and Frederick G. Kilgour. "Moderately and Heavily Used Biomedical Journals," *Bulletin of the Medical Library Association* 52:1 (January 1964), 234-241.

671 Richard J. Hyman. "Medical Interlibrary Loan Patterns," *Bulletin of the Medical Library Association* 53:2 (April 1965), 215-224. **(108, 109)**

672 L. Miles Raisig, Meredith Smith, Renata Cuff and Frederick G. Kilgour. "How Biomedical Investigators Use Library Books," *Bulletin of the Medical Library Association* 54:2 (April 1966), 104-107. **(155, 160, 163, 213, 250, 259, 260)**

673 Helen Crawford. "Centralization vs. Decentralization in Medical School Libraries," *Bulletin of the Medical Library Association* 54:2 (April 1966), 199-205.

674 Peter Stangl and Frederick G. Kilgour. "Analysis of Recorded Biomedical Book and Journal Use in the Yale Medical Library," *Bulletin of the Medical Library Association* 55:3 (July 1967), 290-300. **(7, 9, 11, 14, 15, 16, 29, 30, 31, 32, 35, 36)**

675 Peter Stangl and Frederick G. Kilgour. "Analysis of Recorded Biomedical Book and Journal Use in the Yale Medical Library," *Bulletin of the Medical Library Association* 55:3 (July 1967), 301-315.**(45, 46, 47, 48, 50, 51, 52, 207, 208, 209, 210, 211, 212)**

676 Gwendolyn S. Cruzat. "Keeping Up with Biomedical Meetings," *Bulletin of the Medical Library Association* 56:2 (April 1968), 132-137.

677 Joan B. Woods, Sam Pieper and Shervert H. Frazier. "Basic Psychiatric Literature: I. Books," *Bulletin of the Medical Library Association* 56:3 (July 1968), 295-309.

678 Joan B. Woods, Sam Pieper and Shervert H. Frazier. "Basic Psychiatric Literature: II. Articles and Article Sources," *Bulletin of the Medical Library Association* 56:4 (October 1968), 404-427.

679 Reva Pachefsky. "Survey of the Card Catalog in Medical Libraries," *Bulletin of the Medical Library Association* 57:1 (January 1969), 10-20.

680 Janet Barlup. "Mechanization of Library Procedures in the Medium-sized Medical Library: VII. Relevancy of Cited Articles in Citation Indexing," *Bulletin of the Medical Library Association* 57:3 (July 1969), 260-263.

681 Wilhelm Moll. "Basic Journal List for Small Hospital Libraries," *Bulletin of the Medical Library Association* 57:3 (July 1969), 267-271.

682 Lois Ann Colainni and Robert F. Lewis. "Reference Services in U.S. Medical School Libraries," *Bulletin of the Medical Library Association* 57:3 (July 1969), 272-274.

683 Vern M. Pings and Joyce E. Malin. "Access to the Scholarly Record of Medicine by the Osteopathic Physicians of Southeastern Michigan," *Bulletin of the Medical Library Association* 58:1 (January 1970), 18-22. **(76, 77)**

684 D.J. Goode, J.K. Penry and J.F. Caponio. "Comparative Analysis of *Epilepsy Abstracts* and a MEDLARS Bibliography," *Bulletin of the Medical Library Association* 58:1 (January 1970), 44-50.

685 Robert Oseasohn. "Borrower Use of a Modern Medical Library by Practicing Physicians," *Bulletin of the Medical Library Association* 59:1 (January 1970), 58-59. **(228)**

686 Joan M.B. Smith. "A Periodical Use Study at Children's Hospital of Michigan," *Bulletin of the Medical Library Association* 58:1 (January 1970), 65-67.

687 Jean K. Miller. "Mechanization of Library Procedures in the Medium-sized Medical Library: XI. Two Methods of Providing Selective Dissemination of Information to Medical Scientists," *Bulletin of the Medical Library Association* 58:3 (July 1970), 378-397.

688 Stella S. Gomes. "The Nature and the Use and Users of the Midwest Regional Medical Library," *Bulletin of the Medical Library Association* 58:4 (October 1970), 559-577.

689 Donald A. Windsor. "Publications on a Drug before the First Report of Its Administration to Man," *Bulletin of the Medical Library Association* 59:3 (July 1971), 433-437.

690 Charles L. Bowden and Virginia M. Bowden. "A Survey of Information Sources Used by Psychiatrists," *Bulletin of the Medical Library Association* 59:4 (October 1971), 603-608. **(154, 161, 173, 174, 178, 179, 193, 194, 196, 199, 200, 201, 204, 220, 221, 247, 250, 251, 254, 261)**

691 Ruth E. Fenske. "Mechanization of Library Procedures in the Medium-sized Medical Library: XIV. Correlations between National Library of Medicine Classification Numbers and MeSH Headings," *Bulletin of the Medical Library Association* 60:2 (April 1972), 319-324.

692 Anne Brearley Piternick. "Measurement of Journal Availability in a Biomedical Library," *Bulletin of the Medical Library Association* 60:4 (October 1972), 534-542. **(29, 30, 31, 32, 33, 34, 61, 62)**

693 Isabel Spiegel and Janet Crager. "Comparison of SUNY and MEDLINE Searches," *Bulletin of the Medical Library Association* 61:2 (April 1973), 205-209.

694 Fred W. Roper. "Special Programs in Medical Library Education, 1957-1971: Part II: Analysis of the Programs," *Bulletin of the Medical Library Association* 61:4 (October 1973), 387-395.

695 Norma Jean Lodico. "Physician's Referral Letter Bibliographic Service: A New Method of Disseminating Medical Information," *Bulletin of the Medical Library Association* 61:4 (October 1973), 422-432. **(144)**

696 Wilhelm Moll. "MEDLINE Evaluation Study," *Bulletin of the Medical Library Association* 62:1 (January 1974), 1-5. **(139, 140, 142)**

697 Pamela Tibbetts. "A Method for Estimating the In-House Use of the Periodical Collection in the University of Minnesota Bio-Medical Library," *Bulletin of the Medical Library Association* 62:1 (January 1974), 37-48.

698   Joan Ash. "Library Use of Public Health Materials: Description and Analysis," *Bulletin of the Medical Library Association* 62:2 (April 1974), 95-104. **(281, 282, 292, 294)**

699   Ching-Chih Chen. "Current Status of Biomedical Book Reviewing: Part I. Key Biomedical Reviewing Journals with Quantitative Significance," *Bulletin of the Medical Library Association* 62:2 (April 1974), 105-112.

700   Ching-Chih Chen. "Current Status of Biomedical Book Reviewing: Part II. Time Lag in Biomedical Book Reviewing," *Bulletin of the Medical Library Association* 62:2 (April 1974), 113-119.

701   George Scheerer and Lois E. Hines. "Classification Systems Used in Medical Libraries," *Bulletin of the Medical Library Association* 62:3 (July 1974), 272-280. **(119)**

702   Jo Ann Bell. "The Academic Health Sciences Library and Serial Selection," *Bulletin of the Medical Library Association* 62:3 (July 1974), 281-290.

703   Ching-Chih Chen. "Current Status of Biomedical Book Reviewing: Part III. Duplication Patterns in Biomedical Book Reviewing," *Bulletin of the Medical Library Association* 62:3 (July 1974), 296-301.

704   Ching-Chih Chen. "Current Status of Biomedical Book Reviewing: Part IV. Major American and British Biomedical Book Publishers," *Bulletin of the Medical Library Association* 62:3 (July 1974), 302-308.

705   M. Sandra Wood and Robert S. Seeds. "Development of SDI Services from a Manual Current Awareness Service to SDILINE," *Bulletin of the Medical Library Association* 62:4 (October 1974), 374-384. **(151, 152, 153, 262, 263)**

706   Margaret Butkovich and Robert M. Braude. "Cost-Performance of Cataloging and Card Production in a Medical Center Library," *Bulletin of the Medical Library Association* 63:1 (January 1975), 29-34.

707   Donald A. Windsor. "Science-Speciality Literatures: Their Legendary-Contemporary Parity, Based on the Transmission of Information between Generations," *Bulletin of the Medical Library Association* 63:2 (April 1975), 209-215.

708   Helen J. Brown, Jean K. Miller and Diane M. Pinchoff. "Study of the Information Dissemination Service—Health Sciences Library, State University of New York at Buffalo," *Bulletin of the Medical Library Association* 63:3 (July 1975), 259-271. **(75, 76, 78, 85, 86, 87, 88, 103, 105, 110)**

709   Rachel K. Goldstein and Dorothy R. Hill. "The Status of Women in the Administration of Health Science Libraries," *Bulletin of the Medical Library Association* 63:4 (October 1975), 386-395.

710   Janet G. Schnall and Joan W. Wilson. "Evaluation of a Clinical Medical Librarianship Program at a University Health Sciences Library," *Bulletin of the Medical Library Association* (July 1976), 278-283.

711 Anne B. Piternick. "Effects of Binding Policy and Other Factors on the Availability of Journal Issues," *Bulletin of the Medical Library Association* 64:3 (July 1976), 284-292. (**31, 32, 33, 34**)

712 Richard B. Fredericksen and Helen N. Michael. "Subject Cataloging Practices in North American Medical School Libraries," *Bulletin of the Medical Library Association* 64:4 (October 1976), 356-366.

713 Paul M. McIlvaine and Malcolm H. Brantz. "Audiovisual Materials: A Survey of Bibliographic Controls in Distributors' Catalogs," *Bulletin of the Medical Library Association* 65:1 (January 1977), 17-21.

714 Bette Greenberg, Robert Breedlove and Wendy Berger. "MEDLINE Demand Profiles: An Analysis of Requests for Clinical and Research Information," *Bulletin of the Medical Library Association* 65:1 (January 1977), 22-28. (**186, 187, 188, 236, 237, 238, 240, 241**)

715 Renata Tagliacozzo. "Estimating the Satisfaction of Information Users," *Bulletin of the Medical Library Association* 65:2 (April 1977), 243-249. (**139, 141, 142**)

716 Ruth W. Wender, Ester L. Fruehauf, Marilyn S. Vent and Constant D. Wilson. "Determination of Continuing Medical Education Needs of Clinicians from a Literature Search Study: Part I. The Study," *Bulletin of the Medical Library Association* 65:3 (July 1977), 330-337. (**244, 246**)

717 Ruth W. Wender, Ester L. Fruehauf, Marilyn S. Vent and Constant D. Wilson. "Determination of Continuing Medical Education Needs of Clinicians from a Literature Search Study: Part II. Questionnaire Results," *Bulletin of the Medical Library Association* 65:3 (July 1977), 338-341.

718 Donald J. Morton. "Analysis of Interlibrary Requests by Hospital Libraries for Photocopied Journal Articles," *Bulletin of the Medical Library Association* 65:4 (October 1977), 425-432, (**76, 78**)

719 Patrick W. Brennen and W. Patrick Davey. "Citation Analysis in the Literature of Tropical Medicine," *Bulletin of the Medical Library Association* 66:1 (January 1978), 24-30.

720 Theresa C. Strasser. "The Information Needs of Practicing Physicians in Northeastern New York State," *Bulletin of the Medical Library Association* 66:2 (April 1978), 200-209. (**130, 150, 161, 162, 179, 180, 189, 197, 241, 242, 254**)

721 Inci A. Bowman, Elizabeth K. Eaton and J. Maurice Mahan. "Are Health Science Faculty Interested in Medical History? An Evaluative Case Study," *Bulletin of the Medical Library Association* 66:2 (April 1978), 228-231. (**144**)

722 Maurice C. Leatherbury and Richard A. Lyders. "Friends of the Library Groups in Health Sciences Libraries," *Bulletin of the Medical Library Association* 66:3 (July 1978), 315-318.

723   Bette Greenberg, Sara Battison, Madeleine Kolisch and Martha Leredu.
       "Evaluation of a Clinical Medical Librarian Program at the Yale Medical
       Library," *Bulletin of the Medical Library Association* 66:3 (July 1978),
       319-326. **(119, 120, 121, 150)**

724   Gloria Werner. "Use of On-Line Bibliographic Retrieval Services in Health
       Sciences Libraries in the United States and Canada," *Bulletin of the Medical
       Library Association* 67:1 (January 1979), 1-14. **(99, 100, 188, 242)**

725   B. Tommie Usdin. "Core Lists of Medical Journals: A Comparison," *Bulletin
       of the Medical Library Association* 67:2 (April 1979), 212-217.

726   John A. Timour. "Brief Communications: Use of Selected Abstracting and
       Indexing Journals in Biomedical Resource Libraries," *Bulletin of the Medical
       Library Association* 67:3 (July 1979), 330-335. **(268, 286, 287)**

727   Rachel K. Goldstein and Dorothy R. Hill. "The Status of Women in the
       Administration of Health Sciences Libraries: A Five-Year Follow-Up Study,
       1972-1977," *Bulletin of the Medical Library Association* 68:1 (January 1980),
       6-15.

728   Richard T. West and Maureen J. Malone. "Communicating the Results of
       NLM Grant-supported Library Projects," *Bulletin of the Medical Library
       Association* 68:1 (January 1980), 33-39.

729   James A. Thompson and Michael R. Kronenfeld. "The Effect of Inflation on
       the Cost of Journals on the Brandon List," *Bulletin of the Medical Library
       Association* 68:1 (January 1980), 47-52.

730   Carol C. Spencer. "Random Time Sampling with Self-observation for
       Library Cost Studies: Unit Costs of Reference Questions," *Bulletin of the
       Medical Library Association* 68:1 (January 1980), 53-57.

731   Justine Roberts. "Circulation versus Photocopy: Quid pro Quo?" *Bulletin of
       the Medical Library Association* 68:3 (July 1980), 274-277. **(17, 18, 20, 38, 39,
       62, 63)**

732   Dick R. Miller and Joseph E. Jensen. "Dual Pricing of Health Sciences
       Periodicals: A Survey," *Bulletin of the Medical Library Association* 68:4
       (October 1980), 336-347.

733   Jacqueline D. Bastille. "A Simple Objective Method for Determining a
       Dynamic Journal Collection," *Bulletin of the Medical Library Association*
       68:4 (October 1980), 357-366. **(78)**

734   Mary H. Mueller. "An Examination of Characteristics Related to Success of
       Friends Groups in Medical School Rare Book Libraries," *Bulletin of the
       Medical Library Association* 69:1 (January 1981), 9-13.

735   Scott Davis, Lincoln Polissar and Joan W. Wilson. "Continuing Education in
       Cancer for the Community Physician: Design and Evaluation of a Regional

Table of Contents Service," *Bulletin of the Medical Library Association* 69:1 (January 1981), 14-20. (**124, 125, 144, 145, 154**)

736   Gary D. Byrd. "Copyright compliance in Health Sciences Libraries: A Status Report Two Years after the Implementation of PL 94-553," *Bulletin of the Medical Library Association* 69:2 (April 1981), 224-230. (**268, 269**)

737   Ester L. Baldinger, Jennifer P.S. Nakeff-Plaat and Margaret S. Cummings. "An Experimental Study of the Feasibility of Substituting Chemical Abstracts Online for the Printed Copy in a Medium-Sized Medical Library," *Bulletin of the Medical Library Association* 69:2 (April 1981), 247-251.(**115, 116, 140, 141, 142, 143**)

738   Doris R.F. Dunn. "Dissemination of the Published Results of an Important Clinical Trial: An Analysis of the Citing Literature," *Bulletin of the Medical Library Association* 69:3 (July 1981), 301-306.

739   Cynthia H. Goldstein. "A Study of Weeding Policies in Eleven TALON Resource Libraries," *Bulletin of the Medical Library Association* 69:3 (July 1981), 311-316. (**293, 295, 296**)

740   K. Suzanne Johnson and E. Guy Coffee. "Veterinary Medical School Libraries in the United States and Canada, 1977-78," *Bulletin of the Medical Library Association* 70:1 (January 1982), 10-20.

741   Suzanne F. Grefsheim, Robert H. Larson, Shelley A. Bader and Nina W. Matheson. "Automation of Internal Library Operations in Academic Health Sciences Libraries: A State of the Art Report," *Bulletin of the Medical Library Association* 70:2 (April 1982), 191-200. (**4, 5**)

742   Elizabeth R. Lenz and Carolyn F. Walz. "Nursing Educators' Satisfaction with Library Facilities," *Bulletin of the Medical Library Association* 70:2 (April 1982), 201-206. (**131, 132, 134**)

743   Ruth Traister Morris, Edwin A. Holtum and David S. Curry. "Being There: The Effect of the User's Presence on MEDLINE Search Results," *Bulletin of the Medical Library Association* 70:3 (July 1982), 298-304.(**141, 187, 188, 189, 239, 242**)

744   James K. Cooper, Diane Cooper and Timothy P. Johnson. "Medical Library Support in Rural Areas," *Bulletin of the Medical Library Association* 71:1 (January 1983), 13-15.

745   Susan Crawford. "Health Science Libraries in the United States: I. Overview of the Post-World War II Years," *Bulletin of the Medical Library Association* 71:1 (January 1983), 16-20.

746   Susan Crawford and Alan M. Rees. "Health Sciences Libraries in the United States: II. Medical School Libraries, 1960-1980," *Bulletin of the Medical Library Association* 71:1 (January 1983), 21-29.

747   Susan Crawford. "Health Science Libraries in the United States: III. Hospital Health Science Libraries, 1969-1979," *Bulletin of the Medical Library Association* 71:1 (January 1983), 30-36. (**18, 20, 110, 111**)

748 Mark E. Funk and Carolyn Anne Reid. "Indexing Consistency in MED-LINE," *Bulletin of the Medical Library Association* 71:2 (April 1983), 176-183.

749 Michael R. Kronenfeld and Sarah H. Gable. "Real Inflation of Journal Prices: Medical Journals, U.S. Journals and Brandon List Journals," *Bulletin of the Medical Library Association* 71:4 (October 1983), 375-379.

750 Jane McCarthy. "Survey of Audiovisual Standards and Practices in Health Sciences Libraries," *Bulletin of the Medical Library Association* 71:4 (October 1983), 391-395. **(284)**

751 Rajia C. Tobia and David A. Kronick. "A Clinical Information Consultation Service at a Teaching Hospital," *Bulletin of the Medical Library Association* 71:4 (October 1983), 396-399.

752 Elizabeth R. Ashin. "Library Service to Dental Practitioners," *Bulletin of the Medical Library Association* 71:4 (October 1983), 400-402. **(197, 244, 245, 246)**

753 Peter P. Olevnik. "Non-Formalized Point-of-Use Library Instruction: A Survey," *Catholic Library World* 50:5 (December 1978), 218-220.

754 Susan A. Stussy. "Automation in Catholic College Libraries," *Catholic Library World* 53:3 (October 1981), 109-111.

755 R.M. Longyear. "Article Citations and 'Obsolescence' in Musicological Journals," *Notes* 33:3 (March 1977), 563-571.

756 Ann Basart. "Criteria for Weeding Books in a University Music Library," *Notes* 36:4 (June 1980), 819-836. **(15, 26, 35, 293, 295)**

757 Richard P. Smiraglia and Arsen R. Papakhian. "Music in the OCLC Online Union Catalog: A Review," *Notes* 38:2 (December 1981), 257-274.

758 William Gray Potter. "When Names Collide: Conflict in the Catalog and AACR 2," *Library Resources and Technical Services* 24:1 (Winter 1980), 3-16.

759 Rose Mary Magrill and Constance Rinehart. "Selection for Preservation: A Service Study," *Library Resources and Technical Services* 24:1 (Winter 1980), 44-57. **(285)**

760 Sally Braden, John D. Hall and Helen H. Britton. "Utilization of Personnel and Bibliographic Resources for Cataloging by OCLC Participating Libraries," *Library Resources and Technical Services* 24:2 (Spring 1980), 135-154.

761 Cynthia C. Ryans. "Cataloging Administrators' Views on Cataloging Education," *Library Resources and Technical Services* 24:4 (Fall 1980), 343-351.

762 Thomas Schadlich. "Changing from Sears to LC Subject Headings," *Library Resources and Technical Services* 24:4 (Fall 1980), 361-363.

763 Elizabeth L. Tate. "For Our 25th Anniversary...," *Library Resources and Technical Services* 25:1 (January/March 1981), 3-7.

764 Barbara Moore. "Patterns in the Use of OCLC by Academic Library Cataloging Departments," *Library Resources and Technical Services* 25:1 (January/March 1981), 30-39.

765 Judith J. Johnson and Clair S. Josel. "Quality Control and the OCLC Data Base: A Report on Error Reporting," *Library Resources and Technical Services* 25:1 (January/March 1981), 40-47.

766 Edward T. O'Neill and Rao Aluri. "Library of Congress Subject Heading Patterns in OCLC Monographic Records," *Library Resources and Technical Services* 25:1 (January/March 1981), 63-80.

767 Elizabeth H. Groot. "A Comparison of Library Tools for Monograph Verification," *Library Resources and Technical Services* 25:2 (April/June 1981), 149-161.

768 Elizabeth G. Mikita. "Monographs in Microform: Issues in Cataloging and Bibliographic Control," *Library Resources and Technical Services* 25:4 (October/December 1981), 352-361.

769 Lee R. Nemchek. "Problems of Cataloging and Classification in Theater Librarianship," *Library Resources and Technical Services* 25:4 (October/December 1981), 374-385.

770 John Hostage. "AACR 2, OCLC, and the Card Catalog in the Medium-Sized Library," *Library Resources and Technical Services* 26:1 (January/March 1982), 12-20.

771 Robert H. Hassell. "Revising the Dewey Music Schedules: Tradition vs. Innovation," *Library Resources and Technical Services* 26:2 (April/June 1982), 192-203.

772 Patricia Dwyer Wanninger. "Is the OCLC Database Too Large? A Study of the Effect of Duplicate Records in the OCLC System," *Library Resources and Technical Services* 26:4 (October/December 1982), 353-361.

773 Stephen R. Salmon. "Characteristics of Online Public Catalogs," *Library Resources and Technical Services* 27:1 (January/March 1983), 36-67.

774 Thomas E. Nisonger. "A Test of Two Citation Checking Techniques for Evaluating Political Science Collections in University Libraries," *Library Resources and Technical Services* 27:2 (April/June 1983), 163-176.

775 John Rutledge and Willy Owen. "Changes in the Quality of Paper in French Books, 1860-1914: A Study of Selected Holdings of the Wilson Library, University of North Carolina," *Library Resources and Technical Services* (April/June 1983), 177-187. **(285, 286)**

776 Jim Williams and Nancy Romero. "A Comparison of the OCLC Database and *New Serial Titles* as an Information Resource for Serials," *Library Resources and Technical Services* 27:2 (April/June 1983), 177-187.

777 Mary E. Clack and Sally F. Williams. "Using Locally and Nationally Produced Periodical Price Indexes in Budget Preparation," *Library Resources and Technical Services* 27:4 (October/December 1983), 345-356.

778 Victoria Cheponis Lessard and Jack Hall. "Vocational Technical Collection Building: Does it Exist?" *Collection Building* 4:2 (1982), 6-18.

779 Virginia Witucke. "The Reviewing of Children's Science Books," *Collection Building* 4:2 (1982) 19-30.

780 Margaret F. Stieg. "The Information Needs of Historians," *College and Research Libraries* 42:6 (November 1981), 549-560. (**125, 126, 128, 149, 157, 158, 159**)

781 Howard D. White. "Library Censorship and the Permissive Minority," *Library Quarterly* 51:2 (1981), 192-207. (**117, 118**)

782 Judith Serebnick. "Book Reviews and the Selection of Potentially Controversial Books in Public Libraries," *Library Quarterly* 51:4 (1981), 390-409.

783 Richard W. Scamell and Bette Ann Stead. "A Study of Age and Tenure as it Pertains to Job Satisfaction," *Journal of Library Administration* 1:1 (Spring 1980), 3-18.

784 Robert M. Hayes. "Citation Statistics as a Measure of Faculty Research Productivity," *Journal of Education for Librarianship* 23:3 (Winter 1983), 151-172.

785 William Skeh Wong and David S. Zubatsky. "The First-Time Appointed Academic Library Director 1970-1980: A Profile," *Journal of Library Administration* 4:1 (Spring 1983), 41-70.

786 James Rice, Jr. "An Assessment of Student Preferences for Method of Library Orientation," *Journal of Library Administration* 4:1 (Spring 1983), 87-93.

787 Frank William Goudy. "Affirmative Action and Library Science Degrees: A Statistical Overview, 1973-74 through 1980-81," *Journal of Library Administration* 4:3 (Fall 1983), 51-60.

788 Thomas G. English. "Librarian Status in the Eighty-Nine U.S. Academic Institutions of the Association of Research Libraries: 1982," *College and Research Libraries* 44:3 (May 1983), 199-211.

789 Nathan M. Smith and Veneese C. Nelson. "Burnout: A Survey of Academic Reference Librarians," *College and Research Libraries* 44:3 (May 1983), 245-250.

790 Floris W. Wood. "Reviewing Book Review Indexes," *Reference Services Review* (April/June 1980), 47-52.

791 Herbert Goldhor. "Public Library Circulation up 3%; Spending Jumps 11%," *American Libraries* 14:8 (September 1983), 534. **(19, 20, 28)**

792 Laura N. Gasaway and Steve Margeton. "Continuing Education for Law Librarianship," *Law Library Journal* 70:1 (February 1977), 39-52.

793 Michael L. Renshawe. "The Condition of the Law Librarian in 1976," *Law Library Review* 69:4 (November 1976), 626-640.

794 Susanne Patterson Wahba. "Women in Libraries," *Law Library* Journal 69:2 (May 1976), 223-231.

795 Jean Finch and Lauri R. Flynn. "An Update on Faculty Libraries," *Law Library Journal* 73:1 (Winter 1980), 99-106. **(54, 56)**

796 Robert D. Swisher, Peggy C. Smith and Calvin J. Boyer. "Educational Change Among ACRL Academic Librarians," *Library Research* (*Library and Information Science Research* since Spring 1983) 5:2 (Summer 1983), 195-205.

797 Michael D. Cooper. "Economies of Scale in Academic Libraries," *Library Research* (*Library and Information Science Research* after Spring 1983) 5:2 (Summer 1983), 207-219. **(18)**

798 Virgil Diodato. "Faculty Workload: A Case Study," *Journal of Education for Librarianship* 23:4 (Spring 1983), 286-295.

799 Jerry D. Saye. "Continuing Education and Library School Faculty," *Journal of Education for Librarianship* 24:1 (Summer 1983), 3-16.

800 Maurice P. Marchant and Carolyn F. Wilson. "Developing Joint Graduate Programs for Librarians," *Journal of Education for Librarianship* 24:1 (Summer 1983), 30-37.

801 Barbara L. Stein and Herman L. Totten. "Cognitive Styles: Similarities Among Students," *Journal of Education for Librarianship* 24:1 (Summer 1983), 38-43.

802 Marilyn J. Markham, Keith H. Stirling and Nathan M. Smith. "Librarian Self-Disclosure and Patron Satisfaction in the Reference Interview," *RQ* 22:4 (Summer 1983), 369-374.

803 June L. Engle and Elizabeth Futas. "Sexism in Adult Encyclopedias," *RQ* 23:1 (Fall 1983), 29-39.

804 David F. Kohl. "Circulation Professionals: Management Information Needs and Attitudes," *RQ* 23:1 (Fall 1983), 81-86.

805   Kevin Carey. "Problems and Patterns of Periodical Literature Searching at an Urban University Research Library," *RQ* 23:2 (Winter 1983), 211-218.

806   Beverly P. Lynch and Jo Ann Verdin. "Job Satisfaction in Libraries: Relationships of the Work Itself, Age, Sex, Occupational Group, Tenure, Supervisory Level, Career Commitment and Library Department," *Library Quarterly* 53:4 (October 1983), 434-447.

807   Louise W. Diodato and Virgil P. Diodato. "The Use of Gifts in a Medium Sized Academic Library," *Collection Management* 5:1/2 (Spring/Summer 1983), 53-71.**(28, 29, 65, 66, 67, 68, 69)**

AUTHOR INDEX
TO BIBLIOGRAPHY OF ARTICLES

Note: The index is arranged alphabetically, word by word. All characters or groups of characters separated by spaces, dashes, hyphens, diagonal slashes or periods are treated as separate words. Acronyms not separated by spaces or punctuation are alphabetized as though they are single words, while initials separated by spaces or punctuation are treated as if each letter is a complete word. Personal names beginning with capital Mc, M' and Mac are all listed under Mac as though the full form were used, and St. is alphabetized as if spelled out.

ABOUT THE AUTHORS

DAVID F. KOHL is currently Undergraduate Librarian and Assistant Director for Undergraduate Libraries and Instructional Services at the University of Illinois-Urbana, with the rank of Associate Professor. Dr. Kohl did his graduate work at the University of Chicago. He has taught library administration at the University of Illinois Graduate School of Library and Information Science and has published numerous articles and monographs on library management and automation. His wide range of service in library management includes active participation in the ARL/OMS Library Consultant Program, the Washington State University's Managing for Productivity Program, and the Assessment Center Program for Potential Managers, sponsored jointly by the University of Washington Graduate Library School and the Washington State Library.

THOMAS E. ALFORD has been the Assistant City Librarian at the Los Angeles Public Library since November 1980. He was previously Director of the Macomb County Library in Michigan. His activities in the American Library Association include serving as chairman of the Committee on Program Evaluation and Support and the Circulation Services Section and as a board member of the Public Library Association and the Library Administration and Management Association. Mr. Alford currently serves on the Cooperative Library Agencies for Systems and Services' board of directors. He has authored several articles on library issues, including a chapter in *Libraries in the Political Process* (Scarecrow Press, 1980).